On Be(come)ing a Woman of Wisdom

Memoir of a Modern-day Tantrika

Volume 1

Patricia Spinoza

On Be(come)ing a Woman of Wisdom
Memoir of a Modern-day Tantrika
All Rights Reserved.
Copyright © 2022 Patricia Spinoza
v4.1 r1.0

The opinions expressed in this manuscript are solely the opinions of the author and do not represent the opinions or thoughts of the publisher. The author has represented and warranted full ownership and/or legal right to publish all the materials in this book.

This book may not be reproduced, transmitted, or stored in whole or in part by any means, including graphic, electronic, or mechanical without the express written consent of the publisher except in the case of brief quotations embodied in critical articles and reviews.

Tantrika Press

Paperback ISBN: 978-0-578-25359-6
Hardback ISBN: 978-0-578-25360-2

Cover Photo © 2022 Isaiah Fleming. All rights reserved - used with permission.

PRINTED IN THE UNITED STATES OF AMERICA

PRAISE FOR *On Be(come)ing A Woman of Wisdom: Memoir of a Modern-day Tantrika – Volumes I & II*

Spinoza is a fearless storyteller. The searing honesty in the relating of her life from childhood to cronehood leads the reader into the author's private world as she seeks to manifest her full *Shakti Energy* (the divine feminine). As she recounts the #MeToo experiences of her life and lineage, the joy and excruciating challenges of motherhood, her heart break and ecstasy with lovers, her exquisite story telling never falters. Spinoza's courage to share what is often not revealed inspires and invites the reader to undertake her own spiritual journey to wholeness. Thank you Patricia Spinoza!
    -- Nisha Zenoff, MFT, PhD author of *The Unspeakable Loss: How do you live after a child dies?* A gold medal award recipient in Grief, Death, Dying by Living Now Book Awards

Narrating one's life is a complex task. As Patricia's narrative effortlessly unfolds the ebbs and flows of a life fully lived, we are taken into moments of poignancy, of excitement, of softness. We enter the magical realm of her story - the mythical journey into woman empowerment, of *Shakti Energy*. We move with the rhythm of her breath, of her body and of her emotions as she shares her childhood and her lineage, her relationships, her woundedness and her path to healing. Patricia transports us into the making of life itself and invites us to see how our life too has unfolded in its own tender, wounded, and victorious way.

    Her story reads like a fascinating page-turner - her life, our life.
    -- Francoise Bourzat, M.A. Somatic Counselor, author *Consciousness Medicine*

-- Referencing Volume II

"Right there I found my warrior's stance; feet planted apart, feeling the earth rising through feet and vagina, arms spread wide, face gazing out to the horizon. From that place of power, I spoke...."I vow to leave the mouse in me here in the foothills of the mountains. Thank you earth for accepting it."

My friend Patricia's superb power tantrika memoir opens a third eye to her transcendent feminine energy. I was fascinated to follow her journey, challenges she faced even embraced, and the call for all of us to discover our own paths to divine *Shakti Energy*.

-- Gerard Sarnat, author of four collections - *HOMELESS CHRONICLES: from Abraham to Burning Man, Disputes, 17s, and Melting The Ice King*

Patricia Spinoza, a wise crone, shares with us her long journey, the mysteries of the feminine, and the complexity of life, in a rich, enchanting language and story.

--Ben Hanah, a fellow traveler, psychologist, teacher, and writer.

*In loving memory of my mom, Marian, who always
understood even when she didn't.*

*For my children, Ron and Pam, who
bring boundless joy to my quest.*

Table of Contents

Introduction: *My Tantric Quest* i
Prologue: *Medicine Journey* 1
1. The Dark Labyrinth: *#MeToo Beginnings Forced to the Light*..... 3
2. The Sun Room: *A Shattering Decision That Binds My Heart*.... 25
3. Transition: *Blessings and Banes of a Budding Tantrika*............ 29
4. Stirrings: *Sexual and Spiritual* **Shakti** *Tremoring*...................... 33
5. Junior High: *Hell and Heaven Seamed Together* 55
6. High School: *Intuiting Freedom* OR *It's All About Sex* 71
7. San Francisco Dreaming 91
8. The Prodigal Daughter Returns: *Marriage-Children-Taking Responsibility* 116
9. Jackson: *The Sacred Tremor Grabs Hold in Her Soft Iron Grip*... 159
10. The Dream Fades: *Joys of Anchorage Life Dissolve into Loss and Grief*... 210
11. Vicente: *My Mettle Is Tested – Adventures on the High Seas*..... 240
12. Emancipation of the Dreamer from the Dream 285
13. End of an Era 300
14. France: *The Chrysalis*... 302
15. India and Nepal: *My Heart, My Body, My Soul Succumbs*.... 314
16. Paris to Denmark: *Shakti - Open Heart and Sexuality*............ 333
17. Full Circle: *Ricocheting across the Globe*.................................. 346
18. Hiatus: *Ordinary Life Enriched by the Unpredictable*............ 373
19. Love Stories: *The Innocent and the Vulgar* 388
20. Tipi Living: *Healing Alone In Nature*... 409
Epilogue: *Dayton's Death* 413
End Notes.. 420
Characters 422
Acknowledgements 426

*Contemplating on supreme consciousness
is the practice of the tantrika.
What resonates spontaneously in oneself
is the mystical formula.*
                    Vijnanabhairava Tantra #145

Introduction
My Tantric Quest

Throughout the years, friends, partners, children have encouraged and suggested to me, "You ought to write your life's story." My life story? I would ask myself. I'm an ordinary person growing up in small-town America; a wife, mother, student, therapist, and yes, a seeker, doing my best to fight for psychic health. To reach for awareness, free-flowing energy, and follow the call of spirit no matter where it may lead. If there is anything that adds an unusual flavor to my story, it is that last phrase "to follow the call of spirit no matter where it may lead."

Several years ago, in response to these entreaties, I felt an impetus to write my story. Buried at my computer, I responded to this impulse, but after 100 pages or so, my writing felt boring. I dragged the pages into the trash bin of the computer and dumped the trash.

A year or so later, my partner, William, suggested I write my story as fiction. Well, that caught my fancy, it would give me distance, I could embellish or erase as I wanted, so I started again. . .Once upon a time. . .

Along with his suggestion to write my story as fiction, he described how he saw my life from the point of view of *Shakti Energy*. How was he using the word *Shakti*, I wondered aloud? This question engendered lively conversations over breakfast about the idea of *Shakti Energy*, the enlivening feminine energy in the universe. One morning he got up from the table and rummaged through the stacks of boxes on the floor of the yurt that, like us, were awaiting the completion of our home here in Hawaii.

"Ah-ha, here it is." He handed me a book of an ancient text, *The Vijnanabhairava Tantra*. I randomly chose to read a sutra (an aphorism) from this appendix to the main text.

> *24. The highest Shakti reveals herself when inbreath and outbreath are born and die at their places of origin. Thus, between two breaths, experience the infinite Bhairava.*

Meanings vied for attention as I contemplated the words I had just recited: *Shakti*? Infinite space? The path of Tantra? William seeing me as a particular expression of *Shakti*? Over the next few days, as I avidly immersed myself into this hidden treasure, like an eternal torch of the ages, I felt an ember ignite inside of me. Then I came upon Verses 68 and 69.

> *68. When you practice a sex ritual, concentrate in the quivering of your senses and reach the infinite bliss of ecstatic love.*

The next verse, like bees to a field of sweet clover, aroused my foraging attention.

> *69. At the start of the union, be in the fire of the energy released by intimate sensual pleasure. Merge into the divine Shakti dissolving duality, avoiding the ashes at the end. This delight is that of one's own Self.*

Shakti Energy? The Self? Hum-m..... I point to this text to introduce a primary lens through which I understand the unfolding of my passage on earth: the tantric path. But I'm getting ahead of myself, much more of that to come.

I named this second attempt at the book, this fictionalized version, *Athena and Artemis (Diana)* after the two goddesses that seemed the archetypes that defined my identity. With my Jungian Psychology background, the concept fit like a glove, and for my Western mind it was more easily understood than *Shakti*. I found it exciting to sit down each day and unfold the story of these two parts of myself, and it unlocked the reticence in me until one day, I didn't know why I was writing. The intention, the impetus had dissolved away into a wisp of wind carried into the ethers. Nearly 300 pages, I mused to myself, I'd actually written 300 pages! Trouble was that it didn't feel honest to fictionalize and play with facts and events, so these pages too went into the trash bin. However, there was residue from this second attempt - a vague, undefined intuition of why I might want to share my life story.

Nearly two years flew by as, with my partner, I tended the garden paradise we were planting here in Hawaii and tended the garden of our shared passion, reveling in its delights and the celestial consciousness it was opening in me.

In May 2018, Anna, a dear friend visiting with her husband, inquired, no demanded, to know of "the book." She knew I had made stops and starts with writing, and like a dog with a bone, this sister would not let me slither away into my doubts, my lethargy, my fear. Perhaps, this was simply and finally the right time. During their visit, I would listen to her, sometimes stonily, often with a hidden smirk that I knew what I could and couldn't do, and writing a book fell into the tried-it-can't-do-it column. As she harangued about "your book" on walks and at the dinner table, I reluctantly let fall little morsels here and there.

On a peaceful tropical morning, the four of us sat at the breakfast table inquiring of each other, "What shall we do today?" We quickly reached a consensus, and soon we were in the car, leaving our sea-level home and climbing to the 4,000 ft. elevation of Volcano National Park. Pausing at the Visitor's Center to introduce our friends to the park, we soon drove the few miles west to the Jaeger Museum. There at the edge of the outlook, we joined locals and visitors gazing enthralled at the Halema'uma'u Crater on the flank of Mt. Kilauea. Usually one could see the steam rising out of the crater, and on one visit, William and I had been awestruck at the bubbles of lava that occasionally burst into view from the elevated lava lake. But this day, as we stood with eyes glued to the lake, we could see and feel the constant bulging bubbling visceral red torrid lava as it sent glowing hot lava bombs into the air. We were transfixed at this audacious display of Pele's power, as oh-hs and ahh-hs escaped unbidden from the lips of each person there. None of us standing enthralled that day could imagine what was to come.

When we could finally tear ourselves away, we left the Jaeger Museum outlook and drove a mile or two to Volcano Village for dinner at the Kilauea Lodge and Restaurant. Sipping wine, awaiting our food in this quaint "mountain lodge," Anna suddenly exclaimed in one mysteriously magical moment, "Well of course, it's the perfect time. Your book - it fits with the **#MeToo** movement. It's time! You must do it!" Where the hell did that come from, I wondered? A rush from my belly to my heart stopped my inner dialogue. Suddenly the *raison'd'etre* of the book had arrived right on cue.

That night, after our conversation and her timely introduction of the **#MeToo** movement, sleep refusing my entreaties, I arose and traversed the 100' long wooden walkway between our house and our sleeping yurt. Leaving the walkway, I meandered along the driveway, through the orchards, the nearly full moon casting my shadow as I strolled and danced in the moonlight. I kicked a leg watching its sinuous movement, fuzzy at the edges, clapped my hands over my head, once again watching the shadows play at the edges of space around the garden landscape William and I had created. Though their faces were closed, I imagined the brilliant pink portulaca bursting from the black lava crevasses off to my left. In the full moon, I could make out the purple morning glories and yellow hibiscus as they sought to outdo the riotous display of the other. The aroma of the night-blooming jasmine wafted in the air.

Passing under the glorious pink powder puff tree that graced the driveway entrance, I took a few more steps and paused to marvel at a dragon fruit blossom in its audacious open beauty - green spidery tentacles spread out generously around the base cradling the abundant white petals glowing iridescent in the moonlight. Nestled in the bed of white, hundreds of feathery yellow stamens, each one waving its banner of powdery pollen, gathered together in a circle as if to consult about how to send their pollen to the top of the thin pistil stem that almost reluctantly split out into a few wispy tendrils, echoing the spidery green below. In a mysterious act of nature that placed the stamen with its fertilizing pollen below the pistil, the blossom can only become a fruit if a wayward night moth or a human hand comes along to help it pollinate; so beautiful, so vulnerable, and so dependent, and yet commanding in its dazzling ten-inch span and complexity. In a heartbeat I understood my quandary with writing: I hadn't dared risk opening my heart and mind, showing their vulnerability, power, even dependence since I needed the hands and minds and love of friends and partners and children to propagate my story to fruition. That night, I knelt before the sensuality of the dragon fruit flower, touched it tenderly, and I knew the only way to tell my story was to share my own beauty and vulnerability, my own ugliness and despair, my own wisdom and foolishness, and to hold nothing back. I found myself asking the question, "If I am breathing my last and haven't written my story will I have regrets?" The answer came back instantly, "YES!"

In one of those inexplicable synchronicities, the day after Anna and her husband flew home on May 2^{nd,} I sat down at my computer to begin the Prologue, and Kilauea erupted. Like the explosion of *Pele* from the molten depths of the earth under our feet, this book exploded out of me. These pages will unveil how sex, my love of sex, my joy in sex, and even my need for sex has all along been the stirrings of *Shakti Energy* intrinsic in my heart. The pages will reveal how poverty, spirit, violence, and even self-hate drove me relentlessly to discover my own particular *Shakti* energy, which is quite simply the appreciation and engagement of the sensual, especially the erotic beauty of sexual joining. These driving experiences and feelings have been hard to trust over the years, but on that morning, as I sat down to my computer, trusting this internal command, supported by the energy and beauty of nature around me, and my partner, my fingers flew across the keyboard. I write not a fictional story of real life, but my real-life story because I believe our earth and we humans are desperate beings longing for an elusive unknown that seems to hover just out of reach. What a beautiful and healing act for our earth and we beings who have stewardship of this marvelous planet if each of us were to strive to fully manifest the call of *Shakti Energy*. It is the birthright of all. It pours from the skies, flutters up from the earth, surrounds us in the very air we breathe, permeates our beings and pulls us to our own fierce expressions of our connection……..to **Source**, to **It**, to **The immensity**, to **God**, to **Goddess**, to **Bhairava,** to **Allah** – the names are diverse but one-pointed in their meaning. This then is the gift of birth into the earth realm if we simply open to it, receive it, and thrill at its contents!

Building Blocks: The Foundations of Be(come)ing

It seems to me that each of us comes into the world with what one might call a blueprint or a vague architectural form that animates the contours of a life. In my case, this organic architectural form coalesced around a powerful, dissonant parental triad, a nearly debilitating poverty, an undefined sensuality, the power of nature, and a hazy, formless *Restlessness*.

The infrastructures that defined my adulthood were introduced into my life in a particular chronology: Christianity, Jungian Psychology, the teachings of J. Krishnamurti, Process Oriented Psychology, Sorcery - or as I shall interchangeably refer to it, the tradition of Seers - Medicine Work, and finally Kashmir Shaivism. This last one, Kashmir Shaivism, differs from the others in an essential point. Rather than studying a tradition and doing my best to adhere to its precepts, I saw how it articulated in great detail who I already was in my core. Though the words, *path of tantra, a tantrika,* would only surge into my life like a *Janey-come-lately,* and will only be fleshed out in the final chapter of Volume II, I would discover I was already living the tenets of this tradition. There was nothing new to follow. For now, I set this chronological order aside, as each structure will emerge throughout this narrative as the narrative demands. All of these stones and structures will insist their voice be heard.

I suspect that Kashmir Shaivism and, by extension, *Shakti Energy*, unlike Christianity or Jungian Psychology, is a somewhat foreign concept for many Westerners. I ask the reader to rest a bit in the unknown with the relaxed knowledge that clarity and depth about these concepts will be woven into this story. However, as a starting point, *Shakti* is a word from the Vedic scriptures of the East used to describe the universal enlivening feminine energy that manifests us, surrounds us, and that we all carry inside of us. Its myriad manifestations are endless. In my life, it will assert itself as tantric sexual energy.

We'll journey on this path to absorb, reflect, and hopefully delight in how that enlivening, feminine energy runs and dances between hearts and vaginas, hearts and penises, heart to heart, genitals to genitals, and finally, bodies to spirit. It is one girl child's, one teenager's, one young woman's, one middle-aged woman's, and now one crone's story of how a devastating, terrifying childhood brought the awakening of *Shakti* within and that now releasing it out to others is my greatest joy.

Dreaming the Shakti

For a moment, we skip back to a day in a bookstore in San Diego, California, summer of '75. I have always been curious about "the way we work" and that day, in the bookstore where I was browsing, my eyes landed on Carl Gustav Jung's last book, *Memories, Dreams, and Reflections*. The door of psychology was thrown open, and I stepped across the threshold into a world that would animate me for the rest of my life and eventually segue into an understanding of this elusive affectionate *Shakti Energy* that animates the earth realm.

I started my first dream journal in 1975, attempting to interpret my dreams and also noting what was occurring in my external life. Mysteriously, in 2008 when I moved to Hawaii, only a few times a year would a dream find its way to consciousness. This commitment to my dream life has been a curiosity to me. I've marveled at how through all my travels, most often with a backpack slung across my shoulders, I've carried those dream journals, all shapes, sizes, colors with me, faithfully recording strange, beautiful, and often nightmarish dreams. I have read, reflected, and interpreted those dreams from a Freudian view, a Jungian view, a Process Oriented Psychology view. About a year or so ago, I undertook a final review so I could close my journals with a golden key, turn them to ashes in a fire pit on one of our old lava flows, and let go of the stories.

Late evenings, sitting in my favorite chair in my space - an out-of-the-way room on the second floor of our house - I would read the journals, be horrified, ecstatic, curious, and put markers on pages of enigmatic dreams and scenes. Then inexplicably, about six months into the review, I stopped. I would think of the 25 journals stacked in the corner of my room with the reviewed in one stack and the to-be-reviewed in another. And so I waited and I waited.

As I began to write this narrative, like a long-buried treasure fortuitously and unexpectedly uncovered, I understood that these dreams are the storyline of the teleological intention of *Shakti Energy* weaving through the unconscious into consciousness and full manifestation. It is through this narrative that their *raison'd'etre* comes to light.

C. G. Jung wrote in his autobiography, *Memories, Dreams and Reflections*:

> A book of mine is always a matter of fate. There is something unpredictable about the process of writing, and I cannot prescribe for myself any predetermined course. Thus this "autobiography" is now taking a direction quite different from what I had imagined at the beginning. It has become a necessity for me to write down my early memories. If I neglect to do so for a single day, unpleasant physical symptoms immediately follow. As soon as I set to work they vanish and my head feels perfectly clear.

I humbly borrow Jung's succinct expression of his process of writing his autobiography as a description of my odyssey. Unlike Jung, there is one more crucial point I must touch on as we begin, and that is the relationship of my story with the **#MeToo** movement and how it plays throughout these pages. The **#MeToo** movement is the early dream of emerging power and truth-telling by women. In my lifetime, there hasn't been a cultural web to support the predilection of women with powerful sexual energy, nor our defiance of the victimhood with which the society wants to imbue us.

It is a story at times, joyful, painful, beautiful, ugly, sublime, and hellish – just like all of our stories. This is the tale of my life, simply one of an infinite number of *Shakti* patterns that I now bring to you in the hopes you can recognize the power of your own *Shakti Energy*.

Two things to note before we begin - Any author presenting her autobiography must, by the exigencies of the undertaking, make choices. In my case, the most significant stories, chosen from a lifetime of stories, will be in service of the unfolding of *Shakti Energy*. Second, my given name was Diane, and I will use that name until I change my name to Patricia in the fifth decade of my life.

And so dear reader let us begin.

Prologue
Medicine Journey

Journey Experience May 2015

    Amorphous play of the gods and goddesses. Formlessness is, yet little gusts of momentary gathering begin to form. An intention ripples through the formlessness, and like a thought, it begins to grow, gathering unto itself, giving form to the intention. The intention pulls at the formlessness, insistent, and in a brief instant, a slight gust materializes enough to lend its "thought" to the ripple of purpose. The ripple begins to take form, the "thought" of other little gusts of form attaching themselves as the ripple of intention moves among the formlessness, calling to itself other indistinct intentions vaguely hinting at manifestation. There is no time, no beginning, no end, no ownership, but at a given moment in moment-less space, as the intention grows, begins to manifest solidity, a probe is borne of the infinite will of Shiva *and* Shakti *in an embrace moving in and out of timelessness.*

    As Shiva *and* Shakti *fade back into formless oneness, into emptiness, a form is borne entering into the world of duality. The tap of infinity that momentarily touched an intention moves into the finite world of time and space called earth. SHE is born and thus begins her journey as a probe to bring back form to formlessness.*

    The stamp on the probe has children; the stamp on the probe is fecund sexuality, a stamp that will be initiated by a man who is her father. The intention of this probe, intrinsic in its configuration, as well as the curiosity of the gods and goddesses, is to discover all the possible ways this birth could unfold. It happens instantly, yet with the stamp of time that all probes carry, it "arrives" to the earth realm.

Can this probe re-enter the world of the formless, able to leave her form, its triumphs, its tragedies, its pain, its joy, its fetters? This probe enters the earth realm in the moment of earth time when most of humanity is engaged in what would come to be known as World War II. It enters as a girl baby whose father will play a role in the Tantric Shakti *intention of the probe; the mother will bear silent witness with unspoken pride and love to the unfolding of this daughter.*

1

The Dark Labyrinth

#MeToo *Beginnings Forced to the Light*

Coming Into Being

My story begins in a rented house on the Bakerview Road In Bellingham, a small town in northwest Washington. In the bedroom, as Marian and Dayton joined to conceive me, sleeping in a crib beside their bed was my older sister, Rochelle, a tender four months old. She would play a perhaps over-size role in the seminal years of my life. Like any newlywed couple and new parents, Marian and Dayton were proud of Rochelle, their curly auburn-haired daughter with brown eyes in a round cherubic face. They thrilled at the admiration the three of them inspired as an attractive young family. (Ah-h those persistent stories that enter the realm of myth in a family.) The idyll changed on February 13, 1943, just over an hour before midnight when I announced myself with a loud cry to the world. That innocuous little fact of my birth time engendered the oft-repeated lament, "You just missed Valentine's Day. You just missed being a Valentine's baby." It was a painful reminder that I had somehow fallen short of an idealized land of specialness. However, my birth carried a certain welcome specialness for my parents: my arrival was added insurance against Dayton's being called up by his alma mater, the U.S. Navy, to fight in the great war. As the war raged on, even the arrival of a third child couldn't keep him out of the fight. In my baby book, *Our Baby Book,* Marian wrote the following, "Second Xmas was spent at Grandpa Johnsons, Xmas Eve at Uncle Franks. Pappa was in boot camp in San Diego."

My Mother Marian

Marian would live to be 102 years old. Her longevity was a great gift to me. How fortunate I was to have countless years to talk with her, process with her, learn from her, love her, and be loved by her. If being close to another is measured by the honesty between them, the communication they undertake, the empathy of understanding, then I was the child with whom she was close. On the other hand, I was a bit of a mystery to her; our female essence was diametrically opposed, I was undeniably my father's favorite (a strike for or against me?), and yet I seemed to be the only child daring to break through her resolute reticence to share secrets. Indeed, my tenacious burning desire to know and understand her and thus to know and understand myself was unflappable. And way beyond this quest, the sharing space we created fostered my natural predisposition to listen that would one day find its professional niche.

Marian also gave me the gift of the papers she kept as though they were riches hidden away for an unknown time of need. It is through these papers collected across generations that I gained unexpected and unknown information that has enriched this telling.

Marian's Secrets Revealed

One weekend sometime in 1991-92, I had gone to spend a week with my mom where she still lived in Bellingham, Washington, the city of my birth and upbringing. A compelling urge to recapitulate the town, the schools, my birth hospital, the neighborhood – all the places that provided the setting for the early years of conditioning - drove this trip to the north. (Recapitulation is a term used in the seer's world to describe a process of reviewing life events, and through the use of breath, take back energy expended in the event under review.)

First and foremost was a burning question for her. "Mom," I asked as we sat chatting over morning coffee, "what was your mood when I was conceived?"

That she was taken aback is an understatement! This was an odd question even from me. She frowned, "What do you mean, my mood when you were conceived?" The tone of her voice affirmed this was a truly weird question, but it was at these dissonant moments that my mother would surprise me the most. I reiterated the question and further explained that this wasn't a salacious curiosity but rather I was examining a precept of the seers of ancient Mexico (the tradition she knew I was currently aligning with), namely that the mood of the parents at the moment of conception affected the overarching temperament of the child.

Undaunted I continued, "The seers suggest that the mood at conception establishes a child's stance in the world and one's basic energy." I rushed on to explain that in numerous talks I had attended, the women teachers and Carlos Castaneda himself had reiterated that most of us were "bored fucks." (Back in those days the word fuck easily flowed from my mouth, and I hoped the shock factor would energize her.) I pressed on, telling her that they proposed that most parents weren't energetically, emotionally, or otherwise fully engaged with the sex they were having when they conceived a child. My mini-lecture concluded, I waited.

"Hum-mm I don't know." Undeterred by this, her default response to most any question, I carried on by giving her choices; happy, sad, passionate, upset, engaged, angry. These were all met with a negative shake of her head. But, when I suggested resignation, she brightened. "Yes, that's it. I didn't ever much enjoy that part of marriage. You know it's just what women had to do." She wasn't naturally conversant about sex, periods, bodies, but over the years I think she had grown accustomed, even comfortable, with our intimate conversations, so had related bits and pieces, tidbits of hers and papa's sexual relationship.

This morning in the midst of the conversation of my conception and birth, she suddenly segued into a long-buried secret of her sexual relationship with Dayton. When I look back I'm amazed she shared this story with me. It must have always weighed heavily on her psyche and to finally share it with someone must have been, in and of itself, the lifting of a heavy burden.

At the time of the telling, she was in her 70s, about the age I am now, and I would have been in my 40's. At the time of the event, she would have been in her late thirties and I would have been a pre-teen. Her emotions were always contained, even in the telling of this horrendous event. She began the narrative of how, this particular night, like many in her years of marriage to Dayton, she had waited up for him till past midnight and then resigned herself to the obvious conclusion that he would undoubtedly drink till the bars closed. "You know," she said, "I hated those nights when I knew he'd come home drunk and was afraid how he would be. Anyway, I finally fell asleep and dimly woke up as Dayton drunkenly fell into bed on top of me. I looked at him trying to gauge his state – would he collapse and be asleep or would he want to have sex or was an argument and beating brewing." Here she looked closely at me, undoubtedly gauging how I was taking in this information. I must have had the right look on my face as she continued, "I was so shocked when I found myself looking into the face of one of Dayton's friends. He was staring at me as he lay stretched out on the bed fumbling under the covers for me. When he tried to kiss me, to stick his limpid tongue into my mouth, his alcoholic breath almost gagged me."

As I listened, I fought to hold an open expression, though I wanted to howl with outrage and sorrow. She continued, "I pushed him away and he rolled off the bed onto the floor. He barely got up and staggered to the door, falling into it." With the next words, I at last heard outrage in her voice. "I looked away from the sight of him and saw Dayton peering through the slightly ajar door."

The picture she painted shattered my reticence. I couldn't contain my fury, but it was my sadness and compassion for her, not anger that cried out. "Oh Mama, I'm so sorry for what he did." There was silence

THE DARK LABYRINTH

and yet the picture demanded the last brush strokes be painted.

"When Papa's friend smashed into the door, it flew open and he fell into Dayton who managed to shut the door as the two of them disappeared." Her voice broke ever so slightly, "I couldn't move. I was so afraid." And using that well-understood phrase, she added, "I was like a deer in the headlights, frozen in abject horror so I just curled up and drew the covers over my head." In that hushed ocean where we swam together, I had no words.

We got up from the table and busied ourselves with washing up the dishes in the kitchen and let the quiet return us to some sense of normalcy. As we worked side by side, I asked her what she had done the next morning when she awoke to face Dayton. She was vague. Painfully, I could fill in the blanks, guessing she had been unable to do anything but deepen her hate and feeling of helplessness. It's hard to imagine that years later, when she finally dared to divorce him, there was even a hint of love and understanding left toward this man who had been her husband and abuser for over 20 years. But eventually, there would be a lightning strike from the blue that would belie my assumptions about her feelings. Who can understand the laws of attraction? The question of my conception was rendered irrelevant.

The family continued to grow. Laura came 20 months after me, and my brother David two and a half years later in 1946. Papa was ecstatic to have a son. Following what he'd done with his favorite daughter, he named David so his initials matched his own. **D**ayton **L**awrence **J**ohnson, **D**iane **L**ee **J**ohnson, **D**avid **L**awrence **J**ohnson, and finally **D**on **L**ester **J**ohnson, the brother that came after David.

David's birth and conception held a special place in Marian's memory. I once asked her when she had been happy with Papa, as she was always claiming in her later years through selective memory that she had never been happy. "There must have been some time you were happy?" I couldn't bear the thought that in my mother's memory my parents had never found happiness together.

"Well, I think I was happiest the September when the war ended and I went to San Diego to visit Papa where he was stationed, as he hadn't been sent overseas after all. On the train the air was festive, lots of people were drinking and celebrating the end of the war. When I disembarked from the train and saw him, well, we were so happy to be together. Everybody around us on that train platform was ecstatic and smiling. Dayton bought me that ring of pink stones (she carried it in her purse until she died) and that's when David was conceived. Yes, that was a joyful time, and Dayton wasn't drinking, so there wasn't even a hint of violence. You know," she added, "he would sometimes stop drinking for months at a time, but he always went back to the bottle, and each time he stopped, he seemed to come back meaner than ever when he drank." She sighed as she stopped talking, closed her eyes.

We jump ahead nearly 20 years to 2012. Four of us, my daughter Pam, grandson/son Isaiah, Pam's boyfriend, Joe, and I had driven the 10 hours to eastern Oregon from Bellingham to visit mom/grandma/great-grandma where she lived with my sister Rochelle and her husband Bill on their ranch. The two of them had built their ranch home in 1962, during the second year of their marriage and every piece of furniture, dish, and knick-knack was original from those early years. The family room, where the floor boasted a mosaic of the ranch's brand embedded in the tile, was now used to bring calves, born in the winter's freeze, inside and place them in front of the fireplace to be sure they survived the night. In the bedroom and bathroom area they had recently built a large shower with two shower heads for mom to sit and shower. Rochelle showed me this newest addition, "Bill and I still love to shower together – turns out we use it more than mom!"

We laughed together, "That is so great. I love that you and Bill, now in your 70s, are still so intimate together after 50 years of marriage. You know, you and I are miles apart in our relationship life, but I have always appreciated the longevity and abiding love the two of you have for each other."

The living room carpet was the original orange shag, and the

THE DARK LABYRINTH

heavy drapes with orange and green flowers matched perfectly. The piano that now stood idle most of the time, but where their daughter had played in her growing-up years, occupied a wall where, in another home, a TV set would have installed. (Like many Adventists, they have never had a television set in their home.) Whenever I visited them, I always felt I had stepped into a time warp with every detail authentically intact. It was a little like walking into a childhood memory.

The large kitchen Rochelle had designed boasted countless dark cupboards hanging over three long counters and a ranch-size stove, where over the years, she had prepared meals for her family and lunches for the ranch hands. Against a partial wall was an ancient dishwasher that walked across the floor with thunderous noises when in use and was a constant source of jokes.

One evening during our visit, the seven of us sitting around the old-fashioned chrome table that separated the kitchen from the living room, we carried on a delightful after-dinner conversation of family memories that brought laughter and sighs. I admit that I was often a rather mercenary provocateur with my family, using every opportunity to dig into our psyches, to satisfy the restlessness to understand myself and my lineage and the history into which I was born. I turned to mom who sat beside me in her wheelchair pushed up to the table, and finding the question somehow fit in the conversation, I asked her if she had any regrets in her long life. A pregnant pause as we all waited. "Well, yes, just one, I regret that Dayton didn't live long enough for me to tell him how much I hated him."

Shock waves reverberated through the stunned silence. Eyes suddenly found empty dinner plates fascinating, a few throats were cleared, but no words relieved the deafening hush that settled over the table. What does a family do after a moment of truth like this? I wasn't as shocked as the others. Mama and I had been here before, but I was deeply saddened and finally spoke into the hush. "Mama you don't want to die hating anyone, even Papa." She mumbled something unintelligible. Someone filled the silence with an innocuous statement.

ON BE(COME)ING A WOMAN OF WISDOM

Another rushed in to add their own space filler and then another. The family tension was relieved. It was clear we would go no further into the rubble of this land mine dropped into the middle of our convivial family façade. Later that evening, Rochelle pulled me aside and in a near-whisper said, "I had no idea mom felt that way. She's never ever said anything like that before."

I sighed, "Well, perhaps now that the hint of dementia has reared its sad and fearsome head, the dementia has allowed her to find and express real feelings. It's also a testament to how well she has hidden her inner life from us, her family, and the world-at-large."

We return now to births and children that defined so much of Marian's life. After David's birth, there was the hemorrhaging loss of a 5-month-old fetus. With this interruption, their fifth child, Don, came a whopping three years after David. With nary a pause, Dayton insisted on pushing his macho dream of a dozen kids, so onward towards that goal our family welcomed a sixth child; a girl born on Valentine's day 1951. They named her Gayle Anna after Marian's mother. Then in the last cold December days of 1953, the last child born alive arrived. He was the only boy not given the initials **D.L.J.** Instead, he was named Martin Peter after Dayton's grandfather and Marian's father.

Marian had one more full-term pregnancy, bringing her pregnancy total to nine. It took many conversations between my mother and me for the full story of the birth to emerge, though the detail of the phone call was one my grandmother, Anna, confided to my sisters and me with the idea no doubt of cementing our antipathy toward Dayton.

In July 1955, our family had been living with Grandma Trotto for nearly six years, and Dayton had been living in Seattle for the last two of those years where he had recently started a new job at Boeings. He theoretically came to Bellingham on weekends, though that had wordlessly shifted to every other weekend. Early in the morning of the 11th of July, Marian bolted upright from a sound sleep. She quickly ascertained the baby was coming. When the next contraction came, a piercing sustained pain, she knew this one was different. And then she saw the blood. She called out to her mom; Anna rushed into Marian's bedroom. "Call Dr. Z and get a taxi." Anna sprang into action. She was a small, physically unremarkable woman but had the inner strength of a giant. She was easily at her best meeting an emergency.

As the taxi sped toward the hospital, Marian's belly roiled in an unfamiliar way. She wanted to cry out, scream from the pain, but she fought hard, not wanting to scare the driver, though the low moaning that escaped her lips no doubt reverberated throughout the cab. What a relief for both of them when they arrived at the emergency room. Dr. Z, sensing an emergency, had called ahead, so the orderlies were there with the stretcher and wheeled her right into the operating room.

Meantime, Anna telephoned Dayton in Seattle, "Marian's gone to the hospital, the baby is on the way, you best come."

"Well, maybe I'll wait till the weekend. It'll be hard to get the time off right now because I'm so new on the job."

Anna's fear and anger vibrated through the wire, her voice was low, commanding, "I think you better come now. Marian was in a lot of pain, there is blood. Something's not right." He wasn't used to his mother-in-law asserting herself and he felt the edge of fear in her voice.

"What seems to be wrong? I mean she's had so many kids and they all have come easily."

Anna was relieved, even a little self-righteous when she heard concern come into his voice. "I don't know Dayton. I just know she was in extreme pain, could hardly walk."

"Ok, I'll get the next bus north I'm not sure when I'll get there, but I'll go directly to the hospital when I arrive." The relief was palpable on each end as the phone line went dead. Though it had been many years since our family had moved in with Grandma Trotto, Anna and Dayton were never comfortable having to talk directly to one another.

Dr. Z, who had delivered all but her first two children, was at the hospital to meet Marian. She was vaguely aware they didn't take time to prep her, and she felt Dr. Z examining her. He quickly determined why she was in such extreme pain; the afterbirth was coming first, otherwise known as placental abruption. "Mrs. Johnson," she heard his voice close to her ear, "there is a problem with the baby." Though she heard words, she could make no sense of them. She simply closed her eyes and drifted into darkness.

At that moment, Dr. Z made a crucial decision. He could try a caesarian section and maybe save the baby, but he knew the risk of losing Marian was extremely high, her body and energy dangerously weakened from the multiple births and the beatings (she'd briefly hinted at the beatings in his office a few months earlier when he expressed concern for her physical and emotional condition). Or he could let the birth go as it was unfolding, the afterbirth coming first. He chose the second, and as soon as the afterbirth was cleared out and he had the child in his hands, he confirmed what he had guessed. The baby boy was stillborn. And then, as her doctor and perhaps only confidant, knowing she didn't want more children and knowing she probably wouldn't survive another pregnancy, he made another crucial decision. He tied her tubes.

Marian made no secret over the years of her gratefulness to Dr. Z. "I'm so glad he wasn't a Catholic doctor who would have decided to save the child first before the mother. That's what they do you know. Had he chosen to save the baby, my seven children, or maybe eight, would have lost their mother. Imagine," she'd say to us, generally my sisters and me. "I hate to think what would have happened because, well, you girls know Dayton, he isn't/wasn't much of a father, and I was so thankful I'd never have to go through another pregnancy. I was tired, just bone-weary tired."

She never got to see this son. Before she had come out of the haze of the sedatives and painkillers, Dayton had arrived from Seattle and spirited the tiny body away and had him cremated. All she had left was the little note from the funeral home that they'd received the body of baby boy Johnson, $10 had been paid, and the body had been cremated. Decades later when we siblings were going through mom's mementos, we would find that receipt and the newspaper announcement of the death of baby boy Johnson at birth. I sent a little prayer of acknowledgment that evening to remember this being who lived only in his mother's womb and never himself gave a lusty cry as he entered the earth realm. None of my siblings wanted these little slips of paper. They now find a home in my mementos until I myself can add them to the fires of released memories.

I am eternally grateful that my mother shared her dangerous stories. Her act of bravery nourished a need in both of us - mine to know our story and hers to speak her story. One time, I asked her directly how it had been for her in the household with Grandma and Papa. She haltingly described what an uncomfortable arrangement this powerful split between the two had been for her: the deeply religious, pious to a fault, mother/grandmother she so loved and who helped the family to survive, and the atheist, fun-loving but violent alcoholic husband/father she had married. "I was always caught between the two, always trying to please them both, not knowing where I fit. And you know," she would whisper conspiratorially, "my father would never have approved of Dayton."

Living well into old age, buffeted by circumstances, she seemed to have her own version of a peaceful heart. Marians wasn't an easy life, but she had an indomitable feminine spirit, a quiet potent center that chose to hang out in the earth realm for over 100 years. I am in awe seeing how she and thousands, no millions, of mothers are indeed the embodiment of the earth itself.

I sense the powerful resonance between my two mothers - the earth, that despite how we humans abuse and use her, continues to support us however long she can. And Marian, who, despite being used and abused, is not an object of pity, but rather the powerful energy of the earth itself. She loved the world around her and quietly held her children in her heart. When I asked her what she was most proud of in her life she instantly replied, "My children. You've all turned out well. That makes me proud."

For centuries, the dominant expression of feminine *Shakti Energy* has been that of Marian and her mother Anna – passive acceptance and long-suffering forbearance, seeing to the needs of men and children, not taking "a seat at the table." It's not bad nor wrong, just limited. Today, a hitherto untapped expression of feminine *Shakti Energy* is emerging. I experience this energy as a celebration of the body, the power of sensuality, loving stewardship of the earth, and challenging the patriarchy - daring we humans to live in connection rather than separation.

The Dark Labyrinth of My Matriarchal Lineage

We children grew up believing that on our mother's side, we were one-quarter Italian descended from Grandpa Trotto and one-quarter Scotch from Anna's side of the family. I loved to listen to and dream about the oft-repeated story of Peter Trotto's flight from a depressed little village in "the boot of Italy." How he ran away from a violent father, stowed away at the tender age of 12, and arrived in New York where a distant uncle lived and took him in. How he worked hard for two years saving his money and returned to Italy. What a hero I imagined he was as he presented himself at the doorstep of his family hovel dressed in his cheap ill-fitting suit that his uncle had passed down to him, the shoes he'd shined to bring out the little remaining luster hidden behind the scruffs. Yes, he was proud. He'd gone to America and the dream was alive in him. As the door handle turned to his knock, he drew in his breath, the chest of his slight frame puffed out. As the door opened cautiously, he peered hopefully into the eyes of his father, "Papa!" the hint of joy at seeing his father bursting forth.

The voice that blasted him, as he was about to step across the threshold, was gruff and angry, just as he remembered. "I have no son." Fourteen-year-old Peter caught a glimpse of his mother's face, eyes sad beyond comprehension, her hand raised slightly as his father slammed the door forever shut. It would only be after his father's death that Peter's mother sought out the village scribe who wrote letters for her to her son in America. When the letters found their way to America to her equally illiterate son, it was Peter's wife Anna, who could neither read, write nor speak Italian that would do her best to phonetically read the letters to him. It is these same letters that I would one day carry with me to Italy in search of our family roots.

It isn't hard to imagine Peter's despair, the loneliness of being cast out from his family, the hopelessness of his smashed dream of coming home to his family, grown to be a young man, able to help his family, only to be met by his father's fierce hatred, his mother's sadness. How it must have torn the joy and shining beauty of his young and proud eyes and passed a shadow over his soul. I imagine him with leaden feet turning and shuffling away from his family home, the coaxed-out luster of his shoes mocking him as he stumbled off the door stoop onto the brown dust of the Italian soil his family tried marginally to farm.

He still had the money in his pocket he'd brought with him to share with his family. Once more his eyes turned west to America, the unquenchable hope of the immigrant restoring some of the shine his father had so ruthlessly destroyed. This time he booked his ticket, yes in steerage, but no longer a stow-away. He must have taken some pride in this change of circumstances.

This, I thought was one half of my matriarchal lineage. I happily identified with my Italian nature: the passion, the gesturing hands, the world of Fellini. It gave me a sense of identity throughout my life, a way to categorize my underlying passionate nature.

But there was a mysterious story my sister Gayle had shared with we siblings after Grandma Trotto died. It seems that one afternoon, in the last year of her life, Grandma was trying to write a letter, but her hands had grown too weak. Gayle, with whom she was living at the time, offered to help her write it. Grandma replied, "Well no, it's a personal letter to Mama." (She often referred to our mother this way.) She added, "I'll talk to Marian when she comes to visit next week."

Gayle continued with her story. "When Mom left, I asked Grandma if she had been able to talk to Mom and Grandma replied sadly that she had told Mama there was something she needed to talk with her about, but that Mama had rebuffed her." Incredulous and curious, I asked Gayle if she had pursued the matter further with Grandma. She said no, it hadn't seemed to her that Grandma wanted to talk about it.

Time passed and once again, unable to halt my curiosity, I questioned our mom about the incident, asking what she thought Grandma wanted to share with her. Mom claimed not to remember Grandma ever wanting to talk to her about something personal. I asked her one more time about a year later, but her story remained the same. I asked, "If Grandma had needed to talk to you about something private, what would it have been?" With a frown, she insisted that she couldn't imagine what on earth Grandma might have wanted to talk with her about. The mystery lay idle.

The answer to this mystery would pierce through the secret darkness in my mother's 99th year. With her dementia deepening and her hips unable to support her, Gayle and Rochelle, who had been caring for our mom - six months with one then six months with the other - could no longer manage her care, so we decided to move her to a small home for women in Bellingham. To help with the transition, we seven siblings had gathered in Bellingham where my three brothers lived. David, who had been single for years, and Don, married to Alene, had lived in Bellingham most of their adult lives. Martin, the youngest and divorced from his wife, had recently moved to the area from northern California. In his high-tech job, Martin was on the road weeks at a time, so his company had given him the choice of where he wanted to be based and he'd chosen Bellingham.

My sister Gayle and her husband Keith were ranchers in Montana, as were Rochelle and Bill in Oregon. Both ranch operations were in full swing, harvesting alfalfa crops, grain, corn, and hay, and the men couldn't leave the farm, so Gayle drove mom to Bellingham, and Rochelle drove alone. My sister Laura had moved to Little Rock, Arkansas in 1972 after her marriage to Jim, a structural engineer. He ran his own company and seldom found the time to travel to the northwest when Laura would come to family gatherings. In my case,

THE DARK LABYRINTH

since William, my partner, had minimal history with my family, we readily agreed he stay behind. I was content to go alone. Thus, in the designs of fate, the seven siblings, all without partners except for Don's lovely wife, Alene, gathered together in Bellingham. With no partners and despite the sadness at our mom's failing health, the seven of us settled into an easy camaraderie of appreciation and laughter - re-telling old family stories of which we never tired and sharing new stories of our children and grandchildren.

One of us was always with mom at the home as she struggled to adjust. They were hard days for everyone because she couldn't quite understand what was going on, and in the first few days, she felt we were betraying her by leaving her with strange people. And then, like a gift from the dementia gods, she determined that her roommate, Ethyl, was actually Grandma Trotto. Ethyl was thin and of small stature. Her round face with rimless glasses and her long gray hair braided and pinned at the back of her head rendered a likeness to Anna. Overnight, mom's lifetime tranquility returned. She wasn't to be swayed from her conviction of who Ethyl was, and Ethyl, as quiet as Anna had been, never objected to Marian's fantasy. Over the three years she was there, when I, or another sibling, was taking leave of her after a visit, she'd say, "Say good-bye to Grandma."

Afternoons or evenings of the week together, we would gather at Pam's cozy two-bedroom home, where she had moved a year before from Port Angeles, Washington. I was staying with her for the duration and had co-opted her living room for the task of going through mom's things. Pam had close relationships with her aunts and uncles and loved having this family activity in her home, where every corner of her living room was filled with boxes of memorabilia to be gone through, as well as new piles for each sibling's personal relics. Both Anna and Marian had squirreled away keepsakes of their lives right down to the tiny cards that had accompanied flower arrangements at Peter's funeral! We unpacked boxes of pictures, objects, letters, legal documents, many dating back more than 100 years. We even found a couple of almost titillating love letters from an early boyfriend of moms, as well as pictures of the two of them together which wowed us as none of us knew anything of this man before Dayton, who had asked her to marry him and she had rejected. We indulged in "what ifs," and I remarked to myself it had never occurred to me to ask her about boyfriends before Papa.

But the most giant WOW by far was the crisp November day when Don found the marriage license of Peter and Anna. It was stuffed into a box with hundreds of other pieces of paper including mementos dating back to Anna's early days, even to the days of Anna's parents. I saw Don peering closely at the marriage license. "Wow, look at this," he inhaled sharply, " someone tried to smear the marriage date to read January 1, 1915. I can make out that it was January 1, 1918."

"What?! No way. Let me see!" our babbling voices grew insistent, and Don relinquished the paper. We passed it around, aware that baby Marian, our mother, was born on October 17, 1915. It seems that the Italian immigrant, Peter Trotto, was not our grandfather after all!

As one after the other we fingered the brittle paper, peered closely at the smeared date, each one confirmed for her or himself that the marriage had indeed occurred in 1918. To say that each face registered consternation, and not a little denial, is to put it mildly. It was Rochelle that confided to me the next day that she hadn't slept all night thinking of what we'd uncovered. I guessed that for her and Gayle, the other Adventist in the family, the idea that mom was illegitimate was a dark stain in their Christian consciousness and hard to swallow. For me, after the initial shock and loss of my Italian identity, I was wildly curious about who our real grandfather was. What a grand mystery! In the obfuscation of Peter and Anna's marriage license, I wondered about the hidden antecedents to their marriage. Mom's dementia made it impossible to ask her if she knew anything about who had tried to change the date on the marriage license. Collectively, we wondered aloud if she'd known these details and had perhaps been the one that had tried to change the year of the marriage to 1915. Then again, maybe Grandma was the one trying to change the story of her daughter's birth.

My brother Don's dedicated sleuthing would eventually locate our mother's birth certificate in the records of the state of Idaho. Opening the email attachment he'd sent, I stared at the word written with a light hand as though the doctor was loath to have to stain the life of this young woman, Anna and her firstborn. **Illegitimate**, screamed out at me. Beside the word, "Father" was a quickly scrawled,"?".

Though I never knew Grandpa Trotto, mom's "adopted" father who died in her 18th year, I believe he was a good man. The story will always remain a mystery, but he did take into his heart this woman, Anna, and her daughter, and never in any family story was anything different even hinted at. In my mother's family of origin, there were five siblings - Marian, and four brothers, Frank, Tom, Sam, and John. Group pictures of the five, taken over the years, show four curly-haired, swarthy-skinned Italians and one very pale Scotch-looking sister. It was always said that Marian took after the Scotch side and the boys took after the Italian side.

Soon after locating the birth certificate, Don and I decided to send off a saliva sample to *Ancestry.com*. He tried to get mom to spit into the vial but she wasn't having it, so Don sent his saliva. For two years he researched and checked new people coming into the *Ancestry.com* system. It's a time-consuming undertaking, but Don was captivated. The first official confirmation that Peter wasn't our grandfather occurred when our first cousin, Brian, showed up in the *Ancestry.com* system as Don's second cousin. (First cousins always show up sharing the same two grandparents of either the matriarchal or patriarchal line. Don and Brian only shared one grandparent, Anna Trotto.)

On Christmas Day 2017, the day after mom passed away on Christmas Eve, Don was reviewing his account on *Ancestry.com* when the ancestral line of our true grandfather was revealed. Someone showed up in the system as a second cousin, which meant he shared a grandparent with us. What a synchronicity! Mom had refused the knowledge of her lineage and then magically, the morning after she left the earth, a matching DNA of a cousin appeared. It turns out our lineage runs right through the UK from England to Scotland and Wales. Don contacted the cousin and confirmed the shared grandfather, F.F. We were sad to learn the family had no pictures of him. Apparently, this grandfather and his family had moved to Canada, and according to this cousin, at some point, his grandmother had taken her children and left her husband (our grandfather) in Canada and returned to America. Don and I guessed that F.F., our grandfather, wasn't a very nice man if the family had chosen to forget him.

I spent a few days lamenting the loss of this favored and very relatable Italian identity, but in the end, I acknowledged the fact of our racial heritage. And while the family's treasured story of an Italian immigrant was no longer technically, factually my story, I nevertheless carry the spirit of Peter's story in my heart – a cultural inheritance from Anna and Marian.

But now the flashpoint that burned inside of me was the question of my mother's conception. The same desire to know and understand burned in my brother Don's psyche as well, and together we dared delve into the story rather than sink into the comfort of denial. And thus we pieced together the story.

It seems that Grandma Anna at the time of Marian's conception was a housekeeper (birth certificate information). For unskilled young women of the time, thrown on their resources (Anna's father had died in 1912 when she was just 21), housekeeping would have been a job available to her. Her employer was most likely our grandfather, F. F., a farmer bachelor ten years her senior (census information). For my blue-eyed brother Don, alone amongst the brown-eyed siblings, F.F. had blue eyes (army papers), which also explained Marian's hazel eyes.

Was it consensual? No! I have no doubt it was rape, pure and simple. That Grandma was shy and retiring around others was instantly clear to anyone who observed her. In pictures of her as a child and a young woman, I see someone who can barely look at the camera. (The only exception to that is a mysterious photo of her laughing as she holds onto her hat from an unseen wind, standing next to a smiling man, clearly not Peter, who holds Marian. Someone had written on the margin of the picture, "Anna and Marian with guide.") Ah-h the secrets that will never be revealed.

Among the mementos stashed in mom's closets, there was a postcard from Anna to her sister Agnes, sent from Sweet Sage, Idaho. Anna would have been about one month pregnant. Then there is one from Agnes to Anna. The postcards are vague. In one, Anna asks her sister to come visit her. Next, we tracked the sisters to Colt, Idaho (census), when Anna would have been about three months pregnant. Don and I couldn't discover anything of the sisters, Anna and Agnes, for the next six months. (When I was growing up, looking at pictures of Anna's youth, her younger sister Agnes was a mystery for me. She had severe asthma and in her 26th year, she informed Anna that the next time she had an asthma attack she wasn't going to fight for breath. She was going just to stop breathing. Sadly, Agnes did die from her next asthma attack. Mom would tell us that Anna was bereft without her sister and confidant.) Marian's birth certificate shows that Anna gave birth in Colt, Idaho, close to Idaho Falls, the town Marian always identified as her birthplace. At last we had pieced together our mother's conception and birth as far as we could.

In speaking of Marian's youth, her young adulthood, I speak out now of her **#MeToo** experience as it aligns with Grandma's **#MeToo** experience - those experiences in the life of a woman when a man with power abuses her and, in the case of Anna and Marian, rapes them.

I learned the story of Marian's rape on one of my summer visits to Bellingham. When Marian's second husband, Bill, passed away in 1992, she sold their home in rural Whatcom County and moved into town, where she now lived in a quiet residential trailer park in a double-wide trailer she had proudly purchased herself. On my visits "home," we would often hang out together over breakfast, talking and reminiscing and planning the afternoon activities. This morning, from where I sat in the dining area that gave onto the ample living room, I remarked to myself how the living room furniture, pillows, and throws she'd crocheted or knitted, reflected her fondness for fall colors and patterns. Orange, yellows, browns, and splashes of greens in leaf and flower shapes of all sizes competed for my attention. "Not my style," I remarked to myself, and out loud, "Mom, you really get the morning sun through the front windows. It's great how the colors get so bright."

"Yes, you're right," she smiled almost sheepishly, "though I didn't plan it that way."

"Well, planned or not, it's a wonderful feature of your home and makes the room feel warm and cozy. The sun always relaxes me. I guess that's why I left the northwest for California," I added with a laugh. "But I know you like the northwest weather, right?"

"Yes, some people don't like the rain, but I do. Like your sun, the rain relaxes me."

"Yeah, I guess we are different in a lot of ways." With barely a pause I continued, "You know I'm in a new relationship with this guy, Frank, who I met through Nisha. You've met her right?" She nodded yes. "Well, he's pretty amazing. You'll meet him at some point." I added jokingly, "Assuming we stay together." Then with my insatiable curiosity about my history, I jumped, "Mom, tell me again how you and Papa met. I know you met him when you were in secretarial school, but not much more than that. Were you attracted to him right off?"

"No!" her retort was instant and caught me off guard. Then a pause, "Well a friend at the secretarial school talked about him and that he was in the Navy. One time when he came home, she introduced us, and we all went out together."

"He was her boyfriend?" I queried, titillated by the implication she had stolen her friend's boyfriend.

"No, they were just friends. He was fun to be with and in his Navy uniform, very handsome. We started going out, but that's not why we got married."

"So then it was loving not just his handsomeness?" I teased with a smile.

"No, it wasn't really because I <u>loved</u> him. . ." the emphasis on the word love hinting at something. Though I was impatient as she paused for what seemed like forever, she finally continued. "One time when we went out Dayton forced himself on me. I didn't know how to stop him. He was strong, a little bit drunk so he seemed even stronger and more insistent. Earlier, at his urging, I'd had a beer, so I wasn't clear-headed. I don't remember much about it, but after that, I felt dirty. I hated him and I hated myself. I didn't think I had any choice but to marry him because I didn't deserve any other man. I wasn't pregnant or anything, I just felt so sullied and unworthy and filled with regret and hate." As she repeated the words, "I felt so dirty," her pain held me as her voice broke. I understood then that the feeling had never left her and had intensified over the years she was with Dayton, and it explained the inexplicable – why she had tolerated the ways he continued to sully her: her profound and heart-breaking belief she deserved no better.

I held my tongue and distress for as long as I could, but I had to ask. "Mom, are you saying that he forced you to have sex? But that's rape! He date raped you. Today, that's what it's called." I couldn't stop my outburst or join her in her self-hatred. I ranted on indignantly at this new wrinkle in the mosaic of my mother's life.

"Well, yes I guess so. I've never really allowed myself to use that word."

"Yes, I understand it's an ugly word, rape, but that's what it was. Him forcing himself on you is rape!" Her eyes glazed stolidly into the distance, mine burned with fiery outrage. "I get now why you hate him, though as far as I can tell this was only the beginning of his violence toward you. I hate him for what he did to you."

I felt her shrink away and knew I'd gone too far and had sucked out all the air in the space where perhaps more could have been revealed. Though I gently tried to hold open the door to talk further, I had slammed it shut with my outrage and lack of control. She could go no further. We had touched the debilitating pain of her life with Dayton, and she hastily floated back into the darkness of unknowing.

There would be times later on when I'd try to broach the subject, but she had locked the door into that memory. It pained me that I couldn't help her exorcise that ghost, but that was not her path.

I continue to reflect on this matriarchal lineage even to this day. What a tragedy that for both my mother and grandmother, the first sexual experience of intercourse was rape. I broke that thread in my lineage when as a starry-eyed teenager my best friend Peggy and I made a pact to "go all the way" with our boyfriends. Now it's true I didn't choose the young man with eyes wide open as to who he was, but I did choose. And there was a point where his and my intentions merged: I wanted to lose my virginity, and he, a testosterone driven and insecure young 17-year-old, wanted to have sex with a virgin!

The weight of my female lineage of self-hatred around sex was cracked open. Rather than self-hatred, I would embrace sensual transcendent sexuality even when I didn't have the words to explain it. Ultimately, the power dynamic of men and women I carried inside of me, originating beyond my matriarchal lineage back into ancient ancestral DNA itself, would resolve itself into the full light of understanding and wisdom when, with a future partner, we would reach the limitless through the tantric path.

2
1946

The Sun Room

A Shattering Decision That Binds My Heart

Young Street and 621-23rd Street were the abodes of my youth in Bellingham, Washington. The Young Street house still stands kitty-corner from Bellingham High School, which I, and most of my siblings, attended. Over the years, I've occasionally driven by the house, admiring the simple architecture of the early 1900s. Nearly square in shape with a dormer window atop the roof surveying the neighborhood, a small green lawn edges a narrow sidewalk, with three steps leading up to the front porch. On each corner of the modest porch stands a post with scalloped trim, and window seats occupy two sides. Three small bay windows wrapping around the living room complete the façade of normalcy.

The front door opens into the sunroom that, during the occupancy of our young family, was designated the girl's playroom where we were allowed to leave toys scattered about. Even though an archway opened into the living room, the space had a hidden yet out-in-the-open quality that suffused it with a mystery that satisfied a deep longing in me for internal quiet. Though I didn't have words to describe it, this longing was simply my innate introversion.

Playing, imagining, and daydreaming in that room, with the sun filtering in through the windows, I could touch a light and carefree place inside. When the sun couldn't melt away strange shadows playing about the corners of my mind, and a somber mood would fill the room, I would listen attentively until I was sure Mama was busy in another part of the house. Then quiet like a little thieving mouse, I'd open the door to the small closet off our playroom where a 50-pound bag of sugar beckoned me. In the faintly lit closet, tucked away in a dark corner, I'd unroll the top of the brown paper bag, wet my finger, and dip into that sack of whiteness, and no matter what my mood, that taste would bring a secret smile to my sweetened lips. One more dip, or maybe two, reluctantly sliding my finger from my mouth, loath to leave the treasured grains, I'd slowly push down the top of the sack, creep back out, shut the door ever so carefully, and reprise my spot among the toys. Eyes closed, I'd savor the lingering sweetness, and when only the echoes of that tryst remained, I'd open my eyes, surprised to find myself in a nearly forgotten reality.

Fittingly, the room held, on a far-reaching fate-filled day, a heart-wrenching decision precipitated by my new position as the middle daughter. My younger sister, Laura, sent from an unknown source, had landed in our family five or six months before this event. When Mama brought this tiny creature with fingers and toes home from the hospital, she was a novelty for my nearly 2-year-old curiosity. Standing by the bassinette, peering in through the open lattice, I would stare at her, and when she would wrap her tiny fingers around mine, my delight in having a baby sister knew no bounds. In my parents' faces, with eyes alight, big smiles, and the cooing sounds they'd make when they held her, I grasped that they were equally enthralled. I mean I really loved my little sister, but I felt, with confused affection, how the adults just couldn't get enough of darling Laura. . .so sweet, so quiet, and she seldom irritated Mama with unwarranted crying.

When Laura arrived, I was already fighting hard to feel seen and loved in the shadow of Rochelle, my adored older sister. Though I couldn't articulate concepts at the time, I admired her, and though different in our essences, I ached to be like her. I was envious of how she brought ready smiles to adults with her giggling laughter, her red ringlet curls, her ready smile of confidence in the world around her. In pictures of our years on Young Street, Rochelle smiles engagingly back at the photographer, curls ringing her round open face. Conversely, my dark impenetrable eyes stare off in the distance—thin strands of reluctant hair frame my narrow face.

I felt squeezed between these two sister bubbles of parental joy and attention and judged there would never be space for me. I was a nearly deflated bubble of vital life that, no matter how hard I pushed against the sister bubbles on both sides of me, I was squeezed out. There was an unerring certainty inside of me that I would never be seen and loved like they were.

Was the sun shining through the windows that day when I sat in my "hidden" corner in the sunroom? If so, its rays couldn't penetrate the shadow I felt pressing me down. And so it was, at the dawn of my 3rd year, I made the momentous decision that I would never fall prey to the need to be seen and loved and touched by others. I was an island, and no one could ever cross the ocean around me and hurt me. The pain I felt in my lost corner of the sunroom was more than my child's body and mind could bear. It was so dark, so scary, like being in a cave that unknown hands had sealed up, forgetting whatever lay behind that cave door. Unconsciously, I drew a heavy veil around me, one that would let me be a critical observer of the world, giving me protection from the pain and heartache, a thin veil of transparency that would allow manageable impressions, feelings, sights, and sounds to filter through. (The understanding and complexity of this memory would come in my adult life.)

From that barely conscious moment, the unintended consequence of my decision was that I would never be 100% present in my life. From my teen years right into adulthood, living always behind the veil, I'd limit and restrict myself during interactions with others: a boy that had rejected me or perhaps smiled at me, a friend that had gossiped about me, a party I'd attended, an adult critical of me. No matter what the tone, good or bad, I'd hold my reactions and words inside until I was safely sequestered back home where I would "go to the sunroom" and re-enter the experience, make-up stories, revise interactions, creating a deadening enchantment. I built an insular world of survival that protected me, and yes, of course, limited me.

I have come to comprehend that this decision was an element in the manifestation of tantric *Shakti Energy* fomenting inside me. Simply put, the need to connect in mind, body, and soul did not go away. This basic drive found its expression through my natural sexual predilection. I would use the ecstasy of orgasm to open, not only to another, but to who I was in my core. As the orgasm would fade the veil would drop, and I would retreat inside and jealously guard my love, my fear, and my power from the world.

I believe that all of us, with few exceptions, desire to love and be loved and know the power of our wholeness. I would even propose that this drive is in our very DNA. There are infinite paths to this wholeness, and I have been destined to fulfill this ancient covenant through immense sexual energy. Today, in my 77th year, as I ride this particular train to the manifestation of *Shakti*, perhaps my train ride can smooth the passage of women, young and old, whose energy, like mine, manifests through sexuality, bodies, and the sensate.

Today is the moment of **#MeToo.** That is the train that has roared out of the long dark tunnel of ignorance. I'm infinitely grateful for the women of today, and the endless generations of builders before, that have brought the **#MeToo** train thundering across this country, nay the western world and beyond, and has given me the courage and context to tell my story.

3

1949

Transition

Blessings and Banes of a Budding Tantrika

In the bright and orderly Young Street home, right around my 6th birthday, a conversation that had been floating through the rooms and activities solidified into "The Move." Even though still innocently young and not understanding completely, it filtered down to Rochelle and me that Papa had been drunk on his job driving a truck for Standard Fruits Company, had crashed the company truck, and had been fired without ceremony. Driving truck would be the last steady job Dayton would have for more than half a decade. With no steady income and the hungry mouths of four children and another on the way, the family was forced to move in with Marian's mother, Anna, our Grandma Trotto. Papa borrowed a truck, and in just a few trips, he'd moved everything from the furnished house on Young Street, across town to Grandma Trotto's place in the area known as the South Side and more specifically Happy Valley.

When our family arrived in 1949, Happy Valley was a low-lying area broken here and there by meandering hills. Nestled throughout were simple, modest homes, many built in the early 1900s by their owners, just as Anna and her husband Peter had done. Peter's death when Marian was 18 had left the family with few financial resources to maintain the property, leaving the house and outbuildings run-down. Though Grandma had done her best to repair damages, the door to the cluttered garage hung lopsided on its rusty metal runner, the rickety stairs and railings felt almost unsafe, and in front of the garage, a woodpile begged to be stacked in the woodshed. Jumbled bushes and tall grasses ran right up to the half-buried basement. When we arrived, my excited 6-year-old eyes didn't register dismay and embarrassment at our new home. That would come later in junior high when my eyes, enculturated by the collective, saw disrepair and destitution.

At 621-23rd Street, the 3-story house structure demanded new strategies. Marian and Dayton's bedroom would be the west-facing room on the first floor. It had been Marian's room when she was growing up, and now only a short hallway separated Anna's bedroom from that of her daughter and son-in-law.

The children's bedrooms were upstairs except for the latest child – he or she slept in a crib in our parents' bedroom. David and Don were assigned the smaller south-facing room. Rochelle, Laura, and I had the larger north-facing room where in winter the nor'easters would howl through the walls and window. (In the cold of winter, with icicles hanging on the inside of the windows, Laura and I would sleep in one bed with all our covers and quilts piled over us.) In spite of the winter's chill and summer's heat, the three of us proudly took ownership of the expansive room with sloping ceilings and various nooks and crannies. Over the years we would rearrange our personal space and create new spaces. We bought a record player together and paid for a phone in our bedroom. We bought paint and painted the room a bright yellow. Though there was competition between us, our room coalesced us into a sister unit of love and support, creating an invisible barrier to anyone that might encroach on our space.

Within Grandma's land and numerous buildings were treasures to be used and explored. We kids loved to creep into the room above the root cellar where family stories were hidden away in mementos held in steamer trunks. We discovered letters written between people we didn't know, so we dreamed up imaginary stories about them.

We'd wander among old furniture and discover weird treasures from the travels of Marian's brothers, like a painted, 4-foot-tall wooden cut-out of a hula dancer wearing a grass skirt hanging in tatters. A hillside rose up behind the house topped off by the chicken house filled with clucking hens, a shed where we would hang a basketball net, and the old one-cow barn on the other side of the hill that in our teens we would clean and convert to a sleep-over space. When we were old enough to imagine a baseball diamond and do the work of hand-mowing the wild grasses in the yard beside the house, we would create our own baseball field.

Beyond where the house sat in the middle of an acre of fruit trees, berry bushes, and garden there was a direct path through neighbors' yards to Sehome Hill Park where adventures for our young minds and bodies were endless. We wandered across the manicured green grass where swings hung for our body-pumping flights, and when that was too tame, we ascended the hill into the wooded area where we climbed rock "mountains," found caves, and reveled in the tall surrounding evergreens. Though Bellingham was often overcast and gray, it was nevertheless a sprawling land of unruly green and blue, a fecund wildness that, unknown to me at the time, echoed my *Shakti* energy. As I look back, I am convinced that the move to Happy Valley was the essential ground-of-being for the nascent tantrika that lay beneath the bewildered child.

An unexpected outcome of the move was that our parents decided Rochelle and I should finish out the school year at our old school. Each day, Rochelle and I would take a cross-town bus three miles to school, and at noon I'd ride the bus back alone to the Garden Street stop, then trek the mile home from the bus stop. The first time, though I was nervous and scared, I was proud of my burgeoning maturity. I have metaphorically taken that first bus ride over and over again, daring, throughout my life, to brave a vast unknown. I remember a phonograph record we had of a character named Little Audrey. From that 45 rpm record that I'd repeatedly play, one refrain resonated in my child psyche, "*Little Audrey says, 'look before you leap,' but she doesn't look cause it's more fun to be surprised when the leap is done."* Living my life as Little Audrey advised has always made perfect sense to me! She was my first heroine.

The move to 23rd street signaled a cataclysmic shift in our family dynamics. There were now three adults in the household. (Today, I view them through field theory as merely three roles in a field, but back then, it wasn't a theory, it was a living story.) Grandma, the matriarch, owned the house and would now be a defender of the weakest one, Mama. (Time would make me doubt this supposed bulwark against Papa's violence that would reach dangerous levels.) Papa was the ostensible male head of the family with a silent adversary, and he was living in her home. On the religious front, Grandma a Seventh-day Adventist, Papa an atheist, Mama neither. On the character front, Grandma the responsible and duty conscious adult, Papa the irresponsible and irrepressible indulger, Mama clinging to simple physical survival. Grandma, the hard-working, self-effacing, could do a man's job any day from plumbing, building, hauling manure – the list goes on and on. Papa happier to play than work yet delighted to work when it was creative and noticeable. Mama, the daughter, and wife, worked hard to serve both master and mistress. I think it was a time of terrible disquiet and despair for Mama, though she never openly defied either of the other two.

When I look back, I recognize how Anna and Marian had no choice but to create a <u>much-needed</u> bulwark against Dayton's anger and unpredictability. Unfortunately, with the new family dynamic, Dayton would begin to turn to his daughter and affairs to feed his starving manhood. This relational backdrop would be the stage for what would be much of the blessings and banes of my struggle toward manifesting my sensual feminine *Shakti* core.

4

1951-1955

Stirrings

Sexual and Spiritual Shakti Tremoring

I was in my element at grade school. I excelled in my studies, played team sports with passion and skill, found my place amongst my schoolmates, and even a little power in the social scene. Entering the halls and classrooms at Larrabee Grade School was my salvation from the craziness of home.

Though the Sun Room decision propagated internal dialogue like, "I don't care about anyone anyway," referring to the big three and my sisters, the truth was, I did care. However, my psychological survival depended on pretending to myself that I didn't. And while this decision not to care gave me a freedom that cannot be underestimated and encouraged my somewhat reflective nature, another outcome was a quiet seething energy - the *Restlessness* that encompassed a deep river of rage flowing inside. As I look back, I can trace its twin headwaters to my father and my grandmother. There is no blame. I recognize and even identify with Grandma's conundrum of being competent, intelligent, independent, and deeply religious, yet always having to submit and accept men's power: from her father's decision to leave the well-appointed family home in Missouri to homestead in Idaho, to the man that raped her, and even her husband of whom Marian, her daughter said, "My dad expected Grandma and me to serve him and my brothers." Most galling of all was to be victimized by the violence of her son-in-law. Though Grandma found quiet and solace in her religion, the shadow of her outrage hung around the house and found a home in my psyche.

My father's rage is more challenging for me to understand, but I have come to know that it was the rage of a weak man who didn't have the guts to go for his big dreams, and so he raged at the culture, his birth, the life he had chosen with his wife and children. My father's rage was that of a man of his time, who, by virtue of his gender, had an inalienable right to power, and yet he was incapable of tapping into that birthright.

My rage, not so different from either of these two adults, boiled just below the surface of my façade, and I could not always deny its expression. It would erupt like a fiery solar flare sending out wild energy that I had no control over. Stories of my exploding rage entered into the family myths told and retold at family gatherings. In the telling and retelling, we would laugh and joke about my just desserts when I would lose control, though I didn't laugh quite so hardily as my siblings.

The most powerful of these rages occurred in my 9th or 10th year. Summertime had rendered the tall grasses on the hillside high and dry. Each of us girls had our piece of cardboard, and with shouts and laughter, we were summer sledding down the hills. Our little brother, David, now 6 or 7, was with us either by Mama's orders or our sometime generosity that let him tag along. He was patiently waiting his turn, waiting for one of his older sisters to share their cardboard sled as his had disintegrated. After one of my runs down the hill as I laughingly rolled off the cardboard, David darted in, grabbed my summer sled, and crawled and slipped his way to the top of the hill. Gleefully, he jumped on my sled and zoomed down the slick burnished grass right into my ankles and knocked me off my feet into the thistles lining the sled run. I shrieked at him as I struggled to crawl out of the thistles that were attacking me with their powerful prickly thorns. He wisely took off as fast as his little legs would carry him, fearing the penalty his rage-filled big sister might inflict as she'd been known to do.

He was a fast little bugger, tearing out across the yard with me fast on his heels. He ran across the driveway, and with only about ten feet left to the bottom of the stairs, I knew I couldn't catch him. Help came in the form of a heavy tow chain with a big hook that I spotted in the driveway. Like Hercules, I reached down and slung it over my shoulder as I ran. As we both dashed up the stairs, he for his life, me for my rage, I called forth all my raging warrior energy and heaved the heavy chain up the last few stairs just as he opened the door and darted into the safety of the house yelling at the top of his lungs for Mama. A loud crack, the softer sound of glass shattering, and the harsh grating of the chain brought my mother instantly to the doorway. She stared in shock at the scene before her, and her eyes, alight with a fire I'd never seen before, burned through me. "Get up here Diane. What have you done?" Well, it was obvious what I had done. I climbed the last few stairs, head bowed, eyes glued to the ground. I started to protest, "He. . ."

Mom wasn't having it. With her finger piercing my chest, she directed me, "Go to the back porch right now!" There was no mystery as to what would happen next. The back porch was where the wood was stacked in the wood box and where both parents meted out punishment. She stormed into where I waited and with one hand, grabbed a stick of wood, and with the other she grabbed my arm, whose great strength I had used to mete justice to my little brother. As she swung, I counted, like I always did when either parent spanked me. She had never hit me more than five times, so though I howled and yowled, I knew it wouldn't last forever. She went the full count this time and unexpectedly added one more for good measure. Undoubtedly her adrenalin was running like fire at the thought of what I might have done to my little brother. "Get upstairs and no supper tonight. You will pay to replace the window! Don't come down till morning. Now go."

I didn't need further orders, figured I better get while the getting was good. I comforted myself that I didn't hate having to stay upstairs – my books were there, my diary, my bed. (Though into the dinner hour with my stomach growling, I would feel like the punishment was unjust.) As I lay on my bed, my howls reduced to offended sniffles, sanity returned. I was grateful David's little legs had carried him swiftly out of harm's way. I was scared at how seriously I could have hurt him. "Maybe I would have killed him," I reflected morbidly. Then mom's last words sunk in. "You will pay to replace that window!" Where would I get the money? We didn't get an allowance, and I knew exactly how much money I had frugally saved from my birthday. As my anger drained away, I lay like a wet dishrag, feeling sorry for myself. When my indulgence in self-pity abated, my rage dropped to the bottom of the well of repression. It would lie like a sleeping giant until one day I would join with a partner that dared to enter, with me, into this violent creative energy.

Though scuffed and scarred by years of poverty, Grandma's big ole run-down house was at times a place of refuge from the world-at-large. Before our arrival, she'd painted the living room walls a soft turquoise and the wainscoting a deeper turquoise. Soon after our move, Papa built floor-to-ceiling bookshelves along one wall to hold the collection of books that included Grandma's old and tattered religious books and childhood novels, as well as books left by her sons when they had left home. Alongside Papa's novels and carpentry and mechanic's guides were Mama's treasured, *The Harvard Classics*, that she'd bought on a two-year monthly installment plan. When I wasn't reading teen romance novels in high school, *The Harvard Classics* was the reading source that opened my mind beyond small-town concerns. Equally prominent on the bookshelves was the *Encyclopedia Britannica* our parents had bought, also on a long-term monthly installment plan from a door-to-door salesman. Those volumes were the source for many a school assignment. Because books held such a prominent place in our family, nurtured by Mama and Papa, Christmas and birthdays, each child received a book. These books too joined the august company on the bookshelves.

In an extended corner of the living room stood a console sewing machine, where over time, all the women and girls in the family would sew clothes. An old-fashioned fold-down couch filled out the remaining wall space. In the future, this is where Don, my husband-to-be, and I, would sleep with our newborn son for the two weeks after his birth. Along the fourth wall was a cluttered dining room table where kids would deposit their junk and valuables of the day. The floor linoleum, whose symmetry had long been obliterated by generations of footsteps, became a playground when, joy of joys, on wet winter days, Mama would allow us to chalk a hopscotch pattern and play hopscotch right in the center of the living room. In the last corner, like an open temple, hovered the smoky stove and chimney. On cold days, we would fight over who got to sit beside the old-fashioned wood-burning stove that provided little warmth in the far reaches of the large living room. Over time we would each have our personal, not to be shared, blanket to wrap in as we watched T.V. or did homework. In winter we'd wait our turn to heat our blanket and race upstairs and crawl in bed wrapped in the blanket's warmth.

Though a communal center of comfort, the living room nonetheless witnessed and held intimate stories from a shadow world. Confrontations, overt and covert, repeatedly occurred over the years as a mini undeclared war played out, fueled by Papa's alcohol-induced violence, Grandma's passivity, and Mama's debilitating fear.

A promising shift occurred around my 10th year. Papa, Mama, and six kids, the seventh still in Marian's belly, boarded the local bus to the Greyhound Bus Station to see Papa off to Seattle. As our parents explained, he had been accepted in a tech school and would do a 2-year course in electrical engineering, and once he had finished school and had a new job, he would move the family to Seattle. I was thrilled and began to dream of an alternate life. In this new life, Papa would earn a lot of money, and we would move to Seattle to a new neighborhood and a new school. Papa and Mama would be the perfect "Father Knows Best" parents in middle-class life. There would be no parental triad, no violence, no drunkenness. But the reality of this dream of ordinariness promised by Papa's departure was anathema to the reality of weekends at 621-23rd Street.

While the drunken nights of violence decreased in number, they grew in intensity. Friday nights, when Papa came home for the weekend, he usually stopped off at *The Log Cabin Tavern* beside the bus station. By the time he took the last local bus home and stumbled through the door, he was possessed by an alcoholic rage. On these fearsome nights, Grandma would occupy the role of the peaceful one, Mama took on the heroic victim role, the shield between Papa and her children, and the children would tremble.

Often on these nights, drawn by the battle sounds floating upstairs from the living room, the three of us girls would creep down the stairs and huddle behind the stairwell curtain. Even as we plugged our ears, we listened in fascinated terror, caught and held as if by a nightmare monster. Indelibly stamped in my brain, I hear Papa's slurred and lurid voice demanding of Mama why he shouldn't kill her. "What do you have to live for anyway?"

"I have seven kids to live for." The words echoed in a surreal oceanic roar; my chest constricted, I gasped as a river of tears gushed forth. I was terrified that in the morning Mama would be dead. This night like others before, Grandma came out of her room to the living room, called softly to my sisters and me and motioned us to her. We sidled along the dining table, an interminable gauntlet through the war zone of Mama and Papa. In abject terror, casting furtive glances through tears at the scene taking place across the room – Mama crying, Papa yelling and hitting her – we were relieved to reach Grandma's outstretched hands. "Come, come," she whispered, pulling us into her room as she shut the door. Gayle, who had moved into Grandma's room when Martin arrived, huddled in the bed.

Gathered together in her room amidst the shouts and tears of that thunderous background, we kneeled with her and prayed to our Lord Jesus to somehow stop the nighttime terror. In my heart, I prayed Papa wouldn't kill her, and yet I couldn't comprehend the possibility. Grandma's supplications to God were faint sounds in an alternate reality. With eyes closed and hands in prayer, I drifted, untethered. Grandma's "Amen" pulled me back, and Rochelle, Laura, and I fervently added our, "Amen." Trying to shelter from the noise, the three of us joined Gayle and Grandma under the covers. I hovered close to sleep but only truly slept when Papa had exhausted himself, gone into their bedroom, and passed out. Hearing a rustling in the bathroom, I sobbed to know that Mama was still alive. We three girls crept upstairs to our own beds.

The next morning the three of us got dressed and headed to the kitchen where Grandma was cooking the daily 7-grain cereal breakfast for us kids. The silence after this event and similar ones was deafening and baffling. We were required to act as if everything was normal and that this is what families did. Inevitably, later in the day, first Mama and then Papa would be up, both acting like the night hadn't happened. To maintain his façade of normalcy was an enormous energetic and psychological drain on each of us.

At the time, I had little awareness of my brothers, David and Don, alone in their room and Martin in the crib in our parents' room. What terrifying nights they must have suffered through in their vulnerable and tender lives as they surely shuddered and cried alone in their beds. It breaks my heart to imagine the fear and loneliness of the three of them. How does a child digest the sounds and terror of a scene like that? I'm not sure, and though memories blur over the years, feelings stay locked up in our bodies. What I do know is that we siblings would have to fight, each in her or his way, to emerge out of the tangled brambles and detritus of this war-torn village that was our family.

For most of my adult years, I found it incomprehensible that Grandma allowed Papa to beat her daughter, assuring myself that I would have killed him if it was my daughter. That's my rage. I don't think it ever occurred to Anna to confront him, and who knows, it might have enraged Dayton even more. I don't know even today what was or would be "right action."

Like the tulips that grew in our spring garden, closing at night and in the mornings opening their brilliant, inverted bell-shapes to the sun, so ran the behaviors of Dayton with his wife and children. In those moments in the sun, I would forget the dark and scary nights and shine in the rays of his attention and the fun he brought to our household. He loved to swim in the lake with us kids and one afternoon at Bloedel Donovan Park, he taught me how to do a backward somersault off the diving board. Though I was scared I wanted to make him proud, and that I hit my head on the diving board in the attempt and was momentarily knocked unconscious hardly mattered. I showed off the cut and goose egg on my head as if it were a medal.

Sunday play often included acrobatics. A photo, taken in my 13th or 14th year, shows me standing on Papa's shoulders with arms outstretched against the sky - a powerful testament to my total faith that I was safe above the world on his shoulders.

On Sundays when the family would pile into whatever old car we had - Papa driving, the youngest child on the seat between him and Mama, and the rest of us stacked together in the back seat - we kids loved to sing as the car followed the country roads to Grandpa and Grandma Johnson's farm. After greeting our grandparents, we'd dash outside with Papa's youngest sister, our aunt Ronnie, who was a few months younger than I was. Racing around the farm, we'd undertake adventures into the woods nearby, or, disregarding the admonishments of Grandpa Johnson, we'd chase down the calves trying to ride them or steal into the hayloft to leap and jump.

Early afternoon we'd watch in fascinated horror as Grandpa killed and skinned a rabbit for Sunday dinner. Once satiated from the gourmet farm meal, adults and children would gather in the living room for music. This after-dinner ritual when Uncle Les would sit down at the piano and Papa and his sisters, Marge and Arly would gather around the piano and sing beautiful harmonies together, warmed me through and through. I was flush in the joy and pleasure of the music, my full belly, and the afterglow of dashing around on the farm and forest, all the sensual delights of a budding tantrika.

Johnson family gatherings at our grandparents were a stunning contrast to the sober propriety of the holiday gatherings at Grandma Trotto's, those being the only time the Trotto clan would gather. Sitting in a formal arrangement in the shabby living room, if there wasn't song and laughter, there was deference and appreciation for Anna, the family's matriarch. I remember the respectful esteem her children showed Anna and how she humbly basked in their appreciation. Mama and Grandma would serve the food they'd prepared. Us kids, with our one cousin, Mary, would hang out upstairs quietly playing board games or chattering.

Grandma Trotto was the adult that sustained Mama and us seven kids through thick and thin. Grandma was the one who nurtured our minds and bodies with homework help and meals. She was my first spiritual teacher. And finally, with her patient commitment to duty, she shared her love. Plain and simple, our family wouldn't have survived without her. And yet, I basked in the guilty stolen moments in the familial camaraderie of Sundays with Papa's family, mesmerized by his *joie de vivre*.

in my 41st year, during the month-long spring vacation from Brockwood Park where I lived and worked, I visited Grandpa Johnson, where he still lived on the farm with his second wife, Inez, whom he had married when Grandma Johnson died of cancer. This tiny 5'4" man, with his irrepressible good humor and quiet acceptance of what life sent his way, was one of my favorite relatives. We were reminiscing, talking of Papa, who had died that winter. In his sweet thoughtful voice, he volunteered, "You know you were a plain-looking child. Dayton called you his ugly duckling and he'd always add, 'You'll see. In the end, she'll be the most beautiful swan of all.'" Grandpa's words touched me beyond the moment from beyond the grave. The internal tape of Grandma Trotto reiterating to me, "You were such an ugly child. . ." had met its match. I know Grandma meant no harm, and from what Grandpa had just related, the adults in both families acknowledged that I was, if not ugly, rather plain-looking. Many years would pass before I could see my beauty, and yet sitting with Grandpa that day, I felt the possibility. "Thank you Grandpa for that, thank you." Though he gave a little chuckle, I saw his eyes get watery. As a child, I'd known, even before the overt sexual episodes happened, that I was special to Papa, and when later I could give voice to this, I also hated that I was his favorite. But that day, listening to

Grandpa talk of his son, my father, in a loving yet dispassionate way, brought a little grace into my understanding of Papa and me.

And while the bane of the parental triad still reigned in my inner kingdom, that day the blessings were intimated, and a chink in the castle walls was chiseled away.

Daring to Remember

As I write of these pre-teen years, I have skirted around the incident with Papa I most remember. Unrelentingly curious about my psyche and that of others, I feel I am on a perennial *walkabout* to open my heart and mind. To eat, swallow, and digest both personal and universal imprints and be gathered up into perceptual possibilities that even today expand and challenge me.

I felt early on my attachment to my father. I loved my mother and depended on her, but my dashing father I loved in a whole other way. Though I feared him when he'd come home drunk and prayed he wouldn't be so violent and angry and hurt our mom and sometimes me and my brothers and sisters, he was so handsome and joyful when he was sober. Then again, indelibly etched in my psyche above any other memory of my interactions with him is the manifestation of the dark and dangerous shadow of this man, my Papa.

I was eleven and a half years old. It was a Saturday. Grandma and my brothers and sisters had all gone to church. Mama was in town and would pick the others up after church and bring them home around 12:30. I'd stayed home, happy to curl up on the couch with a slight fever that made the world around me a little fuzzy. As I lay on the couch still in my nightie, my thoughts drifting among clouds and shapes on the walls and ceilings, I was soon fast asleep. Unbidden, a repeating childhood dream from which I always awoke yelling and afraid rolled into my drifting dream world. At its grossest level, it was about to play out.

Repeating Childhood Dream

There is a giant mass of fluffy white clouds on the left. Off to the right, there is a small mass of clouds, white like the other accumulation but tight and dense. I understand that little mass is me. The two masses, both white but so different in substance and texture, are moving toward each other. Feeling myself the little cloud, I'm excited about it, curious, wondering about it, because except for the color, it seems so different, more significant but kind of older, and there's a lightness. I realize it is drawing me toward it. The clouds move closer and closer toward each other. Suddenly, as the soft edges of the immense cloud touch the firm and dense little cloud that is me, my excitement turns to terror. I awaken yelling as the gigantic mass envelopes me.

This time, awakened from the dream, I was yelling and whimpering like a quivering scared puppy. At that moment, I heard the front door opening and Papa came through the door. Before he was aware of me, I watched him and knew right away the familiar signs of his drinking; the sloppy way he came through the door, the shuffling feet, and even from the couch, I smelled the alcohol. The door closed, and he turned and saw me. "Oh," his eyebrows raised in momentary surprise. "Hi honey, whadda ya doin here? Not in church?" He was just managing to keep the slur out of most of his words.

"I stayed home cause I'm sick."

"Oh whas's wrong?"

"I have a temperature and my head hurts."

"So sorry. I gotta go take a piss, be right back." I was surprised he used that word. A little nervous tremor rose and ran up my back right into my neck where a shiver erupted and shook me. I felt I should run upstairs, but I didn't know why and stayed frozen. I watched as he shuffled out of the bathroom, passed through the hallway, then across the worn linoleum floor of the living room. He eased himself down into the chair next to the woodstove. There was a fire burning to take the October chill from the room.

Papa looked across the room where I sat huddled under my special blanket. I averted my eyes, picking at some fuzz. I dared glance across the space between us, wishing there was something, a table, a chair, anything that would obstruct the way he was looking at me. "Com'mere," he said softly, "come and talk to yur ole pop, it's warmer over here by the stove anyways."

I felt myself sitting up slowly, feeling light-headed. The floor was cold on my bare feet. I slipped my feet into my slippers. As I pushed myself up, I glanced back at the couch where I'd been resting, wishing I was still there, yet drawn inexorably to Papa. As I got close, the smell of alcohol nearly gagged me, making me feel dizzy. He reached out and pulled me close to him, my body between his legs, his arm around me. "There, isn't that warmer?" I nodded yes with my eyes downcast. Quietly he slipped his free hand under my nightie. He tightened his other arm around me, and his other hand slid slowly across my breasts. He squeezed them both, gently at first, then he began moving his hands around more roughly.

"Ah-hh, you're getting to be a woman now," he said as he kissed me lightly on the forehead. I could only nod agreement. "Are you wearing a bra yet?" I shook my head no. "You know, you're my favorite daughter." His lips brushed mine. That kiss was different from the ritual good-night kiss we had with Mama, Grandma, and Papa at bedtime. I didn't know whether to nod agreement or not. To do so seemed dangerous, but I felt good to know I was his favorite, and I liked his touch on me. I nodded my head once, my eyes locked on the floor, searching for the pattern in the linoleum, not daring to look directly at him. There was never much hugging in our family. I couldn't think of when my Mama or Grandma had ever really hugged me, only my Papa from time to time. His hand slipped down my tummy to my private place. As he began to rub me down there, he asked, "Have you started your period yet?" I shook my head no. His hands continued to touch me, pressing and rubbing, and then his finger slipped inside of me. He put his head on my shoulder. "I love you," he whispered in my ear. I froze. What he was doing wasn't right, what was happening? Something in me felt that truth but mixed in with that knowledge was how good his touch felt in some dangerous, scary way. I had no power to move or say anything.

Suddenly he pulled his hands away from me and was undoing his belt and unzipping his pants. His knees squeezed tighter as he locked his feet to keep me close. I'd never seen that part of him before. It was sticking straight out as he opened his pants. He reached out and brought my hand to touch him. My hand stiffened. Sensing my resistance, he paused momentarily, "It's okay honey, it's okay, just feel it" He gently wrapped my fingers around his penis, and putting his hand around mine, he forced me to hold tight, not just touch him. "See Honey, that's it, that's it. Isn't that nice? Yes, yes, ah-ah." As he leaned back, his eyes closed, his hand once again slipped under my nightie, and he grabbed my tiny little breasts and squeezed hard. I gave a little cry of pain. "It's okay, it's okay," he assured me, and he lightened his touch. "Just squeeze me a little harder, honey, okay." I tried to comply but couldn't. A little voice inside me cried out, "Oh Papa, what are you doing?" But like in a dream, when one tries to yell, and nothing comes out, the words were just pains in my chest unable to find their way to the surface. Words seeming to drown in an ocean of both pleasure and pain.

His hand wrapped around mine pushed my hand back and forth, back and forth, faster and faster, and he was once again squeezing my breast hard until I cried out in confusion, pain, and a strange pleasure. I didn't know what I was feeling. My head started to swim, and I had to lean against him to keep from falling, "We're almost there, almost there." He pushed my hand harder along his penis, brutally squeezed my tiny nipple. Suddenly he let out a long groan, and stuff came pouring out of his penis. I was scared. What had I done? Had I hurt him? What was that sticky stuff on my hand? I felt like I was going to throw up. My tears began to flow uncontrollably. Papa suddenly came to his senses, "Oh sorry, hon, it's okay, really it's okay, it's just your Papa who loves you. I love you Diane." His arms encircled me with the sticky mess between us. "Come on into the bathroom." He led me into the bathroom and put my hand under the water.

I wished the water could wash away the bad feelings in me, but the cleaner my hands became, the more shame I felt. When the water ran clear from our hands, he cleaned up the rest of him. "There," he said, "all good, great, it's okay, it's okay. It was good, wasn't it?" I stared up at him, bewildered at what he was saying. "See, you're becoming a woman." His words were making no sense to me, but what he said next did make sense. He zipped up his pants, buckled his belt, and knelt in front of me, his eyes locked on mine, piercing me to my very soul, "Honey, what happened today was special. You're my girl, right, my favorite girl. You shouldn't talk with anyone about it, not your sisters or Mama, okay, and not your Grandmother. Understand? Promise?"

I stared silently back at him, my unstoppable tears blurring his face. He implored me further, "It is special between us, no one else should know, okay? What happened is special just for us." His hands on my shoulders tightened as he gave me a little shake, "Promise?" Mutely, I nodded yes. "That's my girl, that's my girl." He pulled me to him, my arms immobile, rested against my rigid body while his arms encircled me. "That's my girl," he whispered as he hugged me tighter, "That's my girl."

We both heard the car turn into the driveway. I wanted to run upstairs and hide in shame, but he insisted, "You go lie back down on the couch and rest. Just close your eyes and sleep. Remember, not a word." I nodded again, numb and mute, becoming a co-conspirator in his deception. He turned into the kitchen, and I found my way back to the couch. I wiggled my feet out of my slippers, held my nightie tight around me as I sat down, swung my legs onto the sofa, laid down, and turned my face to the wall. I drew the blanket up tightly around my neck. The family clambered up the stairs, noisy voices and laughter as they burst through the door. Papa strode out of the kitchen. He seemed sober and greeted them all joyfully. He hugged his wife; she pushed him away as she smelled the alcohol.

"It's okay, hon. I just had a beer while I was waiting for the bus." She turned toward me. He quickly added, "She's been asleep since I came in. I think she's still asleep, though how she could sleep through all this commotion, I don't know," he added with a laugh.

Taking his cue, I pretended to be just waking up, turning groggily, "Hi, mom."

"How are you feeling?" she asked.

"Okay, I guess. I just been sleeping. Maybe I'll go upstairs. I'm not hungry, just thirsty."

"I'll get you a glass of water," my father quickly offered and turned to the kitchen. I heard the water running, and then he came across the room, space I had crossed minutes, hours, lifetimes ago. He handed the water to me with a smile as he brushed my hair from my face. "How's that? Better?" I nodded and handed the glass back. I pulled the blanket tighter around me so no one would see my shame.

My mother came over to where I stood and felt my forehead. "You're still pretty warm. I'll come upstairs and check with you as soon as everyone gets fed. That okay?"

"Yes, okay. I think I just need more sleep till my temperature goes down," I said bravely. "Will you take my temperature when you come up?" I always liked having my temperature taken, holding the thermometer gently under my tongue for five minutes, Mama pulling the thermometer out of my mouth and turning it until it was in just the right light. Then she'd announce a number and show me how the mercury had risen just to that spot to reveal my temperature – a magical moment in the mind of a child.

"Yes, of course," my mama assured me. "I'll be up in an hour or so. You sure you're okay?" she frowned as she looked down at me.

I tried to figure out if she sensed anything. "Yes, I'm okay." I heard a strange finality, almost belligerence, in my voice and wondered if my mother noticed it. She didn't seem to. I wished she would. If only Mama would come up with me now, maybe I could find a way to tell her. But she was headed toward the kitchen to feed the hungry children just returned from church. Feeling desperately alone, I turned and trundled up the stairs to the bedroom I shared with my two sisters. In bed, I sobbed quietly as a cacophony of ambiguous bewildering images and feelings threatened to overwhelm me. I drifted into a hazy floating mist. Mama's footsteps on the stairs, her concerned voice calling me, pulled me gratefully back from the mist. Mama took the promised temperature and affirmed I still had a fever. To my wan smile, she brushed my hair out of my eyes and smoothed the covers over me. That day, planted in my pubescent body, was a tightly congealed knot in my belly and an undetectable vibration that settled into my core.

First Love Brings Balance

As if to bring balance to my world, the infinite universe gave me the gift of innocent childhood love. He had arrived at our grade school mid-way through the first grade. "Students, this is Bob. His family just moved to Happy Valley." She came over to the table where I sat with four other classmates and added a chair next to mine. "Bob," she continued as he sat down, "this is Diane, and Alice and Charles." I turned in my seat to stare at him. Most striking was his heavily freckled face and his dark brown piercing eyes that scanned the classroom and classmates. I may not have had the words yet, but the feeling, as I stared at him, was of a powerful intelligence. My impression was soon borne out when one day the teacher asked the class this simple question, "How far can we see?" Instantly, with the enthusiasm of our youthful ignorance, many of us, including me, raised our hands waving insistently, sure we had the answer. I had thought of how far I could see in the neighborhood and guessed maybe three miles thinking of being on Sehome Hill and seeing the town off in the distance. Another volunteered his experience, guessing five blocks. Miss Swinton, our teacher, continued to call on a few more students, and we guessed on with our limited vision. Then she called on Bob who had quietly raised his hand.

He pronounced simply and boldly, "Millions of miles because we can see the stars." My mouth dropped, and the other students stared their mouths agape. That had never occurred to any of us.

"That's right Bob," the teacher beamed at him, and I felt a stirring in my chest, a heart flutter. That he could think and see like that was mind-boggling. My child's admiration and adoration blossomed at that moment. The two of us would roam together in a circle of innocent first love all through grade school, from being square dance partners at the school's spring festival to our attempted secret double-date in the fifth grade when somehow a parent got wind of our scheming and put the kibosh on our much-anticipated evening in a dark movie theater.

At the end of the 6th grade, our last year of grade school, a much-anticipated school patrol picnic would cap off our final grade school year for those of us who had been privileged to be on the school patrol team. When the day arrived, we boarded the school bus just after 9:00. Chatter and laughter and excitement reigned as the driver headed out of town to Birch Bay, a sweet little resort center that played largely in the Johnson clan's summer days. But this day in my 12th year, as the bus arrived and disgorged its passel of 6th graders, a tantalizing prospect took center stage. The chaperones were few, and besides, we were the best in the class, so they trusted us not to go too gaga with our freedom. After lunch, while swimming with classmates, Bob and I quietly slipped away and walked down the beach until we were out of sight of chaperones and classmates.

He threw down his towel and we arranged ourselves self-consciously on the soft sand under the towel. Every movement felt like a commitment to forever. We rushed over the awkward move of turning to face each other, his arm lay across my shoulders, and quicker than the flash of the big bang, I leaned into him and awkwardly initiated our first kiss. We pulled back slightly, and then daringly, his arms encircled me, mine wrapped around him. Though unripe and ungainly, youthful passion seized us, and our lips pressed harder as our embrace tightened. And right there, with our panting breath roaring in my ears, feeling our hearts pound together, like the whisper of a soft morning breeze, bliss caressed me ever so lightly. Entwined together on that sandy beach, a longing arose in me for more and I sensed the same in him, but we didn't dare further intimacy. Our lips tested, pressed, clung together until the faint sound of the chaperone's whistle tore into our passion and startled us into action. We gathered up our towels and joined the others. Even today, the memory of those first kisses, the sweetness of that afternoon, bring a secret smile to these same lips that were inflamed that summer afternoon.

Baptism Into Spirit

As my body awakened, there came an equally powerful spiritual awakening. Grandma, the guardian of our spiritual life, suggested to Laura and me, ages 11 and 12, that we were old enough to be baptized and become church members. I was terribly excited. Baptism was a rite of passage into the church circle that held my spiritual energy, and I couldn't wait for membership. Each Wednesday evening, through the winter and spring, Laura and I trudged the three miles to the church to meet with the Pastor and sat with rapt attention as he taught us what it meant to accept Jesus Christ as our personal savior as well as other church doctrines. We took in the words, and I felt the holy spirit move in me. I was a true believer, and the warmth emanating from the Bible lessons stole my heart. I dreamed of belonging at last to this earthly expression of spirit, the Seventh-day Adventist church.

On a Sabbath afternoon in early June at the lakeside home of one of the church elders, Laura and I were baptized. To be baptized in Lake Whatcom was unique and only occurred because a new church was being built, and church services were held in the school gymnasium. Though I knew the lake would be cold, I secretly felt superior to all the others who had been baptized in a baptismal font. Laura and I were being baptized just like Jesus had been by his cousin, John the Baptist - outside in natural water flowing directly from the earth, not through metal pipes into a baptismal font.

STIRRINGS

The Lord sent a beautiful sun to bless the day. The lake was quiescent, devoid of wind and waves that might mar the ceremony. The lawn shone green where it sloped down to a small sandy beach where the parishioners were gathered to witness the blessed event of these two young souls taking Christ into their hearts. In the house basement that led directly onto the sloping green lawn, the women elders, the deaconesses, helped Laura and I change into our white baptismal robes, checking to be sure we had an extra pair of dry panties to change into after the immersion. Hymns of praise drifted gently to our expectant ears and our open souls. We bowed our heads with the others as the Pastor said a prayer of blessing and praise. "Amen," he intoned.

"Amen," the parishioners' fervent echo resonated in my heart, and I opened to this deep spiritual commitment Laura and I were making.

The Pastor motioned to us, and a deaconess accompanied each of us to the water's edge. As I walked, I looked over to Grandma. I seldom saw her express much emotion, but today her eyes met mine, and the proud smile that passed between us warmed my heart. Being the oldest, I went first while Laura waited at the lake edge. I stepped into the water, barely noticing the coldness of the liquid that softly swirled around my legs. Meditatively, my eyes on the Pastor, I walked out to where he stood in almost hip-deep water and took his extended hand as he guided me to stand sideways in front of him where he faced the worshipers at the lakeside. My two hands firmly grasped the Pastor's wrist. He held a pure white cloth in his palm.

Raising his right hand, he offered my soul, my whole being to Christ, and asked God to accept me into his grace. His upraised right hand came down and firmly cupped the back of my head and neck like one holds the head of a newborn babe. It was my signal to take a breath. I inhaled deeply and held that breath in my heart. His left hand brought the white cloth to my face, and he laid me backward until he immersed my whole being into the holy water of the lake. As he raised me up from the dead, born into Christ, my feet stumbled a bit, but I quickly caught myself. The Pastor took the cloth from my face, and I breathed my first breath as a true child of God. I turned to the shore, my face glowing, smiling, and gazed at the gathered community of like souls that had come to witness the most sacred moment of my life thus far. Their faces reflected my deep joy, some even with tears in their eyes as I walked out of the water to the shore where Laura awaited her turn. Her immersion mirrored my own, and when she emerged from the water, we walked with Jesus beside us to the basement room where we changed clothes. Rapturous, though a little shy, we gathered with the church members to share a potluck meal and be welcomed into our new family.

These two seminal events, one with my father and one with my grandmother, tumbled in agitated concert, right to the core of my psyche. My father awakened my earthy *Shakti* energy, my sexual predilection, and then stole it from me for his perverted satisfaction. The stealing left an undefined longing. My grandmother awakened the spiritual *Shakti* energy and spirited it away to imbue it with the oppressive Seventh-day Adventist Church religious doctrines. This stealing equally left a longing. Each, in their way, captured the two most important facets of my diamond essence, my spiritual affinity and my sexual affinity. It would be my task in an unimaginable future to integrate these two seemingly disparate and conflicting entities. As surely as the earth rotates around the sun, the resolution would come, and the two essences within would flower into a miraculous oneness, earthly and sublime, breathtakingly beautiful in its symmetry and unity, the full manifestation of *Shakti Energy*.

Preview of Shakti *Awakening*

As in every family, secrets lie hidden in the crevasses of shared family stories; secrets float about in darkened rooms. These secrets lie buried until someone, driven by what Jung calls the teleological function of the unconscious, finds her light, turns it on, and begins to illuminate the darkness. When one dares to open to and integrate the shadow world, she not only does the work for the individual woman or man, but for the lineage, and for the web that connects all of us. Though I had no way of knowing or understanding this concept when this inner conflict was set up, I would emphatically embrace this undeclared task.

We jump for a moment from my thirteenth year to some twenty years into the future. In 1979 I was living in Aix-en-Provence, France, where I had just moved. In those years, as I began deep psychological work, dreams of dying and killing were almost commonplace, and most often, I'd awaken myself with yells, fear, crying. The following dream stands out because I didn't awaken yelling or crying, and it speaks of the coming integration of my deep-seated fragmentation.

>Dream Nov. 19, 1979
>
>*"We" are facing a firing squad. I wish they would hurry and get it over with so I won't have to continue thinking of it. We are all relatively calm, and it seems as if we are a kind of collective consciousness and what is in my brain is also in everyone else's brain. Finally, "they" the firing squad, fire, and we all fall. Then I discover to my horror that I am still alive and in pain. The pain seems as much mental as physical. There is also a guy that hasn't died, and we are of one mind. I/we think they will shoot again and finish us off. This thought comforts us. Then I see to my/our horror "they" are leaving; that they aren't going to fire again. It seems they have no more ammunition and that it doesn't matter to them anyway.*
>
>*Then another dream image intrudes. Peggy, my best friend through childhood, is sitting in the basement of the 23rd Street house cradling a little stuffed animal in her arms, her face buried in it. She won't come out, and I'm talking with her through an open window, telling her it's okay, it's safe to come out.*

In the first dream sequence, some parts of myself are ending. The dream further informs me that all the inner parts are connected, and though some aspects will die in the process of this psychological unfolding, some parts will be alive to carry on. This prescient dream hints that in the integration to come, the immature feminine and the immature masculine, while terrified at the thought that the killers (consensus reality) haven't destroyed them, will be transformed into oneness. This idea is beautifully described in this sutra.

> *Worship does not mean offerings, but is a matter of focusing the heart on supreme consciousness, beyond dualistic thought. Then in perfect ardor, Shiva/Shakti dissolve into the Self.*
>
> Vijnanabhairava Tantra, #147

In the 2nd dream image, the young me, scarred and hurt by the event with Papa, by the family dysfunction, poverty, and violence, is scared to come out of the 23rd street basement (unconscious). Now working with compassion and curiosity, my adult part is talking with her, encouraging her to come out. The dream world is giving support to this process of shining light into the dark, chthonic places inside where spirit and sexuality have been abducted and artificially separated.

5
1955-1958

Junior High

Hell and Heaven Seamed Together

In 1955, Fairhaven Junior High School, with its brick façade, sat proudly on a sizeable triangular, shaped corner. Long sloping lawns converged at the lowest point of the triangle, framed by an archway supported by two columns. Lanterns sat atop the two columns, and the words, FAIRHAVEN JUNIOR HIGH SCHOOL, were emblazoned in a metal and brass banner suspended between them. I walked under the banner, turned, and ambled backward, staring beyond the archway. "Hurry up," Rochelle insisted. I turned and caught up with her as we followed the long curving walkway and climbed the stairs, thrilled to be a mature 7th grader. I was in glorious ignorance of the collective's full weight that hovered just inside the doors like a hell-bent tsunami whose events and personages would conspire to shape and form me from a naturally engaged and sometimes rowdy child into a reluctant and insecure teenager.

In the boiling cauldron of junior high school, we young teens would become agents of consensus reality and blithely enter into and unwittingly establish a school society that reflected the world-at-large. Money mattered, home address mattered, clothes mattered, looks mattered, respectability mattered. Everywhere I looked, I was found wanting. I was puzzled by this new culture that seemed only to want to quash me, didn't seem to appreciate what was inside me, and didn't value the sensual *Shakti* underpinnings, barely conscious, at my core. Insidiously, the economic reality and the secrets of our family, which had been unremarkable at Larrabee Grade School, would, like a malevolent ghost, eat away at my thirteen-year-old bravado.

The first semester, I was naïvely thrilled to be accepted as a student worker in the lunchroom. In exchange, I would receive a hot lunch, which seemed the apogee of good fortune. (I'd always envied the students at grade school whose parents could afford to buy them lunch and didn't have to carry a sack lunch, which in my case, was a peanut butter and jam sandwich with an apple or pear from the root cellar.) I was assigned to the milk dispensing machine. Students would come with their trays, and I would lift the handle of the milk machine to dispense the milk and then carefully place the full glass on the tray of the waiting student. I soon noticed that my smiles at the students as I put the glass on the tray weren't reciprocated. By the end of the semester, I realized that other students looked down on me as one of the poor ones that had to work in the kitchen. I was embarrassed and ashamed of this clue that gave away the penury in which my family lived. I couldn't bear the weight of my self-imposed and student-imposed judgments and quit the lunchroom job after the first semester. I would do whatever it took to have a place in mainstream culture. Borne of our family's poverty, violence, and secrets, this longing to belong, to have a place in middle-class America, dominated my thoughts and fantasies. Even as I searched for ways to belong, a shy, less conscious part of me clung to my natural sensuality and spiritual aspirations. As if to reward that shy part of me, I discovered dance!

Dance! It was a panacea to my hungry sensual soul. Dance shook the ground of my being and would keep alive the undulating ocean of *Shakti Energy* that had been hinted at in those stolen moments with Bob. To fully embrace this fledgling expression of my tantric *Shakti* energy, I severed from my mind the church's prohibition against dance – just cut it away. The music danced my body; the rhythm vibrated inside of me. I felt an unfettered freedom as I shimmied and shook with abandon on the dance floor. When the music played, I let

JUNIOR HIGH

the pure vibration and bliss bury self-judgments and shame. I whirled around with other girls as the boys were timid about dance. (Looking back, I sense how dangerous my ecstasy must have seemed to them.)

In grade school, we had square danced, but the world of bebop and rock'n'roll, of Chuck Berry, Jerry Lee Lewis, Little Richard, and finally Elvis, the guitar and drums, the saxophone were something else! If square dance was a firecracker, rock'n'roll was an exploding Roman candle lighting up a night sky, and I was riding those rockets higher and higher as I burst into my teenage sensuality.

I learned the art of flirting and yet found only rejections to my smiling-eyed glances. Till then, I hadn't entirely absorbed the words deigning me ugly, but they slammed me hard in those years. Grandma's oft-repeated litany of what an ugly child I was with a big nose and stringy hair; Papa's words, though I didn't hear them directly; the apparent agreement in the family as to my ugly mien burned my young brain. A child has only so many resources to combat an assault from the unconscious adults around her.

An exclamation point to this family-held belief about my ugliness came from my friend Peggy. On an autumn day in our 9th-grade year, Peggy and I rustled and shuffled through the fallen dry leaves as we headed home from school. I loved the crackle and swish as I slid my feet over and under the leaves, lost in the sensuous youthful joy of sound and color. With my mind dangerously distracted, I confessed to Peggy that I was afraid I would never get married because I was so ugly no one would want me. It was an unlikely confession from the likes of me to Peggy, who, from the moment she came to Larrabee in our 3rd-grade year, was considered the cutest girl of all, and the boys were besotted. She was petite, had light golden-brown hair, dancing blue eyes, and wore frills and bows and soft colors. She didn't say anything, just grabbed my hand and began to run through the leaves. She always had that ability to lighten heavy moments, and as we ran, we left the words hanging in the bare branches that had shed their summer green and gold.

The next day, when we saw each other in the hall, she excitedly grabbed my hand and pulled me out of the flow of students hurrying to class. As though declaring a proclamation, she breathlessly exclaimed, "I talked to my mom last night about what you said about not getting married, and she said that looks aren't everything, that even if you're ugly, there are other things that count, and you'll find someone." I didn't know whether to laugh or cry, be relieved or devastated. I looked around furtively to see if anyone had heard her.

"Oh," was all I could utter, "Oh, okay." I looked down at my hand that she held tight. It seemed to belong to someone else. I pulled my hand away to cover my belly. "Gotta go, see you after school. We'll walk together, okay?" Not waiting for a reply, I turned and fled outdoors. Relief and dismay at this news played havoc with my brain creating a strange moment when I was no longer in my body. As I bent over to catch my breath, like a malign spirit, this moniker, ugliness, firmly lodged itself in me. For decades, I would look in a mirror and reaffirm the decree handed down from the high court, "Diane is ugly."

Rite of Passage

In the miasma of junior high life, I waited anxiously to become a woman. Helpful and honest information about my body was years away. I remember our 8th-grade health education teacher who crazily informed us that we could get pregnant taking a bath after a man, that there could be sperm lurking around and waiting to swim up inside of us. Fortunately, she taught more accurately, if not with slight embarrassment, about menstruation. I was jealous of the girls who couldn't shower because they were "having their period." I waited and waited for that first sign of blood.

At last, toward the end of 8th grade, the longed-for day arrived. After a P.E. class, I was showering away the sweat and saw red blood on my hands. I quickly dressed and slipped into the toilet stall to confirm. Blood still flowing! I made a pad of toilet paper, and the 2-mile walk home seemed to go on forever. By the time I got home, I could

JUNIOR HIGH

feel my panties were wet, but I didn't care. Once home, how to tell Mama? She had never talked with us girls about our bodies, our budding breasts, or the period that would come, hoping no doubt we'd learn from friends or school or someone other than her. I changed my panties, hid the bloody ones, and mustering my nerve, went down the stairs, through the stairwell curtain, through the living room, and through the kitchen door to where she was preparing dinner. Just get the first words out, I told myself. "Mom," I stammered, "I um umm started my period." Staring at her, I waited. She rinsed her hands from the potatoes she was peeling, went into her bedroom, and came out with two one-dollar bills. "Here, take this to the store and buy some pads and a belt to hold them. You know what you need, don't you?" She sounded almost angry.

"Well, yes." My already soft voice dropped even more as though we were whispering about a terrible secret.

"Go to the ragbag and use a rag for the blood till you get back." And that was it. She turned back to the potatoes, more intent than ever on peeling them for the pot. I hung around the kitchen until she finally ordered me, "Go now. It'll be dark soon." I dutifully went to the ragbag on the back porch, retrieved a rag, and pinned it in my panties.

There was nothing to do but take my 13-year-old shame and embarrassment to the little local grocery store, *Grant's Groceries*, named after its owner. I hurried along the route, wondering how much I would bleed before I could make it back home. The half-mile walk felt daunting – one block down the street, turn off onto the path with the little bridge that ran over the stream, hurry on through the wooded hillside and along the neighbor's fishpond, merge onto the sidewalk on 21st street and traverse the last block to the store's entrance. As I almost stomped along the path, my anger at mom intensified, "How could she not drive me to the store and buy what I needed? It's not fair that she'd just abandon me to do this myself the first time. I'll be so embarrassed in front of Mr. Grant." At the store, I pushed through the wooden screen door with the spring that pulled it shut behind me.

The sharp bang echoed the anger hiding my embarrassment . . .well almost. Mr. Grant, who knew all of us neighborhood kids and who sometimes extended credit to low-income families like ours, greeted me by name, then asked congenially, "What do you need today?"

I looked around and spotted where the women's items were. I pointed and walked over to the shelf. Fortunately, there was only Kotex back then. I didn't have to stay and ponder which size, which thickness, which brand; it was one size fits all. I grabbed the smallest pack and thank god the elastic sanitary belts were hanging just above the pads. I pulled one off the wire and carried the belt and pads to Mr. Grant. Tuning in on how shy and embarrassed I was, he quickly put them into a bag for which I was grateful in case someone I knew should come in. He counted the change into my outstretched hand. "Thank you," I mumbled. I even dared to glance up at him as I turned and hurried out the spring-loaded door, trundled along the sidewalk, skirted the neighbor's fishpond, and headed down through the woods, emerging into the small depression where the little stream flowed. I could feel the wetness seeping through the cloth pad I had fashioned. What a relief to be home, though tears of unmitigated anger at my mom accompanied this small comfort. As I handed her the change, she said, "If you have any blood on your panties, rinse it out with cold water because soap and hot water will set the stain." And that was it. Never to be spoken of again. I bought my sanitary pads with babysitting money from then on, fighting against the shame. In my mother's time, there was so much ignorance and self-hatred around anything that hinted at body genitalia, a woman's cycle, and especially sex. I know today that she could only act and feel as women before her had done. Back then, I felt no such forgiveness.

Spirit Renewed

As a young tantric teenager, though I occasionally found my spiritual aspirations burdensome, I was a faithful Christian in my heart. Miraculously, in the summer after 8th grade, my faithfulness to Christ was rewarded. Each summer, thousands of Seventh-day Adventist church members from across the state gathered at the Adventist boarding school in Auburn, Washington, for camp meeting. On the soccer field and surrounding school property, the Washington Conference of Seventh-day Adventists erected hundreds and hundreds of army tents. Most of the congregation attended these camp meetings, even if only on weekends, leaving a minuscule congregation back home. Being too poor to attend, coupled with our parents' indifference, even antipathy to the church, we were the ones left behind, and I hated this depressing reminder that Grandma and her flock would never get to partake of that exalted religious gathering. Those Sabbaths I stared hard into the mirror of our poverty that was like an open wound that won't heal. A wound inflamed every Saturday morning when Grandma, with her pathetic passel of grandchildren, had to trek the nearly three miles to church. Worst were winter days plodding through rain or snow, carrying our high heel shoes, nylons, and garter belts in a bag. Arriving at church, Rochelle, Laura, and I would dash to the bathroom and change from our wet tennis shoes into our church-going finery.

Sweet relief came when Mama passed a milestone - she got her driver's license. We were grateful on the cold, wet mornings when she would drive us to church, but even then, my dignity was assaulted when most mornings, the car wouldn't start. We'd take off our white gloves, climb out of the car in high heels and special Sabbath clothes, and push the car the block or so it took to turn the starter over. If today I can look back and smile and feel no shame, even have a kind of admiration for how our family met and conquered adverse circumstances, back then I was ashamed and even a little angry at our wretched poverty.

But this summer of '56, this extraordinary summer, Grandma announced that we – Grandma, Rochelle, Laura, and I - were going for the whole ten days of camp meeting. I was so committed to the teachings of the Seventh-day Adventist religion that with this announcement, I was caught up in the Rapture. Grandma rented one of the army tents, four army cots, half a wooden floor (cheaper than a full floor), a food cupboard, and a 2-burner cook stove.

Mama drove us the 100-plus miles from Bellingham to Auburn in our old car, all of us praying it would make it there and back. Arriving at this storied place, I thrilled at what my eyes took in. Happy people walked the grounds, stood together in groups, and I soaked in the religious fervor of the very air we breathed. The school buildings were off to the left (dorm rooms rented out to the V.I.P.s). To the right stood the big spherical main meeting tent. I could make out the hundreds and hundreds of chairs lined up like ranks of soldiers at attention. Beyond the tent were several cream-colored buildings, specially constructed for the yearly gathering, that housed shower facilities, toilets, and sinks for morning ablutions. By far, the most arresting part of the scene was the rows and rows of olive-green surplus army tents, each one 16' x 12'. One of them was ours! "Why don't you girls go find our tent and get one of the hand carts to move our things." We were off like a shot.

Four cots had been placed side-by-side at the back of the tent with just enough space between to walk and sit on the edge of the bed with soft grass underfoot. With Friday sundown just a few hours away, Grandma and us girls quickly settled in and prepared food for our dinner and tomorrow's lunch and dinner since observant Adventists didn't cook on Sabbath. Glowing, happily busy, I whistled and hummed and smiled unashamedly. My buck teeth, which had come in with a black hole in the center of one, and that I usually tried to hide with my upper lip, would be a prominent feature of my radiant face for the next ten days, my self-consciousness washed away by spiritual alchemy.

As if a fairy godmother had waved her magic wand, I saw Grandma transformed before my eyes. Her face, lined with the cares and concerns of almost single-handedly trying to support her daughter and family with her part-time $.70/hour job, dissolved into softness. She never complained of the burden imposed on her, and I know she was grateful in her stoic way to have family around her, to feel the life of the young ones enlivening her home, but this duty she bore every day,

JUNIOR HIGH

all day, couldn't have been easy. Now, for ten days, though no doubt she wouldn't have expressed her experience with quite my exuberance, she was in heaven!

The announcement of Friday evening service boomed out over the loudspeakers calling us together just before sundown. The four of us put on nice clothes, not quite our Sabbath best, and walked together to the big tent. As she always did at our local church, Grandma took chairs near the back, and we sat down with her, though the stage was far away. The service began with a prayer and hymns. The conference president welcomed us and preached this most important opening service. Today, I imagine back to that evening, and guess at the thrill for Anna, to be carried back to when she had first found Jesus at a tent revival meeting.

The ten days passed in a heartbeat. At the last Sabbath service, I answered the emotional call to come forward and re-dedicate my life to God. Standing proud and tall, *en masse* with the others that had come forward, I cried tears of gratitude for spirit in my life.

With reluctance on Sunday morning, after the last gathering under the big tent, Grandma, Rochelle Laura, and I packed up our things. We stowed them in the trunk of the car, and Mama drove us back to ordinary life. In my case, it was my last year of junior high and its inexorable sexuality.

Fueled by books of teen romance and imaginings, some nights, after faithfully saying my prayers, pleading with Jesus for my mother's soul and a peaceful world, I would settle into the comfort of my bed. In the quiet of the night, I would touch my vagina in furtive and daring exploration and guiltily dare to push my finger up inside of me. It generated a feral frisson inside and was even a little frightening, and I was naïve about what to do. In those days, though we knew of boys and masturbation, the idea that girls could touch themselves and masturbate and that I had something called a clitoris seemed not to exist in the collective knowledge of our town. (The publication of Masters and Johnson's revolutionary research into men and women's sexuality in their 1966 groundbreaking book, *Human Sexual Response*, was years away, and Bellingham wasn't exactly a hotbed of revolutionary ideas!)

But happily, I was beginning to find my footing in this junior high world. Two activities, sports and academics, had kept the door open as I sought my place in the confusion. Competing on the girls' volleyball, softball, and basketball teams, often being elected team captain, brought a fierce shine to my eyes, and my body reveled in the physical demands. And each semester, when the Honor Roll list was posted, I was proud to read my name, Diane Johnson.

The grace of friendship also salvaged those junior high years from the junk heap of teenage angst. In the 9th grade, it would be Theresa who would soothe the rough edges. My friendship with Theresa, one of the wealthy hill girls, gave me a place, if not at the center of the illustrious hill girl clique, then at least on the periphery, hiding the shame I felt about our family's day-to-day existence.

Theresa and I knew each other through the school orchestra. Our friendship deepened when, in 9th grade, Theresa was designated the first chair of the cello section, and I was named the first chair of the viola section. Another friend, Adele, was designated the first chair of the violin section. Adele joined forces with Theresa and me, and in the natural order of things, we formed a formidable trio. We soon thought and acted as one.

That orchestra became the most exciting activity that year was due to our trio and the newly hired music teacher, Mr. B. He was young, handsome, newlywed with a baby on the way, and sweet with the added grace of forbearance, the last of which we would test to the limit. Driven by our shared crush, the three of us flirted outrageously with Mr. B, and acted out in foolishly creative ways to generally harass him with our unwanted attentions. To his credit, he was impeccable in navigating the onslaught, never once inviting us forward with sexual innuendos. In class, as first chairs, we joyfully gave him our best. Under his guidance, the orchestra not only thrived but was stellar. As the first chairs and self-identified acolytes, we were proud.

The Friday night before the last week of school, in collective madness, the three of us crossed a line that forced him to seek the intervention of the school counselor. That infamous night, giggling, pushing, and daring each other, we found his address in the phone book, took a cross-town bus, and in the cover of darkness, we walked the two blocks to his house located in a quiet neighborhood. As if casing the joint, we circled the house peering in windows, whispering and giggling, trying to get a glimpse into his private life. Fortunate for us, the curtains were closed, so we settled with leaving him a note brazenly signed by the three of us. (Thankfully, the grace of time has obscured what we wrote.) At the time, we considered it a lark, a harmless adventure, yet looking back, I grok how we let our collective teenage libido run amok. We had indeed put our beloved teacher in an untenable situation.

The following Monday afternoon, the three of us were called out of class and ushered into the conference room where the 9th-grade counselor sat stern-faced and unmoving, along with our mothers. The counselor indicated we were to sit across from them. Looking across the conference table at my mom, seeing her somber and angry countenance, was a bucket of ice water thrown over my drunkenness and sobered me up in a heartbeat. Theresa and Adele were doused in the same chill immersion. As the counselor laid out our crime in the light of day, we were deeply embarrassed, our eyes cast down in shame, shocked when we realized the vertiginous heights of misplaced passion in which we had indulged. We were honestly repentant, but our apologies could not deter our mothers who, collectively and firmly, allied with the counselor's penalty. Theresa, Adele, and I had to individually sign a contract saying that if we caused any trouble in our sophomore year in high school, we would be summarily dismissed. Period! It was sobering to enter high school with this humiliating contract glued on our backs like a scarlet letter.

Some say Love it is a hunger, an endless aching need.
    "The Rose" by Amanda Bloom (sung by Bette Midler)

The summer between junior high and high school, this hunger felt all-consuming. I would dream, imagine, flirt, and send out a silent call, "Come dance with me. Come play with me," but my silent entreaties failed to beckon a prince. Then, though disguised by the mantle of camp meeting, my prayers were answered.

Grandma had quietly worked out with several church members for the three of us girls, the Johnson sisters, to return to camp meeting with various families. I would be with the Craigs, who had a daughter, Shannon, about my age. There can be no doubt of grandma's intention to save our souls. (Ultimately, she'd save one out of three.)

As we packed the evening before Friday's departure, the three of us girls chattered excitedly. Rochelle confessed that she was dreaming of romance. "You know, whenever I'm talking with Barry (referring to the new pastor's son), it seems like his mother comes up and takes him away. His parents are so old and out-of-date and so strict. Barry and I have agreed that at camp meeting we'll see each other more even if we have to sneak around a little bit."

"Ah-hah," I thought to myself, "I wasn't the only one thinking of romance." The excitement in her voice about her and Barry's future trysts not only drew my yellow fangs of jealousy but activated the old refrain inside of me that there was no one out there to love me, that I was ugly, and no one would ever want me. I fought the voice, insisting to myself that with the hundreds of kids at camp meeting, there would be someone for me. In my nighttime prayers for Mama and the world, I dared asked the Lord for someone at camp meeting to like me, to be my boyfriend.

Once again, the wonder of that huge encampment entranced me. The Craigs had taken two tents. One was the sleeping area for Mr. and Mrs. Craig and their younger daughter, and the other was the cooking and eating tent with two cots for Shannon and me. We all settled into the rhythm of meetings and meals and teen activities. I was always deeply touched by the sermons, and though this year I didn't go forward to stand at the feet of the preacher when the call came to re-dedicate our young lives to God, I stood proudly with other young people. But at night, lying in my cot, I fantasized about how I would meet *Him*, not the Jesus Him, but my young man, *Him*, how we would walk together, sit in meetings holding hands. For what it was worth, the religious messages, for which grandma had sent me, held their own against this dreaming, my devotion to Christ still powerfully intact.

On the last Wednesday, just four days before camp meeting ended, when I'd almost lost hope, my wish was granted. Teenagers had boarded several busses after breakfast to go to a nearby lake for an afternoon of swimming and water-skiing. In the late afternoon, we were patiently re-boarding the bus, counselors checking that all were accounted for before we headed back to God's tent city. As I looked for a place to sit, I saw him sitting alone toward the back of the bus. Divinely inspired and emboldened, I asked if the seat was available, to which he nodded yes. I sat down, confident in the Lord's guiding hand. It didn't take long to introduce ourselves. His name was Harry; we tested the waters and jumped in. Half an hour later, as the bus rolled to a stop at the camp meeting grounds, Harry asked me to go to the evening meeting with him. "Yes, yes, I'd like that." We arranged by which tent pole we would meet.

My heart beating wildly, half afraid he wouldn't be there, I spotted him leaning against the tent pole. My heart took flight into the stratosphere. I took in once again his black curly hair, his pale white skin with the faintest of freckles, his shy demeanor; not quite handsome, I thought, but nice looking. And thus, our all too brief camp meeting romance began. Most of the details of each encounter over the next four days are lost, but our last night together etched itself into my body and mind.

I waited impatiently for the Saturday night meeting bell, and when the sound rang out across the campground, I joined the faithful streaming out of our tents to the big top. As we reached the edge of the sacred meeting tent, with Mr. and Mrs. Craig's permission, Shannon and I hurried off, her to find her boyfriend, and me to find Harry. He and I sat down as close to an exit point as we could. The pressure of this last night together subsumed all else.

We slipped out of the tent as soon as dusk deepened to the dark of night. Free of the encumbrance of the speaker's words from on high, we walked to a neighboring field where the lights from the encampment were the *mise-en-scene* for this play of young lovers. Overhead the stars were the twinkling guardians of the night. We smiled shyly at each other as he produced a blanket and spread it in the tall grasses. I knew I wanted him to touch me this night. He'd started to before, but the fear of peer and divine retribution would assert themselves, and I'd resolutely pull away or remove his hands. But this night belonged to the unfathomable, to the dreams of teenage love.

We lay down, and he pulled me to him. Our arms encircled each other, our kisses instantly feverish, carrying both of us to a passion I had never known. He slipped his hand under my blouse, and his tentative caresses of my breasts, meeting no resistance, boldly transformed into a powerful squeezing. My lips parted as I gasped and shuddered, felt my back arch as I pressed my body to his, and for the first time in my life, I felt a man's, a boy's, erection against my groin. His lips were painfully crushing mine in his ardor; the pain was simply background accompaniment to the sweet symphony of my pleasure. Each kiss, each touch animated every inch of my skin, and I opened for more. I felt his hand slip from my waist, softly exploring under my skirt. There was an explosion as his hand broached the cloth barrier of my panties and touched my wetness. I was afraid in a deep unknown place inside of me, but my fear only fed my willingness, and my legs spread apart, almost timidly, to invite his exploration. When his fingers pushed inside of me, a shock shot through my body, and by its own volition, my body rolled over onto him, and his hand slipped away as I pressed my body into his hardness, and he moved against me. I wanted his hand inside of me, but we couldn't stop the wild movement of our bodies moving together. Our breath grew harsh, and my belly contracted in spasms. Suddenly tears were wetting our cheeks. For a moment, I didn't know if the tears were his or mine, but they called us back, and we swam to the surface.

"What's happening? What's wrong? Are you okay?" his voice pleaded for reassurance. I realized then the tears were mine.

"It's okay, I'm okay," I managed to whisper. "It's just that what I'm feeling is so strong and almost overwhelming. I'm good, really, I am. I want more." For one long sweet protracted moment as our bodies moved more gently, I savored the wonder and danger of our passion, of his body, of that hardness, of our lips and tongues pressing and seeking, of my body vibrating. I lingered in his embrace and his touch as long as I dared. A reluctant feeble intuition told me that the big tent had darkened. I pulled away. "We have to go," I whispered raggedly, "the meeting's over, and the Craigs are going to be looking for me." He briefly tried to pull me back, his begging desire pushing at me. "I've got to go; come on, walk me back to the tent." Lovingly, though half-heartedly, he acquiesced. I forced myself to stand up. "Do I have any grass in my hair?" I asked with a regretful smile. In the faint glow of the lighted lanterns of tent city, I reached over and pulled dried grass from his dark black curls as he ran his fingers through my hair. "It's getting late. Mrs. Craig is going to be mad. She was upset last time when I got in so late. We better go."

"Yes, you're right; we have to, but I don't want to." In the fading light of quelled passion, I shyly straightened my blouse, pulling my bra back to cup my breasts protectively, then reached under my skirt and adjusted my underwear where his hands had slipped into forbidden territory. He reached to his crotch, straightening what lay hard and erect. We stood and kissed one more last lingering time. He gathered up the blanket, and we walked quickly back to the campground and the Craig's tents. A kerosene lantern still burned in the tent where Shannon and I slept. I breathed a muted sigh of relief when I saw that the second tent, where the parents and their younger daughter slept, was dark. "See you tomorrow before you go," he whispered.

"Yes," I whispered back as I slipped into the tent where Shannon lay awake.

"Mom's so mad," she whispered. "Where were you?"

"With Harry, we were just walking and walking. It was hard to say goodbye, you know, the last night and all." We blew out the lantern, and in low tones, Shannon and I talked and giggled in the night. The next morning at breakfast, Mrs. Craig was understandably outraged. I apologized profusely, and I knew another invitation would not be forthcoming. It was a small price to pay.

As Harry and I had agreed, I wrote to him at Auburn Academy, where he was a student. About a week later, I arrived home from school and saw the much-anticipated letter lying on the table. I grabbed the letter and ran upstairs to our bedroom. Savoring the pregnant moments, I unhurriedly broke the seal, and as I read, every word burned into my romantic soul. My eyes lingered on the closing, "Love, Harry." Oh, how I capitalized on the romance of those two words. I wrote back at once, and he replied. Was it three or four exchanges? I don't remember, but then the mails fell silent. I learned through a friend at the academy that he had a new girlfriend.

This foray into touch and tremor, as dramatic as it was short, ended in the still silence of a void. I was heartbroken. I couldn't comprehend why God had taken away what he had so briefly allowed me in the desert of my loneliness. Lying in bed at night, I would quietly weep and long for Harry, his touch, that random vibration that had been almost more than I could bear. My dialogue against myself over the next few months was vitriolic at times, the inner voice affirming I was too ugly for anyone to love me after all, telling me how pathetic I was, reminding me that I was, after all, unlovable. Blessedly, from those brief weeks of feeling loved and seen, I dared to doubt the voices inside.

6
1958-1961
High School
Intuiting Freedom OR *It's All About Sex*

Built in 1938, Bellingham High School, with its art deco façade, is a landmark. Fronted by green lawn and trees, with its twin landmark, the Catholic Church and Parochial School posed just across the street, the two structures serve to enrich the neighborhood's architectural impression. During the years our family lived on Young Street, I would gaze at both structures from our porch. The young kids and nuns that would appear outside the Catholic school's doors held a frowning curiosity for me, but the teenagers, as they entered and exited the high school, held the real magic for my young mind. The sculpted solidness of the building with the students chatting away had seemed a dream far away in the future, yet I could almost imagine myself that grown-up someday. And now that day had arrived! The simple stateliness of the building drew me in. Passing by two imposing pillars, I joined the flow of students as we entered the building through three 15-foot-high doors of glass, brass, and wood. Stepping across the threshold, I soaked in the dark wood wainscoting of the interior and crossed the expansive foyer. Everything . . or nothing. . . was promised.

  First semester, I survived on a limb of loneliness. I didn't share a class or lunch period with Theresa or Adele, or Peggy, who were my trusted confidants and friends, and I seldom saw them in a school day. Second semester, the gremlins of teen angst took notice, and reassignments of classes and lunch periods delivered Peggy and me together - before school, after school, on the phone at night, we were happily joined at the hip.

During the summer between junior high and high school, my friendship with Peggy - yes, the cute one in grade school, the one with whom I'd had the "ugly" conversation - had deepened as we prepared for high school. With her daring and curiosity, I discovered in Peggy a like soul. Her sexuality, like mine, was pushing up through the hard soil of convention, and together we whispered and fertilized each other's innate feelings. Our budding sexuality was growing like twin blossoms.

Just remember in the winter far beneath the bitter snows
Lies the seed that with the sun's love
In the spring becomes the rose
    "The Rose" by Amanda Bloom (sung by Bette Midler)

An unlikely duo, we were a study in contrasts, some of which you the reader are already acquainted with - Peggy petite, me tall and gangly; me intellectually smart, Peggy average; Peggy's family lower-middle-class, my family off the lower end of the economic scales; boyfriends vying for Peggy's attention, my dance card empty; Peggy cute, me ugly. But those differences were as nothing when held alongside the insatiable desire for an elusive, vaguely defined state called freedom. They were nothing when held alongside the powerful stirrings of our sexuality. Fate gave us the gift of each other, and together we would fertilize the sensual *Shakti* germinating in the soil of our psyches. We were like spirits joined to explore our sexuality and seek freedom from our small-town cultural restraints. My teenage years took on a new hue: a riot of unfettered shades and colors. We would dare much together.

We jump some 20 plus years in the future to February 1982, when I had a dream that presages a battle to come, and it reflects this time of boldness in the summer of '59. In the dream, I know I have to kill my grandmother, though it isn't clear why. I smother her and hide the pieces of her body in a field. At one point in the dream, the family discovers that Grandma is dead and that whoever killed her also burnt her marriage certificate and other papers (I didn't yet know of the hidden story of Anna's marriage to Peter.) The family decides I'm the one to go to the underworld, find Grandma, and ask her who killed her.

The dream announces the process of killing off the internal grandmother, i.e., the accusing voice of my ugliness, my feelings of impoverishment, my mistrust of men, and the hold of the Seventh-day Adventist church that had hijacked my spiritual yearnings that were destined to find expression in the Tantric path. I will go into the underworld and search to connect unabashedly to my true self. Only I can undertake the journey. Throughout the dream, there's an unknown person in the room (this presence will appear in other dreams, always in the kitchen on 23rd street.)

A Virgin No More

In the hot summer of '59, whooping and hollering as one body, students dashed from the imposing doors of Bellingham High into the promise of summer. The promise for Peggy and me lay with her steady boyfriend, Tommy. He had a friend, Willy, a close neighbor who was one year ahead of us and had a car. Though Tommy and Willy had outgrown their childhood affinity, the vehicle kept their friendship alive. They were as different as night and day: Tommy handsome and charming, Willy with Mickey-mouse ears and a cynical smile; Tommy's laughing teasing blue eyes, Willy's narrowed scorpion-like eyes; Tommy's light brown hair styled just a little bit long, Willy with a military crew cut; Tommy a track star, Willy never daring to test himself in sports; Tommy brimming with self-confidence, Willy a quiet introvert; and finally, Tommy with girls in line, Willy, like me, with an empty dance card. Tommy, enlisting Peggy's help, set about bringing Willy and me together and briefly introduced us in the hallway one day at school. I noted all the things that I have described and then searched out those scorpion eyes; I saw a flicker of interest. My eyes reflected the same.

From the time I was eleven years old, each summer, my sisters and I and other young teenagers would head to the strawberry fields to earn money. For my sisters and me, it wasn't a choice. We needed the money to buy school clothes. Now, in my 16th year, like all the years before, the Linns (Peggy and Sherry) and we Johnson girls boarded the noisy and crowded converted truck that transported us out of the city to Wakefield's Berry Farm in rural Whatcom County. It was simple back then. The field owners needed to harvest their crops, and young people needed to earn money.

In this field of hard work and hot summer sun, Tommy and Willy began to show up at lunchtime. Peggy and I would hurriedly eat our lunch under the shade of one of the giant evergreens that dotted the farm, then the four of us would sneak down to a cluster of trees where a stream bubbled through the countryside. The air itself breathed sensuality, just like the scenes in my teen romance books. We'd kiss and touch until the whistle called us back to work, truncating our trysts. I intuited, well, just barely, that Willy didn't <u>love</u> me, but I felt he liked me a lot. This story I was caught in - best friend Peggy's boyfriend, Tommy - his good friend, Willy with a car - girlfriend needed - I happily stepped into and insisted to myself that I really liked Willy. I thrilled at the promise of entering the beckoning world beyond shy caresses.

Brief lunch encounters in full daylight weren't enough, so we soon set up a real date at the drive-in movie, which would be the first of many, and for the next two months, the four of us celebrated this summer of freedom with dates and outings at every opportunity. Regardless of the activity - the beach, a movie, parking at Bunk's drive-in for hamburgers and milkshakes - the night inevitably ended with us parked in some dead-end road or other hidden corner of the city. Peggy and Tommy were now going steady, which opened up the parameters of how far they dared go sexually. I was happy to ride the coattails of their "going steady" status. Our mutual teen lust smoldered, the very atmosphere of the car vibrated with our libidos, and each night, the scene would repeat itself with slight variations. Parked on a dark road, Willy and I in the front and Tommy and Peggy in the back seat, I couldn't wait for the first kiss and the moment, with my mouth open and summoning, when Willy's tongue would slide inside pressing and slithering into my cheeks, almost into my throat. His hands would slip under my shirt, first feeling my breasts through my bra and then, reaching behind, he'd unhook my bra and free my breasts that longed for his hands to touch my flesh. My nipples, perhaps remembering Harry's touch, were hard as his hands first brushed the contours of my breasts, then began to squeeze. My skin was on fire, and every cell quivered for more sensation. His hands pushed my pants down with no resistance from me, and his fingers found my wet crotch and pushed inside. Groans escaped my lips, and though a little embarrassed at the noises, I let them trail into muted sounds of invitation. I'd been turned on with Harry, but now with time not limited by the shadow of parental oversight and with my body maturing, I was carried way beyond the experience of those stolen kisses and shy touching in the fields of the summer camp meeting.

One night, Peggy and I, as one mind, decided it was time. Yes! It was time to "go all the way," this being the euphemism of the times to distinguish actual penetration of penis in vagina as opposed to hands and fingers. Emblematic of the 1950s in a small northwest town, oral sex was way too daring: it barely existed in our sexual lexicon. When we made this rite-of-passage decision, though the fear of God's retribution still hovered at the edges of my mind, it had no power over the desires of my body. Peggy, who had none of my trepidation born of religion, scoffed when I hinted of god's wrath. There was the possibility of pregnancy, but we had selectively gleaned from books and magazines that no one ever got pregnant their first time . . .well hardly. In truth, nothing could deter us from this intention we had set; desire obliterated all obstacles.

We didn't directly communicate our decision to the boys. Still, when we informed them that Peggy and I would be babysitting together, and the parents of our charges were planning to celebrate a birthday in a neighboring town and would be gone for hours, and they were welcome to come over, we all knew. Eyes locked in mutual accord, we entered, not just willingly, but enthusiastically into this shimmering vibration of teen sexuality that summoned us. We had no desire to escape this fantastical land of teenage sexual lust.

On the appointed Friday night, Peggy and I arrived at the house at 7:00, and I met the parents. The kids greeted Peggy and took her hand to show her their activity for the night. I took in the setting of our assignation - the kitchen through an archway where a chrome table and chairs sat with a plastic flower arrangement in the center of the table. Opposite the kitchen, a stairway I assumed led up to kids' bedrooms. The door to the parents' bedroom on the first floor was open, and I could make out the double bed with matching dresser and night tables, and the living room, where the kids had dragged Peggy, boasted matching couch and chairs.

The man and his wife gave last-minute instructions and a phone number to reach them in case of emergency. "See you around midnight or one," the wife threw over her shoulder as with the other couple, they disappeared through the door. The next hour the kids demanded our full attention, then it took half an hour to get them into bed, then an impatient 15 minutes to read them a story, and at last, we turned out the bedroom lights saying good-night.

"Finally," Peggy said, rolling her eyes. We waited another 15 minutes, crept into their room, and called their names softly. Their measured breathing told us what we impatiently sought to confirm - the kids were sound asleep. As agreed, Peggy picked up the phone and called Tommy at home where they were waiting. (Cell phones were still more than a decade in the future.)

"Finally!" Tommy impatiently echoed Peggy's words. "We'll be there in fifteen minutes." Willy parked the car a block away so the neighbors wouldn't report that Peggy had company. We had pulled all the curtains closed with only one small lamp burning, and the television turned on. There was a soft knock. Peggy opened the door

HIGH SCHOOL

carefully, and the two of them slipped in as she locked the door behind them. When Willy and I kissed, I smelled the hint of beer on his breath. We had to keep shushing the guys as their voices would rise, no doubt to hide their nervousness. Looking back, I realize that their anxiety was way more elevated than mine and Peggy's. The four of us sat together in the living room, Tommy and Peggy on the couch, me on Willy's lap on an overstuffed chair. We talked for a few minutes, but with teenage hormones muskily permeating the air, words died on our lips as kisses and touches become more intense, breaths louder, and little moans filled the air. Willy whispered, "Let's go upstairs."

"Okay," I whispered back, and quietly in stocking feet, we climbed the stairs. I held tight to Willy's hand as I led us to the empty bedroom I had scouted out earlier. We quietly shut the door. I was glad to see it had a lock on it just in case a kid woke up. In the moonlight streaming through the gauzy curtains that hid us from outside eyes, we lay down, and the kisses and touching, the pleasure and excitement of it all was everything I had imagined.

At last, we could take off every stitch of clothing and throw everything aside. For the first time, I lay side by side, fully naked with a man's naked body next to mine. I didn't have to dream it or imagine it; I could feel it. Our hands roamed freely in the darkness, and my hand sought his hard penis, and I gave free rein to the natural way I caressed and stroked him, his moan buried and held by our entwined lips and tongues. When his fingers slide down my belly and found my vagina, and he buried them deep inside of me, my body pressed hungrily into him as a soft, barely audible moan tore my lips from his.

In that moment, with no questions remaining about the outcome, our breathing the panting of animals, he hard and erect, me wet and impatient, he rolled on top of me and grabbing himself he jammed his penis inside where his fingers had been. When his penis met resistance, he unrelentingly pushed harder. I knew this was part of it, this breaking of my hymen as I gave up my virginity. I hadn't known it would hurt so much. I spread my legs wider, hoping to open more, but the pleasure of his touch, our kisses, and my erect nipples vibrating with new sensation was suddenly conflated with the burning ripping pain. "It hurts, it hurts," I whimpered into his ear. He didn't want to stop, and his first response was to push more insistently. I realize now that he was as unprepared for this wrinkle as I was.

Our breath grew hoarse and jagged. "Hang onto the bedposts," Willy whispered huskily, as he directed my hands overhead and behind to where I could grab the iron whorls of the fancy bedstead and hang on. Hardly pausing, once I was positioned with my legs open, my arms stretched overhead, my hands squeezing the cold iron, he pushed and strained his way inside of me. I lost all sense of time, of myself, and was aware of the pain in some distant way and of his pushing and his muffled groans. Suddenly he gasped, and I knew he had come. (With friends, we had often giggled together about how men always needed to come, and there'd been laughter at the expression, "They shoot their wad." It always brought me the image of water balloons exploding when they hit someone or something. But this night, there was no laughter.)

Willy lay panting on top of me with his face buried in my neck. His hands had found mine where I was holding onto the iron bedstead, and now his outstretched arms pinned my arms to the mattress as we lay like matching Christs on a crucifix. We stayed like that for an eternity, my tears falling softly, head turned away from his, waves of shock and dismay coursing through my whole body, any hint of pleasure flown away. At last, his breathing returned to normal. He lifted his head, glanced down at me, surprised he was holding me down. He quickly released my arms, and our lips came together in relief and, yes, even satisfaction. We'd done it! The joy was fleeting as within moments, he rolled off the bed and hunted around in the mottled moonlight for our clothes. He separated the various pants, shirts, underwear and handed me mine. Still laying on the bed, I stared at him intently as he pulled on his underwear and gathered the rest of his clothes, "I'm going to the bathroom. I'll see you downstairs," he whispered as he rose from the bed, tip-toed to the door, turned the lock and slipped out. I heard running water in the bathroom and guessed he was washing up.

I lay there feeling lost, as unbidden questions and even recriminations flooded my mind. "Does he love me? What if I get pregnant? Was it supposed to hurt that much? What will he think now that we "did it"?" I felt warm wetness in my crotch and realized his come was flowing out of me. A strange awareness hit me that his come was inside of me. That, too, was an unimagined piece of the puzzle of losing my virginity. I stood up, clutching my crotch with my hand so I wouldn't drip on the bed or floor. I waited for the water to stop and the bathroom door to open, then slipped silently from the bedroom to the bathroom and, with the door locked, sat down gratefully on the toilet. I looked down in fascination as the milky pink fluid flowed out of me, attesting to a broken hymen. Surreal words came, "Yes, I guess this proves I was a virgin." I cleaned up, put toilet paper into my panties so I wouldn't stain my white shorts, and quietly crept down the stairs, anticipating a moment of joyful complicity when our eyes would find each other in the light. I paused at the bottom of the staircase; the house felt different, strangely quiet. By the lone light in the kitchen, I confirmed he wasn't there. I was disappointed but reassured myself he had simply gone outside to have a cigarette. I idly wondered if he had the sense to be discreet, to hide between the garage and house from neighbors' prying eyes.

When he came in from outside, I tried to read his face: embarrassment, triumph, happiness? I smiled tentatively at him; he responded with a quick smile as he sat down across the table from me. I felt so overwhelmingly relieved. In the disquiet of that moment, did I guess he was already leaving me? I don't know, but this night, having just given up my virginity, sitting across from him, that thought was inadmissible. I debated what I should do. Sit on his lap? Reach across the table and kiss him? Talk? I longed to feel his arms around me, hear reassuring words, to have him smile at me and lovingly kiss me. Despite his smile, I felt a coldness like a winter front blowing across a prairie, so I settled for reaching across the table and taking his hand in mine. My fears were eased when he didn't pull away. We sat together, hands joined, not speaking until Tommy and Peggy came out from the master bedroom arms around each other, smiling. Tommy leaned down and kissed Peggy tenderly, squeezing her close to him. "How you guys doing?"

"Good," I replied too quickly, wondering if they could read in my face that in the upstairs bedroom, going all the way had had a different flavor than going all the way in the downstairs master bedroom.

"I'm great," Willy said, looking at his watch. "Hey Tommy, I gotta get home. My parents, you know, midnight is the magic hour," he said lightly, jokingly.

"Oh, sure, hey man, I need to have a cigarette, then we'll go." Tommy always spoke in a way that admitted of no argument.

Willy shrugged, pulled his hand away from mine, and stood up. "I'll wait for you in the car." He came to me and brushed his lips against mine. There was so much I wanted to say, but I could only manage, "See you tomorrow," to reiterate the beach date the four of us had made.

"Yeah, sure," he said as he turned and walked out the door, his back disappearing into the darkness. It was the last time I would see him as my boyfriend and lover. Over the days and even weeks that followed, I would shed tears in the night, but mostly I was numb with disbelief and self-hatred. It's a testament to my innate sensuality that I didn't shut down after this humiliating rejection of my sexuality and desire.

Peggy and I orchestrated a series of sad and pathetic attempts to make Willy be my boyfriend, even going so far as to intimate to Tommy that I was pregnant. I just wanted to know that Willy had felt something for me other than the triumph that he'd "had a virgin," which, I would learn from Peggy via Tommy, was Willy's attraction to me. Looking back to those hot summer days, the four of us did have fun together, and I remember the thrill of being someone's girlfriend, sitting beside Willy in the front seat of his car as we drove the teen "look at me" route through Bunk's Drive-In and the A&W Drive-In. In the end, Willy and I both got what we'd come for: I wanted to lose my virginity, and he, a testosterone-driven and insecure young 17-year-old, wanted to have sex with a virgin.

Some say love, it is a razor, that leaves your soul to bleed
"The Rose" by Amanda Bloom (sung by Bette Midler)

It was just a couple of weeks after this initiatory rite that Peggy, Rochelle, Laura, and I hatched a camp meeting plan. That Grandma joined us in our dubious scheme is astounding and attests to her total commitment to saving the souls of her granddaughters. She signed the application for tent space, and we girls sent it off with the fee. We were appropriately subdued and grateful to Grandma when the tent assignment came back. But once upstairs, in our sister inner sanctum, we were giddy with excitement. For the third year in a row, the Johnson girls would attend the Seventh-day Adventist camp meeting.

Mom drove the four of us the 100 miles to Auburn Adventist Academy; we unloaded our stuff and waved goodbye. It soon became known among a circle of teens that we had a tent without adult supervision. Guys were in and out of our tent, the lanterns burning bright past the curfew hour, and our voices and laughter rang through the tent-town neighborhood.

Among the male visitors was Lawrence, the coolest, most handsome guy. I longed to bury my heartbreak from Willy's rejection and competed with Rochelle for Lawrence's attention. Rochelle captured the prize. I felt jealous and rebuffed. "The same old story," I thought bitterly to myself. "She always wins." I kept my feelings to myself and joined in the laughter and play. Laura soon hooked-up with Lawrence's younger brother, Ted. Though going steady with Tommy, Peggy flirted outrageously with the whole stable of young studs. I joined her half-heartedly.

The neighbors quickly complained to us and harangued us with their inquiries. "What's going on? Where are your parents? You're making too much noise. This is camp meeting, not a party place." Naturally, we lied and reassured them we'd quiet down and that our parents were coming on the weekend. Wanting no further investigation of our situation, and definitely wanting to stay the whole ten days, we shooed guys out early and turned out the lanterns.

I can trace my shifting relationship with church doctrine and my body's innate desire across the three years of camp meetings. The first year my focus was centered on religious inspiration and my spiritual soul, and a longing for heaven. The second year, while the meetings and the message inspired me, I was enamored and curious about my body experience and concomitant cravings. By the third year, the meetings and messages were barely present in my awareness. The religious teachings of the Adventist church and its strict Christian morality were on a collision course with the demands and desires of the Tantric spiritual path that dwelled in my very soul. In church on Saturdays, I found it more challenging to listen to the minister's sermons or be interested in Sabbath School classes with other teens. Neither seemed to have relevance to what I was feeling inside. While the minister's voice droned on, I drifted in fantasy and excitement about going to the dance that night. I couldn't find a fit with the Christian teens or the Christian adult admonitions, and in typical teen revolt, I grew disdainful.

In my junior year, a perfect storm cast this opposition in full relief. With much fanfare, a local radio station kicked off Saturday night dances at the gymnasium at Bloedel Donovan, the community park on Lake Whatcom. Local DJ's spun records non-stop. The Saturday Night Dance became a must! Rochelle, Laura, and I joined forces to unmercifully lobby our mom to be allowed to fully enter high school social life and go to the dances. She struggled mightily to walk an invisible line once again. Though she wasn't an Adventist and showed not the slightest inclination to enter the church, even in her 40's, she was unable to disappoint or overtly challenge her mother, our grandmother.

We, the younger generation, had no such compunction, so almost every Saturday night, we cajoled mom, knowing we would win in the end. When she capitulated, she would add, "Don't tell Grandma,

HIGH SCHOOL

say you're staying with friends." Eventually, Grandma found out we were going to "that place." When she'd say those words, her voice intimated a doomsday cult meeting. I was unfazed. At those Saturday night dances, to my amazement, boys were asking me to dance. I wasn't a wallflower! Out on the dance floor, twisting and turning or snuggled in close, the sensuous music and movement transported me to a place where I longed to be. I was happy.

One night, a few minutes before the last dance, a group of guys I more or less knew, came noisily (they'd been drinking) through the door drawing all eyes in their direction. As I watched, one of the guys broke away from his pals and came over and asked me to dance. I knew his name was Don, he'd been a star football player at Fairhaven Junior High, but I knew very little else about him. I did my best to follow his awkward, dipping style of a waltz. What he lacked in rhythm he unabashedly made up for in happy, confident prancing around the dance floor. When the last dance ended, we girls, friends and sisters, gathered our coats and bags and headed out the door. His voice called to me across space, "See you at school on Monday."

Lo and Behold! Monday, when I exited the lunchroom, I saw him lounged lazily against the wall waiting for me. I had been so thirsty for so long in the desert of invisibility and desire that his being there, waiting for me, wanting to see ME, was abundance in the bleak landscape that had been my relationship life. We met most every lunchtime and sometimes after school. When someone had a car, several of us would pile in, and Don and I would make out in the back seat. I didn't feel passionately in love with him, but then I hadn't with Willy either. Only Harry held my feelings in that way. What mattered was that, at last, a boy seemed to honestly like me and want me. A boy who was attentive and kind, good-looking, and if he wasn't attending classes and couldn't quite meet me intellectually, what did I care. We double-dated through May with other couples that had access to a car. In June, he flew to Alaska to work on a commercial fishing boat, with a promise to write. Our letters were steady throughout that summer of 1960.

My Prince Stays True

In July 2017, when our family gathered in Bellingham for Pam's wedding, I gave my son, Ron, then 55 years old, the scrimshaw ivory bracelet that Don had brought me from his Alaska fishing caper. Arrayed across each ivory square is the story of an Eskimo man walking out on the ice, killing a seal, and bringing it home: the cycle of life in the frozen tundra of Alaska. When Don asked me to go steady, we agreed it was our "friendship ring," and I wore the bracelet every day. Going steady, being genuinely attracted to each other, gave me internal permission to consider "going all the way."

Don had bought a car with some of his Alaska fishing money and hidden it away from his parents at a friend's house. He was 16, unlicensed, uninsured, and barely knew how to drive. But we were immortal teenagers, and we loved that car as we gamboled around town on a Saturday night, he sitting proudly behind the wheel, I snuggled up close beside him – the apogee of teen life in Bellingham.

On a crisp fall night, the temperatures edging toward freezing as Halloween approached, Don and I sat enclosed in the metal warmth of the roomy Oldsmobile, heater softly humming. The big bench-type front seat was perfect for young lovers to stretch out in the fever of lust and love. That night as I allowed, even invited his hands to roam, caress, explore my breasts, my belly, and I felt his hand slide down the front of my panties . . .that was the moment. I rolled out from under him, twisted to sitting, eyes watering, "I, I have to tell you something," I threw the words out in the open space between us, protecting myself from what I was sure would be recriminations and rejection. (In 1960, though many couples were having sex, and Peggy and I had passed that milestone over a year ago, there was still the cultural more slithering around in my brain that good girls shouldn't have sex before marriage: that no man would marry a fallen woman.) Squeezing my eyes, willing my voice not to fade away, I stammered, "Don, ummm, ummm." The words were burning in my throat, a fire wanting to rush out and something equally strong trying to quash the fire. "Just say it," I said to myself, "just open your mouth and say it."

HIGH SCHOOL

A breath, shallow, but a breath, and I plunged on, "Don, you aren't the first one. There was another. I'm not a virgin." I rushed on. "It was with Willy S, one time, it was awful. I'm so sorry. I'm so sorry." My tears gushed forth, tears of shame, relief, even challenge.

"I know," he said softly, "and it doesn't matter. I love you. Willy bragged about it, his virgin conquest, and he made sure I knew when we started dating."

I was mortified, furious, ashamed, and at that moment, I was enraged not only with Willy, but Don as well, enraged against these boys bragging of their conquests and dissing girls. And just like that, without my conscious awareness, another brick was mortared into the wall named, Mistrust and Hatred of Men, a hatred began with my father's betrayal, built stronger when Harry found another, and cemented by Willy's dishonest ambition. Though unconscious, to build this wall was in direct and painful opposition to my honest, open drive, my desire, to express this glorious *Shakti* energy at the core of my being. Though unknown to me at the time, this exquisite desire would be the font of transcendence and wholeness.

Don simply held me tenderly as we sat there. I didn't have words as I slowly took into my heart his clear words of acceptance. When words did come, I mumbled a simple thank you and raised my face to him. Our kisses, filled with longing, buried stories, and fear became an impassioned avowal of our love. His caresses became more urgent, and this time, when his hand slipped under my panties, I reached down and pulled them off of one leg. He, a little frantically, unzipped his fly and shoved his pants to his knees. As he entered me, it hurt a tiny bit, and I winced a little, but as he moved gently inside of me, the pain dissipated, and I gave myself over to new, unknown sensations. Later at home, I even discovered a little blood. I was elated – I had been a virgin for him and felt exonerated by that great judge in the sky who resided in my psyche.

In my diary, throughout my senior year, I dared not write that we'd had sex, suspecting, even though it had a tiny lock and key, that a sister or even my grandmother might read my diary. I fooled myself that no one would guess that the word "*DON,*" superimposed across the page of daily scribbles, was code for "SEX." I liked to thumb through the pages and think of our lovemaking hinted at by that word written across the page. Just reading and remembering would make my vaginal juices flow, my belly flutter. Of those pages with *"DON"* written across them from corner to corner, two scenes stand out.

On a Friday night after a movie, impatiently driven by the full folly of our passion, Don and I parked in the driveway of my home just under the living room window alongside the porch. We stretched out on the front seat of the car, unclothed, having surged past inhibitions, loving the feeling of flesh on flesh. Suddenly, the porch light blinded my eyes as I lay on my back looking up through the windshield. It was a spotlight highlighting us entwined, my legs spread in the air, Don's white butt pumping hard. Startled rabbits, we bolted up, scrambling for our clothes. At that moment, I looked up and saw Grandma outlined in the front room window. "Shit. Shit, shit," I exclaimed to Don. In the next moment, I heard Mom come down the front stairs, open her car door, start the car, and leave. (I learned later that Rochelle had called begging Mom to come pick her up from a party because she'd gotten in a big fight with her boyfriend.) Mercifully, an invisible hand doused the porch light. I suspect Grandma couldn't bear the sight that had assailed her sensibilities. When the whole house was dark, I slipped out of the car whispering, "Call me tomorrow," and carefully climbed the front steps to the porch, cringing when the screen door squeaked. I tip-toed swiftly up the stairs to our bedroom.

I learned two things about myself that night and the next day. One was that I had the capacity to lie – not little white lies of convenience like permission to go to a dance, but bold-faced out-and-out lies. I'd never dared lie to any of my three parents – additionally, I prided myself on my truthfulness before God. But that Sabbath afternoon, when mom trekked upstairs, which in general she studiously avoided, her discomfort was palpable. As she stood beside my bed where I lay stretched out reading, I smelled her fear and knew hers was more devastating than mine. When she haltingly said, "Grandma saw you and Don with your clothes off," I looked her in the eye and indignantly retorted, "No, that's not true. We didn't have our clothes off. We were just talking. She just didn't see clearly!" My vehemence stopped my mother cold. She looked down at her clasped hands, muttered okay, and turned and left the room. At that moment, I discovered another unknown truth about myself; I had power.

On Saturday night, I reaffirmed my discoveries. As we kids walked with Grandma to a church social, she managed to separate me from my siblings and said in an anguished voice, "You don't want to have to marry Don. I saw what you were doing."

"You didn't see anything, and I'll never have to marry Don!" I snapped back at her and hurried to catch up with my siblings. In that moment, I had no clue of Anna's story that lay buried under a mountain of shame, nor of my own murky future. As I elbowed my way between my sisters, I marveled at my audacity to lie twice, and on Sabbath to boot. Though I didn't understand it at the time, those lies, the proverbial one small step, were a giant leap into liberation from my maternal lineage of passiveness and repressed energies.

The second incident was equally empowering but in a whole different vein. Today, I picture my 18-year-old self and laugh at the potent energy of my tantric nature. However, back then, an unearthly bolt of lightning had simply left me giddy with wonder. This night, Don had driven his Oldsmobile to a hidden spot in Sehome Hill Park where, unlike other make-out spots known to high school lovers, the word was the local cops didn't patrol.

Feeling unconstrained and reckless, we climbed into the back seat. In seconds we shed our clothes as our lips desperately sought each other. His lips fastened onto my nipples that responded joyfully to his fondling, nipping, and sucking and carried me to pre-coital tension. Ah-h, the exquisite entry and moving together. Each time we made love, the pleasure of his penis moving inside of me, his hands touching me, gripped me in a thrilling passion, but this time I felt a storm gathering more and more force until I ached with desire. Time seemed to pause and then speed up – an other-worldly explosion rippled through me, and I collapsed into pure sensation. When at last we lay together quiescent, I knew without a shred of doubt - I'd had an orgasm!

The following day as we boarded the bus to school, I pulled Peggy into an isolated seat in the back of the bus and whispered, "You'll never guess what happened with Don last night. I had an orgasm!" Unable to contain my excitement, I gushed on, barely able to keep my voice down, "It was so rare. You can't believe it. I mean, oh my god . . ."

"Oh my god," her words echoed mine, "tell me, tell me, what was it like?"

"I don't know how to describe the feeling. There was a strange ripple that moved through me and carried me somewhere - a wave of vibration just took over. I don't know . . .? What else. Well, actually, it was almost overwhelming, like being in a tornado with the wind tearing up trees around you, and you're trying to stay on the ground. Kinda weird really - in a good way." We continued exclaiming together, and she was justly impressed. Throughout the day, as I sat glowing through Spanish, math, English, geology, the words of the teachers couldn't erase the lively babble circulating in my head. "My orgasm was unbelievable, so pleasurable, and IT'S FREE! IT'S FREE!" For a teenager living in the lap of poverty, this was a revelation. The sensual, *Shakti* pleasures offered by movies, sodas, dances all demanded I spend my hard-earned babysitting money, but this . . .nothing could compete with this newfound pleasure. Over the next few months, I noted that I couldn't make an orgasm happen on demand. The elusive orgasms engendered a bit of consternation for my tantric soul that longed for the indescribable sensations, but there was a promise that eased this yearning. It was the promise of San Francisco, California.

San Francisco. Though technically only a town on the map of the U.S.A., our mothers feared those words, and Don was distressed by them. But for Peggy and me, those two words, San Francisco, were an irresistible siren call. What tantalizing mysteries, what romantic adventures, what glorious unfolding awaited us there? We'd planned, saved our money, talked of nothing else since we'd decided to embark on freedom from small-town life. In our high school annual, alongside our graduation portraits, seniors stated an ambition. Beside Peggy's and my pictures, these words appear **Ambition - Perennial Wanderer**. An unwavering wanderer spirit had captured us. We dreamed of grand adventures, with San Francisco the launching pad into our glorious unknown future. By land, sea, air, we would see the world, gather knowledge, grow wise in the ways of the world. In those months before graduation, our dreams restlessly incubated in our shared psyche space. Unbeknownst to us, lurking in the margins, a life-changing event was about to steal our dreams.

The night before our departure for San Francisco, Don came to visit me. Sitting together with my family watching T.V. and talking like so many other nights, Don and I followed a secret routine we'd set up. "Mom, I'm going to walk with Don to the end of the road, okay?" (By now, his parents had discovered Don had a car when he'd had a run-in with the police. They'd had the car towed and kicked him out of the house. His transportation was his legs and hitch-hiking.)

"Okay," she replied, rather disinterestedly as Don was nearly a member of the family, and she generously allowed us this private time together.

"Going to get my coat," I said loudly to Don.

"Okay," he replied, "I'll wait outside."

I dashed upstairs, pulled my sleeping bag out of the closet, and threw the bundle out the window where Don waited. Football player that he was, he easily caught my pass.

Back downstairs, I called to mom, "Be back soon," and joined Don outside. It was a beautiful June evening with a clear sky, which wasn't always the case in northwest Washington. I looked up, drawn into the romance and mystery of that night sky. This night, my last with Don, felt perfect. We walked the block to the tiny one-room adorable dollhouse that had belonged to old Mr. Clark, who had passed away a year or so before. His daughter, who lived several blocks away on our isolated road, would check on the house occasionally, but otherwise, the cottage stood empty and free. In those days, no one in our neighborhood locked their doors; our house didn't even have a lock on the back porch door.

With the sleeping bag under his arm and me holding his hand, with a hint of caution just in case, we opened the door to what we'd come to call "our house." Mr. Clark had been the delight of the neighborhood, and the house still exuded the warmth and goodwill of this delightful pixie man. Don and I were the lucky recipients of the charm and ease of his home. Through the window, light from the half-moon illuminated our little love nest. Tucked away in one corner was the old-fashioned wood-burning stove Mr. Clark had used for cooking and heat. Under the east-facing window was a table with two chairs and across from the entry stood the door to the bathroom.

On our left was a narrow bed covered with a clean, though worn quilt. As we'd done so many times before, we pulled the single mattress onto the floor, and Don spread the sleeping bag over the mattress. Relishing the freedom this little house provided, we quickly undressed together, and naked and hot, arms wrapped around each other, half laughing, we entered into our bubble of bliss.

We had no condoms - they were illegal to buy until you were 18, and Don wasn't quite 17, so unless I had my period and we knew we were safe from pregnancy, we practiced *coitus interruptus* or, more simply put, "pulling out." That night I knew it was near my fertile time, but whether out of guilt or pure generosity, or the designs of fate, I chose to make a parting gift to Don. As our passion built and our bodies writhed together, I whispered in his ear the fateful words, "You can come inside of me." My whispered words snaked through our panting and pulsing, and together we shared a sweet and poignant orgasm. I lay in his arms, my head resting on his chest, blissed out in the orgasmic afterglow. An intuited time-awareness intruded, and we knew it was time to go. We slowly retrieved our clothes, often pausing as we dressed to linger over a kiss. We rolled up the sleeping bag and restored the mattress for the last time onto the cot. Exiting the little cottage, we walked back to my place to say our goodbyes. As his footsteps crunched across the gravel to the road, and I climbed the stairs, I was already dreaming of the morrow, of boarding the train to freedom.

7

Summer 1961

San Francisco Dreaming

The train chugged slowly out of the Bellingham train station. Peggy and I waved goodbye to our mothers and friends standing under the portico. Our enthusiastic waves were echoed by those of our friends, though theirs were tinged with envy. In contrast, our mothers raised their hands only slightly, their faces showing parental disapproval of our journey. Months ago, when they had vociferously objected to our adventure, Peggy and I had pronounced, with the arrogance of our imminent freedom, "We're 18, so you can't stop us." They had acquiesced and given their halfhearted approval. I like to think that perhaps they even admired our audacity in some little corner of their being, especially my mom, who that same year had herself grabbed her centimeter of chance to flee toward freedom. She'd found the guts to divorce Dayton. (What drove her emancipation was that she had a job! About a year ago, the brand-new Redden Net Company had hired her, and now, with Grandma's continued help, the two of them were raising the family out of abject poverty. Best of all, she loved her job.)

Peggy and I pushed the envelope of community conformity in our small, protected town wherever we could - skipping school, losing our virginity at 16, and deciding to get drunk in our senior year. To this end, we enlisted the help of a generous 21-year-old friend to buy us cheap Thunderbird wine and babysit us while we got drunk at the drive-in theater. Oh, the puking and swearing and hallucinations that moved through us that night! When we had sobered up a little, our friend drove the vehicle to an alley behind another friend's house and left us passed out in the back seat. In the early morning light, rubbing our blurry eyes, we awoke to the putrid smell of our vomit and cheap booze and were sick all over again. Gathering our wits about us, we drove to a neighborhood park, washed in the kiddies' pool, threw the bottles into the bushes, and cleaned the car as best we could with paper towels from the park bathroom. When we returned the smelly old vehicle to Earl, Peggy's dad, he was generous and didn't mention the smell and our wretched appearance. "How was the movie?" he asked, with an indulgent wink to let us know he knew and would be our partner in crime. I'd always envied Peggy her dad; that day, my appreciation of him multiplied immensely, and I felt his empathy for our *Luna*-driven spirits.

One night and two days later, disembarking from the train into the city of our dreams, a smoldering blast of heat slammed us. That day, June 14, 1961, is recorded as one of the hottest days in San Francisco's history, 101 degrees. The feverish air we breathed matched the fever burning in our hearts and brains. Nervous, doing our best to hide our country bumpkin-ness beneath a pseudo-bravado of imagined sophistication, we hailed a taxi and gave the driver the YWCA address where we'd booked an alcove with two beds for the allowed limit of three days.

There was a wildness, a hunger burning inside us to experience everything, to risk, to court danger. As soon as we'd showered and changed into "city clothes," of which, in fact, we were woefully ignorant, we exited the doors onto Powell St. Imagine for a moment you hold a lottery ticket in your hand. As each number is read and matches your ticket, your excitement grows, and when the last number is read, and it is a match – well, no words can describe that moment. Such was the feeling of those two 18-year girls yearning to become young women as they stepped into the red skies of a hot sun setting over the city. *Shakti Energy* burned in their very souls. Every horn, siren, the whistling wind was a magical call to go forth.

We felt no fear. We had each other for safety, and we shared a sisterhood of love and trust. We thought as one; we risked as one; nothing could dampen our free spirits breathing in the enchantment,

SAN FRANCISCO DREAMING

the endless vistas beckoning.

When we'd checked into the YWCA, the woman at the desk had given us free tickets to the Ice Follies for that night. Wow, our very first night in San Francisco, we were going to a show! When we took our seats, the colors, sounds, music, and movement of the swirling, twirling ice dancers assaulted our senses and carried us in a sensual balloon. Floating out onto the street after the final curtain had dropped and the applause faded, lost in wonder, we soon got lost in the city. We took the wrong bus and had to take the next one back to where we had begun. We waited impatiently until the right bus pulled into the stop. We arrived at the YWCA a few minutes after the 10:00 curfew. The matron on the night shift harrumphed as she answered the bell and unlocked the door. We apologized quickly, explained about the busses, and ran up the stairs to our alcove. Undressing, slipping into our flowered nighties, we collapsed onto our cots and fell asleep. This first night in the city, a promising step into our future, danced and swirled in our dreams.

We'd heard of the USO, and happily, the YWCA gave us tickets to go and volunteer. We weren't sure what we'd find, but we liked the idea of dancing with soldiers, sailors, marines; basically, handsome men in uniform. In 1961, the USO still retained the spirit of the 1940s and 1950s.

They wanted middle-class, mostly white women who were considered sexually respectable," said Winchell. "The USO knew women mattered to morale—the men needed company of women. [But] they didn't want them having sex." USO hostesses were prescreened "good girls" who could provide comfort in the way of conversation, dancing and the occasional picnic outing. Young women had to be approved by a committee to volunteer.

Retrieved from uso.org (See appendix)

We arrived at the nearby venue, presented our tickets, and cheerily submitted to a brief "interview" to ensure we fit the bill of "good girls." We qualified, and the interviewer gave us open passes. 50's music was playing, uniforms were everywhere, and young women like ourselves mingled and talked and danced. Peggy and I shared a "cat that caught the canary" smile. The USO was definitely not the scene of my junior high school graduation dance where I'd suffered the indignity of standing throughout the night in the wall-flower line. Girls were boldly taking the initiative, pulling young men onto the dance floor, whirling with abandon. In that "nostalgic hour," we danced, talked, and at the end, we agreed to meet two young men, Nicky and Steve, outside; girls were not allowed to leave with the servicemen.

Nicky was a short, swarthy curly-haired Italian from New York and Steve was a blond, blue-eyed Swede from Minnesota. I got Nick, Peggy got Steve or Nick got me, Steve got Peggy. They took us to a local café and bought us dinner. Though unspoken, Peggy and I shared the thought, "This is so rare, just like we imagined." During dinner, the four of us carried on the ubiquitous conversation of couple encounters everywhere, who we were, who they were, where from, how old, etc. Dinner eaten, bill paid, the requisite conversation over, we left the bright lights of the café and entered shades of darkness where the boys, as if by a pre-arranged signal, took our respective hands. Steve and Peggy dropped a few feet behind Nicky and me as we walked the city streets.

Then once again, right on cue, our sailors guided us into an alleyway. The kisses quickly moved to hands testing how much of our bodies they could touch, first over our clothes, then Nicky's hand slipped under my blouse. On cue, this time from Peggy and I, we gently pushed those hot male bodies away, straightened our clothes, and one of us said, "We need to go; there's a curfew at the Y." The other echoed, "Yes, yes, let's go." The boys exhaled an exasperated sigh, but with no further protest, walked us back to the YWCA, where they left us a block from the building.

We rang the bell and the matron in charge appeared, speaking into the 2-way speaker, "You girls are late. We can't have this."

"We're so sorry," conjuring up our most contrite mien, "so sorry, we lost track of time, we were just walking."

"Don't you know it's not safe for young girls to be walking alone at night? You foolish children!" Lips clenched and jaw muscles contracted, she noisily jangled her key ring, jammed the key in the lock, and let us in. "You girls broke the rules, and this is the second night you didn't respect the curfew. We can't have this. It's unacceptable. Tomorrow you will have to find another place to stay." She paused from her breathless diatribe.

With eyes lowered, seriousness etching our faces, voices a little panicky, we begged, "We are so sorry we didn't get here before curfew. Please, we've paid for one more night. Could we just stay one more night so we can have time to find a place to stay? Oh, please, please let us stay one more night. We're so sorry, we for sure won't break another rule. We promise." How contrite must we be? We held our breath. Finally, shaking her head and glaring at us, she agreed to give us one more night. Whew, our relief was palpable as we turned and ran up the stairs before she could change her mind. The next day we found a room in a sleazy run-down hotel just off Market Street.

As I reflect on those two months in San Francisco, I believe there was a spirit of cosmic innocence guiding us, or perhaps it was the benign zeitgeist of the late 50s, early 60s. Just a couple of days later, a new male twosome from the USO entered our lives, and on seeing where we lived, they grew alarmed. "This is a dangerous area. You're right in the middle of the "red-light" district. You can't stay here!" We were terrified. They insisted on walking us to our room and made sure we locked the doors and windows. When they left, they warned us, "Don't open your doors to anyone. Tomorrow we'll help you find a new place." We packed everything and slept fitfully till we heard the knock and voices, "It's us, Lyle and Art." Our saviors were there to carry us to safety. Lyle knew the city and helped us find a room in an equally dilapidated neighborhood, but kindlier and safer.

We were virgin explorers in the city, and every discovery felt destined for the history books. We'd never imagined anything as grand as Golden Gate Park could be hidden in the middle of a big city. We marveled at a park so big that it boasted stately buildings, including an art center. Whether basking in the warm sun or bundled up in rain slickers, the park was a favorite destination. We rode the cable cars, swam in the invigorating ocean, climbed the stairs to the top of Coit Tower, walked across the Golden Gate Bridge - we just couldn't get enough of the infinite flavors, sights, and moods of the city.

From today's vantage point, I recognize *Shakti's* vibration in that city held by the vast Pacific Ocean and the surrounding hills. Though burned to the ground in 1906 after the earth goddess shook and flexed and tore the land apart, the city then and now thrives in the material world. Equally impressive, San Francisco plays host to gatherings of myriad spiritual seekers, including the transformative energy of the '60s that found its center in the Haight-Ashbury district in the *1967 Summer of Love*. (In 1968, to the far north in Bellingham, Washington, San Francisco's *Summer of Love* would reverberate through me as I struggled to find the courage to separate from Don. It would be a long untangling – marriage, kids, money, intellectual ambitions.)

In the summer of 1961, though the revolution hadn't yet come to San Francisco, Peggy's and my personal revolution was in full swing, so it'll come as no surprise that our aspirations for that indefinable freedom landed on the words, "Greenwich Village." New plans erupted. After calculating plane fare to New York City, a few days lodging at a YWCA, and a few days of food, we decided we'd stay in San Francisco until our money reserves reached the calculated point. Then we'd board a plane for the new promised land. We'd be beatniks in Greenwich Village, New York City. What drives young women like Peggy and me to keep seeking an unnamed, unknown, utterly foreign experience? For us, it was freedom - we just didn't know the full meaning of the word.

We were living dangerously and found safety in making decisions together. We eagerly agreed to include Lyle and Art in our lives. Lyle was 32 years old, Art around 25. Art was cute and sweet; Peggy could have him. I was drawn to Lyle. He was a Robert Mitchum doppelganger right down to the broken nose. I liked him instantly – well, at 18, perhaps I was in love with the bad boy image of Robert Mitchum. He was undeniably attracted to me, and my gosh, he was such a mature man. That he was recently divorced only added to his allure as a man of the world. The two were army buddies, and at first introduction, Lyle said he was a photographer in the army and offered to develop the extravagant number of pictures we were taking. He promised he'd get us jobs within a few days. (None of this proved to be true.) We believed he was an angel heaven sent. I recently read a letter I had written to my mother during this time. I wrote most innocently, *"I've met this really nice man, well two men, Lyle and Art. Lyle is a photographer and he's going to develop the colored film for us and I'll send you pictures. He said he'll get jobs for us in a couple of days."* I wrote so honestly, and I have often wondered what, if anything, my mother projected onto those words.

Meantime, toward the end of June, an unwelcome hint of a new drama unfolding in my body troubled Peggy and me. Each time I went to the bathroom, I prayed for blood. Peggy would holler, "Anything?"

"No, nothing, " I would call back disconsolately as I wiped and hoped. My period had always been on time, so I should have been bleeding by the end of June. I reassured myself that the excitement of our move to San Francisco, or perhaps the summer heat, must account for the lateness of my period, but each day my period was overdue seemed like forever. Peggy alternated between sympathy and anger that I might be ruining our plans, our dream of going to Greenwich Village to be part of the beat generation, meeting poets and musicians and artists. We debated our future, refusing to give up our dreamy ambition of liberating our true selves.

Don and I were wonderfully innocent and tender lovers, exploring man-woman sex from a place of inexperienced teen love. But this man, Lyle, so much older and experienced, initiated me into the world of intoxicating, sensuous lovemaking. When he took me powerfully and confidently in his arms, it took my breath away, just as had happened those years ago with Harry.

If I was a flower waiting for the spring sun and rains to blossom into a thing of beauty, Lyle was the spring sun and rain, expanding the beauty of sexual expression in me. He loved being my teacher in the man-woman sex story, and my wonder and the innocent responsiveness of my body brought out a loving tenderness in him. From the first time, as he undressed me slowly and his hands brushed across my breasts as he pulled off my shirt and unhooked my bra, I was aflutter from my head to my toes. The way his hands explored my body left me breathless. My back arched, begging him to touch me more intimately, to squeeze my nipples as his fingers slid easily across my erect clitoris. Yes, like finding a diamond buried in the earth, with Lyle, I discovered the existence of this thing called a clitoris. I was a small-town girl and was elated with Lyle's knowledge of female genitalia that was much broader than mine!

This new, almost revolutionary passion made me hungry to dissolve into something, but in my youth, I knew not what. (One day I would know this "something" as "oneness.") But wait! Even as I wanted to open my body to Lyle without restraint, I wondered if I had the right. I was dimly aware that perhaps another path awaited me.

Two parts of me made an agreement with my future. Until I started my period, I wouldn't allow Lyle to penetrate me with his penis. Everything else was acceptable. After all, a missed period doesn't equal a baby . . .but just in case. This rationale was decidedly a fine line, but it gave me the permission I needed to joyfully invite Lyle's attentions – I just wouldn't "go all the way." I prayed for my period to start and fantasized about him entering me. When I reflect back, I am astounded beyond words that he respected this boundary. This acceptance by Lyle, a powerful and mature man, reaffirms even today, nearly 60 years later, that a cosmic innocence must have protected Peggy and me.

In this moment of my 18-year-old self, with Lyle lovingly and expertly playing my body, his hands and lips ranging over every crevasse with exquisite timing, it didn't take me long to overcome any shyness of his penis. In the full light of day, he instructed me on how best to pleasure him as he patiently awaited my, "Yes." Lyle's touch and tender words overrode the old memory of Papa's touch and words, and my tears and mixed emotions - that day at 621-23rd St., a barely remembered story. With Lyle, I was simply a curious and happy student in the intrigues of sex. He brought me to orgasm through my clitoris and vagina. I unashamedly brought him to orgasm by jacking him off. Like a glorious piano duet, we improvised and played each other's bodies right through to climatic orgasm. Lyle taught me about oral sex – that too brought me to orgasm. And then one afternoon, I was so aroused that I dared to bring him to orgasm with my mouth. It was the first time I had tasted and swallowed a man's semen. Conflicted and guilt-ridden, I was like a street person who feels the eyes of the world judging her and feels that same judgment within herself, and yet can find no way out of her homelessness, and perhaps doesn't want to.

As though bedazzled by a magician's wand, I never doubted Lyle, and when he introduced Peggy and me to Tamara, I trusted her as I did him. When we met her, Peggy and I were impressed by her sophistication and flattered when she took the time to be interested in us. One afternoon, I was home alone when there was a knock at the door. I opened it cautiously, as we didn't have unexpected visitors. I was surprised to see Tamara and opened the door wider, "Oh hi Tamara, come on in."

"Hey, I'm just hanging out with a couple of friends who are staying in the same hotel. Come on up and meet them. There may be jobs for you and Peggy."

"Oh, OK. Give me a minute." Wanting to look my best, I quickly changed clothes, ran a brush through my hair, put on lipstick and a little eye shadow. Gazing into the mirror past my reflection, I noticed Tamara looking around the room, taking in all the details.

"Where's Peggy?"

"She's at her job."

"Oh, OK. Why don't you leave a note on the door and tell her to come up when she gets home?"

"What's the apartment number?"

"325. It's the next floor up."

"OK." I dutifully followed her instructions and left the note on our door as I locked it behind me.

And here, at last, I share my **#MeToo** experience. The elements were all there: a man of power, a young woman needing work, money, naïveté, and trust. Except for Peggy, who sadly passed away a few years ago, no one else knows this story. It has stayed hidden in shame until now. I've always been too embarrassed to speak of it; embarrassed about my naïveté, ashamed about what happened, sure it was something I'd done wrong.

We ascended the stairs, walked some ten feet down the hall, and I followed Tamara into room 325. Closing the door behind us, she introduced me to her friends, first to a dark-complexioned Latino man with a closely cropped beard and glittering, searching black eyes. His black hair was pulled into a ponytail, and he wore a flashy outfit – over a black shirt, a black leather vest with silver bangles on the chest pockets. Around his waist was a black leather belt with a large silver and turquoise buckle. Black leather jeans completed his outfit. I felt danger and an unstoppable curiosity about this outlaw right out of a gangster movie. He was almost menacing, but I relaxed in the knowledge that he was Tamara's friend. The other man I see less clearly. His soft round body contrasted markedly with the outlaw's sharp angular body, as did his loose-fitting, almost sloppy shirt and pants. He was solicitous and friendly. I marveled at finding myself standing in a scene right out of a movie.

The apartment was larger than ours. Tamara and I had entered into the living room, and ahead a doorway led into the kitchen. To the right was a set of double doors, fronted by a threadbare couch, thrown open, allowing easy access to the large bed on the other side of the threshold. Tamara was chatting away as she introduced us. I remember her prompting the outlaw (I have no memory of his name, so I shall simply leave him anonymous) to tell about Mardi Gras where the two men had been some months before. Then she prompted him to show me something in his suitcase. He acted reticently, then finally opened the lid of the suitcase, moved aside a shirt or two, to reveal a revolver. Before what I saw fully registered, he unhurriedly drew the perfectly folded shirts over the weapon and asked, "Would you like a whiskey and soda?" I'd never drunk hard liquor before.

In my dissociation from what was going on, wanting to be as grown-up and sophisticated as the three of them, my answer came quickly before I could change my mind. "Sure."

"Sit down here with me," Tamara said, patting the spot beside her on the couch. The outlaw mystery man disappeared into the kitchen and returned with drinks. He handed me a glass and served the others a drink as well. Someone made a toast. This strange fantasy of being in a movie wowed me again. I raised my glass and drank deeply. The ice-cold liquid burned as it rushed down my throat and took my breath away. "Bottom's up!" the outlaw commanded, and I quaffed my drink to the bottom. There were vague words from Tamara that we could work for him . . .as what? Prostitutes? I couldn't make sense of the words. They all seemed to be smiling. I smiled a lopsided smile, though I wasn't sure why. That smile is the last thing I remember.

I groggily opened my eyes, my body fighting something, someone. Whispered words from the outlaw, "Shh-shh." I must have been fighting with my voice as well. He was on top of me, his pants off, my breasts exposed, he working on getting my pedal pushers down. I surfaced like a rocket through the drug-induced haze, and pushed at him with one hand, held tight to my pants with the other. He swore, called me whore and bitch, and rolled off me. He retrieved his pants and jerked them on as he stood up and thrust a hateful frustrated stare right through me. I was terrified and embarrassed and angry. He exited the bedroom. I lay on the bed, looking fuzzily through the still opened double doors into the living room. In my sideways view, I saw the friend and Tamara. I turned away as I fumbled to get my bra back on and my blouse. Standing shakily, I reached down, tugging my pedal pushers up, and stumbled into the living room as I fastened them. I resolutely refused to notice their accusing glares, their disbelief that I hadn't understood the game. And then, like the grade B movie it was, there was a knock at the door. Tamara pushed past where I stood, disheveled and confused. She cautiously opened the door.

"Hi," Peggy said gaily. "I saw the note on the door and came up." She nodded to Tamara and brushed past her into the room. A reprieve. Saved. I was racked by a flood of indecipherable emotions. Only the sight and feel of Peggy standing so close kept my unsteady legs from collapsing.

I roughly grabbed her arm, "We need to leave right now. Let's go." Remembering the gun in the suitcase, finally understanding I'd been drugged, and frightened out of my wits, I turned her on her heel and steered her to the door. She looked curiously back over her shoulder; a questioning sound came from her. I ignored her look and pushed her out the door, yanking it closed behind us. Holding even tighter to her arm, terrified, I hurried us down the stairs, into our apartment, and locked the door.

"What is going on?" Peggy questioned. "You left me the note to come up."

"I'm so scared. You'll never believe what happened." Our room felt strange as we stepped across the threshold. When we looked around, we understood why. Clothes were thrown on the floor, the content of our drawers strewn about, our purses dumped out. Our two sets of eyes surveyed the chaos and then turned to stare at each other. It took only a moment to confirm our worst fears. Every dollar and travelers' check was gone! We were penniless. I quickly told her the story, and we figured out that while I was drugged, the accomplice to the outlaw had taken my keys that I'd set down on the coffee table and come and robbed us. Our shared fury and outrage was the catalyst we needed. We pulled ourselves together and headed straight for a Traveler's Checks office. We had been prudent where our funds were concerned and kept the record of check numbers in a safe place. At the Traveler's Checks office, the women were solicitous and listened as we related only the most salient point, that someone had robbed us. They soon restored the stolen checks. Most of our nest egg was intact. As we left, one of the women in the office admonished us, "Now, young ladies be careful. It's a big city." We thanked her for the advice and help. We were no longer wide-eyed innocents.

By the time Lyle came over that evening, I was livid. With clenched teeth, I demanded an explanation of his and Tamara's plan to turn us into prostitutes. He vehemently insisted he was innocent and acted as outraged as I had felt when Tamara's intentions dawned on me. When I challenged him as to what the jobs were he'd promised us if it wasn't to turn us into prostitutes, his self-righteous indignation that I would dare even think such a thing of him obliterated my doubts. Even today, it boggles my mind that this man, who was so protective of Peggy and me, had set up such an arrangement. Back then, I needed to believe him, and so I chose to do just that. I hadn't yet learned of his pathological ability to lie shamelessly. The next day, the two men upstairs had disappeared, and we never saw nor heard of Tamara again.

It was an ugly sordid affair, as I encountered for the first time and first-hand the world's slime. There's no clean or comfortable way to talk about it. I felt victimized, but bringing it to the light of day, I can acknowledge that, though innocent, I had nevertheless chosen to enter that theater. At the time, my youthful folly allowed me to see the episode as a little drop in the bucket of water called "freedom in San Francisco," where events were unfolding, unraveling like a massive tsunami. I chose to ride the wave and land on whatever rocky or sandy shore it would drop me.

With the mobility Lyle's car afforded us, we ranged beyond the bounds of San Francisco proper. On an early morning, Lyle drove us all north across the Golden Gate Bridge, and we wound our way up the coast into wine country. Another day Lyle decided we should all see Half Moon Bay, so we four climbed in the car and headed south to the quaint little town and inviting beach. Though the water was cold, we swam with pelicans diving around us. I lay in contentment on the beach beside Lyle and sensed a shadow pass over my closed eyes, then his lips touching mine, and laughingly his hand slipped under my bikini. The days flew by; Lyle was in the foreground of my thoughts as I anticipated the moments when our lovemaking, without my conscious awareness, was stirring the seeds of tantric *Shakti* energy.

Concurrently, with the barely heard whisper of the child growing inside of me, I indulged in an emphatic denial, compartmentalizing my present relationship with Lyle, and my possible future with Don and the child I was carrying in my womb. Lyle was a gift of my youth, of my resolve to experience all the sensuousness of life and live with the consequences – the same resolve that had enticed me to that ultimate moment with Don in the little house "to go all the way" no matter what the consequences.

Like a clock ticking away the minutes and hours, each day the unavoidable fact that I was pregnant and would undoubtedly be returning home to marry Don brought the pressure of time. Peggy and I set out to pack every experience we could into the three weeks before we must go back to Bellingham. Longing for one more storied city, though Los Angeles was a pale compensation for New York City, we decided to go south. Talking with Lyle and Art one night, sharing our intent, Lyle, apparently on impulse, volunteered to drive us to this next shimmering outpost of our aborted flight to freedom.

A few days later, Peggy and I packed everything we'd brought with us from Bellingham into our waiting suitcases. Mine was the large, light green suitcase that Papa had given me for my high school graduation on learning of our travel plans. I was heartened by his support of my dreams of travel, even though I had come to despise him for most everything else he did.

As Lyle drove south, Art, Peggy, and I scoured travel brochures and outlined our excursion. We'd drive straight through to Tijuana so Peggy and I could see first-hand this place of exotic stories. After Tijuana, we'd go to San Diego to stay with some friends of Lyle's, north to Knott's Berry Farm, and then Los Angeles. As we drove south, Lyle and I in the front, Art and Peggy in the back, having long conversations, confirmation of a niggling suspicion began to darken my joy. Lyle lied. I mean big lies, unnecessary lies, all the time lies, lies, lies, and as my attention engaged with his stories and lies, I realized how compulsive his behavior was. At 18, decades away from being a psychologist, I didn't understand what could happen if I confronted him. Still, his lying had become burdensome, profoundly affecting my feelings and trust in him, and the internal pressure to clear this issue was mounting. I kept my feelings hidden until on the drive back north from San Diego, I took a deep breath and, with the earnestness of the naïve 18-year-old, small-town girl I was, blurted out, "Lyle, I like you so much. I love who you are and everything we do together, so there's no reason for you to lie to me about anything. Really, it makes no sense. I think you're great. I love being with you, so please stop telling me lies all the time."

His rage, like a dark beast eerily filled the car. The beast extinguished Peggy and Art's soft murmuring in the back seat. My mouth dropped open as he spun the wheel and swerved off the road, sending gravel and dirt flying. He slammed on the brakes just inches off the road and inches from a deep ditch. I couldn't entirely stop the scream that filled the silence. He reached across me and flung open the door, "Get out of the car," he roared, "Get out now, you little bitch. Who the hell do you think you are?" I didn't move - self-preservation kicked in.

"No, no," I stammered. "I'm sorry. I'm really sorry. I don't know what I was talking about. Really, I didn't mean it. Please Lyle." I sat with head bowed, even praying a little, worried he'd hit me as Papa had so often done to Mama, or worse yet, shove me out of the car and drive off, carrying with him my best friend and all I owned in the world. "Jesus," I thought to myself, "I can't believe this is happening. What if he actually kicks me out of the car. . ." Under the fear, my anger began to boil. I held it in check, not daring to look up and risk him seeing the fire in my eyes. We waited.

Art leaned forward from the back seat, putting a hand on Lyle's shoulder. "Hey, she's sorry, what a stupid thing for her to say. We're all tired. Let's just get to Buena Vista, find a hotel, and rest. Come on Lyle. It's OK." Art had a soothing voice, and they were friends. Perhaps, perhaps it would work. Not daring to move a muscle to turn toward him, I glanced out of the corner of my eye; the three of us held our collective breath. Every second, as he considered Art's words, or perhaps was working on calming himself down, was spring-loaded with unbearable tension. Art's voice gently floated from the back seat. I detected even the hint of a smile in his words, "Hey, I'm hungry, let's find a drive-in and get hamburgers and milkshakes. I'm buying."

Moments passed, "Shut the door," Lyle growled at me. My hand shot out and grabbed the door handle, and I slammed the door shut, relieved to be inside and not outside. "OK," he muttered as he started the car. Spinning the wheels out of the gravel, he merged aggressively onto the highway. Restrained sighs of relief filled the vehicle, and all eyes stared hard out the window, looking for a drive-in.

As we ate, Lyle seemed to recover his usual mood and conduct himself as if the blow-up had never happened. That scared me even more as I began to have dark fantasies of Dr. Jekyll and Mr. Hyde. I mentally calculated how many more days we'd need to be with them, how many more days I would still need to be his attentive consort, always rejecting his want to be inside of me. I was scared and felt myself on sinking and dangerous ground. My mental wheels whirring, I swore to myself to hold my tongue, and with mature understanding, stay the naïve 18-year-old for two more days and two more nights. Lyle's rage had retreated to a hidden corner of his psyche, and the caring man I was so attracted to, even nearly in love with, had reasserted himself. The lies didn't stop. I acknowledged attentively everything he said. Not a whisper of dissent escaped my lips.

In Los Angeles, with the help of our guardians, Lyle and Art and our unseen guardians of the beyond, we found a large room in a working-class neighborhood on the first day of looking. Large windows across two sides let in the southern California sunshine, and under the bank of windows was a couch with a battered coffee-stained table in front. In one corner was a bright, clean kitchen nook, and in another corner, the bed and closet. We moved in right away, and

Lyle and Art crashed on the floor for one night. In the morning, my voice tinged with sadness, I thanked Lyle profusely for all he had done for us. In the compressed two months with him, the good had far eclipsed the bad.

I didn't verbalize my feelings directly to Lyle, but I was grateful that though it was challenging for him, and he'd tried to push the envelope from time to time, he had nevertheless honored my request that he never be inside of me. I had told him about my pregnancy, and it's very likely that held him back as well. Mine had not been the perfect solution, but it had helped me navigate through the conflicting demands and needs of my mind and body, the demands of present and future.

In our sun-filled room in Los Angeles, I awoke many mornings with anxiety and uncertainty, yet Peggy and I were determined to play and find joy. The destination highest on our list was Disneyland. The park had opened just over five years earlier. Back home, when I had watched *The Wonderful World of Disney*, as Tinkerbelle sprinkled fairy dust over the castle, the theme song drifted right from the television into my heart. I was no longer Diane, the young girl living in a worn-out house that broadcast our impoverishment to the world. Watching the magical fairy dust float, hearing the promise of those alluring lyrics, my dreams soared like an eagle flying across a sky of infinite possibilities; my heart swelled, joy and hope shone in my eyes. Those words of promise to the mythical Pinocchio were equally true for young Diane, who, for a moment, wholly, sincerely, and against all odds, believed in the promise of these words.

> *When you wish upon a star*
> *Makes no difference who you are*
> *Anything your heart desires will come to you*
>
> *If your heart is in your dream*
> *No request is too extreme*

With our trip to Disneyland, I would relish my youthful innocence one last time. Peggy and I boarded an early bus and arrived just as the keepers threw open the gates of the kingdom. From our dwindling stash, we splurged and bought "unlimited rides" tickets. How we laughed and played that day: rides, shows, songs, and the Disney characters roaming the make-believe streets of this magical kingdom. We weren't too old for any ride, any experience. It was a sharp contrast to the risqué alien world of Tijuana that Lyle and Art had taken us to where we had gone to dog races and strip shows and drank Tequila - all at our request, to be sure! "Oh, we want to see a strip show. Oh, let's have Tequila. Oh, let's buy stuff. Oh, greyhound races. . ." Peggy and I had felt taken care of by the guys, and they didn't fail us, keeping us safe, laughing at our naïveté, enjoying showing us another side of life. But Disney World was the fulfillment of a dream that would dream me forward! Peggy and I were the last to leave the kingdom that night.

After Disneyland, I went to a doctor to confirm what I already knew; I was pregnant. With this unassailable confirmation, I knew it was time to write home to Mama and Don. Don was thrilled beyond measure at the news, and he began preparations for our future together. Since his dad had kicked him out of the house, he'd had no job and had been living in a tent in the back yard of a friend and depended for food on the goodwill of his friend's mother. The news that I was pregnant, and we would marry transformed Don from a lost young man into a marvelously maturing young man. He excitedly wrote that he loved me, that I should come home as soon as possible, and that he'd found a job. I hesitantly began to dream of a future married to Don, sometimes smiling with ironic compassion at the memory of the young Diane who believed she was too ugly ever to get married.

In 2014, going thru my mother's things, simultaneous with when we'd found the marriage license of Anna and Peter, I found the letter from me telling her I was pregnant and saying I understood if she didn't want to help me or support me. I'd written that I understood

SAN FRANCISCO DREAMING

if she didn't want me home, that I was sorry to disappoint her as a daughter, and that she was the best mother ever. When I read the letter all these years later, I realized I hadn't given her credit for her love and understanding. My letter reflected my internalized cultural bias about my out-of-wedlock pregnancy. I rejected myself before she could. I'm sure she didn't welcome the news, but, as I said at her memorial when she passed away, "I always felt Mama had my back."

Also, in the "Diane" box (she had one for each of her children of things she'd saved over the years) was a yellowed telegram. I laughed as I read it aloud to my siblings, and I was shocked as well, almost not remembering how desperate those weeks were. It read, "WIRE FIVE DOLLARS TO MARTINEZ IMMEDIATELY WE ARE HUNGRY NO MONEY HOME NEXT WEEK SP STATION=DIANE JOHNSON." Peggy and I had decided to spend everything and do everything we could to compensate our adventurous spirits for losing our Greenwich Village dream. We kept just enough money for our tickets home and food, but we had cut it too close. The $5 did arrive, as did $5 from Peggy's mom. The following week, our spirits deflated, our pockets empty, we closed the golden door of our grand adventure as perennial sister wanderers. The dream didn't die in me; it simply, like a bear hibernating in a hidden cave, silently awaited the springtime.

In some ways, as a teenager coming of age in the late 50s, early '60s, where sexual *Shakti energy* was masked and cast out by a hidden Puritanism, I am today warmed and feel blessed. Somehow, during that time of repressed sexuality in the American culture, my sensuous spirit striving toward wholeness not only survived but began to manifest in an unstoppable trajectory. When I think of the delightful innocence in grade school with Bob, the initial shock at the feelings in my body with Harry, daring to go all the way with Willy, discovering with Don a sweetness and a loving affirmation of these vibrations in my body and mind, and finally with Lyle encountering the dizzying heights of this powerful vibrational stirring, I am at peace with these beginnings of the manifestation of *Shakti Energy* in me.

Any woman, young, old, or in-between, who has had a powerful orgasm with someone she loves, knows that moment when she touches the sublime - knows that moment when the mysterious energy of creation extends its finger and touches her and opens her to receive: to be a vessel, not only for a child but equally for transcendence beyond the mundane world.

Today when I look around at our human greed, the materialism that has turned this sacred enlivening energy into a crass misrepresentation of its true meaning and possibilities for humanity, at the uncompromising abduction of *Shakti Energy* by the "bottom line" of dollars, yuens, rubles, the euro, I am saddened with where humanity is and where we could be.

And then I remind myself that *Shakti* is energy. This feminine creative energy is the most potent energy enlivening our earth. As women, as sisters to the planet, we know and feel her wisdom. Our gift and challenge is to discover, each woman for herself, how best to manifest this feminine wisdom in her ineffable richness and most glorious.

Marian - early 20s

Dayton – early 20s

Diane and Rochelle 1943

Anna circa 1953

Oh so serious at 2 1/2 years

Marian and Dayton with daughters
Laura, Rochelle and Diane 1945

Anna in her favorite chair

The Family 1956
Back Row: Rochelle, Papa, Mama holding Martin, Diane
Front Row: Laura, David, Gayle, Don

Me standing proudly on Papa's shoulders as Gayle and Don look on

Peggy and me at Knott's Berry Farm, California

High School graduation portrait

Our young family: Me, Pam, Ron, Don 1964

Pam and Ron 1968

8
1961-1969

The Prodigal Daughter Returns

Marriage-Children-Taking Responsibility

The train pulled into the Bellingham train station. The pungent salt air from the waterfront assaulted our senses; the smell, the feel, the sound of waves lapping at the shore, the overcast gray hues were all so familiar. Peggy and I were back where we had started just under three months ago. I half expected things to be radically changed as that's how I felt inside, but it all seemed unnervingly the same.

Not wanting to face my mom at the train station, I was relieved when I saw Mr. Linn was alone in the car. When he dropped me off at our driveway, I pulled my still pristine suitcase out of the trunk, waved goodbye to Mr. Linn and Peggy, and turned to look up at the house - faded, weathered, shabby, just as when I'd left. I climbed the sixteen stairs to where my mother stood, holding open the screen door. Searching her eyes, I found neither recriminations nor disappointment. Dropping my suitcase on the porch, I ran to her and gave her a quick hug; we'd never hugged much in our family.

The two of us wandered into the kitchen where I went directly to the side cupboard, cut myself two slices of bread from Grandma's homemade loaf, and made myself a peanut butter and jam sandwich. Mom and I didn't share a cup of tea or coffee. That ritual had never been a part of our household. Perhaps I held a cup of water in my

THE PRODIGAL DAUGHTER RETURNS

hands to wash down the sandwich. We sat at the table, cluttered as it had always been. My eyes drifted to the slightly sagging windowsill where objects of different shapes and sizes, deposited and forgotten over the years and covered with a thick layer of dust, arrested my attention as though I'd never seen them before. Gazing around the room, I felt I was on an archeological dig: the old wood-burning cookstove; the outdated heavy metal hot water tank that never provided enough water for a real bath; the deep sink, chipped on the corners with a faded curtain around it to hide the plumbing; the never-used mangle in the corner, collecting objects just like the windowsill; the original floor linoleum, it's design scuffed beyond recognition; the scarred cupboards, an old toaster, rusted metal canisters, and the bread cabinet with the cutting board and bread knife lying alongside. I tenderly breathed in this room that was both strange and familiar, noticing that I was neither judgmental nor ashamed, the age-old poverty not pressing itself on me.

I idly wondered who did dishes now that both Rochelle and I were gone. I guessed Gayle had had to step in and take alternate weeks with Laura. Other odd and discrete thoughts came as Mom and I sat there together, me on one of the familiar old wood chairs, and Mom in "Mama's chair" at the end where she always sat when she and us kids had gathered for dinner.

Settling into the hard curve of the old wooden chair, I remembered the unique family ritual our mother had devised for dinner meals. Every six months, each of us six older kids would draw a number that matched a place at the table, and that would be the sitting arrangement for the next six months. On the first day each month, we'd move one place to the left. This ritual settled any argument about who got to sit next to Mama - we'd all get two months each year in that exalted position. Martin, the baby, had a permanent place beside her. I saw us sitting around the table, each of us excited to tell Mama about our day at school, talking over each other till she would bring order to the chaos. I saw how she had patiently listened to each of us. The meals were simple fare using garden harvest wherever possible and eggs or beans for protein. These memories of our family warmed my heart.

"Mama, I just remembered how we'd draw numbers twice a year for the seating arrangement. I loved the suspense as we'd each draw, waiting to see who I'd sit next to for six months. I can't imagine what it must have been like for you, seven of us all vying for your attention." She smiled a mysterious Mona Lisa smile that seemed to take in my belly. I looked up at her, and in that instant, I felt a companionship that obliterated the rebellious teen. Though perhaps a little overdue, going forward, the baby growing in my womb would be what I cared about most. Just over two months along, the hints of change in my immature woman's body were still subtle, but my hands sought my belly, and for the first time, I could genuinely imagine the being growing inside of me. I had left Bellingham an adventure-seeking 18-year-old and returned home pulled into a domestic adventure, equal in its allure, to San Francisco.

That evening, when I opened the door in answer to Don's knock and paused to look at him before our questioning hug, another transformation burst forth. I fell in love all over again. San Francisco faded, its phantom luster no longer shimmering. Yes, nostalgic moments would resurface, but held in Don's arms, I was baptized and reborn into a new identity. I believe it was the power of the child growing inside of me that pushed me, insisting I make this quantum leap to motherhood and wifehood.

A few days passed. One afternoon I was in the kitchen with my mom canning peaches when she asked the burning question. "Have you and Don decided what to do?"

I proudly revealed our plans. "We're getting married soon. You know Don has been working at Wallace Poultry for over a month now, so with his first $50 paycheck, he bought a car, the next check he bought me a ring, and with the 3rd check, we'll look for a place to live." I added, "You know, Don is only 17, so his dad will have to sign for us to marry. Don's going to talk to him in a couple of days." Relief flooded her usually stoic demeanor.

THE PRODIGAL DAUGHTER RETURNS

Things didn't turn out as I'd confidently assumed they would. When Don arrived at his parents' home, he'd knocked, a stranger to the house since his dad had kicked him out. He unfolded the story more or less as follows. "Dad and Ginny and I sat at the table, and I told him you were pregnant, that I couldn't wait for them to meet you, and that I needed dad to sign for us to marry. I was shocked that dad didn't immediately say yes. He asked me how I even knew it was my baby because you'd been in California. Then he said that I'm too young to marry and he wasn't about to start supporting me and you and a child. He said he absolutely would not sign for me." I sat in stunned silence, incensed at these strangers that had so much control over my life. I spared no words in telling Don how angry and furious I was.

"I know, I know, but we'll figure something out." Having an unwarranted trust in Earl, his dad, Don saw the disapproval as a minor setback, a feeling I did not share. Undeterred, he wanted to give it one more try and proposed we get a note from the doctor and go together to his parents. I went alone to see Dr. Z. He confirmed I was pregnant and readily obliged with kindness and concern, writing a note to Don's parents saying I was almost three months pregnant. Note in hand, Don and I went together to his parents' house. As we walked up the sidewalk, my eyes widened in dismay when I saw their lovely ranch-style home surrounded by sculptured gardens, the entryway set off by two gorgeous climbing clematises. The well-kept freshness was a sharp contrast to our old and decrepit family home, and I felt intimidated by the perfection it implied.

Don knocked. We waited. Ginny answered the knock. Seeing us, she called out to Earl, who was in his woodworking shop. Don introduced me to them, and I unobtrusively sat with my hands in my lap, trying to keep eye contact with Don as he handed his dad the note. Earl quickly scanned the note, and with what I felt was unwarranted anger, lashed out at us. "You two can't possibly know what love is or what it means to be married. You'll never make this work. How the hell are you going to support a child? You're too young to be married, and I'm not going to be a party to this predicament you've gotten yourselves into!" An eerie calmness displaced his anger. "There's nothing more to discuss here." With a last withering look at us, he stood up from the table, turned his back, and disappeared into his workshop. In the stunned silence, Ginny mumbled an apology.

The words were barely out of her mouth when I stood up, burning with the question I dared not speak aloud, "What the hell does he expect us to do?" My vision blurred by tears of rage and dawning desperation, I grabbed Don's hand and held tight as we lurched out of their upper-middle-class home carrying between us the heavy and emphatic "NO." At that moment, I made a vow to myself that I would prove Earl wrong. That we were in love and would stay in love and married and that we would never divorce. Though silent and spoken only to me, one day, this vow would seem an insurmountable roadblock to an ill-defined dream of freedom.

Looking at our limited options, Don and I formulated Plan B - we'd elope to the neighboring state of Idaho. We mapped out a plan to drive the 7-8 hours to Coeur d'Alene, Idaho, just across the border from eastern Washington, and get married, hoping the falsehoods we'd need to concoct would pass muster with the powers that be. On a Thursday evening, we packed overnight bags, filled the old Oldsmobile's gas tank, and hours before dawn, on a wing and a prayer, we headed south to Seattle and then turned east onto I-90. Our nerves frayed as the car heated up over Snoqualmie Pass - not only because of the old car that we'd never intended to carry us such great distances, but also because Don was driving without a driver's license, and I didn't know how to drive. We were on a shaky mission at best. Events piled up to thwart us – twice the worn tires blew out, and we had to pull over so Don could change them. Then somewhere on a deserted stretch of road, a water hose burst. Don left me in the car and hitchhiked back to the nearest town. Despair set in as I sat alone in the car, doors locked, crying my eyes out, graced only with the company of the little being inside of me. A fresh torrent of tears, this time of relief, burst out when, in the rearview mirror, I saw a car pull over and Don climb out with a new hose in hand. Time began to compress and stretch, our stress level by now at a fevered pitch. Don drove like a maniac. I stared at the clock as the minutes ticked by, wondering if we even had a prayer to get to Coeur d'Alene before the courthouse closed for the weekend.

Relief and new fears surfaced as we drove into the town and down the main street. What if we were too late? We had to get married this day, Friday, or it all ended in the hearts and minds of two young desperados. We saw it at the same time, **The Hitching Post**, and under that, **Minister. Weddings**. We parked the car, jumped out, and dashed through the still-open door. "We want to get married today," Don blurted out.

It's a blur now, but somehow the minister, Rev. Scott, pulled our marriage out of the proverbial rabbit's hat. He sent us two doors down for blood tests, made a call to the clerk at the courthouse asking her to stay open past closing, and, unbeknownst to us, asked her if she'd be a witness to our marriage. We raced back from the blood tests to the minister. "Go across the street to the courthouse. The clerk is waiting for you." Ignoring a red light, our hands squeezed tight together; we ran across the street and up the stairs to a woman waiting impatiently in an office. She looked askance as I showed her my birth certificate that proved I was the required 18 years of age. She turned to Don, "Let me see your ID." The telltale moment that would decide our fate had arrived.

"I couldn't find my birth certificate," he lied/replied to her, "and I don't have a driver's license." He looked older than me, and our threadbare hope all along was that officials would assume I wouldn't be with a younger man.

"How did you get here?"

"She drove," he nodded toward me. The clerk paused. We held our breath waiting for her decision. There is no doubt she knew something was amiss, but spirit touched her heart.

"Okay, I'll go ahead and issue your license. Take the license over to Rev. Scott and tell him I'll be over as soon as I lock up. I'll bring my son with me as the second witness." We noticed then the young pre-teen sitting behind her reading. He looked up indifferently and went back to his book.

I had brought a blue wool suit to get married in, but there was no time to change. Don and I stood before Rev. Orland Scott in our wrinkled and dirty jeans and sweatshirts. Rev. Scott read the Bible's standard remarks, and we each said, "I do," and promised to love, honor, and obey. It wasn't how I'd envisioned my marriage, even an elopement, but as we stood there in front of the minister, I was a hopeful and in-love bride. Don had stayed so steady through it all, and I took courage and optimism from him. The clerk and her son signed the marriage license as witnesses that on September 1, 1961, Donald Longstaff Carlson and Diane Lee Johnson were duly and lawfully married. We'd done it. We were at last husband and wife with a baby soon to make us a family.

With Don, I entered into another iteration of feminine energy. I would discover that a domestic *Shakti* energy lived inside of me as well as the passionate, sensuous *Shakti*. What comfort our marriage and family provided to the young Diane who had always felt outside in nowhere land: outside of the ring of love of Papa, Mama, Rochelle; outside of the church community; outside of the school culture where money and Sunday worship mattered; outside of middle-class life in America; and most of all outside of normal family life. Our marriage would be a time of growing self-confidence, of gentleness rather than violence, of shared domesticity rather than fractious domesticity, of simplicity rather than complexity.

We nestled into the little one-bedroom furnished apartment we had rented just before leaving. My god, we were so young, fresh out of high school, not a clue about married domestic life. Each day I would unmake and remake the bed, sweep the floors, wash dishes, and play solitaire and read. A couple of hours before Don was due home, I'd take out my one recipe book and begin dinner preparations. Don was patient with the burned meals I presented to him at the end of his workday. Evenings, after I had cleaned up while he read the paper, the high point of the day was when we would happily fall into each other's arms in bed. We learned what pleasured the other and connected through simple, sweet orgasms - simple because we had neither reached the age of full sexual maturity. Hence, orgasm was often an uncomplicated release and confirmation of the love we felt.

Being home alone with no friends, no car, no family, not even a TV, I wandered around our love nest bored to distraction. To assuage my boredom, we moved twice in the first six months of our marriage, each move a homeopathic remedy to my *Restlessness*. Sometime in mid-January, our baby's imminent birth redirected my focus from boredom to the joy of baby preparations. I spent a couple of days with Grandma, and we cut and sewed soft flannel diapers. She'd clearly forgiven me for getting pregnant and "having to marry Don." In her living room, I helped set up her quilting frame, and together we made a crib size quilt for this child about to grace our lives. Sitting side-by-side with Grandma at the quilting frame, laying out the batting between the layers of fabric, neatly pushing our needles with trailing yarn through the layers, cutting the stitches, and lastly tying the ends in a square knot, I knew and sensed my grandmother more intimately and compassionately than I ever had before.

I realize today that what I appreciated most about Don was how much he loved me. For the child-adult who had always felt unlovable for all the reasons described earlier, feeling so deeply loved was an exhilarating experience. When I looked into Don's eyes, I didn't see or feel even a hint of my supposed ugliness. I vividly remember one morning in the eighth month of my pregnancy, Don and I were standing naked in the bedroom after showering, in front of a big mirror on an old chiffonnier. He looked in the mirror that reflected my big belly and full breasts and said, so earnest and loving, "You are so beautiful." I let myself consider the possibility for just a moment and then quickly pooh-poohed him, as I couldn't comprehend what he was seeing and saying. But those words began to exorcise the ghost of "ugliness." I felt almost mystically touched by this man's love for me. In one of fate's inexplicable ironies, held in Don's unwavering love, I inched toward loving myself.

Can the Youthful Commitment Mature?

At last, following the textbook description of a birth, our child initiated its passage. Early evening, the first sign, a backache, was followed by intense back pains that moved around to my belly. Don and I monitored the pains and drifted into an agitated sleep until, in the early morning hours, we two nervous young parents-to-be arrived at the labor room of St. Joseph's Hospital. My textbook labor continued with hours of contractions. Don held my hand until I'd dilated to 10 centimeters and a nurse wheeled me away. Following the barbaric birthing norms of the time, she instructed Don to join other waiting fathers in a windowless hallway outside the delivery room.

"Ah-h, here we are," Dr. Z announced, "it's a George." (His choice of words was due to our boy being born on George Washington's birthday.) I opened my eyes as he placed the tiny, wet, wiggling body on my belly while he cut the cord. The nurses quickly cleaned and swaddled him, and one of them came to where I lay in exhausted ecstasy. She held our precious bundle where I could see him as the doctor was stitching up the episiotomy routinely done in those years. She opened the soft cotton wrapper to show me his ten tiny toes, his ten wiggly tiny fully formed fingers, and his little penis. Her words, "He's all here and healthy," brought a satisfied smile to everyone in the room. A nurse conveyed the news to Don, who, hearing my cries, had been in a high state of tension. A healthy boy! The news soothed away his worries.

Childbirth is an incredible manifestation of *Shakti Energy*. It felt as if this child was an expression of Don's and my love here in the earth realm. Gazing into our child's face, putting his lips to my breast, touching, and smoothing my hands over his body, softly squeezing the tiny little toes and fingers, I soared with this tiny being into a place ridiculously beyond words - I felt the whisper of transcendence.

We named him Ronald, shortened to Ron – not quite Donald (we didn't want a junior) but close enough and gave him my middle name, Lee. This child single-handedly initiated me into an almost unfathomable condition, unconditional love. Ron was a snuggly baby and was most content when I'd hold him close and rock him. I knew I would give my life in an instant to protect our child. I cannot speak for men, but being here on earth in a female body, I can say unequivocally that carrying and giving birth is a gift from the deep space of time itself. I can also assert unequivocally that the gift of transcendence, whatever one's chosen path, comes from that same source!

When Ron was born, Don asked my permission to tell his parents. We'd had no contact with them since the day we'd left their home after their emphatic "NO." I wanted to take revenge, to shut them out of our life, to punish them. We weren't even sure they knew we were married, having no idea if our grapevine tangled with theirs. I acquiesced to Don's pleas, and he carried the news one evening to Earl and Ginny. I don't know how the evening went, but in the end, our child's birth accomplished what our marriage had not - they opened their hearts to us. Along with my family, though our families would never meet, Don's family came to play a significant role in our lives – Sunday dinners, holidays, summer outings. We were the quintessential, traditional, extended American family.

Don emerged as a hero in my struggle with Papa when on a Sabbath afternoon, another of Papa's drunken dramas played out. I was still attending the Seventh-day Adventist church with Ron, not yet willing to overtly disappoint Grandma. Don had picked us up from church, and we'd gone to Grandma's for lunch. My recollection is like a moving portrait at Hogwarts. My brothers, David, 17, and Don, 14, are lounging on the couch. Martin, not quite 10, is sprawled beside his older brothers. Don Carlson is standing by the table holding Ron, and Grandma, Mom, and I are laying out a lunch spread on the table. There is a brief, brutal knock on the door, and within seconds it is pushed open, and Papa lurches into the room.

As though the shutter had been clicked, this Hogwarts-like snapshot came alive, and everyone was startled into action. Papa wasn't entirely falling down drunk, but "he's drunk," registered collectively. His presence blackened the living room where we were gathered, the same room where we had all experienced his violence toward his wife and children - Mama's beatings, the youngest brother, not quite a year old, held by his feet out the open window as Papa threatened to drop him on his head to the cement below, us girls crying, once daring to enter the fray and beg him to stop beating Mom. At that moment, all those scenes came flooding back.

Papa turned to Mama, "I'm here to get David, to take him to Seattle away from this house full of damn women and teach him to be a man. He's going to be a sissy if I don't take him." He turned menacingly toward David, "Go now and pack everything; you're going with me." David's bravery at that moment was something to behold. Papa was bigger and stronger, but David stood his ground, looked Papa in the eye, and gave his answer. "No. I'm staying here. I'm not going with you."

At David's refusal, Papa countered, "Let's go outside and fight. You're a wuss, c'mon now." He grabbed David's arm. Though lacking in size and bulk next to our father, David pulled his arm away from Papa's drunken grasp.

From across the room, I spit the words out at him. "What kind of a father have you ever been anyway? You know Earl, Peggy's dad, was just killed in a car wreck. He was a real father. You aren't and never have been."

He turned, "I s'pose you wish I'd been killed steada him."

"Yes, yes, I do. Earl was more of a father to me than you ever were or could be."

Turning from David, he came at me with his fist raised. In one fluid movement, Don handed Ron off to me and stepped between Papa and me. "If you want to fight, let's you and I go outside and fight you son of a bitch." As my husband stood there, his 6'2" frame towering over Papa, restrained violence in his voice, Papa backed down. Like a beaten dog, he mumbled some self-pitying refrain and slouched out the door. It was the only time I ever witnessed one of Papa's drunken outrages end by someone confronting him and sending him away in defeat.

"Come, let's eat," Grandma quickly interjected as the door closed. Even as Mama and Grandma bustled about, my brothers seemed unsure and moved slowly to the table. For better or worse, they had made an unintentional choice to stay in the house of women. It would have been a gift to all three boys to have a father in their lives, but this offer from a violent drunk who had abandoned his family was not the man to show David nor Don nor Martin how to be a man. I held Ron close as my husband's arms encircled us. He was my hero. He had protected me from Papa's violence. We ate silently at first, but the irrepressible chatter of relief took hold, and we gossiped and recounted the incident putting a safe distance between the scene and us.

Even the actions of a hero don't last forever. A niggling feeling, the same one that had driven Peggy and me to flee our little hometown and seek experiences in the wide world, hijacked my restless psyche. The idea of satisfying that discomfort through an affair didn't occur to me – that would come in the next go-round. Though I'd hid it well, I was deeply unhappy with the pedestrian quality of our life, with the fading teenage love that was being replaced with a deep like and respect for Don, but not the in-love quality of my youth. Conversely, Don was unquestioningly happy with our apparent idyllic life.

I kept my own counsel. I didn't yet have tools like meditation to quiet my mind, and the idea of praying to god was anathema to who I was struggling to become. I didn't have any spiritual principles or guidance to replace what had been my fervent belief in Jesus Christ. As a young teenager longing for a connection with spirit, the Seventh-day Adventist religion was my only avenue to affix this overarching longing. This aching desire is what I would come to call the *Restlessness*.

By this time, 1963, I had split with the church. In a meeting with the pastor, I demanded he formally strike my name from the church membership list. He demurred, asked to kneel and pray with me. I demurred and said, "No, I'm no longer a believer."

Over the years, I had learned that the church rules I endeavored to follow weren't a recipe for happiness. I would learn that much of what made me feel happy and excited were things to which the church said "NO." Dancing, movies, sex, secular romance books, all the things that set my heart beating. The more I connected with the sensual awakening in my body, the less connected I was with the Christian God. I particularly hated the punitive nature of my grandmother's religion. The mind-twisting part of that was that as a child, Grandma had been the haven from the violence and abuse of Papa, and she was the only one that offered succor to my spiritual yearnings, and so I had jumped on the church's spiritual wagon.

When I jumped off, I hadn't yet found what would eventually be my spiritual path. Still, something in me knew that my path lay with my body, with the feelings when a lover touched me, the ecstasy of orgasm, the joy I felt when I moved on a dance floor, the delight of relationship with a man, not with a God. As I was maturing, I was learning something of who I was at my very core.

I couldn't articulate most of this in my early 20s when I left the church. It was girlfriends like Peggy, women friends like Rebecca that sustained me - not my mother, grandmother, and certainly not my father even though our spirits were aligned in the Tantric path. But oh my god, that was all far away in a future of which I couldn't even conceive. All I had in this moment were my feelings, body aching, and intellect with which to question and consider. I reached a decision and clumsily delivered an ultimatum to Don.

I had picked Don up from work after dropping Ron off at Grandma's as that night we were going out with friends. It was getting on toward dusk. In the waning light, I could see Don's face as I turned to look at him, my eyes barely able to meet his. I vividly remember the dark blue wool coat I was wearing that I had proudly sewn. Don was still in his work clothes. By now, he had moved from Wallace Poultry to Bornstein Fish Company, where he once again stood before a conveyor belt, this time pulling dead fish off the moving train and filleting them. The pay was better, and with my supplemental income from my nurse's aide job at O'Cain's Nursing Home, we could just pay our bills.

The fish smell from his clothes hung in the closed air of the car. I rolled down my window to the cool rush of the fall night and put my hand on his shoulder before he had a chance to open the door and exit the car to head for the back porch and shed his smelly clothes and shower. Afraid I'd lose my courage, I dare not wait for this cleaning ritual. I clenched his shoulder a little tighter and blurted out, "Don, I'm not happy. I don't like our life as it is. I think we should think about divorce or possibly have another baby. We just have to change something."

Though I had been reflecting on this for weeks, those words were all I could get out. Even today, I am astounded at the unfeeling brashness, born out of nervous fear, with which I blasted Don, not to mention the outrageous choice I gave him. For Don, oblivious to my well-hidden discontent, my words were a shock that dealt a searing blow to his heart and mind. I couldn't ignore the deep pain that registered in his dark brown eyes as we stared at each other. Though I've tried many times to reconstruct what was said, the only detail that remains is that opening salvo. God knows how that conversation went, but that night, as we sat together in the car talking while dusk turned to darkness, we made the momentous decision to have another child. I stopped taking my birth control pills, and by the next month, I was pregnant.

In about the fourth month of my pregnancy, we moved into a quaint home with the look and feel of a miniature English country home. It was on Portal Drive in the Lake Whatcom area of Bellingham. There was a fireplace in the living room, and many were the nights that Don and I would open the double doors of the bedroom onto the living room and savor the romantic warmth and beauty of a fire whose flames warmed our naked bodies as we made love.

The second bedroom, Ron's room, with knotty pine walls and a built-in bed and drawers, enhanced the impression of a miniature country home. The kitchen opened onto an extensive dining area that provided ample space for kids to play, and an expansive terraced lawn provided space for outdoor adventure.

In that house of happiness for our young family, our daughter roared into the world on July 13, 1964. She announced her arrival with a pain that blasted me out of a sound sleep. My water broke before Don was even awake. We loaded Ron into the car, sitting him in the front seat between us. Don drove like a crazy man to the hospital as I groaned with full-on contractions. Nestled in close to me, Ron looked at me with fear and worry. I managed my best smile. "Everything is fine," I assured him, putting my arm around him. He snuggled in closer to my big belly. "Remember we've been talking about a new baby that will join our family, and, well, it's coming now. Dad will drop you off at Grandma's after he takes me to the hospital to bring your new baby sister or brother into the world." Ron, seated between the two of us, hearing reassuring words, took the event in stride as kids do and responded with a sleepy mumbled, "Okay."

Don handed me off to the waiting nurses at the hospital. This baby wasn't waiting, and before Don could get back to the hospital, she entered the earth realm arriving within 90 minutes of my water breaking. Her cries before she ever exited my womb were lusty. There was no sweet moment of laying her on my belly. She was out of my womb, and amidst her healthy howls, Dr. Z quickly cut the cord and handed her to the nurse. "She's fine," our family doctor assured me, "We had to pay extra attention because she came out so active, but she's fine."

I rested nervously in the hospital room, wanting to see my baby. Dr. Z came in and reassured me with these words, "When you first see her, she will be blue, then the next time you see her, she will be yellow. She's not a blue baby or a jaundiced baby, it's just that she came so fast and so active and was crying before she left your womb and breathed air, but she's a big healthy baby." Each time the nurse brought Pam to me, no matter her color, I marveled at this beautiful little girl that now graced our family. My heart swelled with unutterable joy and love, and I couldn't wait to get home and introduce her to her older brother.

Pam's impatience, exemplified by her birth, would sometimes turn to temper tantrums throughout her childhood. As young parents, Don and I would struggle, as would she, to manage this internal angst that would erupt from her. I would do my best to see it coming and try to redirect her impatience. After an episode, when I would hold and comfort her, her big brown eyes would turn tearfully to mine, "Mama, I don't know why I do that. I can't help it." How I wished I could bear her pain for her. As she grew older, her warrior spirit found outlets to express this deep, inexplicable anguish. From elementary school through high school, she would often protect classmates who were being bullied. All her life, right up to today, she fights against cruelty to animals.

Ron's love for his new baby sister gave the perfect expression to his sensitive nature. He'd sit in the big, overstuffed chair at feeding time, and cradling her carefully in his arm, he'd proudly hold her bottle with the other while she noisily sucked the nipple. We were bottle-feeding her, as I had no desire to risk another breast infection as had happened when I nursed Ron. Ron was never jealous of his baby sister. He was the big brother, patient, and lovingly protective of his little sister. She was the little sister that loved and trusted her older brother to be by her side and have her back no matter what! He planned adventures, and she followed, she jumped into adventures, and he followed.

For a few sweet and poignant years, Pam's arrival accomplished what I'd hoped it would. We were an affectionate family together, I had recommitted to our marriage, and Don's new job at Georgia Pacific paper mill paid well enough for us to live without running out of money a few days before payday. Unexpectedly, it was while we lived in our little dream house that I found an outlet for my untamed sensuousness through our new neighbors, Rudy and Annie Ralston.

Rudy and Annie were about ten years older than we were, and I saw them as the perfect expression of a white American wholesomeness that I envied. They had a modest yet lovely home, Rudy made good money, and Annie, oh my god, to me, she was the perfect wife and mother. I began to emulate her down to the smallest detail. Like her, I'd clean up the house each evening, I practiced adoring my husband as she did, and I made sure I had on fresh clothes and make-up when Don came home from work.

Rudy and Annie loved to drink and party, and we lustily entered into their social world. They loved alcohol in all forms, so beer, whiskey, martinis dominated every get-together. When we went out drinking and dancing with them and their group of friends, I observed that little flirtations were acceptable. Tightly squeezing someone's husband or wife on the dance floor was okay. Once I watched with curiosity as Annie came off the dance floor, landed on Don's lap, and planted a big kiss right on his lips. Her action gave me permission, and predictably I pushed the envelope, occasionally slipping out of the dance hall with some husband for a few furtive kisses and feels. It was through these little forays into this mildly titillating and out-in-the-open flirtation that my restless, sensuous *Shakti Energy* began to yawn and stretch from a long deep slumber.

Ah-h, but there was a way to keep it at bay. I was fully onboard with fulfilling America's promises and dreams, and one of those dreams was owning our own home. We settled on a comfortable two-bedroom house on Lindberg Avenue in a middle-class neighborhood. With no down payment and only $500 in closing costs, we became proud owners of our first home. It boasted a fireplace and bay windows, two modest bedrooms, hardwood floors, and best of all, a large open backyard for the kids to play. The house was situated just up the hill from Bellingham Bay, where, as they got older, Ron and Pam would roam.

Like many, if not most tradition-based marriages, the evening routine was warmly predictable. Around 4:00, the kids would be in the living room watching cartoons while I prepared dinner. Don would come home from work and greet me with a kiss and the comment, "Umm, smells good." He'd change his clothes, and as I finished

THE PRODIGAL DAUGHTER RETURNS

cooking and got dinner on the table, he'd roll on the floor with the kids accompanied by their screams of delight and laughter. Their joy warmed my heart and fanned the wavering flame of love for Don.

On weekends we'd get together with friends to drank beer and play competitive games of Canasta while the children entertained themselves. Summer weekends, we'd pack up our truck and go camping either just the four of us or with friends. We'd sit around a glowing fire at night, nature alive around us, roasting marshmallows, and then tuck the kids snugly into our small camper. Don and I and the other parents would sit around the fire, cradling whiskey drinks, telling jokes and stories that blissfully obliterated the demands of daily life.

In the bedroom, our lovemaking was maturing, both from knowing each other's body and from years of sharing our most intimate joys, fears, and challenges. It was comforting to sleep together after making love, and on weekend mornings, we welcomed Ron and Pam into the bed to joust and play in another family ritual.

A couple of years after we moved into Lindberg Avenue, my brother David recently discharged from the Army, came to stay with us for a few weeks while looking for a job and an apartment. He and my husband, Don, fellow grease monkeys, were already good friends, I adored my younger brother (even though as kids I'd tried to kill him with a tow chain!), and Ron and Pam were delighted to have their Uncle David living with us. He readily integrated into our family while at the same time having a full life of his own. He would live with us for well over two years while he went to community college on the GI Bill. His friends and ours easily intermingled. In fact, Annie would have a little crush on him at one point.

David and I were easily identified as brother and sister: the same brown hair, brown eyes, same average nose that fit our faces. He didn't have my buck teeth, his beautifully straight and white. When he first arrived, we teased him about his nose that an Army doctor had operated on for a deviated septum just before his discharge, and he assured us as it healed, his average nose would go back to its original shape. Well, when the swelling went down, so did his nose, flattened out like a boxer's nose, as it is to this day. He was and remains a gentle, sensitive soul. He and Ron share a common spirit that way.

At some point, Don and I had to acknowledge a fly in the ointment - our expenses were increasing, and we couldn't pay our bills. I hated fielding phone calls from the power company, the phone company, and creditors for overdue payments in a way that was so deadly reminiscent of my childhood. I vociferously complained to Don, who remained unfazed by the monthly shortages until my complaints turned to laser-sharp anger. I proposed getting a job and was surprised to realize my proposal threatened his male machismo. He caught me off-guard when he said, "no," he didn't want his wife to work. Necessity demanded a compromise, so I created a licensed home-day-care center. Five days a week, 4-5 children would descend on our home into my care. Ron and Pam kind of enjoyed the additional playmates but didn't like sharing their mom with others.

Though we successfully met these day-to-day challenges in the Loch Ness of our marriage, the monster lurked. I overly anticipated the evenings going out with couples to drink and dance and indulge in flirtations, both covert and overt. And finally, my young adult self forced the romantic teenager to acknowledge that though I liked and respected Don, appreciated and loved him as a father and husband, and got along well with him, the teenager who loved him had matured. The passion of youthful love was gone, and I could not find anywhere inside me a mature love to replace what was lost. I was more and more frustrated that he didn't share my love of books and learning, and I surely didn't share his love of cars. "But," I would remind myself, "I am so blessed. Ron and Pam are healthy, happy kids, we have a close circle of friends, and surely the family joy and wellbeing must be enough."

My mind would wander to my mother, Marian. When she was hired at Redden Net and finally divorced Dayton when I was a senior in high school, she had found a circle of women at the net company to play with and with whom she became life-long friends. The defeated, dejected bearing of a poor, victimized woman with a passel of

THE PRODIGAL DAUGHTER RETURNS

kids, an unfaithful dissolute, now ex-husband who spent his earnings mostly on himself and gave minimal financial support to his wife and kids, was gone. A liveliness I hadn't known in my mother all the years of growing up made her eyes shine, and I have no doubt that her relationships with these women enabled her to open up to the intimate woman-to-woman conversations she and I would later have.

As I saw it, the real miracle came several years after the divorce when Marian had Dayton arrested and put in jail for the thousands of dollars of back child support he owed her. I was so proud of her. A lawyer had a court hearing expedited, and Marian agreed to a settlement with Dayton for the past debt. Going forward, his child-support payments would be sent through the court for tracking. What a mighty victory for her.

Like the stirrings for freedom and independence that urged on my mother, though my situation differed dramatically, the susurration of tantric *Shakti* energy, my path to freedom, crept back into my awareness. Like my mother, I was afraid and frozen and gave my utmost to hide my growing dis-ease until the summer of '69. In the country, the *1967 Summer of Love* had transformed into political and social action and unrest. University campuses were roiling as students protested the Vietnam War. It was amidst this sometimes violent demand for change that I chose to use soft violence to effect change in my life.

Sheltered on Lindberg Avenue, I found myself buried in a "Winter of Discontent." I was frozen, but arrows of heat began to penetrate - simple things like the song, *Is That All There Is*, that Peggy Lee famously recorded in 1969, the year of my escape. I played that record over and over, held it to my heart. It expressed what I felt as no other words could.

> *Is that all there is, is that all there is*
> *If that's all there is my friends, then let's keep dancing*
> *Let's break out the booze and have a ball*
> *If that's all there is......*
>   "Is That All There Is" by Jerry Leiber and Mike Stoller

In these words, I heard a defiant invitation to go out dancing, to drink, and have a ball if life seemed limited and unalterable. I took up the challenge and made a grave, even absurd, decision. Unable to face the prospect of being the wicked woman to break up a happy home, ruining the lives of Don and Ron and Pam, taking responsibility for my future, I came up with a strategy. It wasn't pretty. I'm not proud of the line of reasoning I adopted, but it's what I had the courage for at that moment.

I decided I would act out, be a bad person, make our married life untenable so that finally Don would hate me and ask me for a divorce. Buried in the concept was the convoluted idea that it would be less painful for Don, which, I would be forced to admit, was simply self-serving camouflage. It was a flawed strategy of reckless behavior. I told no one except my close friend and confidant, Rebecca, who would be my companion in implementing my strategy over the next six months.

With Peggy Lee singing in my head, I needed something to break the monotony of familial life and the hassle of the five kids that showed up each morning in my home-day-care center. I joined a women's bowling league at 20th Century Bowling. The bowling alley provided free daycare, so every Thursday, I'd load the passel of kids into my little Karman Ghia, and off we'd go. I loved, just loved those two hours of adult female companionship and moving my body, throwing a ball furiously down the alley, and, always competitive in the world of sports, I excelled. But the real prize was Rebecca.

Though Peggy still lived in Bellingham, we had drifted apart due to time and lifestyle differences and only occasionally saw each other. I desperately longed for a woman friend with whom I could again entrust my deepest fears, hopes, good behavior, and bad behavior. Rebecca was the answer to this yearning. I sensed she was not like the other women in our bowling league, and like magnets, we were pulled toward each other. Over coffee, we revealed our parallel paths - a marriage entered through teen love and pregnancy to men who were more interested in cars and hunting than in books or world

THE PRODIGAL DAUGHTER RETURNS

events, a growing unhappiness and separateness from our partners, and we each had two young children of the same ages. Unexpectedly, our husbands became close friends and Rebecca and I became close cohorts in intrigue, both vague and grand, with no end game in sight. This symmetry quickly made us a foursome – playing cards, going out dancing, and camping.

A benchmark moment in my strategy to make Don hate me began on a Friday "girl's night out." Rebecca and I had gone out with 5-6 other women, the female coven of our couples' circle. These circumscribed outings gave us a chance to drink and laugh and even flirt if the occasion arose while our husbands gathered to play poker and drink. We women met at a local bar, **The Sandpiper,** where there was always a band playing on the weekends, where college students, workers, and even a few on-the-make businessmen mixed and mingled. The atmosphere was local; the bartenders knew the regulars of which we were members.

"*If that's all there is, then let's keep dancing, let's bring out the booze and have a ball . . .* " The words in my head mixed with the band as they swung into other 60s songs, The Beatles, *Hey Jude*, Simon and Garfunkel, *A Bridge Over Troubled Waters*. I found identification with all the songs and danced my heart out, gyrating and moving, letting loose my most sensuous self. And unlike six years ago when I was in crisis, and Don and I had decided to have a second child, an affair was not off the table.

I saw him sitting at the bar alone, black shoulder-length hair, piercing black eyes, skin a tawny brown, slightly hooked nose. I would learn later he was Cherokee. I picked up an empty pitcher from the table, "Hey girls, I'll get this refilled," and sidled up to the bar and stood next to him. As I waited for the bartender to draw the pitcher of beer, I turned purposely to face him. He glanced sideways at me, and my eyes willed him to look closer. "Hi, I'm Diane."

He grinned self-consciously, "Hi, I'm RT." (I would learn those initials stood for Ralph Thompson, the last name belonging to the stepfather who had adopted him when he was young.) God, he was gorgeous. Standing at the bar in my joyful alcoholic haze, I fell in love between one breath and the next with this shy, reticent man with a soft voice. The bartender handed me the pitcher with a sly grin.

"Add it to our tab," I smiled at him and quickly turned my attention back to RT. "Wait here a minute," I charmingly ordered him. I blew a bubble into the universe with that interaction and entered the bubble as it floated iridescent around me.

In the last hour at **The Sandpiper,** I pulled RT onto the dance floor, and as we moved together, I enticed him with seductive smiles and half-closed eyes. Annie, my friend and neighbor from Portal Drive, picked up on the sails unfurling before a wild wind. She pulled me aside and admonished me to be careful and not do anything I'd regret. She kept her eyes on me whenever she caught a whiff of my intention with him. Nevertheless, before I departed **The Sandpiper**, and despite Annie's scrutiny, RT and I made the connection we sought. That connection was a stone dropping into the pool of my life as a wife and mother, into the middle-class American values Don and I had upheld together. The reverberations would ripple out until they touched and tested everyone in my life.

RT and I agreed to meet at the public library the following Wednesday. I'd made the mental calculation that Don would be at the community college in Skagit County that night. I was guarded and hadn't given RT my phone number nor taken his. Driving home a little drunk, I reveled in the memory of the night, of him, of what, if anything, was to come. I reviewed to myself, "I'll take the kids to my friend Shirley's for a couple of hours. I'll have to figure out what to tell Don. I need to hide this from David so he's not put in a compromising position with Don. Am I ready for what I'm about to do?"

Perhaps this is the moment to look closely at Don's and my relationship a year or so before I decided to make him hate me. I had formulated a plan, a last-ditch attempt, in my eyes, to save our marriage. It wasn't as radical as deciding to have a baby. Rather, I pushed and prodded Don to try to be something he was not. And because he loved me, loved our kids, loved our life, and would do whatever he

THE PRODIGAL DAUGHTER RETURNS

could to preserve what we had together, he gave it his best.

One evening after the kids were in bed, I presented my plan to him. He would go to college, get a degree, and a better paying, higher quality job than managing a machine at the paper mill – maybe a teacher, a businessman. We'd have more money, and I could close down my glorified baby-sitting job and go to college myself. Privately, I reasoned we could move in circles more intellectually exciting, and he would become someone else, someone that challenged me intellectually and culturally. Of course, my plan was doomed to failure because my grand scheme was not his nor ours.

Don negotiated with the paper mill where he worked, and, wanting to support his educational goals, they were amenable to his working part-time. Together, we got him enrolled in the community college in Skagit Valley, about a 45-minute drive from Bellingham. I was noticeably more excited than Don (it would turn out I often did his homework for him). I recommitted to our marriage and, surprising himself, Don committed to and enjoyed college classes. We joined together to maintain the status quo. Our family life together was still a "wonderful life." Sex was good – we even had a book that we hid in a closet of positions for lovemaking. We giggled and orgasmed anew as we checked out novel positions. (So that readers of a certain age get a glimpse of those times over 50 years ago, I relate the afternoon I showed the book to Annie. She looked at it with great interest and then closing it, she sighed, "Rudy won't do anything but the missionary position. I wish he'd be open to other positions, but he's not." I was grateful for my husband, who had a more sexually adventuresome spirit!)

Back now to the iridescent bubble that I was to live in for many months to come. I arrived at the library 15 minutes early and took up my station at a table within sight of the doors. I wondered if I would recognize him, and he, me. As the minute hand on the big clock clicked over to 12, I glued my eyes to the door, not blinking for fear I'd miss him. And there he was, just two minutes late. I watched his eyes scanning the library and grinned at his smile when he saw me.

From then on, as I'd refused to give him my phone number or address, he'd wait for my call that usually came on Don's school nights. I'd drop Ron and Pam off at my friend's, make some weak excuse, and drive to the alley behind RT's house where he lived with three other guys. Hearing my horn honk, he'd appear at the top of the stairs, his friends right behind him scanning the car, and dash down laughing. It seems that I had become RT's mystery woman as he refused to reveal my identity.

I'd drive us to a bar in a neighboring town where we were unknown. We'd eat a few peanuts to accompany our beer, and when the metaphorical midnight hour approached and our mythical castle would crumble, he'd pay our tab, and we'd drive to a dark spot along the waterfront. Parked in the obscurity of the night, our mouths and hands traveled over each other's bodies in light-hearted playfulness. I had it timed pretty close – time for us to engage in kisses and touches, but not enough time for intercourse. We were waiting, and we knew what we were waiting for as we talked about it often - my willingness to "go all the way."

I further implemented my campaign to force Don to hate me in small and subtle ways. Dinner wasn't always ready when he arrived home, no smells to elicit his, "Uh-hh, that smells good." I was less available for sex. I treated him with indifference, sometimes to the point of meanness when I would put him down in front of friends. He suffered, and his natural grumpiness deepened as he tried harder to fight an unseen enemy. I felt duplicitous and wicked, and to alleviate my internal self-hate, I judged myself unmercifully. . . and I persisted in my folly.

That infamous spring/summer of my campaign, one of Rebecca's and my excuses to go out was our Bowling League's annual awards dinner at the Yacht Club. As soon as we could gracefully slip away, Rebecca and I left the Yacht Club and headed to the Leopold Hotel cocktail lounge. There a small group of 4-5 businessmen was having cocktails. They latched onto us immediately. We were no doubt exuding availability, and that night Rebecca met the man with whom she'd have an affair. I made my apologies once she was settled in with Reginald and headed out to meet RT. We didn't go to a bar nor park on a dark beachfront. "Let's just drive," he said, "I need to talk." As I drove, he hesitantly broached the subject of "consummating our love." His description made me smile.

"You mean have sex?" I inquired teasingly.

"I'm serious," he said, "I want to make love with you."

"Soon," I said, "soon."

I had been waiting, albeit somewhat unconsciously, for him to push us. I wanted that union as much as he did, but I was wrestling with being unfaithful to Don. And yet, wasn't this the logical conclusion to my illogical plan? The ultimate betrayal? Isn't this where I was unconsciously heading? Over the years, I had had numerous flirtations, a stolen kiss on the dance floor, a quick feel from someone's husband when we'd been out dancing with our circle of partying friends. Once, like a teenage groupie, I'd even gone to a hotel room with an entertainer. But as he shut the door and led me to the bed, I froze. "Look," I said, "you can tell your bandmates we had sex if you need to, but I can't do this, I can't be unfaithful to my husband," and I fled the room. What made RT different were the feelings I had for him. In more sober moments, I couldn't quite pretend I was in love, but liking him a whole lot, along with the titillating lust, was close enough.

The next time I called, I had everything set up. "I have more time tonight," I said.

"How much time?"

"Enough," was my reply, "I'm ready." The trickster of my mind shut everything out except what was to come with RT and me. When I picked him up, the air in the car seemed to glitter and vibrate.

He'd made reservations at a sweet little motel in the nearby town of Ferndale. As I waited in the car while he went into the office for the key, my heart was beating - no, it was thumping in anticipation. There was nothing in that moment but us. Don, guilt, tomorrow, an accounting, didn't exist. There was only the two of us somewhere in infinity about to join our bodies.

As we exited the car, he grabbed a bottle of Johnny Walker Black, which, by now I knew, was his favorite drink. The summer night was warm and soft, the heat of the day dissipated, the evening air fresh. The weather could have been a more typical northwest downpour, and I'd probably have described it the same. We climbed to the 2nd-floor room like shy teenagers. The orange and yellow décor, the pedestrian motel pictures on walls painted a soft green, enchanted me as though we were in the Bridal Suite of the Ritz-Carlton. There were the proverbial two glasses and an ice bucket on the bathroom counter. RT found the ice machine in the hallway, popped two ice cubes into each glass, poured us a shot, and we drank, our eyes locked across the edge of the glasses.

In unspoken agreement, we set the glasses down and reached across time to undress each other. We didn't slowly, sensuously remove each other's clothing. We had waited long for this undressing, so we tore off the other's shirt, and with lips pressed, standing on one foot then the other, our lips never parting, we each shed our underwear and stood there fully magnificently naked in front of each other.

He was almost hairless, I noted and reached out to stroke his smooth chest. He impatiently pulled me to him, and we fell onto the waiting clean white sheets. Stretched out together, body-to-body, lips locked, we hardly took time for foreplay. All I wanted was to feel him inside of me, and he was no less ardent to be inside of me. With my mystical bubble intact, that shut out Don and our family life and tomorrow, what a thrill to finally relinquish myself to RT. He came quickly; neither of us was surprised. We sat up and promptly finished the drinks we'd set on the side table. We took the time now for foreplay, and I quivered at his touch and kisses. He grew hard, and I opened to his slow thrust inside of me. As he pulsed and moved, my fluids flowed, and my orgasm came seconds after his. Under him, I moaned softly and smiled.

We stole that sweet intimacy whenever and wherever we could. I grew more and more fond of RT, daydreamed of our lovemaking, waited impatiently for our next tryst. In my daydreaming, I wondered if he was perhaps my "get out of jail card," that our affair would be a passage out of my relationship with Don. I didn't know how it would play out, how high I would raise the stakes, but win or lose, I was determined to play my hand.

One night at **The Sandpiper,** when Don and I were out with our couples' circle, RT came in, sat at the bar, and ordered a beer. I'd boldly gone up to the bar where he sat, slipped my hand onto his knee, touched his crotch lightly, all the while smiling at the bartender as I waited for the pitcher of beer I'd volunteered to refill. I was getting reckless and daring, trying to push the envelope to some kind of conclusion. That it was disrespectful to Don didn't touch me. I was beginning not to care.

My most audacious act, the ultimate escalation of my intent, began once again at **The Sandpiper** tavern. As I write, I feel the urge to avoid relating this unpleasant incident, but as I see it, this epistle has little worth if it lacks honesty. If I am not honest, then I too begin to denigrate this tremendous sensual *Shakti Energy* that was determined to manifest its power in me. As awareness grows, there are inevitably moments of awkwardness, missteps, and failure. The following story is one of those. And yet, this brazen event forced me to take responsibility for my life and stop manipulating Don into taking responsibility for what I wanted and needed.

On a Wednesday afternoon, Rebecca and I had dropped our four kids off at a summer play day at a local grade school. After a quick grocery shopping trip, we were having beers at **The Sandpiper** when Paul and Connie, the tavern owners, came in. We all knew each other, the regulars and the owners, as they loved to frequent their bar. "Hey, we just bought a new 30' cruiser, and we're going on its maiden voyage to Orcas Island this afternoon," even he laughed at this rather grandiose allusion. "We'll be there and back by sometime this evening. Who wants to go?"

Rebecca and I looked at each other, "Could we?" Since it was a Wednesday and Don drove directly from work to the community college for his night class and wouldn't be home till late, I figured I could go on the boat ride and be back before he was home.

The wheels in my and Rebecca's heads turned in sync. We'd pick up our kids and take them to a babysitter till we got back. "Yes, we're going," we informed Paul. I called RT and told him the scoop, then Rebecca called Reginald, and we dashed out the door. Rebecca took her two boys to her neighbor, and I took Ron and Pam to my grandmother's house.

An hour later, we all met at the harbor where Paul and Connie's newly acquired yacht floated along the visitors' dock. There were seven of us: Paul, wearing his brand spanking new Captain's hat, and Connie, Rebecca and Reginald, me and RT, and Sal, another friend of Paul's who was an experienced sailor. We clambered aboard and found places to sit in the large cockpit and along the deck with Paul at the helm. He started the engine as Connie mixed cocktails and passed them around. Paul carefully navigated us out of the harbor. "All hands on deck," he shouted. We all laughed at his silly skippering attempt. Paul had made no secret of his lack of experience helming a boat, but he'd assured us his friend, Sal, was a seasoned sailor.

The boat slipped smoothly through the water, passing by the tip of Lummi Island, tracked to the lee side of Sinclair Island, then motored slowly east through Obstruction Pass. In the light of day, boisterous laughter sang out across the water, our voices tripping over each other. But in one moment, as the twilight sun sank into the sea, voices one by one, as though tapped on the shoulder into silence, faded and only the low roar of the engine vibrated around us. For one still sublime moment, curled into RT's arms, time didn't exist.

Without warning, a fist of darkness punched me out of the trance I had managed to maintain up until that moment. The situation was suddenly, alarmingly, apparent. Night had fallen, and we were just now on our northward trajectory between Orcas Island's saddlebags to Rosario Resort where Paul was going to gas up the boat. The time estimation had been erroneous and badly so. I doubted we were going back to Bellingham that night. I went below where Paul and Sal were conferring over the charts while RT, who could list a small dinghy on his nautical resume, was at the wheel. I struggled to keep the panic out of my voice, "Hey Paul, so we're going to be arriving in Rosario soon; what about getting home tonight?"

Distractedly he answered me, "We're much later than we'd thought, so we're going to spend the night at the hotel at Rosario and head back in the morning."

"The morning?" I gulped. "But this was just supposed to be an afternoon and evening trip. What happened? I'm supposed to be home tonight. My kids. . ." An accusatory tone crept into my voice.

His voice was harsh, even a little aggrieved as though I'd attacked his competence outright. "Look, that's your problem. We're getting ready to navigate the harbor, so don't hassle me." As I climbed the ladder into the cockpit, he added, "We're staying at Rosario tonight, so get over it."

"Whoa," I thought as I entered the cockpit and looked around for Rebecca. She was entwined in Reginald's arms, lost in a passionate kiss. I waited till they pulled apart, and before they could join their lips again, I interjected, "Rebecca, I need to talk to you. We're not going back tonight. What are we going to do? I have to take care of getting my kids home from my grandmother's house. We need to talk."

She was almost indifferent to me, the circumstances not penetrating her alcoholic lustful haze. I knew she and Reginald hadn't yet slept together and guessed this would be their maiden voyage. It wouldn't be until morning that she would show any concern for the untenable situation in which we found ourselves. I, on the other hand, was panicked. I didn't want to talk with RT, so I went to the bow of the boat and huddled down to think. The night air had turned cold. I pulled my knees in tight against my chest, tugging my sweater around me. I gazed out over the water at the lights on the shore. They shone like an enormous Christmas tree inviting me into a mood of conviviality that I couldn't find. I could hear Sal and Paul yelling at each other, Sal at the wheel, Paul at the bow, watching for the lighted buoys that would lead us through the harbor.

"Of course, it had to happen," I murmured into the night. "Isn't this what I wanted, to push things right to the edge? To do the unforgivable so Don would want to leave me? This act will certainly destroy whatever goodwill he has left in him." I confess that along with my shock and fear, there was the hint of liberation. But I couldn't quite let go, couldn't entirely tear us apart.

Once we'd docked, everyone checked into the hotel. I found a payphone and called home, knowing Don was away at his night class and that my brother David would pick up the phone. "David, hi, this is Diane. Look, I'm in a difficult situation. I'm stranded on Orcas Island. It's a long story, and I'll fill you in on the details, but I need you to go pick up Ron and Pam from Grandma. Can you do that?"

"Well-l-l, I guess so. How the hell did you get to Orcas Island anyway?"

"It's a long story, and I'll fill you in later; meantime, I'm running out of coins. Look, can you explain to Don that Rebecca and I ran into Paul and Connie? You remember them right, **The Sandpiper** owners? Well, we took up their invitation of a short boat ride to Orcas Island and back with a few other friends of theirs. They badly miscalculated the time, and now we're stuck on the island."

"What the hell…..?"

I interrupted his question, "There's one thing more. I know Don works early, so could you drop Ron and Pam off in the morning at the neighbors and come and pick Rebecca and me up at the ferry in Anacortes? There are no more ferries tonight, or I'd be on my way home right now." I raced on, "I'm really sorry to put you in this position. I'll tell you more later." I was almost in tears. "I'm so sorry, really sorry." David was quiet on the other end. We were brother and sister with a loyalty bond, but he and Don were bonded in a guy way. They loved to work on cars together and share a beer and stories, but I knew, in the end, even though I was way out of line, he'd align with me as we'd grown close over the months.

When he replied, he didn't hide his reticence and unhappiness at being my messenger. "Diane, I'm not thrilled with this, but I'll do it. I'll tell Don though I feel a little awkward about it, okay? I think Don's going to be really mad when I tell him. So okay, whatever, I'll go get Ron and Pam and pick you up in the morning." He sighed, "When does the ferry arrive?"

Leaving the phone booth, knowing there was nothing more to be done, I joined the others in the dining room, where everyone was drinking cocktails. Their noisy hilarity definitely didn't match my mood! After dinner, RT and I, both quite drunk by now, stumbled upstairs, fumbled with the key, fell onto the bed, and fumbled our clothes off. I admit there was the laughter of forgetfulness, the uncertain joy of spending the whole night together, but when I awakened in the morning, I felt like I'd rolled in a metaphorical pigsty. I showered, put on clothes still damp with salt spray, kissed RT goodbye as he rolled over sleepily in bed. I went to Rebecca and Reginald's room, knocking lightly then pounding. I had no more patience with anything. "Rebecca," I yelled through the locked door, "I've called a taxi. I'm leaving in five minutes. Meet you downstairs." I was grateful when she arrived in time for the taxi.

That early morning ferry ride at dawn was beautiful, even quieting. Standing on the upper deck of the ferry with salt spray dampening my face and hair, I reviewed the day to come. I would see Don when he got home from his work shift. The kids would be there, so I wouldn't have to talk with him the moment he came through the door. I felt unmoored with no elegant solution to my dilemma.

When Don arrived home from work, I had his favorite dinner of pork chops and baked potatoes ready, and momentarily we pretended all was well. The routine held the evening together until we'd put the kids to bed. Before he could say much, as the two of us sat across each other at the table, I apologized, admitting that what I'd done was idiotic. "I don't blame you for being angry. I am so sorry. I just don't know what more to say. I made the wrong decision to go on the boat ride. I'm just so sorry." He was quiet.

In bed that night, when he reached over and pulled me to him, I felt or imagined he was saying, "Okay, prove the truth to me, make love with me." I acquiesced.

Taking Responsibility

I spent two weeks in excruciating inner turmoil - assuaging my guilt about what I had done and ultimately would do. Accepting the reality that I must take full responsibility for my life decisions and their effect on others. I reached down and relentlessly pulled all the honesty I could from my psyche until, at long last, I was able to acknowledge and accept the folly and hurtfulness of my strategy. It wasn't easy, this growing up and taking responsibility for my actions, not blaming anyone, not judging myself, separating my future dreams from the enculturation of the times. I worked hard to unravel the whole story of Don and Diane. I looked in the mirror of my soul and my history.

Blessedly, through the whole six months of "the plan," I had continued to be an impeccable mother. Though sometimes I left them too long with a babysitter, I was determined to keep Ron and Pam out of the muck of my doings and not burden them with my acting out as I fought my demons. The questions roiled inside, "How could I DARE to throw my marriage away for a future as insecure as my childhood had been?" With Don, I had reached the longed-for sense of respectability and acceptance in Bellingham's small-town white culture. Why would I risk that comfort and ease to which I'd long aspired? What about the defiant declaration to Earl and Ginny that Don and I loved each other forever and ever? What about breaking that vow?" My pride could hardly bear for them to be proved right.

During those two weeks, with another part of my brain not subject to recriminations, I began to build our future - mine, Ron, and Pam's. I would go to university, not only to feed my passion for learning but to earn a teaching degree to support the three of us beyond the poverty level. As I'd strategized to make Don hate me, I now strategized for my and my children's survival and wellbeing. This time I formulated a plan full of hope, not despair.

THE PRODIGAL DAUGHTER RETURNS

I calculated that I could get a job in a nursing home working the graveyard shift, freeing me to attend university classes while the kids were at school, and we'd have evenings and weekends together. I made weird promises to myself like I would never serve them TV dinners, and intelligent promises that I wouldn't bring RT into my kids' life. Meantime, I continued to slip away to be with RT. I dreamed of a time when we would no longer have to sneak around to be together.

Like the calm after a storm, I was ready, and chose the day of reckoning. I'd decided to soften the blow by suggesting to Don that I only wanted to separate. "You just never know," I'd say to myself.

On the appointed day, I took Ron and Pam over to my grandmother's to spend the night. I made sure David was away from the house. About 3:00 in the afternoon, I sat down at the dining table, stared out the front windows at the cars driving by, and opened a bottle of red wine. I poured myself a drink and waited. I had no intention of being sloppy drunk, but I found courage in the bottle. After all, that was my father's way. He'd drink until the alcohol had lowered his control, and his violence and desperation could surface. Happily, it's an imperfect analogy because I needed courage not to bring forth a violent part of me, but a self that believed in my potential for expansion beyond the role I had accepted at eighteen.

I heard Don's truck, listened to his footsteps across the gravel, and held my breath as he opened the door. Usually, the kids would run to greet him, and I would be busy in the kitchen. Seeing me sitting at the table, he frowned, "Where are the kids?"

"They're with Grandma. Don, I need to talk to you. Come, sit down." I didn't give him time to change out of his work clothes. I had the wine bottle and two glasses on the table, mine half full. Pensively, he sat at the table. I filled his glass. Internally, with head bowed, I counted to three as I had practiced. The words tumbled out, "I want a separation. I don't know if I love you anymore." There. As inelegant as it was, it was out.

Like the conversation before, when I'd shared my unhappiness and we'd decided to have a child, only the opening salvo remains clear. There are flashes, his deathly quiet as he reached for the glass of wine, the bewilderment I watched wash over his face. Words, at last, began to echo back and forth in the alcoholic buffer I had created. I'm not sure how long we sat together and talked, but a moment arrived when I saw his expression change to one of acceptance. With that, he dared to point out how obnoxious I'd been of late and that yes, he agreed that things were amiss between us, and now he understood why. I wholeheartedly agreed with his assessment and apologized for my clumsiness.

I gingerly laid out my plans for our separation. I suggested that he stay at the house until he found a place to live, and when we felt ready, we would sit down with Ronny and Pammy and tell them. I would continue with the daycare; we'd find a way to do it financially. The sadness emanating from him nearly broke my heart, and I fought like crazy to hold onto my resolve. Even as he acknowledged to himself the truth, his eyes begged me to tell him it wasn't so.

About a week later, in the evening, after dinner, we gathered the kids to us. It would be the last time Don and I would join together in shared affection for our kids and even for each other. Ron and Pam had had their baths and put their pajamas on. Don sat on the couch, holding Pammy; she faced him cross-legged and momentarily wrapped her arms around him. Don pulled her close, and she wiggled away as she seldom sat still. She turned toward where I sat on a beanbag chair on the floor, Ronny on my lap.

Looking from Pam to Ron, I remarked to myself, as I often had, how if Don and I had ten kids, they'd all look the same because Don and I shared similar features. Our brown eyes were big and round in their young faces. They had our olive complexions, though Pam's skin was showing signs of the vitiligo that spotted Don's skin. We all had narrow faces with lips neither round nor thin. Happily, neither child had inherited my buck teeth. And during our years as a family, we were all slender of stature, though only Ron and I would carry that through our adult years.

"Mom-m," Ronny impatiently shook my arm. "Why are we sitting

THE PRODIGAL DAUGHTER RETURNS

here?"

Don and I looked at each other, hesitant, wishing time would stand still and wishing this was all over. Knowing our revelation would be a shock to them, we'd rehearsed how to disclose our plans to them. But sitting together, with these two beautiful and innocent faces smiling up at us, neither of us knew where to begin. I don't remember who spoke first. One of us said we had something to tell them. "Daddy and I," or was it, "Mommy and I?" Involuntarily, we each hugged the child in our arms as the next words came, "We've decided to live apart, at least for a while. We don't know if it's for good, or a little bit, or a long time. We'll just have to wait and see what happens."

"A hundred days?" Pammy asked, her five-year-old mind having no conception of time.

"No, not that long!" Ronny quickly corrected her.

"Is daddy going to live here?" Pammy queried, unconcerned.

"No, Pammy, being separated means daddy lives somewhere else. He has an apartment at Lake Samish, and he'll be moving there soon. You kids can go and see him whenever you want, and we have dad's phone number so you can call him anytime."

A hesitant shrug and with his voice barely audible, Ronny asked, "How come?"

"We just have some things to work out, and we can do it better if we're not living together. We love you so much, and it isn't anything at all to do with you, not at all, this is just between mommy and daddy." (We'd read that kids tended to think they were the cause of parent's divorce, so we wanted to reassure them they weren't, without suggesting it to them.)

Ronny, being a couple of years older, began to sense the seriousness of the situation. "Is daddy still our dad?" he whispered as tears ran down his cheeks.

"Yes!" we both replied quickly. Don continued, "Oh Ronny, I'm still your dad, and I will always be your dad, and Mom is your mom, and she'll always be your mom no matter what happens. All our disagreements have nothing to do with you kids. It's just between Mom and me. We have some problems we can't seem to work out, at least not while we're living together, so we're going to try living apart and see what we can work out."

"What's wrong?"

"It's . . ." I paused, "well, it's kinda hard to explain."

"But why does dad have to go? Why can't he just stay here, and you can talk here?" Ronny asked, staring up at me from where he snuggled in my arms, his legs pulled up into my lap, his brown eyes begging for an answer. Silence fell as the logic of his suggestion was incontrovertible.

My eyes met his as I tried to find words. "Well, we've tried. We've had long talks in the night, but we can't come to any agreement, and so we need distance to sort things out."

"What things!" This time it was Pammy demanding an answer. I knew I had to respond as honestly as I could.

"Well, hmm, well, things like what we want in the future, how we feel about each other. What our dreams are for the future." I paused, then added with a light-hearted touch, "We know how we feel about YOU TWO, we love you beyond anything in the world."

I looked over at Don, who, like me, was fighting tears. I knew, as surely as the sun rises, that I was on my own and only my resolve could carry me through. Could I hold my center amid the pain and heartache swirling around the four of us, hold it for an elusive fate that I didn't yet see clearly? I implored Don with my eyes, "Don't cry, please don't cry. We must be strong for them." In truth, I was terrified of drowning in the sea of tears the four of us would shed if he or I started. His eyes filled, spilled down his cheeks. He took a deep breath, sniffed as he bent his head and wiped the tears with his shirt sleeve.

The four of us sat burrowed in familial closeness as we adults continued to affirm our unchanging love for them, even if something had changed between us. Don and I had never fought much, especially around the kids. Now, without warning, they were told we couldn't live together. What words could explain why their world was

THE PRODIGAL DAUGHTER RETURNS

being shattered and their security threatened? How could we give them understanding without burdening them with our problems? We must ensure they wouldn't mistrust us and draw away from us. With a supreme effort, I put aside my fear and halted my flow of words. Instead, I focused on my love for them that was unassailable and steadfast. I think Don did something similar because sitting together in the shared family tension of shock and fear, the susurrus of our infinite family love caressed the four of us. Ronny and Pammy, reassured or unable to bear the tension, began to play and poke at each other and Don and me. Led by their playful jousting, like silly marionettes, we rolled onto the floor, leaving the tension on the frayed couch and chair. The four of us wrestled and tickled each other till we were breathless with laughter. I felt schizophrenic as my laughter turned to tears, and just as suddenly back to strange laughter until the two were indistinguishable. That precious sublime moment, with its jumble of pain and ecstasy, would reverberate in my body as the night wore on.

"Storytime," I announced, "who's night to pick?"

"Mine," Pammy answered. We jumped into the bedtime ritual of me reading a bedtime story while Don perused the newspaper, then Don and I would tuck them in with a hug and kiss. Tonight, carrying out the bedtime ritual, we could almost believe this separation wasn't happening, and for a few more days, it didn't. Don would come home from work, play, and wrestle with the kids while I got dinner on the table. We'd eat, then a little TV or talk between Don and the kids while I cleaned up. Then we'd all enter the bedtime ritual.

Naively Don and I had assumed a couple of weeks to transition was manageable. That we were in a phantom reality soon became apparent. We suddenly didn't know how to interact with each other and sleeping in the same bed was just plain weird. Honestly, I was so happy to be getting this last step over with that I just wanted him gone. He felt the same and in a week, once he'd taken all his things to his new apt, he moved in. During those first few weeks, my brother David, demonstrated a beautiful fluidity, when he became Don's confidant, and they would go out together for a beer. I was grateful for

David's agility and the support he gave Don because though I had hinted to Don that it was only a separation, there was no doubt that this process would end in divorce.

My mother's words when I told her echoed my self-accusations. She was outraged. "What is wrong with you? He's a wonderful husband and father. He doesn't yell or beat you or, or anything like that. How can you treat him that way, knowing how much he loves you and the kids? You have your house, your family. How can you do that to Ronny and Pammy? Diane, you are wrong to do this, just wrong."

I had no answer for her. I couldn't say, "Mom, something is stirring in me that I can't quite define." To say I didn't love Don anymore was nonsensical to her. My whole family adored Don. She was 100% on his side and even hinted at something nefarious she might do, like support Don having custody of the kids because she'd heard that I had smoked marijuana. This same reaction repeated itself over and over as I gradually informed our friends. There were no explanations that could satisfy my mother or anyone else. No one from our circle of couples aligned with me, so the couple friendships we had cultivated over the years were gone. One exception was Peggy. It warmed my heart to know our bond was still intact as she honored our friendship with strength and understanding. Oh yes, there was one other person, and that was my sister, Laura. When I called her, she exclaimed, "I never quite got you and Don. I mean, you just didn't seem a good match." It felt good to have these two women in my corner. Even more reassuring, when Don and I separated, David, who was still living with us, would be my cohort and emotional support, a delightful presence for the kids, as well as a welcome part of barhopping with a new, small circle of friends.

Rebecca's husband, Lane, had forbidden her to see me, as concurrent with the end of my and Don's relationship, she and Lane had nearly followed the same path, and he wanted her away from me. I sorely missed her and her understanding and affection. I was shocked Rebecca had decided to stay and try to make their marriage work. She managed it for just a month, and then she left Lane to fall back into Reginald's arms. Reginald would leave his wife for Rebecca, and they married when their divorces were final.

Just two months after our separation, Don had a girlfriend, Judy. I imagined he was glad to be rid of me and the pain I had brought him. Ronny and Pammy were less thrilled when Don and Judy became a couple. That was to be expected!

Don's birth mother, Doris, who I had come to love as a second mother, was scheduled to visit at summer's end. She was the mother I could share almost anything with, and I was the daughter she'd never had. Don and I called Doris with the news of our separation and insisted that we were all looking forward to her visit despite the split.

With Doris staying with me at the house, I took the opportunity, after Ron and Pam were asleep one night, to head over to Rebecca's, as Lane was out of town. We hadn't had much time together since the wild boat ride. We talked late into the night over a bottle of Chardonnay. Snacking on cheese and crackers, we recalled with laughter and groans the wild Orcas Island night and where each of us was as a result. Though she could barely acknowledge it, I sensed that her and Lane's separation wasn't far off. About 1:00 in the morning, I headed home.

I was driving my brother David's Triumph. It was not in the best of shape, the driver's side door clumsily wired together, and as I came around a corner, the wire gave, and the door flew open. I reached out into empty space to grab the door, and inadvertently my right hand pulled the steering wheel sharply to the right. At 30 mph, I swerved off the road into the cement wall of a deep drainage ditch. My head flew forward, and my mouth met the steering wheel as the car came to a smashing halt. Dazed, in survival mode, with the motor miraculously still running, I backed the car out of the ditch, and though it sputtered dangerously, I managed to drive a few meters and park on the other side of the culvert. The motor died, I turned the key once, twice to restart it, but it was dead. That's when I felt the blood running down my chin and throat.

I gingerly felt my mouth, where my protruding central incisors had been. There wasn't much there. I became aware of pain, yet strangely my mind was sharp. "Shock, I mustn't go into shock," I told myself. With my lips closed, I pressed hard against my gums to counteract the pain and stop the bleeding. Cell phones were decades away, answering machines the same, and whom would I call anyway at 1:00 in the morning? In a house close by, I saw a light still on. I stumbled to the door and knocked, called in a muffled voice through my hand. No answer. I knocked again. Nothing. I turned from the door, descended the few steps, and spotted another house, about 100 yards away, with the lights on. The mute door mocked my knocking. I vaguely sensed no one would be answering his or her door in the night. In an uncanny flash, I realized I was about a half mile from Peggy's house. I began to walk, repeating my mantra, "Mustn't go into shock. Mustn't go into shock." I stumbled across the lawn encircling her home and climbed the familiar back stairs of the dark and quiet house. I knocked and called softly, "Peggy?" No answer, so I dared knock and speak louder, "Peggy, it's me, Diane. I'm hurt." For long seconds the house stayed dark and silent.

Like a lighted beacon on a dark and stormy night, the porch light went on. Peggy cautiously opened the door and peered through the screen where I stood disheveled, dried blood on the front of my coat, my hand red, tears streaming from my glazed-over eyes. "What happened?" Horrified, she pulled me inside, and led me to the bathroom, sat me on a stool, and gently pulled my rigid hand away.

"I had a car accident on Edgemore. Hit a wall. Car's dead. My teeth hit the steering wheel." She continued wiping away the blood and tears. After a few minutes, she handed me a mirror, and the face staring back at me wasn't nearly as terrifying as it had felt. The impact had shoved my two front teeth into my gum, just a sliver of each showing below the rapidly swelling gum, the incisor to the left had broken off, leaving a jagged splinter. The other incisor seemed intact.

Peggy asked the obvious question, "Are you okay?"

"Yes, yes, I think so. I don't know what to do. What do you think?" We consulted and decided I didn't need to go to the hospital right then. She would take me home, and I'd call the dentist in the morning. Peggy woke her husband to let him know what was happening, then took my hand and led me to their car. At my house, she walked me inside to be sure I was okay. We wouldn't see each other often in the following years, but that night I felt the sisterhood we'd shared for over 15 years and was touched by the memory of "us." I silently slipped into bed. I'd tell Doris in the morning as well as explain to my brother David that I'd wrecked his car. (As it turned out, my insurance totaled out his automobile, and David was thrilled about the financial compensation as the tiny sports car was on its last leg!)

Years later, my first therapist, a Jungian psychologist, would observe a pattern in my life loosely described by C. G. Jung. *Synchronicity is the coming together of inner and outer events in a way that cannot be explained by cause and effect and that is meaningful to the observer.* My therapist pointed out in a session, "It looks like each time you make a significant shift in your life, synchronistically, you remove, lose, or something is torn from your physical body." Her words would turn out to be prescient.

Knocking my teeth out had a precedent. I was around nine months old, and Mom had put me in my highchair at the table and placed the steaming hot pablum on the table safely out of my reach. She returned to the kitchen to allow it to cool, but I wanted that cereal now! I managed to push and wiggle myself out of the highchair enough to tip the chair over, my upper front tooth crunching on the table edge. I let out a howl, and Mama found me sprawled on the floor, my mouth bleeding, an upper front tooth hanging by a gruesome thread. (The tooth grew back with a big black hole right in the center, and until the summer before junior high, when mom somehow found the money to have it filled, I would smile awkwardly with my lip clasped over the protruding tooth. Ugly was what I saw if I dared lift my lip to show the black hole.)

And now, some twenty-six years after that first knockout, I sat in my dentist's chair with a throbbing mouth. Dr. Greene examined the damage. "The three front teeth will have to come out, and we probably should take out the fourth one, so there is symmetry in your teeth when we make the bridge." And then, as though he could read my mind, he asked, "Would you like me to shave your front gum back a little and remove the contour of protruding teeth?" I vigorously nodded YES! To think that finally my buckteeth would be gone.

Weeks later, with my new shiny white teeth, I gazed at myself in the mirror. I experimented with smiling, frowning, and laughter. The laugh turned genuine as I stared awestruck. Hallelujah! The dentist had corrected one of my external "uglies!" A few months later I had the large birthmark mole at the corner of my mouth and half a dozen smaller moles removed from my face. When the bandages came off, the stitches removed, and the healing complete, I was thrilled at the face that looked back at me. These changes imbued me with new confidence. Yes, it would take time before my psyche could set aside the moniker, UGLY, but it was an auspicious beginning.

In January 1970, Don and I met with a lawyer who drew up the divorce papers. In early spring of 1970, Earl did for Don what he had refused to do for us as a couple: he reached out and gave Don a helping hand. He arranged a job for Don with Asplundh Tree Company, the company that Puget Sound Power and Light hired to clear their power lines. Within a couple of weeks, Don moved to King County, Washington, where Earl and Ginny now lived, to take the job. I was happy for Don but a little miffed at Earl when I remembered his "No" to us when we'd asked him to sign for our marriage, his "No" when we'd asked him to help us with the dentures Don needed, not to mention his emphatic "No" when we'd asked him to loan us money for the down payment on a house. Within a month after Don's move to the Seattle area, he met his life partner, Carol. They moved to her home in Fall City, Washington, and as soon as our divorce was final, Don and Carol married. By then, I too, was solidly and happily set on my new path – utterly in love with a new man (not RT), attending university, and yes, the hard part, working the graveyard shift at a nursing home. But even that couldn't dampen my high spirits.

9

1969-1975

Jackson

The Sacred Tremor Grabs Hold in Her Soft Iron Grip

We return for a moment to *Shakti*, the omniscient and enlivening feminine force described in Hindu mythology. It is hard to divine, and yet we intuit it. The expression of this feminine energy effortlessly manifests through joining sexually with another. In intercourse, all the senses are engaged, seeing, feeling, hearing, touching, and brushing the divine, if only for a moment.

In the relationship with my next partner, Jackson, the seed planted by Papa, at last falls on fecund earth, and the nourishment of love, expertise, and adventure conspire to initiate me into the transcendent *Shakti*; a state that is beautifully described in the Kashmir Shaivism tradition through the *Shiva/Parvati* myth. Decades in the future, this myth will take center stage with my yet unknown partner, William. But for the moment, I note simply that *Parvati* is the goddess who, once she had won *Shiva's* heart and they married, stayed joined in intercourse for 10,000 years – metaphorically speaking to be sure! This myth's implication, the feminine and masculine entering into transcendence together, can provide a lens into my predisposition of healthy and robust sexuality. This penchant is my true self's teleological drive, enlisting into its service a plethora of beings, both male and female, to entice my sexuality into cultivating the earthly and the transcendent *Shakti*.

In August 1970, just a week after my divorce was final, I enrolled at Western Washington State College, the local 4-year college. As I sat outside in the sun at the university café after the new student orientation, I couldn't help but smile like a big ole Cheshire cat. It was one of those perfect early fall days that grace the northwest. The evergreens surrounding the campus were sparsely interspersed with the maple and birch trees' golds and reds. From where I sat sipping my tea and indulging in a delicious rich chocolate brownie, I could see Bellingham Bay over the treetops, even make out a sailboat or two, as well as fishing boats coming in and out of the harbor. My gaze took in my immediate environment, noting that while most of the students were younger, there were, like the maples interspersed in the evergreens, a few more senior students like myself. As an early morning fog turns the outlines of bushes and trees into blurry suggestions of form and shape, so my thoughts drifted among the shadows of the past and the vagueness of my future. In the plan I'd laid out, I knew there wouldn't be many quiet moments like this, so I relished it like a long-held kiss.

It had taken the better part of a year for Ron and Pam, now eight and six respectively, to adjust to our new family constellations: Don and Carol in Fall City and me in Bellingham. There had been the initial dismay over Don's first girlfriend, and on one of Jackson's visits, as he walked out the door, Pam had shut the door behind him and declared, "I don't want that dirty hippy in our house." Ron, a little more accepting than his younger sister, quickly engaged Jackson in boy adventures. Through the adjustment period and beyond, Don and I stayed amicable, both careful not to be critical of the other, even though we weren't in agreement about many of the ways we cared for our children.

Ron and Pam were maturing beyond their years. They thrived on adventure and were close companions in everything they did. Ron reveled in his role as the circumspect older brother, and Pam loved her older brother and followed his lead, and when sometimes she leaped before she looked, she knew Ron would be there to back her up. I remember what an eye-opener it was for me when two brothers, Ron and Pam's age, came to my home day-care and fought with each other non-stop. I marveled at the harmony and enjoyment Ron and Pam had with each other.

Every other weekend the two of them traveled to King County to visit Don. I'd put them on the bus, see that they were seated right behind the driver, with instructions not to leave their seats until the bus arrived in Seattle. Don would meet the bus, and they'd drive to Fall City where he lived. We adults, Jackson, Don, Carol, and I were delighted with the visits for various reasons – Don had time with the kids, and I had time away from the kids to sleep and renew. On holidays they would have extended visits with Don and his family, and in the summer months, the kids loved spending time in Fall City. They adjusted to the stark contrast between the two households. Our household was loosely organized, with extended family playing an influential role in the kids' lives and with schedules and people shifting constantly. Don's household was conventionally, even predictably organized; Carol's young son went off to school while his parents went off to their jobs each morning. On weekends they would all gather at Carol's mother's house, where she lived just up the street, for a traditional roast beef dinner. This dissimilarity bred in Ron and Pam a fantastic fluidity and acceptance of differences between people and lifestyles that guide them to this day.

Jackson was also on my mind that morning as I sat contentedly at the university café and munched my chocolate brownie. I have vague memories of RT introducing me, his mystery woman, to his curious university buddies when we went for a beer at **The Sandpiper**. That night of introductions, Jackson, one of the buddies, had been shamelessly flirting with me while RT quietly fumed. It was one of the things about Jackson that would fascinate me over the next few years - his flair and self-assurance that bordered on being full-of-himself, yet which he carried with such humor and charm that it never quite crossed the line. When I glanced furtively at him, I liked what I saw - his body firm and upright just a little taller than me, his face tanned and a little rugged, his unruly black hair, full sensuous lips with a smile playing at the corners, visible through his full beard. He exuded a mischievous bad boy quality that attracted me. He must be somewhere around my age, I mused to myself, maybe a little younger . . .but then again, I was with RT. I turned my full attention back to him to soothe the little jealous bump I sensed. I adored RT and had no intention of letting Jackson come between us, but the door had been cracked open, and there was no closing it.

RT's and my relationship began to unwind slowly, and on a frosty winter morning when we were breakfasting out, the proverbial writing on the wall leaped out at us. Hesitantly, yet congruently, and without acrimony, we acknowledged our relationship had run its course. It didn't take time for word to get around, and Jackson called me a few days later. Within a week, RT introduced Jan, his new girlfriend, to the group. I suspected at the time that she had been waiting in the wings. In one fell swoop, Jackson and I were released into the simmering stew of loving lust.

Adrift in my musings, I reluctantly pulled my thoughts back to the present. Seeing a few crumbs of brownie on the plate, I scooped them up and washed them down with the dregs in my teacup. Sighing, with a last glance out over the bay, I stood and slung my backpack across my shoulder and turned my steps toward home.

When I entered university as a mature 27-year-old student, the sexual revolution was in full swing, even in small-town Bellingham. This cultural shift, epitomized by the immortal words, *Sex & Drugs & Rock & Roll* (the title of a song by Ian Dury), was a blessing to the sensuality that is an integral part of who I am. Though it became an overused sound byte, *Sex & Drugs & Rock & Roll* is the perfect expression of the multi-pronged trident that Jackson and I would wield to build and to ignite a sacred tremoring: a tremor that would only reach its full expression some forty years later with William, who at this moment in time, was deeply ensconced in the celibate world of meditation with Maharishi.

Jackson awakened in me a passion and love of life I had no idea was locked away inside of me, and in turn, he was ecstatic with how I loved to make love with him. We were the proverbial match made in heaven. I could never have guessed that our relationship and friendship would last for the next 50 years right up to today.

When we met, Jackson lived alone in a three-bedroom house. The living room was full-on 60s, dimly lit with flashing purple strobe lights, pillows scattered around the room. A hookah pipe sat surrounded by joint rolling papers, incense, and a bag of weed on a low table in the center. On the memorable night when we would make love for the first time, we had gathered in the living room with friends, passing the pipe, listening to music, and talking and laughing in typical marijuana silliness that at the moment seemed profound. Jackson finally kicked everyone out of the house and led me through a beaded curtain into his bedroom. It too, reflected the hippy culture, Indian cloth hanging on the walls, beads and incense burners on the chest-of-drawers. Two incongruous ceramic wall plaques drew my interest. One bore the well-known excerpt from the poem by Sarojini Naidu:

"The bird of Time has but a little way
To fly . . . and, lo! the bird is on the wing"

The other plaque bore a verse from the poem by Mary T. Lathrap:

Just walk a mile in his moccasins
Before you abuse, criticize and accuse.
If just for one hour, you could find a way
To see through his eyes instead of your own muse.

ON BE(COME)ING A WOMAN OF WISDOM

They both arrested my attention, and I guessed a lot about this man from these words that were meaningful to him. Sitting together on the big brass bed, we laughingly exhaled the pungent smoke of a joint into each other's face and succumbed to an earthy animal magnetism that drew us into each other's arms. Never, in the twelve years since that sad and lonely loss of my virginity with Willy and through a range of different sexual experiences, had my body quivered and opened so fully into the loving touch of another. My body rose to his sensual caresses, begging for more as his lips and hands like fingers of fire burned and quenched at the same time. My tongue lovingly slid down his body to take his erect penis into my mouth, my throat. I felt no shyness as I buried my face in his groin, and he buried his face in mine. His tongue released my clitoris and slipped across my belly and breasts where he paused only momentarily, and his lips hungrily found mine. I trembled when he entered me, and as he moved inside of me, I moved with him as we immersed ourselves in a bath of shared passion. Our first orgasm together swallowed me into a mind-boggling sea of sensation. When his penis softened, and he slipped out of me, we lay in utter contentment. Jackson kissed me tenderly, "I'll go get us something to drink."

"Umm, yes, I'd love that," I murmured. He went downstairs to the kitchen and returned with cold drinks of orange juice. The coolness of the liquid had barely cleared our throats when we were ardently in each other's arms. Soon he was inside of me, he was ejaculating into me as his fingers found my clitoris, and I once again exploded into an otherworldly orgasm. We would drift into sleep and awaken together and arouse each other to a near-frenzy of touch and exploding orgasm. I slept at some point because I remember awakening in the morning, marveling at the creature in whose bed I lay. "Yes, yes, and yes," I murmured to myself.

I was sure it wouldn't last more than six months – sure it would calm down. Oh, how wrong I was! As the months passed, our ardor grew exponentially. We could never seem to get enough of each other. I loved when my orgasm would carry me into unearthly colors and sounds, and then he would release his orgasm. Sometimes we'd come together, and I would feel a moment of oneness, a silence whose contours were becoming familiar as Jackson stroked and teased every fiber of my body into a quivering receptacle, and finally unable to contain the sensations of body and mind I'd cry out with ecstatic release. I hungered for that opening into what I would come to call the Vastness, and I longed to sustain that moment of touching the divine – those glimpses where everything was everything in a timeless moment of eternity. I was hungry for every moment I could be with Jackson, share our unbridled passion, and touch that deep yet maddeningly brief place of celestial bliss.

On the alternate weekends when the kids traveled to Don's, and Don would call me that he had picked them up, in the sure knowledge they were safe, I'd fly into Jackson's arms to drink and grow drunk at the fount of the sensual *Shakti*. These weekend trysts, giving my body and mind over to Jackson, daring to drown in our shared passion, pleasuring him and being pleasured by him, fed my hunger for the realm where the goddesses of sensuality and love reigned supreme.

On Sunday night, we'd pick up Ron and Pam at the bus station and go to the drive-in for milkshakes and hamburgers, then Jackson would drop us off at our home, and he'd go to his. Reprising the cycle of work, kids, and school, I'd drive Ron and Pam to my grandmother's for the night. I'd head back home to sleep a few hours before the midnight hour of the graveyard shift at the nursing home.

What mattered most in post-divorce life was the wellbeing of Ron and Pam, so my scheduling centered around them: being home when they arrived from school bubbling with news of the day, dropping them off after dinner at Grandma Trotto's, picking them up in the early morning, still sleepy in their pajamas, going home to have breakfast together, and then getting them off to school, and me to my classes. A couple of times, when depression born of fatigue ate at me, I loaded our 2-person tent and whatever food was in the house into the car, and the three of us went camping overnight in the foothills of the nearby Cascade Mountains. We slept cozily in the tent, waking up with the sun and building a little fire to cook eggs and bacon. After we washed dishes in the ubiquitous stream always found in those foothills, we set off on a hike with them running ahead and exploring. I followed close behind, letting their delight and nature's peace soak me to my core. And I would remember why I was pushing so hard to realize my grand plan. I couldn't have managed the insanity of my life in those demanding days, weeks, months, and years without the joy and loving closeness with Ron and Pam.

When they didn't go to their dad's on the weekend, we had a routine. After breakfast, I'd fall into bed. There was a 2-hour limit on Saturday morning cartoons. They were amazingly disciplined and would turn the TV off as agreed. Weather permitting, they'd invariably go outside to play or if it were raining, they'd pull out the Legos bucket and build, content with the company of each other. At around 1:00, they'd awaken me for lunch. Occasionally, they proudly brought me lunch in bed. There were times when the weight of my decisions as a mother, the exigencies of their life as children of a single parent, an often exhausted one at that, left me doubting, wondering what this was doing to them psychologically. There were times I'd get impatient with them for no other reason than sleep deprivation. And yet, only slightly daunted by these tribulations, we kept on keeping on.

I did homework at night while the patients in the nursing home slept. I sometimes resented having to be interrupted to change wet beds, wipe dirty asses, or answer call lights. I had worked it all out on paper, and it didn't seem too bad, but as the years rolled by, the pace and demands would take their toll. At 28, gray hairs challenged the deep brown strands I had been proud to show off as my hair grew below my shoulders – a true hippy girl I'd laugh to myself. Though still bright, my raccoon eyes peered out through darkened circles in those early morning glances in the mirror, and I understood the expression "bone tired" as I became deeply, unequivocally, exhausted.

And yet, the university environment fed my searching soul. Eastern philosophy hovered on the edges of hippy culture, and books like

Krishnamurti's *The First and Last Freedom* left me almost breathless with wisdom that was revolutionary to me. I added Aldous Huxley, Alan Watts to my awareness exploration and was dumbfounded to discover this spiritual knowledge, anathema to the Seventh-day Adventist teachings, and I understood why I'd rejected the religion of my grandmother. Though my material day-to-day life claimed most of my attention during my college years, in quiet moments, I cogitated on these new ideas and, in rare impromptu moments, investigated them with Jackson.

Some Friday nights when the kids were at their dad's, Jackson and I met up with friends for hamburgers and beers at our new favorite local bar, where there were pool tables and talking circles rather than music and dancing. I reveled in these Friday evenings for the lightness of the mood, the uninhibited laughter among friends at an in-joke, the pool games we played, and then - the moment!

We'd bid our friends goodbye, and at home, wrapped in the wonder of our bodies, we were two eagles soaring into the heavens then plunging to the earth in a death dive. We were the prey caught in the talons, giving ourselves entirely to the capture that would engender tears and laughter of pure joy with no seeming source. Emerging quiescent from bliss, I was like a tired old cat lying contented before a warm fire. Like breakfast with the kids, these Friday evenings warmed and renewed me from the demanding life to which I had committed.

There was, however, a dark side to this ecstasy, one forged from the hunger of the Sun Room decision as a three-year-old, and the furnace of my father's belly where his sexuality burned and consumed my innocence and trust and left me alone in the dark of guilt and longing. This thing would grab my spirit, and like Jacob of old who fought with an angel, I would fight this dark angel with my mind, with activities, with self-pity and self-hatred writings. Nothing, but nothing could wrest me from the clutches of my jealousy.

I found myself mad with jealousy when Jackson would openly flirt with other women. Finally, I couldn't bear my schizophrenic feeling of hatred and love toward him and, worse, toward myself for being so insecure that harmless flirtations made me furious and out of control. No matter how I tried to chase away the feelings, the cause was lost. An inexplicable element of this inner demon is that I would also engage in harmless flirtations for the passing delight of attention and flattery. And yet, my dark angel of jealousy sprung from ancient insecurity and profound love for Jackson, couldn't fathom that this was equally true for him.

One morning, sitting with Jackson at my kitchen table where so many life-altering conversations had taken place, hundreds of meals eaten and where I'd often sat in quiet and felt the table's sympathetic spirit, I was agitated. "I can't stand myself," I announced to him, unable to keep the contempt and anger from those words.

"Wait, wait, okay, okay, but why are you angry at me? I hear it in your voice and feel it's directed at me, not you. Come on Diane, give me some context here."

"Okay, okay, I want to be comfortable with your flirting, with your conversations with other women, and yet I just can't handle it. My mind goes crazy, and I feel ugly, old with children, overwhelmed and tired from work and school, and compare myself with other unencumbered, bright and cheery students, free to go and have a drink whenever, or whatever. I know we've tried to talk this through, you've reassured me, but I can't extricate myself out of this dark enchantment imposed on me by my father and family dynamics." I rushed on like a fire burning through a dry tinder forest, "It's over. We have to break up. I'm going to work on myself and try to get to a place of acceptance, but right now, I'm just so unhappy and angry that I could strike out at you, at the world in terrible ways, even violent ways. That's how it feels inside of me. It's even scary at times the violence that possesses me, the despair, the hopelessness, and I know it's going to destroy this beautiful, loving thing we have together, this gift that you are to me, that I am to you. I look at the road ahead of us, and all I see is destruction, burning, hatred. I know this is all overly dramatic, but it's eating me up inside. I'm so sorry, so sorry." The words trailed off as I held my face in my hands to try to stop the torrent of tears.

Jackson reached across the table's abyss and took my hands in his. I didn't resist because I longed for his touch even as I was rejecting it. "Yes, I do flirt with other women. I enjoy it, it makes me laugh and enjoy the little titillation, but I have absolutely no interest in anything further. You know that, right? There is just no one else for me but you. I don't know how to communicate that to you. If I stop these little flirtations, these momentary acknowledgments of an attractive and interesting woman in front of me, then I give up something of myself. I wish I could say to you that I'll stop, but I can't do that. I would end up resenting this limitation. We've talked about how your relationship with your father and your sisters drives this, and I know you're working hard on that dynamic. And yes, my flirtatious nature is undoubtedly a residue from my dad, from Curley, who was a flirtatious chronic womanizer that I admired even as I saw the pain it caused my mom. But I'd like us to work these things out together. Please, let's try."

I looked up and trembled in the depths of my being. "Jackson, dear one, yes, I tell myself that, and with some part of me, I know it's true, but this other part is way stronger. I'm afraid if we try to work out these parental curses with each other, we may not find our way, together, out of the dark forest of enchantment but will have to leave the other there. I can't bear the possible hurt I could do to you and myself and this relationship. You must understand that our relationship is a gift I could never have imagined for myself. Finally, this is about my wellbeing. I can't abandon it. I must find my way out of the clutches of this dark angel alone. I'm doing it in the hope we can have something better when and if we come back together." I knew I was repeating myself but couldn't stop. I paused and added, "I'm not asking you to wait."

Trying to read him, seeing incomprehension, I realized that this jealous insecure part of me was just something he couldn't conjure up. He seemed not to have a jealous bone in his body. If anything, he would seem delighted, even proud, when other guys flirted with me. He smiled when he saw men admire my wild and unrestrained dancing when, moving, gyrating, I would express my sensuality for all to see. Jackson had shared with me that watching me dance that first time at **The Sandpiper**, he knew he had to find out who I was, how I felt, and yes, what kind of lover I was. He'd wondered if I was all show and actually frigid or was what he saw genuine. And, as he would laughingly tease me, he set his intention that night to find out!

"Well, can we talk? Can I call you?" I detected a strange lightness in his voice. He told me later he knew that we would find our way back together, and whatever I needed to do with this jealousy thing, he was okay with it.

"I'd rather not talk for a while, okay? I'll give you a call if anything changes."

"Well, I don't like it, but I can't make you be in a relationship with me now, can I?" He paused, "and I will be here waiting, I promise you," he couldn't help the slight smile that played about his lips, "though not pining."

That little joke roused the dark angel in me. Was he crazy? The angry tiger of jealousy leaped at him, claws sharp, scratching furiously, blindly. I could barely stand there in front of him long enough to mutter coldly through clenched teeth, "No, I don't expect you'd pine. We're through here."

"Look, sorry," I just meant to say that I'm going to be myself, but I'm not out looking for someone else, okay?" He sensed there was nowhere to go with the conversation at this point, "Okay, I'll wait for your call, though I may check in with you at some point if I haven't heard from you. Okay?" He reached across the table for my hand. I jerked away. He added softly, "Remember, I love you beyond words, I enjoy being with Ron and Pam, and I'm rooting for you, for us. Don't forget those things, okay?" I barely heard his last words lost as I was in righteous indignation about my decision.

We stood up awkwardly as he sought to penetrate the wall I'd thrown up against him, reaching out to touch my arm. I let his hand rest there for a moment, and against all the resolve, all the barriers I'd put up against him, his touch set my heart pounding as though it would burst out of my chest and drive my arms around him. Quickly, I pulled away and began clearing the dishes. The proverbial "last supper," I thought with sarcastic humor, though there was a grain of truth to the image. He found his backpack. We both paused, wanting to say more, but words were pointless.

Over the following days and weeks, I read, talked to my neighbor and friend, Corrine who was now hanging out with David, both in bed and out. Occasionally, on my nights off, with Ron and Pam happily spending the night at Grandma Trotto's, the three of us would go out to party and dance. And true to my pattern, one of those nights, as I gazed into the eyes of a handsome young entertainer, and when his soaring voice singing, *A Bridge Over Troubled Waters*, touched my heart, I was hooked. At his first break, I invited him to our table, and before the night ended, I simply and lovingly took him to my bed. The affair with Grant, this sweet young singer who sang from his soul, would last a couple of months. There was no long-term commitment, no mundane demands, Jackson didn't exist, children didn't exist, and I was free of my inner self-imposed torment of loss and grief and jealousy over Jackson. Our affair was idyllic in a fairytale sort of way. I knew that it wasn't real, but I didn't care. For a few weeks, I simply immersed myself in his beguiling innocence and in sharing with him my uninhibited sexuality. We treasured every moment we could to be together - in his hotel room, in my bed when the kids were at Don's, or most exquisitely of all, on the beach of Bellingham Bay where we'd walk from my place carrying a blanket and bottle of wine, shed our clothes, and make love to the susurration of the waves on the shore.

When Grant's gig ended, and the diversion of him was gone, a dam burst open as the floodwaters of emotion crested. During the long nights at work when I couldn't focus on homework, hated changing wet and shitty beds, or at home where I lay alone tossing and turning in my bed, I would torture myself with images of Jackson with other women. Deliverance would come through my favorite college class of the quarter, **Women's Studies**.

Three women professors taught the class, and though they often had differing points of view, each was a feminist through and through, and this class was a favorite for women. Each quarter there would be two or three men willing to brave this minefield. The three professors were outspoken and encouraged honest discussions on the full spectrum of women's issues: the social mores and internalized limits, including the sexual revolution. In one class discussion, I had taken the view that women can have children and still be fully engaged in following dreams that had nothing to do with being a mother. My position highlighted a bias against motherhood from most of the students and all of the professors. Class that day was a long hour and a half, and I was relieved when it was over.

As I left the classroom, my sense of isolation was acute. I felt my age and differentness from the other students, and I just wanted to go home and hug Ron and Pam, feeling that the women in the class who had spoken out so strongly against me, a mother, had somehow invalidated the kids and me. When Ron and Pam arrived home from school, I greeted them with big bear hugs, "I love you, love you!" I gushed.

"Mom," Pam wiggled away, "okay, okay. I love you too!" Ron paused and melted into my arms. "I love you, Mom," he whispered. I smiled to myself, reassured by their true-to-form responses. Once I'd gotten dinner on the table, I sat with the two of them and listened to the day's experiences just as Mom had done with me and my brothers and sisters twenty years ago. As I gazed from one to the other, lulled by their chatter, my heart swelled with the wonder of these two precious beings, and I was sure I could have it all!

A week or so later, in this same class, one of the professors announced, "One of you wrote an essay for this last assignment, and I want to read some of it and open up a discussion. Turns out from reading your papers, the subject of jealousy is of prime importance to many of you." She paused. "Yes, I see some heads nodding; looks like there's enough interest to talk about jealousy, especially in this post-60s time when many of our parents' cultural mores around sexuality and relationships are coming into question." Heads nodded, some vigorously, others tentatively.

The professor began to read my paper in which I had written, sometimes questioningly, sometimes dangerously, about my relationship with Jackson (nameless in the paper) and what I had gleaned in my readings both for and outside class. I felt proud that she appreciated the paper enough to read it to the class, vindicated somehow. I was excited to hear from my classmates, hoping for clarity and ways to view my struggle.

As Angela finished reading, she identified me as the author. Gina, a young, intelligent, and outspoken student, quickly jumped in. "Personally, I think we should all just get over this jealousy thing. If you all, well, we all, are caught in jealousy, then we're just in a "poor me" mode. I say we just suck it up and get on with it." There were some murmurs of agreement from around the room.

A strong voice from the back of the room turned our heads. It was Fiona, one of the other more senior students. "I agree with Diane and what she wrote. I hate being in the hell of jealousy, but I, for one, haven't found an easy way out of that hell. You really find it that easy? You just suck it up and get on with it? Tell me, how does that work? You mean, you never go to passive-aggressive behavior when you supposedly just get over it?" challenged Fiona. "Personally," she emphasized the word, mimicking Gina, "I don't find it that easy. And I'm not even sure that there isn't some survival reason for jealousy. Look at how our society is structured right now; men control and hold all the power. They make all the rules, they hold the winning hand as far as opportunity and financial wealth are concerned. We haven't many rights as women, so how do we go about protecting what is ours? I mean, think of our mothers; most of them didn't have the training to get jobs, birth control methods were in the dark ages, a passel of kids the norm, so what does a woman have open to her but to jealously fight like ferocious mother bears to protect her survival and her kids. Sure, it's getting easier for us today, but I'm guessing we're still wired like our mothers. When I look around the room, I'm guessing that most of us, dressed in our hippy garb, braless, without make-up, long free-flowing hair, looked in the mirror this morning to check out our image. What's that for except to attract a good hippy man." Her fervor quieted the room.

A voice I recognized broke the silence, "You have a point." The voice belonged to Barb with whom I'd become close friends. Her deep green eyes always seemed to shine from some unknown source, her perfect-size breasts with firm nipples pressed against the confines of her tie-dyed blouses. At the same time, the skirts she wore fell softly around her hips and flared out, undulating and emphasizing her smooth, elegant motions as she walked. Her lips, whether in a pout or broad smile, invited you to share in some secret you weren't even aware you wanted to know. She continued, "Yeah, we all like to look good, right? Who knows, your soul mate may come into your life at any moment. But does this really have to do with jealously? I mean, it's kind of a stretch for me, that I just want to look good so that . . . what? So I can win my man? I mean, maybe it's different if you have kids. But right now in my life, it's kind of a stretch for me to want to possess my man, and I certainly don't want him to possess me."

I frowned slightly, "It's complicated, isn't it? And I'm with you. I don't want my man to be possessive of me, yet I get possessed by my jealousy. At times I feel it's the final relationship frontier for me, that if I can just not be jealous, everything will flow free, and I can live happily ever after with my partner."

Several voices broke in, "You have that fantasy too? I think the same. I dream of the same thing." This response heartened me because one of the fantasies I clung to, as though it was some final truth, was that I would finally reach heaven and be free of my human angst if only I weren't jealous.

Our professor jumped in, "What if, as Fiona pointed out, jealousy is a survival mechanism? And as some of you suggest, is it possible to just move beyond jealousy if it's no longer related to our survival as women and mothers? Or is our internal topography still shaped by our ancestors' experience?"

There were yes's, and no's, and groans, murmuring in waves

around the room, but the discussion was cut short by the bell. Energized by the class debate, excited by a deeper understanding of my jealousy, I decided to skip my next class.

Retrieving my bike from one of the ubiquitous bike racks on campus, I headed down to the waterfront to the bike trail that led along the shore and ended at Fairhaven Park. The park was large, some areas wild with tall trees and a meandering creek, and some parts tamed with a baseball field, playground area, tennis courts, and a community building with a fireplace. As children, on Sabbath, we'd sometimes walk with Grandma to the park. A few times, we had come with Papa, and he had taught us to play tennis with some old racquets that had been in the shed and belonged to my mother's brothers. Both moods of the park, one more reflective and quiet, the other full of activity and laughter, had resonated with me as a child. (In the future, in October 2015, at this same park, in the community building, with a fire burning in the fireplace, decorations gracing every wall and table, a food feast laid out, and a giant birthday cake, our extended family would celebrate Marian's 100th birthday.)

I entered the park, rode up the slope past the wading pond where all those years ago Peggy and I had vainly tried to wash away our drunken vomit. It was dry, as a health department directive, declaring it unsafe, had caused the city to drain the water, and now kids used it for skateboarding. I rode through the center of the park where covered picnic tables were scattered among the tall Douglas firs and sped down the hill away from the park's tailored area toward the creek. Even now, I thrilled to run down the hill, no brakes, picking up speed and then braking suddenly as the bike wheels splashed into the creek. Dropping my bike alongside the bank, I noted how the water still rushed noisily, then came to rest in quiet pools. Even the large rocks in the stream felt familiar from "back in the day."

I waded out to a boulder, one of many I had sat on as a child, and eased myself down, my feet coming to rest on the rocky creek bottom. The cold water, the pebbles I stirred with my toes, the birdcalls, and the muted greens of trees and bushes coalesced to transport me deep into nostalgia. I was a child again, feeling the purity of the space, the sounds, the way nature could wash away everything but the moment. And now, in a silence that descended and ascended around me, clarity emerged. I "saw" that being in Jackson's embrace was to be embraced by this same nature. To connect with him through our bodies was to connect with the sounds of the creek, the birds calling to each other, and the rustling of wind in the trees. In a flash of understanding, I saw that my jealousy was the lack of awareness of this connection, of us, of IT, of timelessness.

I sat with eyes closed while the afternoon sun slipped behind the tall treetops, the mottled sun's warmth finally unable to dispel the coolness of the creek. I opened my eyes, my gaze creating an impressionist tableau of colors and forms flowing ceaselessly into each other. Soon trees took shape, clouds moved overhead, and strewn rocks and the moving stream came into focus. I looked down at my hands beside me on the rock, the wavy forms of my feet, and seizing this precious moment of silence and connection, I committed the experience to my mind and body memory: I would use this as the entry to a peaceful space when I felt overwhelmed by my jealousy. A shiver seized my toes and rose up through my vagina, my belly, solar plexus, my heart, even my arms shook, a final shudder through my neck and head. Sighing, I stood and waded the two feet to the edge of the creek, where I sat down a little shakily. I offered a silent prayer of gratitude and shouted aloud to the skies, "Thank you."

That night, after I had dropped Ron and Pam at my grandmother's, I called Jackson. Oh my god, how the sound of his voice set my heart pounding in my chest. I wondered if he could hear it. I invited him over for dinner with the kids and me the next day, telling him only that I knew we were meant to be together; I'd tell him more later; right now I needed to get some sleep before work. He said simply, "I'm glad. I'll be there."

Ariadne: Their Dream-His Dream-Our Dream

Each slice of my daily life had its place, fitting together like a 1000-piece puzzle, the hours tight, sometimes taut to the point of breaking. At work, standing at the bedside of Mrs. Cole or Mr. Hansen while she or he propped up in bed, washed their hands and face in preparation for breakfast, I would suddenly jerk awake, unaware I had fallen asleep. In classes at university, I was chagrinned when my body would shudder, and I'd awaken and stare at my notebook where the writing had wandered off the page. In the worst of times, I wondered how I could keep going,

Added into our household's intricacies, Ron, Pam, me, and my brother David was the return from Vietnam of my brother, Don, three years younger than David. While Jackson and I joined anti-war protests in the streets, Don was fighting in Vietnam caught body and soul in the fracas. When he returned from his second tour of duty struggling with the carnage of the war he'd fought in, he moved in with us, finding the love and support of family.

My two-bedroom house now gave shelter to five of us. Don and David slept on futons in the living room that they'd refold into couches in the daytime. I added a chest of drawers in the entrance hallway, and we settled in. I liked having my brothers living with me. We helped each other in a million different ways, and Pam and Ron felt they'd won the jackpot – after all, how many other kids had live-in uncles with whom to play, laugh, and learn from? Don and David both enrolled at Skagit Valley Community College. Eventually, we'd all be students at Western Washington University where Don would meet, Penny, his future wife, and they would soon move in together.

That other piece of the puzzle, weekends with Jackson, just the two of us, was a welcome renewal and rejuvenation from my demanding, sometimes draining inner and outer life. What a relief it was to lose myself in him, in us, in the ecstasy of our joining, in the promise of bliss. Sometimes, on these evenings, we would listen to the soft voice of Joni Mitchell or the brash insistent voice of Dylan. But one night, this night before the morning when he would pop the question, Jackson put on the collage tape he had made for me.

As the songs shifted moods - softness, sparkling intensity, moans of blues, the laments of jazz - Jackson insisted on undressing me slowly, touching and kissing each newly uncovered bit of flesh that would quiver under the touch of his fingers and lips. It amazed me sometimes the energy that would course through my seemingly exhausted body. Every fiber of my being was suddenly alive, responding to his touch as though an electrical shock flowed from his fingertips to my center, and I would feel myself open like a flower to receive him, anticipating the moment I would urge him to enter me, or perhaps he would impatiently demand to enter me. I let the music enter my consciousness, felt its shifting moods in my being, and let it propel me deeper into the sensuality of sound, feeling, and *Shakti* vibration, until, unable to bear it any longer, I exploded in orgasm, and Jackson released the intense holding of his own. In that moment of wonder, the vastness swallowed me into its infinite emptiness. Soon, all too soon, the vibration faded, awareness of the bed and wet pooling where sperm and vaginal fluids flowed out of me. I opened my eyes slowly taking in the room, drank in Jackson's face above me – his contented smile, tousled black hair falling across his forehead, and his sparkling brown eyes into which I surrendered. We shared a consummate human moment that made my heart swell . . .and yet I was voraciously hungry for that something I'd only just glimpsed; this thing that captured me, held me in its embrace, and then seemed to eject me from the sublime to the ordinary.

This morning we lazily awoke after spending the night at his house. I was blissfully preparing breakfast while Jackson showered. Our lovemaking through the night had been infused with a mood that hovered enticingly around Jackson, as though something was about to be revealed. I bathed in the mystery and took special care with breakfast cooking the bacon and eggs and pancakes to perfection. Our meal consumed, I sat with coffee cup in hand, dishes still spread out on the table where the sun shone through the east window of his kitchen, the syrup jar emanating golden rays across the butter dish, the pancake and eggs residue presenting a topographical wonder as the light shifted and churned. Jackson wore his usual white tee shirt and blue jeans, which I found sexy in their simplicity. His bright eyes searched mine as he reached across the table and took my hand. With earnestness, melodrama even, he declared, "The dream, my dream of a sailboat has died, the guys and I parted company. Well, Detroit was first to bail, and Lucky and Sheldon followed him right out the door."

The reality is that I hadn't tuned into how serious this sailing dream was for him, what with the demands of my own life of classes, kids, work, sleep, and our relationship. His vision of buying a sailboat and sailing off into a romantic dream with three friends hovered somewhere in the realm of not likely and not relevant. I just figured I'd deal with his leaving when it came to the forefront of my life. Right now, graduating, moving, and finding a teaching job to support the kids and myself was what was uppermost in my mind whenever I had a moment to "future trip."

"You know," he continued, "I felt like a fool and betrayed beyond belief by my so-called friends. When the blowout happened, and they all bailed, I stormed out, yelling, 'Fuck you all. You're just cowards and has-beens.' I've been thinking a lot and, well, I have a new vision." I cocked my head sideways like a curious bird, frowning and wondering.

"I was so pissed. I walked up to the top of Sehome Hill, and looking out across the bay, I saw the four of us, you, me, Ron, and Pam sailing together somewhere." He leaned forward as if to gather me to him, and his voice dropped to a hurried breathlessness. Words sifted out into the space around us and floated down to me, "….sail together……. dream….Ron and Pam…… ." He must have noticed my uncomprehending expression as the words hovered like a silent bee not yet buzzing into the flower of my mind. "Okay," he leaned back, his uncharacteristic hesitancy fading as his voice strengthened, "let me start again."

I laughed, "Yeah, okay good idea."

He shifted, almost shyly, if that could ever be said of Jackson. "What do you think of you and me buying a sailboat together, and with Ron and Pam, sail to the South Pacific, to Tahiti and the Marquesas, and then maybe on to Australia and settle down? I read they need English teachers there. We can follow this dream together. I'd much rather do it with you than the three guys anyway. I've been ruminating over this turn of events ever since it happened and nervous to ask you." He paused then inclining forward, almost jumping out of his chair, he pressed on, "Well, what you think?" I felt his eyes searching mine, penetrating as if expecting an answer right then.

"Shit. I mean, I don't know what to say. It's kinda unexpected, isn't it? I mean, I thought you guys were going through a little disagreement, and you'd all get over it and continue your dream. I'm in shock at what you're suggesting. That's what I think. I mean, I love that you are dreaming this new dream, and I'm in it; we're in it. But I'm not sure it fits with my dream for Ron and Pam and me."

We talked throughout the morning of the adventure, of an exit from the disaster we felt our country was heading toward with the Vietnam War, the Kent State killings, Watergate, environmental destruction. As we talked, our excitement grew, and by early afternoon, our parallel paths converged, and we found ourselves walking one path together into a tropical paradise of sun and sea and freedom. We acknowledged there would be potholes on the road we'd have to navigate, but right in that moment, hands clasped across the table, we vaulted the biggest hurdle, total commitment to each other and a future with the four of us as a family.

Though neither of us had ever been on a sailboat nor traveled beyond the borders of our country except for my jaunt to Tijuana, this monster dream captured us in its beneficent claws. That ecstatic moment of committing to each other, to the adventure beyond our known physical and psychological boundaries, left us as orgasmic as we had been that morning making love. We beamed, smirked even, at our complicity in creating this wild dream. Wide-eyed grins, the glow of our faces melding beyond the confines of our skin, there was only one act left to bolster our vision. With no words, we simply floated from our earthly chairs, leaving all the morning breakfast dregs arrayed on the table, and headed upstairs to the bedroom. Our lovemaking was passionate, our orgasms heralded by a gentle fervor that held the promise of a new uncharted landscape conceived in the beyond and channeled through our now united bodies and minds.

The *Four B's* was the sailboat's name: a thirty-seven-foot-long ketch, broad-beamed like a whale that boasted adequate living space for four. Though she wasn't going to win any ocean races, our new ship was incredibly sea-worthy and forgiving, and with the roomy interior, the boat fit us to a T. As a condition of the sale, Mr. Brown, the owner, agreed to sail the boat from Seattle to Bellingham, and teach us what he could during the voyage north. As we sailed through Puget Sound, Jackson and I did our best to follow our trajectory on the charts. Trying to match an island to an outline on the chart mystified me. Raising sails mystified me a little less as I could touch the ropes and cleats and not abstract them from a picture. I got a little seasick but fought it with every fiber of my being. That was simply and unequivocally inadmissible! Mr. Brown was a generous teacher, and I've no doubt, from a few bewildering questions we asked, he wondered about these two crazy dreamers who had just bought a sailboat with financing, knew nothing of the sea, and were planning a trip to the South Pacific!

We signed up for a sailing class offered through the college. Every Saturday, in a little 12' sailing dinghy, we learned the basics like shifting our weight and position and ducking our heads as the boom swung across the deck when we "came about," reading the telltales tied to the stays for wind direction, balancing the boat when it heeled over. To augment our learning, we invited friends, who were experienced sailors, to sail with us aboard the *Four B's*. We soon graduated to day trips with just the four of us aboard: Captain Jack, First Mate, Diane, and Second Mates Ron and Pam.

The uncreative, but no doubt meaningful name that the Browns, a family of four, had given our boat, wouldn't do for us, so we waited and played with various names but nothing fit. Then one of those Friday nights heading home from shooting pool with friends, Jackson said out of the blue, "**Ariadne.**"

"Oh, the name for our boat?" I asked.

"I don't know. It just came."

"That's it! **Ariadne** who laid the golden thread to lead Theseus out of the Minotaur's labyrinth. That's us, trying to find our way out of the labyrinth of our lives here in Bellingham," was my excited reply. And so she was christened. We didn't break champagne over the bow. Instead, we followed the unromantic bureaucratic process of changing the name with the Coast Guard, as she was a Coast Guard documented ship. It was a proud moment when our artist friend, Steve, palette in hand, painted the name **Ariadne** on both the port and starboard of the stern. And now, when the mysterious cry of the bird of freedom called to me, I would fly with those I loved on the wings of **Ariadne**.

When we bought the boat, Jackson moved aboard to save money. After a year or so, we began to talk about him living with the kids and me. Eventually, when my brother Don rented an apartment with his girlfriend, it felt like the right moment, and Jackson moved in with us. Much to my dismay, David and Jackson did not get along, and strife invaded our household. The tension weighed on all of us. I wished we could all live together, but that scenario was impossible. I felt so sad asking David to leave, but I knew I had to choose between the brother I loved and the man I was in love with. I chose Jackson. David is a sensitive soul, and though he insisted he understood, I felt his hurt and my own as well. We had been through so much together. I'd provided him a home; he'd been my primary support through the divorce, had been there when I needed a babysitter, had shared in household chores and was deeply involved with Ron and Pam. The three of us had been his close family, appreciating and loving him, sharing so many precious moments of laughter and plain silliness as well as challenges. Gratefully, the core of our relationship held firm, and today we continue to be a vital presence in each other's life. With my brothers no longer living with me, our family of four coalesced, and Jackson became a parent to Ron and Pam. Don Carlson would always be their dad, but Jackson was now the father in our unit.

In the summer of 1973, gathering our courage, with our new-found knowledge and trust in our sailing craft, we embarked on a 2-week long trip, just the four of us sailing among the San Juan Islands up into the Canadian Gulf Islands. It was everything we had imagined it would be. Lazy summer days sailing from one anchorage to another, Ron and Pam, proud to be part of the crew, executing their assigned jobs whether under sail or dropping anchor, the four of us meeting the demands of sailing in ever-changing wind and sea, the intriguing shoreline forays into unknown lands, all these essentials cloaked us in a carousel of family intimacy.

From the start of our voyage up the San Juan Straits into Desolation Sound, our senses had been under delightful assault – the sea colors and moods, the smell of the salt air, the taste of the mist on our tongues, our eyes feasting on this banquet nature was feeding us. Sailing into a protected cove, as soon as we'd set the anchors, Ron and Pam would excitedly climb into the dinghy to be the first to reconnoiter the land. Even today, 40 plus years later, they love to laugh and share stories of those adventures when they imagined themselves explorers, climbing in caves, hiking to a lookout. One such foray was on Sucia Island, one of the small islands in the San Juan group. We'd read of its storied history as a hideout for smugglers of everything from opium, whiskey, and even illegal Chinese labor. The kids were excited to explore; sure they'd find the bones of smugglers or at the very least, whiskey bottles. An hour or so later, they arrived excitedly back to **Ariadne** where Jackson and I reclined in the cockpit enjoying the early morning sights and sounds. "Come, come, we found a cave. You have to see it."

Jackson and I jumped into the dinghy and Ron rowed us ashore, where they led us to a cave they'd discovered and explored. Wondering what they had found, Jackson scrambled up a rock and his upper body disappeared. The cave had been big enough for Ron and Pam, but what a sight when Jackson, with his torso inside, freaked out at the low cave roof, contorted his body, and somehow, his head appeared beside his feet. The kids and I doubled over in laughter and then watching him twist himself out – well, we laughed uproariously till tears flowed. We never did learn exactly what the kids found inside. I suspect they'd sat in the cave and imagined themselves pirates and smugglers and concocted the plan to entice Jackson into their theater. Those were indeed idyllic days. Yet etched in my memory of those two weeks sailing northwest waters is the near disaster that almost destroyed our dream.

It was a gorgeous summer morning in Desolation Sound in British Columbian waters: light breezes, the water an unimaginable blue, soft sunlight filtering through wispy clouds, **Ariadne** cutting smoothly through the ocean. I was downstairs cooking breakfast when Jackson called out, "Wow, come see this." I scrambled up the hatch to join him and the kids in the cockpit. In the distance, spread the brilliantly illuminated snow-capped peaks of the Cascades. Forests along the shores, sparkling in varying shades of green, ran almost to the water's edge where narrow sandy beaches, dotted with driftwood, halted their march to the sea. But what had floored Jackson, and now took my breath away, was a magnificent sea stack that loomed straight out of the water, seeming to touch infinity itself. What a defiant act of nature that as wind and sea inexorably wore away the land, this rock had withstood the incessant battering and now towered beyond the reach of the pounding water.

"I'll go down and get breakfast on plates, and we can eat in the cockpit." I tossed back over my shoulder as I descended the hatch. Was it five minutes later, ten minutes? The scrapping crunch, the sudden halt that sent dishes flying as my sea legs sought purchase. The boat began to list, and the propeller spun crazily. I knew instantly we had run aground. But how was that possible? Weren't we in the middle of the channel? Jackson was instantly below. A quick review of the charts and there it was, Stacey Rock, an atoll that disappeared at high tide but lurked below - a sea creature ready to devour unsuspecting or novice sailors. We quickly ascertained the tide was running out, as minute by minute, the listing steepened. No time for long deliberation; we made decisions immediately.

In an adrenaline-stoked burst, I untied the lashings holding the dinghy, and though I can't explain how, I threw the dinghy over the railing. With a strangely quiet splash, the bottom of the dinghy landed on the waiting sea. Ron and Pam, the true sailors they had become, climbed below and quickly donned life vests. Coming back up the hatch, they carefully climbed out of the cockpit, holding tight to the cabin edge, balancing themselves on the angled surface. With knees bent, keeping their bodies low and stable, they joined me amidship. Two sets of big brown eyes stared at me, uneasy yet trusting. "Mom, can't we stay here with you?" Ron asked.

"Honey, Jackson and I have to give all our attention to righting the boat, so the best thing is for you and Pam to wait onshore. It's gonna be fine," I assured them. "When you're on the shore, you watch us, and when the boat's okay, you row back."

They looked doubtfully at each other, "Are you sure that's best?" Ron asked, "Maybe we can help?"

"Sweetie, the best help is for you two to be ashore, okay?"

"Come on, Ron," Pam asserted, "Mom's right. Let's do what she says." I felt their hearts in their eyes as they unflinchingly searched mine. I gazed back, my eyes held theirs, confident and unassailable.

"Okay. You're right, mom. It's best." With those words, Ron and then Pam unsteadily clamored overboard into the dinghy. I noted they chose to both sit amidships rather than Ron in the central rowing position and Pam in the aft seat. My heart swelled, recognizing they wanted to be close together for reassurance. I released the painter and watched proudly, and with fear and trembling as they each took an oar in hand and coordinated their oar strokes that dipped into the sea and emerged in unison. I waved as they rowed away and yelled across the water, "You're doing great - love you." They waved briefly and returned to their oar strokes. I realized I had complete faith in their abilities to meet the situation, and I allowed no further thought except that somehow things would be okay.

Jackson and I decided to get an anchor down in the hopes that it would hold **Ariadne** from listing too far over and taking on water. We dropped the anchor overboard, and it landed on the shelf on which we were perched. I jumped in after it and kept trying to dive to hook the anchor on the rock, but I couldn't get past the surface. "What the hell?" I muttered to myself.

Seeing me struggle, Jackson yelled, "Take off your float coat." Ah-h, good to know the float coats worked. I almost smiled as I tore it off and flung it onto the boat deck. This time I dove unimpeded and managed to secure the anchor, though we had no idea if that would work to hold the boat afloat. Surfacing, I looked to the shore and was relieved to see, off in the distance, the dinghy pulled up on the beach and two tiny figures outlined on a rock promontory. I held my emotions in check to meet this disaster, but seeing them safely ashore, I couldn't stop a few salty tears.

We came to call them, with great affection, the Keystone Cops. A motorboat with 4-5 Italian guys, out for a day's fishing, began circling us. How could they help, they wanted to know, gesticulating at us, at each other, yelling in English and Italian. They brought their boat alongside us and, scrambling over each other, retrieved a rope and handed it into our outstretched hands. Though Jackson and I held out little hope for success, we tied the rope to the stern of **Ariadne,** and they gunned their motor. The motorboat's bow reared up, and they nearly sank their boat. Meanwhile, **Ariadne**, our beautiful double-ended ketch, our home, and our dreaming future, was now listing to starboard at a dangerous angle.

I went below, and my gaze traveled here and there. I wondered what we should try to save. The fevered pitch of voices crashed through my reverie. I rushed up through the hatch. The Italian Keystone Cops were shouting and waving their arms wildly. There on the horizon, we saw the moving dot. With binoculars, it didn't take us long to identify a small inter-island cruise ship. The Italians gestured they would try to hail it to come to help us, and they sped off. Jackson and I stared hard as the motorboat grew smaller and smaller. We lost sight of it as it dipped and crested in the waves. Our eyes held fast to the ship on the horizon, waiting, waiting. We stood on each side of the cockpit, holding onto the boom of the mizzen mast as we strained to stay upright against the boat's list.

Did we detect a movement, a turning? My watering eyes momentarily blurred my vision. I blinked hard, held my breath, waited. I made out the ship's bow turning, turning, and now heading toward us in the dim beyond. Meanwhile, the relentless tide kept running out to sea. I watched seawater rush through the scuppers, the deck kissing the sea.

At last the cruise ship was within hailing distance. A voice came over the megaphone. "This is the captain. Who is the ship's captain?" I could make out the passengers lining the railing of the cruise ship, and my mind spun. "What an exciting tale they'll have to tell if this maneuver works!"

Jackson got our much smaller megaphone. He waved as he yelled, "My name is Jackson Southern. I'm the ship's captain."

"Captain, we will try to pull you off. Will you assume full responsibility for whatever happens? We will have no liability. Do you agree?"

"Yes, Yes, I agree. I agree and thank you." Tears of relief and hope flowed freely down my cheeks as we gazed across the water at the ship, our last glimmer of hope.

The Captain handed the Italians a thick hawser, and their boat skimmed over the surface to **Ariadne**. The voice came again, and we could just make out the figure of the Captain standing on the ship's bridge above where the passengers were ranged on the deck below. "Is your engine still operational?"

"Yes, though it was smoking, and I shut it down, " Jackson answered.

"I'd suggest you start it, and as soon as there's any movement, put it in reverse."

"Thank you. I'll be ready," Jackson yelled back. The Italians handed me the wet hawser. I quickly secured it to two strong cleats in the aft section of the boat. I checked my hitches twice and was satisfied they would hold.

The distant voice of the captain came across the sea between us, "Ok, here we go. I'm in reverse, and I'm going to try to pull you off." Jackson started our engine. All eyes were glued onto the hawser. We watched the rope begin to lift off the water's surface. An uncanny stillness enveloped us. I held my breath. The slack of the hawser tightened. As the rope stretched and tensed between the two boats, a deep thrum vibrated the air, and water flew from the hawser in all directions. We heard the ship's engine rev-up. Jackson pushed the gear lever into reverse and set the prop spinning in empty air. Slowly, oh so achingly slowly, we felt **Ariadne** shift beneath. Would she dip deeper onto her side or slide backward? The sound and vibration of scrapping echoed from her keel as it slid across the rock that held us in. Steadily our lopsided backward motion continued, the prop engaged, and then the boat was floating, sliding backward through the water. I dashed forward and reeled out the anchor line, giving slack to the anchor hooked on the rock below. Jackson shifted into neutral, not wanting to risk cutting the wrist-thick hawser that had gone slack. The Italians jumped up and down, nearly capsizing their boat again, and the passengers' cheers from the cruise ship sang across the water. I turned toward the shore and waved to Ron and Pam, and though I couldn't hear them, I had no doubt that Ron and Pam, patient and distant witnesses, were shouting too. Deep were the cheers in mine and Jackson's chests that though muted, were no less ecstatic.

I untied the hawser from the cleat hitches and passed the heavy rope to the Italians that had come alongside **Ariadne**. They began their run back to the inter-island cruiser as the ship wound in its hawser. Jackson took up the bullhorn, yelling across the ocean and airwaves, our profuse thanks to this anonymous captain and his savior ship. The Captain acknowledged our gratitude and sailed close enough to where we could see his salute as he turned his ship back to its route among the islands. The passengers waved and shouted; we waved back and raised our fists in thanks. When the Italians came alongside, we invited them aboard, but they were anxious to get back to their fishing as it was a competition day. We offered them money, some good Canadian whiskey we'd bought. No, no, they said, though we finally prevailed on them to accept the whiskey.

Turning toward shore, all of us saw Ron and Pam launching the dinghy. The plucky Italians took on one last task and sped toward them. Arriving beside the dinghy, they tossed a line. Ron caught the rope and secured it to a cleat just under the gunnel, and our Italian saviors towed them back to **Ariadne**. We waved goodbye, four pairs of hands in gratitude. It was a tearful reunion with Ron and Pam. There were no words. We could only stand together in the cockpit, the four of us embraced as one. No matter what happened in the future, time would never erase that moment. The depth of connection as family, sailors, adventurers would rest forever in each heart.

We were all shaken, and though we had planned to sail the whole day, we decided to find a place to check the boat damage. I took the tiller while Jackson went below and reviewed the charts. "Look at this," he said as he brought the chart into the cockpit. "There's an anchorage called Grace Harbor close-by. Can you believe it? Let's go there." We entered the little bay, taking in the ubiquitous green forests, the calm blue waters, and a sandy driftwood-dotted beach. When we'd set the anchor and sat together in the cockpit, we felt the grace of our lives. We all quickly abandoned our clothes and jumped in. The water was unusually warm due to the cove's protected nature and filled with transparent jellyfish, with which we decided to take our chances. We were grateful when none of us got stung! Jackson and I donned our snorkeling equipment and examined the damage to the keel. It would need repair, but we determined we could continue our trip.

The near-disaster hadn't dampened our adventurous spirit. Knowing we would one day leave the country, we wanted to show the kids America. To this end, we organized a grand family adventure to travel the country from west to east and back again.

As soon as I put the house up for sale in the late summer of 1973, we bought an old **Snap-on Tools** van, still displaying the logo, and set to work transforming it into a traveling home. The build-out we engineered boasted a tiny kitchen, table and benches that folded up in the daytime, as well as a double bed for the adults. The kids would sleep in a two-person tent they would pitch each day. A friend welded a carrier atop the van, and we attached a 4-bike rack to the front. What a sight that van was! The four of us excitedly planned the trip – well, Jackson and I did with the kid's full approval. We would travel through national parks and national monuments and camp beside streams, pulling off the road until we found a campsite.

For three months that fall, we drove up mountains, the van chugging at a snail's pace across the Cascades, climbing the Teton Range in the Rocky Mountains, and then going at record speeds across miles and miles of corn and barley fields in the Midwest. This trip was the most trouble-free harmonious time I have ever experienced as a family. It felt like we were playing hooky from the world with no time demands, no place demands, no work or school demands. No schedule as we rode our bikes through Yellowstone Park, swam in streams, floated in hot thermal pools, explored caves of the east and southeast, and camped and hiked in Zion and Bryce Canyon parks. We spent days in New York City, Washington D.C., Boston, and Philadelphia: all such storied centers whose historical heft didn't exist on the west coast. There were brief moments - kids picking at each other from time to time, Jackson and I impatient with them, the kids resistant to the school work their teachers had sent with us (Turned out, even with limited "school time," they were ahead of their classes when they rejoined them in November.), the pelting rain at Niagara Falls that left us cold and wet with no place to camp - but those tiny tensions served only as accents to the escapade. It would take a travelogue book to describe all the incredible places and generous people we discovered as we drove and grew and thrived as a family on this farewell tour of our country.

We lived our last year in Bellingham aboard **Ariadne**. I completed my English teaching degree, Jackson had quit his job at the end of the year and completed his master's degree in creative writing, and we both spent every spare moment preparing the boat. Our frugality, including my nest egg from the house sale, reached heroic proportions as we set aside every penny we could for the voyage. With our expenses reduced and a part-time job at the university, I gratefully quit my nursing home job. My long dark brown hair now profusely streaked with gray, the black raccoon circles around my eyes bore witness to the exhaustion I had denied in order to carry on. Gratefully, during that year aboard **Ariadne**, my body recuperated, and in June 1974, I proudly accepted my B.A. in English, graduating magna cum laude. I was gratified that, against all odds, I had managed to fulfill my educational dream. A dream I'd only accomplished through the early companionship and support of my brother, David, the mature acceptance and love of Ron and Pam, the love and belief in me of Jackson, and my grandmother, whose night-time care of my children, put my mind at ease.

As my mind drifts lazily across the landscape of that last year of Puget Sound life, three events, two to add a mind-boggling perspective to the past, and one a harbinger of a far-flung future, stand out vividly.

On a Saturday morning, Jackson and I worked on the boat while Ron and Pam played on the rocks around the harbor. A figure appeared walking the length of the dock where our boat was moored. I heard someone call my name, "Diane?" and looked up. He was much thinner, balder, but there was no mistaking the man ambling slowly down the dock, Earl, Don's father.

"Earl?" I questioned. "Wow, hello, what brings you here? I'm amazed you found us. How are you?" He drew alongside **Ariadne,** where I stood on the deck. "Come aboard, come aboard."

He hesitated, so I jumped onto the dock and extended my hand. He reached out, and we shook hands. "Good to see you, Earl. The kids are playing on the shore. I'll go track them down."

"No, no, it's all right. I just have a moment. I brought something for Ron and Pam." He handed me a brown shopping bag. I peeked in and recognized what was in the bag. I reached in and pulled out two brand-new float coats.

"Oh my god, these are great. They're perfect and the sizes look right. They'll love the colors. These are the best gifts ever. I know the kids will be thrilled. Thank you so much." From the shores of time, his next words blew me away.

"I just want you to know that I think it's wonderful what you are doing, going on this sailing trip with Ron and Pam. It's remarkable, and I wish you well and safe journeys. What an experience for them, well for all of you."

I was speechless for a moment. "Thank you, Earl. I appreciate the gifts and your words." I sensed Jackson close by. "Earl, I want you to meet my partner, Jackson." Jackson popped out of the cockpit, leaped to the dock beside me. "Jackson, Earl, the kids' grandfather."

Jackson extended his hand, "Nice to meet you."

I held up the float coats for him to see, "Look what Earl brought for the kids."

We chatted for a few minutes as if this was the most ordinary of events, said our good-byes, and I watched in wonder as he walked along the dock to the shore and into history. I turned to Jackson, "Amazing, I mean, I'm blown away. People do change. I couldn't have imagined this in a million years."

During that summer, there was another visitation from family. "Ahoy there." I recognized the voice and stuck my head out of the hatch.

"Papa. What are you doing here?"

"Well, we're in Bellingham to see Pop. I'm here with Marlene, my new wife. I brought her to meet Pop and other family, like you. Pop told me about your plans, so here we are. Can we come aboard?"

"Oh yes, sorry. Come on aboard, Jackson is below, and the kids are playing on the shore."

The two of them climbed aboard and came below. "Jackson, you remember my father, right?" Not waiting for his reply, I added, "This is Papa's new wife, Marlene."

"Jackson shook hands with both of them and invited them to sit down at the table. "What can I get you to drink? A beer, water?"

"A beer would be great. Thanks."

I opened four beers, passed them around, and sat down beside Jackson. We were all a little awkward. Papa broke the ice, "Nice boat. What are your plans? Pop thought you'd be leaving this summer. Is that right?"

Jackson grabbed the conversation football and ran with it. I was happy to sit and listen as he outlined our plans and dreams. Then I addressed the elephant in the room, "Well, Papa, the last time we saw you was when Jackson and I visited you in Dayton, and you were married to Gladys. I remember we all went out to a restaurant/bar for dinner and drinks and dancing. I don't think Gladys appreciated us just dropping in! I remember she wanted to show me a letter mom had written to you asking you to come back to her. Right?" Papa nodded his agreement. (When Jackson and I left their place, I'd done mental calculations and realized that mom had written the letter just before she and Bill married in a quiet, very private ceremony - only the two of them and two friends from their bowling league to witness. Bill, like Gladys, was jealous of Mom's family and didn't want us there.)

"Well, what happened?" I prodded him.

Aided by a scrapbook they'd brought with them, full of pictures, scraps of paper, napkins, and even tickets to dog races, they told the story of their flight from Dayton, Oregon, to Mexico.

Marlene and her husband had owned the restaurant/bar where Papa and Gladys had taken Jackson and me out to eat when we'd visited them. Marlene tended the bar, and her husband managed the restaurant. It seems that Dayton and Marlene had fallen in love, and they planned a cowardly get-away. One dark night while all of Dayton, Oregon slept, including Gladys and Marlene's husband, Dayton stole Gladys's Mercedes, picked up Marlene on the street outside her home, drove to the restaurant, and the two of them cleaned out the safe and headed south. They paused only at roadside rest areas for Dayton to get an hour or so of sleep, and they drove on until they crossed the border into Mexico. Though Gladys hadn't called the police, she quickly hired private detectives to find them. Papa and Marlene had planned their get-away well, and even her detectives couldn't trace them. Once in Mexico, they found a justice of the peace and "got married." Of course, it wasn't legal, but it eased their guilty consciences.

When they visited us, they'd both started the divorce process. I learned later that Gladys got her car back and made sure Dayton got none of her money. Marlene's husband settled accounts with Marlene, allowing her to keep the money they had stolen in exchange for her signing over her share of the restaurant and their home. Dayton and Marlene were legally married on Valentine's Day, 1975.

The last event began one morning when our close friends, Fred and his girlfriend Mandy, joined Jackson and me and we set sail for the short jaunt over to a cove on Lummi Island. We dropped anchor, and then we dropped acid. It was the first time any of us had taken LSD, and that day, as I sat outside in the cockpit under a summer sun, **Ariadne** cocooning us, I watched what in my everyday reality I would call trees morph into energy that danced. It was the universe dancing, pure fibers of energy with which I merged. I never wanted to leave that place of energy, but as inevitably happens, the LSD wore off, and achingly the formless dancing energy slowly transformed into trees. I was once again rocking gently in the anchorage, but the drug had cracked open a door. I came back to our consensus reality, but a remembering had swum up through the layers of ego, and I was blessed with the sure knowledge, like thousands of others, that this perception, this state of being, was within the realm of the possible. Unknown to me at the time, this glimpse into formless dancing energy was a door that would be held open for the future.

At last, degrees finished, boat outfitted, a written agreement with Don to reduce child support so he could put aside money to fly Ron and Pam back to the northwest for visits, and homeschooling materials stowed away, we were ready. Because it was our first time out on the big horizon-to-horizon ocean, we decided to make this first trip without Ron and Pam in our nervousness and anticipation of something vast and unknown. They were hugely disappointed but also happy that they would have two weeks with Don and then drive to San Francisco with the wife of one of our crewmembers. A crew of three joined Jackson and me for this long-distance maiden voyage from Neah Bay, Washington, to San Francisco, California. Onboard **Ariadne**, a day before we cast off, we listened and cheered as Richard Nixon resigned as president on Aug 9, 1974. It gave us hope the ship of state would right itself.

The day we finally sailed out of Neah Bay was a surreal dream. Blue August skies, light winds blowing to fill the sails, rippling white caps, **Ariadne,** moving like an ark carrying us out into the sea, beyond the sight of land, ultimately surrounded by 360 degrees of ocean. I was awed to be aboard this minuscule floating island on an infinite sea of blue that only ended where it met the horizon. My eyes followed the sky to the sea, and I imagined I could almost see the curve of the earth. We were anywhere, everywhere, outside of time: Noah sailing to save the world from God's wrath; the Polynesians sailing to the east where they would find Hawaii; Jackson and I and crew of three, sailing into a dream. Sailing about 100 nautical miles west to put distance between us and the land, we turned south.

Three days out, the trip's real challenge came as the winds and waves grew ominously bigger and stronger. We lowered sails, leaving only the stays'l raised, and 12 hours into the storm, we lowered even that sail. Our turns at the tiller were exhausting, and as each one came off shift, we would have a cup of hot coffee or chocolate and collapse into a restless sleep as the boat's pitching threw us from side to side. We were grateful for the bunk's sideboards that kept the sleeper from being tossed out of bed to crash on the floor. When safely through the storm, now feeling like seasoned sailors, we all laughed whole-heartedly when one of the crewmembers described Jackson sitting at the table as the storm raged around us. "Hey man, you were our captain, and you were down below reading what one should do in a big storm. I mean, how crazy was that? I have to say, it made me a little nervous. I guess you read the right page when you decided to put out a sea anchor cause here we are!" Jackson joined in the laughter.

Seven days after our departure from Neah Bay, Washington, having sailed unerringly through a storm with 20-foot waves, navigated our journey with a sextant, caught tuna that we cooked and ate with relish, there, beckoning through a light fog, rose the majestic Golden Gate Bridge. Jackson secured his camera forward of the mainsail, and as we sailed under the Golden Gate into San Francisco Bay, the camera snapped a picture of the five of us smiling proudly in the cockpit with the bridge soaring overhead like a reddish-orange rainbow. Gazing to starboard, I took in Golden Gate Park, the beaches, and the waterfront. I wondered how much I would share of my San Francisco story with Ron and Pam. Should I invite them to slip back in time and meet the 18-year-old Diane? It made me a little nervous.

As soon as we secured **Ariadne** in San Francisco harbor, we found a payphone – they were on nearly every street corner. The first call was to Ron and Pam. "We've arrived safe and sound," I yelled into the phone, ecstatic and relieved to hear their voices – I had kept my own counsel when we left for the vast ocean, not daring to admit the whisper that I might never hug them again. They arrived three days later. Together, we ate chocolate at Ghirardelli Square, wiped the juices running from our mouths as we devoured monster hamburgers at a place called Wimpey's, and gorged on Japanese food in Japan town. We spent days in the park, took the cable cars. Yes, we did all the sightseeing that Peggy and I had done so many years ago. The delight the kids found in the sights, smells, and tastes of the city amplified my nostalgic revisiting of a long-ago time.

The kids would get their offshore sailing legs on the trip to Morro Bay from San Francisco. We'd intended to make a day trip to Monterey, stay a few days, and then go onto Morro Bay. However, as we approached Monterey, ten to fifteen-foot waves were breaking over the deck as the wind whistled through the sails and rigging. We were sailing tight to the wind and agreed that we should head out to sea to be prudent. When we were a good 25 miles out, we headed south once again. It was a long night with Jackson and I taking turns at the tiller while the other grabbed a few winks of sleep. Fortunately,

I now had prescription pills for seasickness, so I was relieved not to be vomiting and miserable.

As the waves lifted the stern, I watched in wonder the glowing, glittering phosphorescence in the rushing water. I listened to the wind whistling through the rigging, rhythm and sound that I could get lost in except for the demands of keeping the boat on course and aligned with the white-crested swells. Though the wind and waves whispered of danger, the ship answered that whisper with one of its own - its broad beam, deep keel, new galvanized rigging, its forgiving nature. Alert as my attention was to boat and sea, my eyes were caught by the hatch cover sliding open. Ron's head appeared. I saw his eyes glazed over, his face white, no smile graced his normally cheerful demeanor. He opened the hatch doors and climbed out of the cabin into the cockpit. He stood up, shut the doors, and pulled the hatch shut. I was proud of his sailing knowledge and his care to follow the protocol the kids had both learned, knowing intuitively that in a storm, battening down the hatches was crucial.

Pam shared with Jackson a constitution well suited to motion; no seasickness ever turned food to vomit. But Ron suffered from seasickness as I did. He sat in the cockpit across from me, his face ashen and eyes glazed. He turned suddenly, leaned over the cockpit to projectile vomit green bile, the only thing left in his churning belly. His pleading eyes sought mine. His voice was soft and muted, "Mom, we have to go to land." He said it so simply, like, well, this is the obvious thing to do. The simplicity of his statement, his demeanor sad and sick, tugged at my heart, and my throat choked up at my inability to make my child's world a better place. Always, in those moments when I couldn't protect my children from disappointment and pain when I had to accept a difficult situation, I felt as helpless as they. That I could not protect them from the exigencies of life was the most painful part of child-rearing. With my head, I knew that was part of life, of being on the earth, but my mother's heart found it almost unbearable at times, and this was one of those times.

"We will as soon as we can, honey. Come here, help me steer."

I pulled him close beside me, putting his hand on the tiller to divert him. "Try to keep your eyes on the horizon," I urged. It helped, but he was so seasick that the diversion didn't last for long. Once again, he leaned over the railing as his stomach churned. "Come on, let's go down, and I'll give you a suppository to settle your stomach." Though the requisite hours hadn't passed between when I should administer the suppositories, I guessed he'd vomited it all out anyway. I called Jackson to take the tiller, and Ron followed me below. The boat's motion in the closed confines of the cabin was predictably amplified. I barely kept myself from vomiting as I held tight to the railings along the bulkhead. I got Ron into his bunk, inserted the suppository, covered him, smoothed his hair from his face, and kissed his sad face, "I love you. You'll rest easier now, and when you awaken, we'll be anchored at Morro Bay, and this will just be a memory we'll laugh about. Okay sweetie?" He managed a wan smile and nodded. "I'm on deck; call me if you need anything." I hugged him and headed out of the fo'c'sle, through the main cabin, up the ladder to the cockpit.

Jackson and I sat together for a while, and the storm began to abate, winds softening their fury. We raised the mainsail that we had lowered to half-mast. Having tracked our speed and heading, we guessed we were pretty much to Morro Bay's latitude and headed east toward land.

As the morning dawned and we approached land, we were dismayed to find ourselves lost in a blinding fog. The saving grace was that the winds had fled. Consequently, we lowered all sails, turned the engine on, and motored cautiously. The low groan of the foghorns wandered aimlessly in the miasma, their location undetectable. I stood on the bowsprit searching for rocks, for foghorns, for buoys, other boats, as Jackson navigated. It was hard to guess exactly where the sounds were coming from, which buoy we were passing. We motored slowly in extended circles until, like a heavenly grace, the sun shone enough to dissipate the fog, and there it was looming portside, Morro Bay Rock! We gasped to realize how close we were. I silently said a prayer of thanksgiving to the spirits of harbor and sea that had brought us through the night and safely into port.

Once we'd dropped anchor, the four of us sat in the cockpit under the early morning sun, held and cradled by **Ariadne**, anchored in the safe harbor of the bay. On the seaward side, the rolling silhouette of soft dunes rose, broken only by The Rock. Fronting the bay on the other side was the town of Morro Bay, with dinghies tied up to its dock. The warmth of the scene called to us, but we took our time, letting stomachs settle, cleaning up the deck and down below, changing out of our damp sea-sprayed clothes into what we jokingly called among ourselves, our town clothes. The kids untied the dinghy from where it was lashed to the deck, and Jackson and I lowered it overboard, tying the painter to a cleat. Jackson climbed over the cable railing first and steadied the dinghy while Ron and Pam scrambled under the railing and lowered themselves carefully, sitting side by side in the aft seat of the boat. I handed the oars to Jackson. Untying the painter, I jumped into the bow seat of our Grumman sailing dinghy, pushed off from **Ariadne's** hull, and Jackson rowed us to land.

We found a local restaurant and, drawn in by the delicious aroma drifting through the open door and the lively talk, we entered and found a booth by the window. After we'd all ordered fresh strawberry pancakes, we watched the people walking by and made up seafaring stories about them. God, it felt good to be sitting on solid ground, drinking coffee or hot chocolate and gazing across the table at Ron and Pam. My heart burst with love and pride at how we had weathered this trip with its unexpected storm. I reached under the table and squeezed Jackson's hand, he turned to look at me, and I knew he felt this special moment in his particular way.

"Mom, mom, look!" Pam laughingly pointed through the window at a man on a bicycle with a chicken in the basket as well as one on his shoulder. Her delight was contagious.

"Here you go," the waitress brought us our food, all four plates balanced on her arms. "Be right back with the butter and syrup." Yum yum, it was the most delicious food ever to fill empty stomachs.

We would spend three months in Morro Bay, where the four of

us played in the sand dunes, flinging ourselves from the peaks, momentarily airborne, letting go of fear as our bodies landed in the fine forgiving sand. Mornings, the kids delighted in going to the docks to fish. On the first day, when they tied off the dinghy and climbed onto the pier, the fishermen sitting with their lines in the water questioned them as to why they weren't in school. Once Ron and Pam pointed to **Ariadne** and reassured them they were homeschooled, one older man took it upon himself to teach them to fish. Ron and Pam were glowing on mornings when they brought home fish to fry. When the kids went to shore, Jackson and I would touch into the ecstasy of our lovemaking, and I would touch the longing for the vastness.

In Morro Bay, living a free and easy lifestyle, we could almost feel we were outside of social and commercial agreements. Jackson and I identified ourselves as members of the hippy culture. What mattered most was love and imbuing Ron and Pam with an inner compass of responsibility for their choices rather than guiding them to adhere to societal rules. We worked to find a balance to living both within and outside of the consumer culture. We didn't hide from the kids that we occasionally used mushrooms and marijuana to reach states of awareness that gave us a window into what might be possible for human beings. When they were curious about marijuana, we allowed them to take puffs from a joint. (As adults, neither Ron nor Pam would show an interest in marijuana.)

Toward the end of the three months in Morro Bay, a tiny crack appeared between Jackson and me. It started as fun and play when Ron, reading Huck Finn, decided to make a corncob pipe like his young hero of adventure and misadventure. Being a natural scavenger, Ron soon found a hollow twig and then insisted I buy corn on the cob so he could dry out a section. It took him a few tries, but he persevered and one day proudly showed his pipe. Conjuring his best Huck Finn voice, he asked, "Ma'am ya have eny tabb'ky round this here place?"

I smiled, "Well, I think we can dig up a li'l sumpin' round this here tub." I went to our stash and pulled out a bit of tobacco we kept around for making horns of plenty (a large cigarette of tobacco and marijuana).

"Well, tank ya ma'am, yu'all mind if I sit in yur cockpit and smoke a few puffs."

"No young man, not at all." I guessed he was unsure about this whole smoking process, but he packed the tobacco in, set a match to it, and lo and behold, the tobacco burned, and he drew in a deep puff. The pipe was a success. He barely had time to smile before his choking and coughing turned his face red as he gasped for breath. When he could breathe, he joined us in our laughter and declared that henceforth, lighting it wasn't necessary. He would simply hold it between his lips and teeth and experience the effect of a pipe in his mouth.

His experiment got Jackson started. By the end of the evening, Ron and Pam had agreed with him that it would be a grand adventure to sail the little dinghy around the point, dock the dinghy at the state park where we took our 25 cent showers every other day, find a campsite, pitch a tent and cook over a fire, just like Huck Finn and Jim going down the river. The three of them began to plan the fantastic voyage; what the kids would take, what they'd eat, how they'd cook, and when was the best time to sail or, if no wind, to row around the point that was about a quarter mile from the boat. The plan was that they'd spend the night and come home in the morning for breakfast. I wasn't worried about their safety. They were now 12 and 10. They knew about the water, were good sailors and strong swimmers, having learned as small children. In the state park, we had all come to know the rangers, and so, my mind insisted, the park was a safe place, but in my heart, I was a little nervous and hesitant. A disquiet arose as I listened to them making plans. "Are you two sure you want to do this," I queried, "really sure?"

"Yes, yes," they answered in unison. "It'll be fun," Pam added. Ron solemnly, like the big brother and protector he was, nodded, "It's an adventure we're going on all by ourselves!" I could sense their excitement. Meantime, Jackson and I began to make our plans for the night. We'd decided to have one of our favorite meals, salad, steak, baked potatoes, and wine, and then get stoned and make love all night long. We carefully guarded our secret plans.

The afternoon arrived for their departure. That morning, Jackson had gone into town to get the food and fare for our night and theirs. Like all the days in Morro Bay, the afternoon sun was brilliant, and the afternoon breeze soothing. By evening the breeze would die down, and the fog would undoubtedly roll in, but the afternoon was full of good cheer as we all set about loading supplies into the dinghy. There was a lot of stuff, considering they'd be gone for less than 24 hours. As the hour of departure approached, I sensed their excitement, and I was already tasting the evening with just Jackson and me in a hedonistic descent into the sensual experiences we loved to share and bring to each other.

We cheerfully gave Ron and Pam big hugs as they climbed into the dinghy with the gear stowed away. Ron took the tiller, corncob pipe in his mouth, looking every bit the captain. Pam raised the little sail and tied off the sheet, and keeping her balance, sat amidship as the sail filled. We were all smiles as Jackson and I waved goodbye from the deck and they from the dinghy as it ran downwind.

We went below, "Where shall we start?" Jackson smiled invitingly as he grabbed me and held me close. There was a hunger in both of us. He was a fantastic father-friend to the kids, but he was also my ardent lover, and we had all been living together on the boat now, with no weekends away, since leaving Washington. While we'd always found times to join our bodies in as much ardor and lust as ever, we hadn't had a whole evening, night, and morning, to make love, orgasm, pause, smoke a joint, laugh and talk and tantalize each other until he grew hard and I was wet with longing, and then bury ourselves in the other.

"Let's make love right now," I whispered, "and then have a glass of wine before dinner and watch the sunset from the cockpit." We knew that we would become uncorked later in the evening, so we simply and hungrily undressed each other and made sweet passionate love, a little appetizer before the main course we knew awaited us. We dressed, well, partially, just shirts and underwear. Jackson uncorked the bottle, poured us a glass of wine. I opened a bag of pretzels, and we ascended to the cockpit. The sky was a swirl of oranges and yellows and streaks of purple as the shadows began to fall over the town, the dunes, turning the bay from a bright blue to a quieter evening gray. I marveled at this moment of both satisfaction and anticipation.

The night was almost upon us, "You hungry?" I asked.

"Yes! Let's get to it," Jackson replied excitedly. We were about to descend below and cook and then play in our voluptuous garden of sensuality when we heard the call across the water, "Ahoy there, mates." The dinghy glided through the water as Ron skillfully rowed toward us till they were alongside the boat. Ron attempted a few words in the Huck Finn vernacular he loved, but he couldn't carry it off. "We couldn't find a campsite," Pam said.

"And besides, we didn't want to leave the dinghy tied up all night," Ron added. But I read relief in their eyes at being back to the safety of the boat as night descended. Nuanced and obvious feelings overlay each other.

Jackson couldn't hide his anger and frustration. "That doesn't make sense," he said accusingly. "The park is never full, especially now that it's September. And I know you can tie the dinghy to the dock. We do it every time we go to take a shower. What you're saying doesn't ring true to my ears." His accusation was harsh and unyielding. I saw the kids' shoulders drop, their heads bowed. Ron pulled the oars out of the water, Pam, standing in the dinghy stern, hung onto the scupper of **Ariadne** to keep them from drifting away. Deflated and chastised, neither of them spoke. "Well, you two better get everything out of the dinghy and put away before it's completely dark," Jackson added as he turned and stomped down the ladder disappearing into the hatch. I followed him below.

Seated at the table, he fumed aloud, "Damn this sucks. Fuck I hate this. I can't stand not having time with just you." His nostrils flared; teeth clenched.

I bit my lip against the words I wanted to hurl at him because I could feel how beyond disappointment he was. "I'm going topside. We'll talk later."

"Come on aboard," I said to Ron and Pam, where they sat in the dinghy, unsure what to do next. "Let's get the things unloaded. I'm glad you chose to come back since it didn't all seem right to you. Good for you. You two hand things up to me, and we'll get it all down below, so it stays dry. We'll sort it all out in the morning." We worked together quickly, finishing up in the dark. As they climbed aboard, I hugged them both tight. "You're brave and wonderful adventurers." I added, "Don't mind Jackson; he's just grumpy." Sneaking peeks below, we saw Jackson sitting at the table holding his head and moaning.

"Are you okay?" I asked going to him.

"I'm fine," he mumbled. "I hit my head on the bulkhead."

"Oh well, okay, just a minute." I turned to Ron and Pam, where they stood in the cockpit, surrounded by the gear we'd loaded up just a few hours earlier. "Let's move the gear down below and get something to eat." The kids were glad for a task to take them out of the tension. Ron, always the peacemaker, tried to make jokes with Jackson as they stowed the gear. His efforts were met with stony silence, Jackson's angry glare flung into the very air of the cabin. When we all nervously ignored him, he sighed noisily, "I'm going up on deck."

Pam ignored him, "What's for dinner?"

With forced cheerfulness, I suggested we all eat steak and hot dogs.

"You were going to have steaks?" Pam demanded.

Jackson paused on the stairway, "Yeah, we were, so what!"

Pam knew not to push it. "I was just asking."

I jumped in, "Well, cooking steaks over an open fire wouldn't make sense, would it? Hot dogs are the perfect campfire food!"

And though I too was saddened that Jackson and I wouldn't have our much-needed night alone, I was secretly relieved that the kids would be with us on the boat that night. Right now, however, I needed all my skill and love to navigate this moment. Taking strength from the reassuring motion of the boat, I poured Jackson and me another glass of wine and set about in the galley. Over good food and chatter, we found our family's equilibrium. Once the kids were asleep, Jackson and I salvaged what we could as we fell into our passion for each other, even if a little more subdued than we'd imagined.

A few days later, over breakfast, we decided to sail onto the next port, Goleta, where my father lived with his fourth wife, Marlene. I, his favorite daughter, was about to sail into his life and inspire Dayton's boating ambitions.

We motored out of the harbor, then set our sails for a southward trajectory, the tension with Jackson swallowed into an abundance of new experiences. We prepared for a rough sail around the infamous Point Conception where winds from three directions battled for supremacy as they blew across the ocean's surface, affecting the near-coast currents and challenging sailors with 20-25 knot winds and fifteen to twenty-foot seas. As the local fishermen and sailors in Morro Bay informed us, "It's going to be a beautiful sail or a hellish sail." They suggested that wind and waves were usually calmer at night, so we set sail just as darkness fell. Clearing the buoys, we raised full sail in favoring winds in a beautiful infinite starry night.

What we all remember most of that night was the cigar-shaped light that appeared in the night sky. "Let's wake the kids up," Jackson insisted. "This is a once-in-a-lifetime event. We're seeing UFOs."

I went below into the fo'c'sle and woke Ron and Pam. "Come quickly on deck. There's something you gotta see."

Stepping into the cockpit, Pam looked up where we pointed and in a voice filled with awe, she whispered, "I never dared dream it possible." We all nodded in agreement, and with our eyes turned to the heavens, we sat together and stared in wonder, as five brilliant white objects left the cigar-shaped mother ship and in an instant, disappeared out of sight. Startled at the swiftness of their departure, we dared not take our eyes from the big cigar-shaped object that hovered. About 45 minutes later, we saw three of the five objects return and merge with the big ship. We wondered about the other two. Had they returned? Had we just missed them? And then, our eyes glued onto the object, we saw it accelerate across the sky and instantly disappear. We talked excitedly into the night until fatigue finally recaptured Ron and Pam, and they went below to sleep. I soon followed while Jackson took the first watch. I would relieve him in a couple of hours.

As dawn broke, we dropped anchor in Goleta, neighboring harbor to Santa Barbara. With everything made fast, we clamored into the dinghy and motored to shore through the rough surf that broke quickly on a steep sandy slope. Jackson punched the motor, and as the little dinghy lifted, he killed the motor and yanked it out of the water. I jumped out into the surf, grabbed the painter, and hung on while the waves washed out, nearly pulling the rope from my hands. At the moment when the dinghy bottomed out on the sand, Jackson and the kids leaped out, and we pulled the dinghy up onto the shore and dragged it to the small dock beyond the waterline. High and dry, we hooked the cable around a post, passed it through motor and transom, and secured it with a lock. Grabbing the oars, we set off, kicking and dragging bare feet through the warm sand. At the edge of the soft sand beach, where we saw a path going up a small, wooded hillside, we stopped to put on our shoes. As we brushed the sand from our feet, we discovered big clots of tar overlaid with sand stuck to the bottoms of our feet. No matter how hard we brushed, the black globs refused our vigorous strokes to dislodge them. "What the hell," Jackson exclaimed.

Taking liberties, knowing they could get away with it at this moment, Ron and Pam echoed him, "What the hell!" The tar felt like an added insult to the oil rigs that ruinously spotted the shoreline. We tore leaves from the low bushes at the edge of the sand and stuck them to the tar so we could don our shoes.

Cresting the hill, we quickly found the duplex where Papa lived with Marlene and her teenage daughter. We had just settled in for a few weeks' stay when Dorothy, Jackson's mom, called him at my dad's to tell him she had to have a second open-heart surgery back in Washington.

"Ok, mom, I'm on my way. When is the surgery?" They talked for a few more minutes, and when he hung up, I saw the worry on his face. "You heard, right? Mom needs surgery again, so I'm going north."

"I'm so sorry, Jackson. How does she seem?"

"She sounds good and optimistic. I wish you could go with me, but of course, you'll need to be here with the boat. Are you okay with that?"

"Yes, yes, of course. We've been here a week or so, and we've securely anchored **Ariadne**. We'll be fine. You just need to be with Dorothy, and if there should be a problem, I've got my dad to help me. I'll miss you like crazy, you know, but I'm glad you'll be there for your mom. She needs you for sure. And I'll be waiting with open arms!" I borrowed Papa's car, and the kids and I drove Jackson to the airport the next day.

Pam was fed up with homeschooling. Sometimes she'd say to me, "You're my mom, not my teacher, so I don't have to do what you say." Inevitably, we'd butt heads over her refusal. Ron was also reluctant to do assignments. Nevertheless, he applied himself in a desultory way. With their agreement, I found a charter school in Santa Barbara and enrolled them. The experimental school matched their spirits, and they made friends – social interactions that the two of them, Pam especially, had been missing. Weekdays I'd row them to shore, and they'd walk the mile or so to school. Ron discovered a unicycle at a swap meet we'd gone to with Papa and Marlene. He practiced for hours and one day proudly rode it to school, earning admiration from classmates. In this separation from Jackson, I found myself enjoying time with just Ron and Pam. This awareness came as a surprise, and I purposefully ignored any message my observation might carry.

On a Saturday morning, I stood at the sink in Papa's kitchen washing dishes, my thoughts floating with the soap bubbles. I noted how, with Jackson gone, the kids and I were having dinner most nights with Papa and Marlene, and then the three of us would head back to the boat for sleep and morning breakfast. I would often join my father and Marlene for gin and tonics in the evening. "Ah-hah," I mused to myself, "this was how he'd managed to bring his drinking under control. He had a wife who drank with him, i.e., would join him as a high-functioning alcoholic. They'd have a gin and tonic in the evening when Papa arrived home from work and then a beer or wine with dinner. Notwithstanding their evident love for each other, I surmised Marlene's on-going participation in Papa's drinking, as well as their shared devotion to each other, avoided the drunken rages and violence that had so marred my childhood.

My feelings were mixed - caught between the past disdain and mistrust of Papa and this reformed version of Dayton, I had to admit to myself I rather enjoyed his company as long as we kept things light. I witnessed how Marlene loved him in a way none of the previous women in his life had. It hit me that Dayton had been surrounded by women who, WITH JUST CAUSE, feared and hated him during the years of my childhood. He was kept outside, and he kept himself outside, the circle of whatever love dwelled within the walls of 621-23rd Street. I pulled myself up short with these thoughts of compassion and understanding, smothering them with remembrances of the nights of dread, tears, and terror. I wasn't ready to forgive and forget.

"Mom?" Startled, my eyes focused from my inner musings to Ron and Pam, surprised to find myself, not at the sink at 621-23rd Street, but in Papa's kitchen, my hands resting in now tepid dishwater. They'd been outside weeding the garden, a weekend task that their grandfather had assigned to them. Though I found myself arguing, just on principle, with my father, about most everything else, I hadn't argued with him when he suggested the task for the kids. It gave them something to do, and my belief aligned with his, that it's good that children contribute to the household in some way. "We're done. Can we go swim?"

"Yes, yes, let's go, sounds wonderful. Get your suits on and grab some towels. I'll get the sun lotion and some cans of soda." We walked the two blocks to the gorgeous beach of fine sand, stepping around the tar blobs that dotted the otherwise pristine beach. As we swam together in the deep blue, slightly warm Pacific, I felt the waves cleansing me, washing over me in ripples of still whispers. I floated on my back, listening to the kids' playful calls and laughter.

I began to shiver from my motionless floating, "I'm getting out," I called to the kids, "be careful, okay? Don't keep following the waves out too deep." I'd seen before how they would go further and further out following waves, then suddenly they were treading water to keep their heads above the pounding surf.

"Okay, we'll be careful."

"And stay together!" I ordered them.

"Okay, okay, we will. Don't worry. We can swim, remember?" They laughed as they turned from me just in time to jump a wave with abandon and dive under the next one. Though they had learned to swim, tread water, and hold their breath underwater from an early age, I still worried. Shaking away morbid thoughts, gazing out to where **Ariadne** floated at anchor beyond the breaking surf, I stretched out, eschewing the towels for the gritty truth of the sand. Angled, so I had Ron and Pam in my sight, I gave my body to the sand and sun, the warmth silencing my questioning, the joyous laughter of Ron and Pam enfolding me in plain and simple unconditional love. Gratitude, gratitude, gratitude. I sighed into this most sublime of moments.

10

1975

The Dream Fades

Joys of Anchorage Life Dissolve into Loss and Grief

The kids and I were elated and relieved when Jackson called to say that Dorothy's open-heart surgery had gone well. Dorothy was an integral part of our ever-expanding family, and Jackson and I had waited together at the hospital when she had her first open-heart surgery. Dorothy was a tiny woman, barely 5'. She kept her hair dyed a reddish-brown and saw to her make-up every day. Her eyes, always questioning, peered out behind large round owlish glasses. She had been a professional cook, so going over to her house for dinner was always a treat, and Ron and Pam loved when she'd send a bag of her out-of-this-world, whole-wheat cinnamon rolls home with them.

Jackson was the only child of Dorothy and her deceased husband, Curly, and to say that Jackson was the "apple of her eye" would be an understatement. She was doubtful at first about his relationship with me, a divorced woman with two kids, but it hadn't taken her long to welcome the kids and me into her heart. Turns out, the only issue Dorothy had was that Jackson and I rejected her desire that we marry. She'd often harangue him, saying he should make an honest woman of me. We skirted around the issue with her, recognizing she was of another generation.

THE DREAM FADES

Jackson stayed with his mom in Bellingham until she was fully recovered from the surgery. Having her son with her those few weeks was such a gift to Dorothy. Though she accepted whatever Jackson chose for his life's path, Jackson, the kids and I, were the only family she had, and she missed us terribly when we sailed away.

(Years in the future, once Jackson had bought property in northern California, he moved Dorothy to a home close to where he lived. She would eventually succumb to Alzheimer's and not recognize him. Nevertheless, he visited her regularly until her death. Unimaginably, Jackson's wife, Barbara, would be diagnosed with early Alzheimer's. He cared for her at home until, when she no longer recognized him, and he couldn't care for her, he had to move her to hospice. Blessedly, though she didn't recognize him, she was cheerful, and every day he'd go and sit with her.)

With Jackson's return from Bellingham, we began preparations for the trip to San Diego, our next port of call, the last one we would make stateside before jumping off west into the vast Pacific – first stop the Marquesas Islands.

My father had asked, and we had agreed, that he and Marlene would sail with us to San Diego. It was an uneventful, overnight trip, the best kind, steady winds, light swell, sunny days. My father observed everything, asked unending questions of Jackson. If he asked me, I didn't have the patience or interest to help his understanding, but Jackson was a proud captain, playing the role to the hilt, that evanescent hint of a smile always playing about his full lips under the beard. My father never pretended to be anything more than a deckhand, eager to learn all he could in the short time aboard. Once we'd secured **Ariadne** in the San Diego Bay anchorage, Papa and Marlene stayed aboard with us for two days and then took the bus home.

During the few days of my precious family and Papa and Marlene living on top of each other, it was impossible to effect any separation from Papa. **Ariadne**, my home, began to feel claustrophobic and unbidden, all the hurts and memories began to foment inside me. I swallowed the bile in favor of harmony. When Papa and Marlene clambered aboard a local bus on their way to the Greyhound bus station, I forced a smile and waved goodbye. I wasn't ready to confront Papa yet again. How many times would it take before the poison I harbored inside of me would be rendered harmless? I was a little sick of the story, and yet it was there, wouldn't go away, and I intuited how much that early pain would pop up in my relationship with Jackson, as my sometimes lack of trust, and my need to diminish his power in order to assert my own.

In San Diego, Jackson, Ron, Pam, and I settled comfortably into anchorage life. The kids were still longing for other young people in their life, so we enrolled them in the local San Diego school. It turned out to be a mixed bag. The conservative bent of that particular school was oil on water with the free-spirited élan of Ron and Pam, and I had more than one meeting with teachers to discuss, "What can be done?" I was little help, as my position lay entirely with the kids. In the end, the pros outweighed the cons, so each morning, we'd row the kids to shore, and they'd walked the half-mile to school. Back aboard **Ariadne,** Jackson and I would scramble down the hatch and into bed, our ardor as powerful and all-consuming as that first night at his house.

We spent our days replacing turnbuckles, making baggy wrinkles to protect the sails from chafing against cables, stitching sails, painting and repairing. Other than occasionally being disgruntled about the school, Ron and Pam loved the freedom of anchorage life where they would work on the boat, row around the harbor in the dinghy, visit neighboring boats, or explore the small peninsula. Our impending departure to the South Pacific provided endless hours of dinner talk as the four of us excitedly planned our getaway to the west.

With reluctance, I'd taken a part-time job at Baskin-Robbins to cover living expenses while we prepared **Ariadne** for the trip across the Pacific. Though I may have been less than enthusiastic about Baskin-Robbins, the kids were thrilled because the owner, Leo, or his wife, would insist on an ice cream cone of their choice whenever they came by after school. We'd found a plethora of sailing friends with dreams like ours – all of us preparing for the grand voyage. Stealthily, as the weeks passed, an undetectable lassitude crept in. And then, in that staid springtime of 1975, a seismic shift shook our world when a transit-worn seafaring sailboat motored into the bay and dropped anchor.

It was dark when I met Jackson on the landing beach where he'd arrived in the dinghy to pick me up at the end of my work shift. I pushed the dinghy off the sand, hopped into the stern, and sat down as Jackson rowed. Barely two strokes in, unable to contain his excitement, he described a sailboat that had arrived in the anchorage that afternoon. "It's from Argentina; these two guys sailed up from Argentina! They've invited us over for a drink. We're going straight there! The kids and I met them earlier and. . ."

I interrupted his excited staccato narrative. "Wait, wait. . .look, I'm tired and sweaty, and I have my ridiculous pink B.R. shirt. I want, at the very least, to go home and change first. Have the kids eaten dinner?"

"Yes, Ron and Pam are taken care of. They know we're going to stop by the **Vikingo**. That's the name of their boat, the **Vikingo**." He barely paused for breath. "You look fine, come on," he begged me as he headed in a direction, not towards **Ariadne**.

I momentarily disappeared into my default silent treatment, pouting at the thought of having to pull it together to meet these two guys in whom I had little interest. I surfaced from my silence, "I'm tired Jackson, don't you get it?" I stared out across the bay, beyond the floating boats, to the city lights glittering in the distance. I could just make out the arcing bridge to Coronado Island.

"Aw, come on," he cajoled. "We'll just say hi, spend a few minutes and then go home."

With a resigned sigh, I relented, "Okay, a quick drink, meet these guys and then go home."

Approaching the Argentinean boat, I could just make out the blue and white tattered flag flying from the stay. As required by international seagoing laws, prominently displayed on the stern was the name

Vikingo. Our dinghy bumped against the hull, and a face appeared out of the hatch. An enthusiastic voice greeted us, "*Hola, hola, buenos noches*, come aboard, come aboard. I'm Emilio."

We climbed aboard and shook his hand. He fairly vibrated with penetrating energy that attracted me with its sheer audacity. The grinning mouth with brilliant, perfectly formed teeth, his nose narrow long and sharp, and a smile that shone in the fire of his black eyes and his dark complexion chased away my tiredness. We followed him down the hatch into the tight interior of the approximately 30-foot sailboat. The layout was typical of small boats: a table that ran aft from the mast, used when under sail as a chart table, and along each side banquettes that doubled as bunks. We halted in the galley area, and I saw the other sailor at the table. He was fairer; his nose, though not as sharp as Emilio's, was also a prominent feature of the face that greeted us. He smiled, not as disarmingly as his childhood friend, Emilio, but with a childish invitation to enter his world. "*Hola*, welcome. I'm Vicente." His hazel eyes danced, reflecting the soft glow of the kerosene lantern suspended above the table. He slipped out from where he was seated. I noted he was taller than Emilio as he squeezed into the two feet of space between the table and where we stood. His hand extended, he greeted me with a light kiss to each cheek. He gestured toward the banquette. Jackson and I slid in together on one side, Vicente on the other. "Pina coladas okay?" Emilio asked.

"Si, si," our voices resounded as one.

I looked around, taking in the boat's interior: the portholes of tarnished brass, the wooden trim, and cabinets needing a fresh coat of varnish, the damp smell of stored sails overlaid by the incense they had lighted in anticipation of our visit. Amidst these sights and smells, the sounds of their broken English, the Latino handsomeness of both of them, I shifted from an impatient sulk to a wide-eyed curiosity.

Sitting across from Vicente, I allowed myself to stare for a moment noting his slight smile, the questioning that played across his features. He wasn't handsome like Emilio, nor did he have that enticing dark, swarthy skin. His piercing hazel eyes lifted to mine, and feeling a

THE DREAM FADES

slight discomfort, I turned to watch Emilio in the galley corner preparing the non-blended pina coladas. (The sailing boats we all owned didn't have electricity for blenders – only enough for running lights.) Emilio poured a generous amount of rum, commenting in his deeply accented English, "We brought this straight from Brazil." Then he opened a can of Dole pineapple juice and laughed delightedly. "And this from America. *Tambien esto*," he added as he opened a can of coconut milk. He pulled ice chips from a bag of melting ice that filled the tiny sink, adding them to the drinks. "*Voila*," he set four glasses on the table and slid in beside Vicente. With a huge grin lighting his face, he pulled a joint out of his pocket. "This'll go great with pina coladas." Among sailors, the ubiquitous joint always surfaced. We passed it around.

I was quiet, though attentive that evening, happy to let the guys go through the getting-to-know-you process. I let myself drift as the conversation floated around me and was aware of how all three men's attention was on me: Emilio and Vicente's occasional furtive glances, Jackson reaching over and squeezing my hand, the two friends watching our interaction with interest and curiosity. Their collective male attention chased away any thoughts of sleep and getting out of sweaty work clothes.

Emilio and Vicente quickly became part of our family. Enchanted with the bigness of America, Emilio and Vicente bought the biggest car they could find: a boat-size sky-blue Mercury station wagon in which they planned to tour the west coast. The six of us would pile into the station wagon for an outing to the local sights and sounds, from the San Diego Zoo and Wild Animal Park to the beaches and downtown San Diego with its heavy military presence. Jackson and I served as guides, explaining all we could of life in America. Their childish delight was a perfect match for Ron and Pam, and their shared joy was contagious.

Emilio was the first to hook into my free-flowing sexuality, flirting with a charming innocence right in front of Jackson and the kids. Jackson didn't care. He was proud that other men were attracted to me, and the flirting? Well, as he had once, fully congruently, said to me, "Why would you want anyone but me? I'm the best you'll find." That statement had floored me. No matter how far I stretched my mind, I couldn't imagine what it must be like to have inner confidence like that. In a perversely jealous way, it almost made me want to prove him wrong.

Some weeks into their stay, as they began to concretize their plans, they mentioned putting up curtains so they could sleep in the car and asked if I would sew them with my hand-crank Singer sewing machine. "Yes, of course, I'm happy to do it." A day or so later, Vicente asked me to go with him to buy the curtain fabric. We used Jackson's and my bikes to ride the two miles to town.

Years later, whenever I remember this next moment, I visualize precisely the spot on the side of the busy thoroughfare where, as we peddled home, Vicente suddenly stopped. I almost crashed into him as I slammed on my brakes. I looked at him questioningly as I took the two steps that brought me beside him. I was about to ask what's up when he reached across our bikes and pulled me to him and kissed me. With no hesitation, as the cars raced by, I kissed him back as fervently as he had pulled me to him. Our lips lingered softly, then pressed together again. Cars honking startled us apart. The glances of passing faces showed smiles of remembered passions.

And so began one of the darkest periods of my adult life that would stretch across the next year.

In his quiet way, Vicente began to seduce me, seduce Jackson, and create the story he wanted. I had never encountered anyone, man or woman, with the ability to mold the world to his will. I had dared much in my life outside of the mainstream, but I always had to wrestle with fear and doubt before following the inner urge to jump beyond safe boundaries. On the other hand, Vicente seemed not to get waylaid by fear or doubt; he'd simply choose his path and stride ahead. I wanted some of that!

I told Jackson about the kiss, about my attraction to Vicente. It barely gave him pause. However, I was tied in knots like a pretzel as

THE DREAM FADES

I tried to imagine outcomes, envision what lay ahead for Ron, Pam, Jackson, and me. I wanted to hold our family unit together, but how? The daily machinations of my mind were overwhelming, and I began to splinter inside. I walked and talked from a murkiness so thick I could only see my path a few steps in front of me. Cracks opened up on the ground I tread. I fought to keep my footing that threatened, at any moment, to slip into the cracks. When I tried to reach out to locate myself, there was nothing there, and I was afraid.

How had it gone after that kiss? At some point, I had capitulated to Vicente's demands about how I felt. Yes, I said, I was attracted to him, though I would always add that I was still in love with Jackson. Details of the Jackson and Vicente months have faded with the years; only a general outline remains.

Emilio was itching to leave for San Francisco. Though the *1967 Summer of Love* was a nostalgic memory for thousands of Americans, it remained a fabled era for an Argentinean artist hungry to experience sex, drugs, and rock'n'roll. (Once arrived in San Francisco, Emilio was "home." He would stay there to become a well-known sculptor, producer of living art shows, filmmaker, and an icon of the San Francisco art scene. All that was still many years away.) Emilio now began to press Vicente. "Let's go," he'd demand, and Vicente would murmur some excuse. They'd sold their boat to someone in Portland, Oregon, who would pick it up at some future date. The money had exchanged hands, the sale was final, yet Vicente procrastinated. One morning, as the two friends were having breakfast aboard **Ariadne** with me, Jackson, and the kids, Emilio announced, seemingly to all of us, but his eyes were leveled at Vicente, "I'm leaving today or tomorrow morning at the latest. Are you coming?"

"I need to talk to Jackson and Diane before I can say for sure."

"Sorry my friend, it's a long drive, and I want to be in San Francisco, not here in San Diego. So, talk to them if you need to, but no matter what, I'm loading the car and heading north with or without you."

"Okay, okay," Vicente replied impatiently as his attention fastened on Jackson and me. "After breakfast, can we talk?" We both nodded yes.

Over coffee, once Ron and Pam had left for school, Vicente pitched his plan. "Look, we all know I am in love with Diane and Jackson, I love you brother to brother, so I've been thinking we could all live together. I've talked to **Vikingo's** new owner and he's fine with me staying on the boat - in fact he's relieved cause I can take care of it. I'll bring **Vikingo** over and we can lash the two boats together. We're all together all the time anyway; the only difference is that she and I can be sexual." What was weird and unsettling about the conversation was that it was a conversation between men, about me, who was sitting right there.

His onrush of words was cut short by Jackson, "Hey, wait, wait a minute." He turned to me. "Did you know about this?" the pained disbelief in his voice struck hard.

"No, no, I promise you Jackson, I've never talked about this with him. Yes, I've told him I'm attracted to him, you know that. I've said I'd like to find a way to spend time with him, but not this." I turned to Vicente, demanding, "What is this? Your proposal feels way out of line, and I don't appreciate you talking to Jackson as though I'm not sitting right here!"

"Well, I didn't want to go behind Jackson's back, so I haven't brought it up with you. I thought it would be best if we all talked together about my plan. It's just in the last few days I've formulated this. With Emilio putting pressure on me to go, I realize that while San Francisco calls, this possibility here with you two calls stronger, so I had to ask. I know it's late in the game, but I wasn't ready to do it till now."

"Yes," I thought to myself, "it's all about you, isn't it?" This thought would become like an evil mantra to me over the next few years, but today it was just a passing thought. I admired, was in awe of his initiative, and his taking a stand for what he wanted. From the boiling cauldron of my brain, I turned to regard Vicente, "What the hell, Vicente? I don't appreciate you dropping this on me, on us, and demanding we make a decision now!"

Jackson echoed my words and then was silent. I felt his inner struggle. He'd always thought of himself as embracing the hippie spirit: free love, nature, poetry, rock'n'roll, all of it resonated with his very essence. When I had struggled with my inability to live these same ideals, he had almost felt sorry for me, being sure there wasn't a jealous bone in his body. But now, plunged into this challenge from Vicente, the silence grew deafening. I heard the now-familiar sniff from Vicente's slight allergies, and it irritated me as I breathlessly awaited Jackson's voice. "Shit." He looked across at Vicente, "Damn," he said, "I didn't expect this. I know you like Diane, but live together? I don't know. I mean if we could just agree to an affair, that works, but this? I don't have an answer right now."

A mitigating relief relaxed my tenseness, and I echoed Jackson. "Yeah, well, I'm not going to make such a major decision just because you demand it, Vicente. You know there are the kids to think about, and I don't know how an arrangement like that can work. NO, Jackson is right. No decision today!"

We closed the conversation, holding its completion for a future date. Through the rose-colored glasses of my lust for Vicente, my admiration of him, my curiosity about him, I had no desire to shut down the idea. The next day, Vicente and Emilio left for San Francisco.

Though each was fearless in his way, Jackson and Vicente were the antithesis of each other: Jackson lighthearted and full of laughter; Vicente serious and quiet; Jackson sensual, Vicente intellectual; Jackson joyfully extraverted, Vicente quietly introverted; Jackson expanding across surfaces, Vicente always searching deeper.

Eventually, with me as the capstone of an arch we sought to build, the three of us reached an agreement: Vicente would come back to San Diego, and we'd give it a try. Our efforts would manifest as a well-intentioned, though ultimately doomed foray into free love. The foray would become a war of passions, a war of ideals versus the all-too humanness of the three of us. It was friendship, toasts to that friendship, sharing of joints, ideas. It was losing and finding, doubts, hurts, and repairs.

I sat down one afternoon with Ron and Pam. "Vicente likes San

Diego, and so he's coming back from San Francisco to hang out with the four of us and take care of **Vikingo** till the new owner gets here to sail it to Portland. We're going to bring **Vikingo** over and tie it alongside **Ariadne**." I paused, trying to gauge where they were, how they were taking it in. They listened attentively, waiting, so I plunged forward. "He'll eat with us; no doubt we'll all be on **Ariadne** most of the time." Then daringly, I added, "You know I love both Jackson and Vicente, and some nights, I'll stay with Vicente on the **Vikingo**." They stirred uncomfortably. My heart grew faint, and I stopped any further explanations, wondering if the sexual part had registered. "What do you think?"

At that moment, I thought to myself, "I'll only sleep with Vicente when the kids are okay with it." Startled at how weird that was, I shut up, shocked by where my mind was running - the depth of my dissociation on full display.

They shrugged. "Guess it's okay," Ron said.

Pam sat there thoughtfully, then added, "I like Emilio better. Why doesn't he come and stay?"

"Well, he doesn't want to be in San Diego. He prefers San Francisco. What do you like better about him?" I tried to keep my voice light.

"Emilio's more fun. Vicente is always so serious, and I don't think he likes us very much. He never plays with us."

"Yes, that's true," I agreed. "Vicente's not as playful as Emilio, but I think if he's with us all the time, that'll change. He's just quieter, that's all."

"Whatever!" Ten-year-old Pam wasn't convinced. "Mom, can we take the dinghy to shore?"

"Sure, go ahead. We'll eat in a couple of hours, so be home about then, okay?"

"Sure, okay." They slid out from the banquette, tumbled after each other up the hatch. I heard them climbing into the dinghy and the quiet dipping of the oars as they rowed away from the boat. I wondered about the conversation they were having vis-a-vis this latest development. As close as they were, I knew it wouldn't go un-discussed: it was undoubtedly the needed discussion, and not play, that had sent them scrambling.

Vicente arrived. We helped him bring **Vikingo** alongside **Ariadne** and we lashed the boats together, both swinging on **Ariadne's** oversized anchor. We all took meals together. I slept either on **Vikingo** or **Ariadne,** according to an unspecified balance we were seeking. As in a desert storm where the path is unseen, winds blowing sand over footprints, where the traveler wonders anxiously if her compass is correct in the directionless vista of the vast landscape, so my psyche would struggle to guide me through the arid desert of our threesome. Trying to please two men became weird and stressful, but I was stubborn.

A few weeks later, just as the sun was rising on a balmy San Diego day, Jackson shook me roughly, "Wake up," he urgently whispered in my ear. "Wake up!"

"What? What's wrong?"

"I have to talk to you, now," he hissed in my ear, "and I don't want to wake the kids. Just get up and come with me to shore."

The near panic in his voice cut through any sleepy argument I might make.

"Okay, okay," I whispered back. I dressed quietly and scribbled a note to the kids in case they awoke before we were back. "Jackson and I went ashore for a walk. Be back soon. You know where the cereal is if you're hungry before we're back. Love, Mom"

We crept up the hatch and slipped into the dinghy. As Jackson began to row, his only words were a curt, "We'll talk when we get to shore." I nodded, nervously shifting in the stern as he rowed through the early morning mist, avoiding the ghostly outlines of the boats around us. Ashore, we secured the dingy and climbed over driftwood shadowed and dark in the low morning light. We crossed through the silent boatyard to the sidewalk that wound around the tiny peninsula. Our footsteps traced this walk I loved, past boatyards where boats were being repaired, past our favorite burger joint on the right, skirting the shoreline, terminating where the land ended, and the sea began. At the end of the spit, wooden benches faced out over the sea where Coronado Island rose on the left, but if one shifted one's eyes just a little, the empty horizon with its promise of unknown lands beckoned.

We found a bench and sat down. I could feel the icy cocoon Jackson had surrounded himself with and knew there was no point trying to melt and penetrate his shield until he was ready. Like a mute who suddenly finds he can speak, Jackson's words came in an uncontrolled rush, "This is the unhappiest month and a half I've ever spent in my life. I can't stand it. I feel crazy. Something has to change, and it has to change now! You have to choose!" After his onslaught of words, silence descended, holding us in unbearable tension. The weight of these weeks pressed down on me.

"I, I didn't know. You seemed to be handling it okay. . ." My barely audible voice fell back into the silence. My throat closed behind the words.

"I was doing it for you, for us, for the kids, but it's all wrong. I hate what's happening. I'm at the breaking point. I'm beginning to hate Vicente, even though I know he's not to blame, that we all have a part in how this is going, but now I'm clear. You have to decide, him or me! Are you going to follow our dream, or seek out some new thing with him? I know I don't have a chance. He's new on the scene, you're newly in love with him, and we've been together for a lot of years, but his threesome is never going to work, especially sailing together! Period! What will it be?"

His sudden ultimatum propelled me into fearsome anger. "You can't just suddenly demand a decision at this moment! You won't bully me into choosing right now!" The inescapable irony that I had delivered ultimatums more than once in my relationship life pricked at my consciousness. The tables had turned, and frankly, I was shocked at how daunting it felt to be on the other side.

"Well, I feel like you and Vicente bullied me into this situation of a threesome. What a joke," he laughed mirthlessly. "We, none of us,

THE DREAM FADES

have the capacity to do this, okay? I thought I could, but I was wrong, and Vicente is so goddamn arrogant. He knows he has the advantage of new love and all that it brings. But look at us. Even now, after all these years, we still have fun together, great sex, and we're a family. I've taken the kids on and come to love them. Vicente doesn't care about any of that. He just wants to barge in and take whatever he wants. You're wrong! I do have the right to demand you decide now." He wasn't backing down an inch. The intense pressure he had been under blocked any retreat.

"Okay, okay, I just didn't know." I paused, and unexpectedly, feelings I'd worked so hard to ignore tumbled forth. "Now that we're talking about it, this arrangement hasn't exactly been a picnic for me either. I feel like I'm always conscious of pleasing not one but two men. I mean, deciding who to sleep with each night has been excruciating. Sitting at the table, I'm never sure where to rest my gaze when I'm talking, wondering who needs attention right now. I haven't had any internal space to think about love." The living hell that I hadn't dared acknowledge gathered momentum as the words poured out. "I've felt you and Vicente like vultures with your claws in my skin, my heart, and you're each tearing away, wanting to get your fair share. I feel like a whirling glob of cotton candy you and Vicente are pulling from, licking off the sweetness, swallowing me. And I, well, I've been lost in my ego of thinking how great it is to be loved by two men that I love and admire. Maybe it hasn't been as hellish for me as for you, but it's at least purgatory. You're right; this arrangement can't go on. I'm guessing the nights when I've slept with Vicente in his boat right next to ours must have been lonely and untenable. Right?" I didn't wait for his reply, "Ach. I couldn't have done it if the situation were reversed, but you've always seemed so sure of yourself, of your place in my heart. You know, no jealousy?"

With that, my anger deflated like a balloon with a slow leak, flattened with nothing left to say or do. With deep resignation and sadness, I added, "It's been so hard trying to navigate the whole situation with the kids. I wonder how it's been for them?" Quiet descended, and in that quiet came clarity. "I can decide right now. Not because you insist, but because, as we're sitting here talking, the choice is obvious. I choose you, our life together, our dream together. We'll go back, and after breakfast, once Ron and Pam have left for school, we have an appointment with Vicente. Please let me take the lead, okay? I don't want you to tell him what I've decided. I want it completely clear that I am choosing you over him."

"Yeah, sure, that makes sense. And, hey, I'm sorry for getting you up so roughly and insistently. I was at a breaking point."

"I get it, really I do. Let's head back. The kids are undoubtedly awake, and the only thing I want right now is to hug them."

"Okay. Me too. Thank you. Thank you for believing in us and holding to our dream and the family we've created."

"Well, thank you for risking everything. I must say it was pretty scary when you said, 'Choose Now.'" I laughed lightly, reached to where his hand rested on the bench, took it in both of mine. I brought his hand to my lips, smiled across our hands, "Let's go home."

The next conversation between Vicente, Jackson and me, wasn't easy. Ultimately, I didn't break entirely with Vicente, saying at the end, "Life will lead us down our paths. Perhaps our paths will cross again someday." I added as I turned toward Jackson, "I am clear that my path is with Jackson." Even as I said these words, I marveled that I was still trying to please both men. Would I ever stop being a slave to men?

That day, I moved psychically and physically back onto **Ariadne** with Jackson, Ron, and Pam. I stopped sleeping with Vicente, though he continued to have dinner with us during the days it took to organize himself to head back to San Francisco. Vicente and I had one more private conversation over a beer at the local pub. I was guarded, careful to keep my mixed feelings behind a curtain of congeniality.

On his departure day, the kids, Jackson, Vicente, and I had breakfast together. Ron and Pam gave him a quick hug goodbye. It was clear they weren't going to miss him! Jackson and I borrowed a friend's truck and drove Vicente to the downtown San Diego train station. It was a poignant parting. We three acknowledged what we had hoped to do and that it was okay we'd failed. There was a deep affection between all of us as we hugged with promises to write. Jackson and I stood and waved goodbye as the train rolled out of the station. As we turned toward the parking lot, Jackson uncharacteristically put his arm around my shoulder, mine found his waist, and we walked together into the horizon of a new beginning.

Life aboard **Ariadne** drifted lazily throughout the spring and early summer. I focused on my mantra, "Life is good!" Ron and Pam delighted in scouring beaches for treasures of glass, stone, shell, and the occasional perfect ocean-carved wooden form. New boats arrived in the anchorage, and one of them carried two kids close in age to Ron and Pam. Ron fell head over heels in love for the first time in his young life. Her name was Tara. She was exotic looking, carrying the genes of her Polynesian mother and French father. At first, Pam found herself feeling left out of Ron's confidence, but soon she joined forces with Tara's younger sister, Francine, and the kids formed a close foursome. Where Tara and Ron were adorably engaged, often glancing shyly at each other, sometimes letting their hands touch, wanting to talk all the time, Pam and Francine found those moments boring. The two younger ones made it their mission to disrupt the older two whenever they could, teasing and being mischievous pests to their elder siblings.

From time to time, a letter came from Vicente. After I'd read his letter, I'd leave it lying on the table for everyone to read. Vicente was circumspect in what he wrote, telling of his adventures in America and the Chilean friends he was living with. With a new vitality, Jackson and I worked to prepare **Ariadne** for the voyage west. We experienced a new tenderness in our lovemaking that acknowledged the fragility of what had seemed firm and stable. The unfettered passion that opened the door to *Shakti* still graced and delighted me, and the glimpses of the immensity still burst forth from time to time. If I had reservations, I didn't reflect too deeply on them.

Break-up

In mid-August, a repeating dream began. I'd started reading more of Jung's collected works and tracking my dreams, and it was as if the unconscious had just been waiting for the door to open. Graphic details stayed with me when I awoke. I began to pay attention to the symbols and bizarre offerings of my dream life. There were slight variances in the storyline, but the feeling experience of panic dominated:

- *There were papers to write for a class that I can't seem to finish.*
- *A long letter from Vicente that I keep trying to read, but something prevents me from reading it, there isn't enough light, or the writing isn't clear enough.*
- *I buy groceries and realize there are too many to carry, so I can't get back to the boat where everyone is waiting for me.*
- *It's evening, and I want to buy flowers for someone waiting for me back at the boat, but the shop is closed, and when I try to gather some from people's yards, young boys start shooting at me, and I throw the flowers down so I can run faster.*

I would ponder these messages from my unconscious but refused to let their meaning unfold. If I felt myself coming too close to some truth, I worked harder on **Ariadne**. Fortunately, there was an unending TO DO list that held Jackson's and my energy and attention.

One night, the dream-maker grabbed my dreaming attention, and in the morning, I couldn't look away from the dream.

> *I was walking up a stairway with my sister, Rochelle, and a friend, and there is someone or something behind us pushing at us. Suddenly the staircase ended in mid-air like it had been cut or broken. There is a huge gap we must jump across to get to the other side and continue up the stairs to a secret meeting. My sister jumps and lands solidly on the other side. Then my friend jumps. She stumbles a bit as she lands but gets*

THE DREAM FADES

her balance and stands up beside Rochelle. Though hesitant, I jump. I almost make it; my fingers scrabble to grab the railing, but I can't hold on, and I'm falling, falling, backward into the abyss. I hear a voice faint and distant, both familiar and unfamiliar, whispering as I fall into forever, "I've seldom found anyone willing to get into this journey and go all the way." I awakened in horrified dread, yelling, "help, help."

Awakening, I pushed myself upright. With pure grit, I managed to emerge from the darkness of the dream, but it plunged me into the dark mood that had been hovering around the edges of my mantra, "Life is good."

I had been doing my best around Ron and Pam to bring joy and attention to our teetering family, and I managed as any "good mother" would. It was more difficult around Jackson. A drop of water in a bucket, many drops, the bucket overflows. Is there a beginning? An end? A moment? Which is the drop that sends the first stream of water over the edge? Unknown, but I finally fell over the edge.

Doubts about my sanity shadow-danced across the thin border to which I clung. Sometimes I would jolt from a dark reverie and look around, not sure where I was. Sliding into the abyss of my dream, I fought valiantly against the falling, but in the end, I lost. I couldn't imagine taking Ron and Pam into that dark and frightening abyss. Whatever alternatives I considered, I ended each time in a prison of despair. Seeing no other way, I decided to write a fateful letter to their dad. "Dear Don,. . ." I can't remember the exact wording, but essentially, I asked him and Carol to take Ron and Pam for a year as I needed some time. I shared with him that Jackson's and my relationship was strained, that the future wasn't clear, and I was searching for a way to bring order and certainty back into my life and just needed a little space. When I was ready to send the letter, I shared with Jackson what I was doing.

The reply from Don came swiftly. "I'll take the kids, but only if I have permanent custody by written agreement." This gut-wrenching blow unhinged me completely. I was furious at his audacity, his coldness, and most of all, his power. Instantly, I reminded myself that he didn't have any control over me. I had asked, and I would decide. As I considered his proposal, I reassured myself that even if I signed his paper, it would be for the kids to choose in a year. I was arrogantly sure that if I arrived on the scene a few months or a year later, things would work out, and they'd be back with me. I was desperate for some space and time. The agony of the decision I had to make crumbled my heart and mind. I saw no way to tell Ron and Pam. The momentous pending decision informed every waking moment. In a deep dark corner of my psyche, I wondered if I'd already made the decision, but a mind-muddling confusion dominated my days. I was losing physical and mental energy, listlessly indifferent to most everything around me, awakening in the morning unwilling to face another day.

One afternoon at work, Leo, the owner of the ice cream shop, stopped by. He liked to come in during the busy afternoon hours to keep his finger on the pulse of his business. Uninvited, like an icy wind of annihilation, the absurdity of working at Baskin-Robbins blew through me. I tore my apron off, and apologizing to Leo, I handed the little apron to him. "Leo, I'm quitting right now. I'll leave the shirt in the back room. I'll pick up my last paycheck on the regular payday. Thank you for employing me." The shocked look on Leo's face followed me as I turned on my heel, walked into the backroom, changed my shirt, and re-entered the shop. As I passed by Leo and the customers and stepped out into the glaring afternoon sun, I had to pause while my body settled into some awareness of itself.

I found my legs and began to walk. I walked and walked and walked, aimlessly, noting at times the beach as I passed by, or the hamburger joint where we often ate. Minutes passed, hours perhaps. Pure mindless walking carried me to resolution as "the decision" pushed from the chaos, over the threshold into my awareness. At that precise moment, I heard the voice of Little John, an admired old salt, whose boat was hauled out of the water as he prepared for yet another sail

THE DREAM FADES

out into the Pacific. He was crusty, handsome, and enigmatic. Little John sparked everyone's dream of sailing away into freedom.

"Hey, hey, what's up with the tears?" His hand reached out for my arm. With his touch, I noticed the wetness of my tears and wondered how long they'd been cascading down my cheeks. I lifted my eyes, looked into the deep blackness of his, and saw my conflicting emotions in a flash. In the way he had guided his small sailboat through myriad storms across the seas, he reflected back to me the sure knowledge that I would find my way through the storm. His compassionate questioning as he scanned my face opened the floodgates. "Oh, Little John, I've just made a momentous decision, and I'm terrified."

A tiny smile caught the corner of his mouth, "Yes? Well, terrified isn't a bad thing. It's what you do with the terror that counts. Will it swamp you? Leave you dead and lost in the water? Or will it spur you to meet the storm, engage with it, wrestle with it, love it, yell forth into its froth and keep on sailing into the maw?"

His poetics wrested a smile from me, and I flung my arms around his neck. "Oh, Little John, thank you, thank the goddess for sending you right at this moment. Thank you for the courage you have given me."

"Whoa, whoa," he laughed lightly. "I don't know what this momentous decision is, but just believe you've made the right choice. No remorse, no regrets, just keep traveling your heart's path." He chuckled to himself.

I did not need to tell him the story, belabor my trials and "the decision," and he had no need to hear it. I registered where we were standing on the sidewalk, just up from the shoreline where I'd left the dinghy for the kids to pick up and row home after school. Suddenly, I began to laugh till tears were once again cascading down my face as I doubled over. I looked up and saw Little John looking quizzically at me. "I just quit Baskin-Robbins, just walked out the door. You should have seen the look on my boss's face!"

Little John nodded comprehendingly, "Good for you!" We hugged goodbye, and I headed toward the dinghy, unlocked the cable, pushed off from the shore, and rowed to **Ariadne,** where Jackson was working on the boat just as I'd left him earlier.

"What are you doing home?" he questioned as I tied up the dinghy and climbed aboard. "I quit, over, finished. What the hell was I doing working there anyway? Ice cream for the kids? Get us a little money so we could hang out in San Diego, dead in the water like half the people we know here?" I rushed on, "I've decided to send the kids to live with Don for a while. You know I wrote to him. I haven't told Ron and Pam, so don't mention it to them. I'll tell them in the next day or so. I don't know what it means for us, but change is here. I'm over the top finished with whatever we're doing here in San Diego. Fuck it all."

"Hey, don't get mad at me, okay? We've planned this all together, so if it's changing, all right, it's changing. Relax."

"I don't want to relax," I yelled at him. "We've been relaxed too long. We should have left to go west a long time ago. I don't know. Maybe it's too late for us. So there, it's all out now, on the table. I don't know where we go from here."

His voice, though controlled, rose in intensity, "Stop right there. Just stop. You can't just start yelling at me. Okay, so you quit Baskin-Robbins, so okay, it's not the end of the world. Just calm down! Stop taking your frustrations out on me!"

His words didn't calm me; instead, my fury grew. I couldn't stop myself, or maybe I didn't want to stop. "I'm sick of our life, and it has to change now!"

"Diane, what you're doing isn't fair. The kids will live with Don, and you and I are finally alone with each other, to find another way to be together. You can't just throw that away. In truth, it's a dream come true for me, just the two of us. I love Ron and Pam, but to have some time just the two of us is, well, I've fantasized about it, never believing it was possible."

"Okay, okay, you're right, I need to relax. Look, just give me a few minutes alone. I'm going below to get a beer and think and clear my head. And I did quit my job this afternoon, oh I already told you that. I'll come up on deck, and we can talk when I've calmed down if you're here, that is. I mean, if you need to go to shore or anything, of course, go. I'll be here whenever you get back, or if you're still here, or whatever, I mean you don't have to go, but if you needed to. . ." My words were becoming incoherent. I ducked down the hatch and pulled the hatch overhead, not quite slamming it, but loudly to let Jackson know he shouldn't follow me.

I didn't write Don right away. I needed to check it out with Ron and Pam. I had decided to tell them separately, but on the same day, to give each of them whatever space they needed to think alone and talk together. Pam arrived home from school first. With trepidation, I invited her to sit down with me. "I have something to talk with you about." Oh, that innocent face framed by her long, tangled, sun-bleached hair, her big brown eyes staring out from her smooth tanned face. I thought, as I often had, that if Don and I had ten children, they would have all had our dark brown eyes, ordinary nose, and mouth, set in an oval face like this endearing mischievous visage in front of me.

"What, mom?"

"Well, I'm trying to figure some things out." (Did her thoughts go back to our living room in Bellingham some six years ago when she, Don, Ron, and I had sat together as Don and I broke the news of our separation?) "I've written your dad and asked him if you and Ron can come and live with him for a while. He said he would be thrilled to have you. I'm not sure for how long . . ." my voice trailed off, unwilling to tell her of Don's conditions. "What do you think?"

Pam didn't miss a beat. "Well, I've wanted to go live with dad and go to school in Fall City, but I didn't want to be apart from Ron. Now, he has to go with me, so it's good. I don't like always being on the boat. I hate the school here, and the northwest is much nicer than San Diego. So great."

Her reply caught me off-guard. I'd no idea she'd been thinking in these terms, that she wanted a more typical middle-class life with clear limits. Her confession reinforced how self-involved I had become. "Oh. Okay. I didn't know you'd been thinking that." We talked a little further, and then she cheerfully asked to go play with Francine. I rowed her over to Francine's boat and then headed to shore to pick up Ron after his school day.

I waited to talk with him until we were seated at the banquette aboard **Ariadne.** I started with the same words. He sat quietly eyes downcast. I could feel him struggling because, unlike Pam, he loved boat life, the free and unstructured days, reading books into the night, *Dune* his current favorite, and especially, he thrived in our family of four. He looked up at me, his eyes sorrowful, his long eyelashes glistening as tears spilled over and down his soft cheeks. "Oh Ron, I'm so sorry," and my tears fell with his.

He didn't let me say anything further. "I gotta go to my job with Brandon. He'll be waiting for me on the fishing boat. Will you row me in?"

"Yes, of course, I'll row you. Are you sure you want to go to work right now?"

"Yes, it's my job, and Brandon will be waiting, and the boat decks have to be cleaned for tomorrow."

"If you're sure……..we'll talk when you're back. I love you." We hugged as we stood up, then ascended the hatch and climbed into the dinghy. I felt the sad and terrible weight of my decision as I rowed to the pier where the fishing boat was docked. By the time we arrived, he'd wiped away his tears, put on his sailor hat, and jumped aboard the fishing vessel with a cheerful, "Ahoy."

I rowed back with a heavy heart. All my doubts surfaced, and that same insistent voice I'd heard so many years ago, "How could you DARE to throw it all away?" subsumed all other thoughts. This time though, the stakes were oh so much higher. I didn't dare let that conjecture find a harbor in my psyche because I saw no other path in my fragmented life.

I picked Ron up at the assigned time. He climbed into the dinghy, and as I rowed us home, he spoke. "Mom, I understand that you need your freedom, so I'm okay going to Dad's. Really, it's fine. I like Fall

City, and I think the school will be better there, don't you?" Those brave adult words tore into my heart and threatened to uproot my tenuous hold on reality. How had he guessed at my deep longing for this thing called freedom? From where came that adult maturity? He continued talking earnestly and with such loving understanding that I could only put the oars aside and reach across and hug him desperately. I, for a moment, was the child clinging to hope that this was going to be okay.

I wrote to Don and agreed to his conditions of signing over custody, with open visiting rights. I told Ron and Pam of the situation and reassured them it was just paper and that we'd see what the future held. I acknowledged that I couldn't promise more because my vision was a blank canvas. I reassured them with words and hugs and smiles from my heart that my infinite love for them would sustain us no matter what.

Don and I and the kids agreed they would go to Don's via my sister, Rochelle, and her husband Bill's ranch in Vale, Oregon. Rochelle had two kids, Monte and Sherry, cousins about Ron's and Pam's age. The kids would stay at the ranch for a month just as they had done the month before we made our cross-country road trip. It would turn out to be a needed transition time for them as they hung out with their cousins and engaged in ranch life.

On departure day, that unforgettable summer of 1975, sitting in the cockpit of ***Ariadne***, we paused to take pictures. Then, for the last time, Ron and Pam climbed over the rail and into the dinghy, sitting in the stern as they had so many hundreds of times before. I handed suitcases to Jackson, and then I climbed into the dinghy, untied the painter, sat down in the bow, and pushed away from ***Ariadne*** as Jackson rowed.

I remember fighting tears every mile of the drive to the airport in a borrowed car, gulping breaths as we walked with the kids to the gate. When they disappeared into the tunnel to board the plane, I wanted to rush to them, grab them from the clutches of my decision, and reverse time, but the ship had sailed. The only other memory of that surreal day is the feeling that I had torn something from my breast and left a hole that I could never heal.

Reflecting on those troubling days, I see how my decision affected my relationships with my sisters. For the next ten years and more, I would live much of my time outside of the USA and outside of the status quo. We never spoke about my decision to send Ron and Pam to live with their dad, and they never openly rejected me - our familial connection stayed intact - but with both physical and psychological fences between us, we would drift apart.

They were, and are today, content in their chosen paths. Rochelle and Laura still live in the first house they bought with their husbands. Gayle and her husband live in a house they built when the original log house they'd built burned to the ground. My drive for freedom is simply not in their lexicon.

Jackson and I, at last, had space, just the two of us, but we were like kids living in a treehouse we'd built and imagined we would live in forever, but the timbers were beginning to rot. We kept visiting our metaphorical treehouse, still shared secrets and dreams, and our passion was undiminished as we could now make unending love and moan our pleasures out into the sea. How long was it? I don't remember.

Over breakfast one morning, looking across the table at each other, we said in one voice, "Let's go sailing."

"Ah-ha," I thought, remembering back to when we had as one mind ascertained our boat's name, "shared consciousness still flowed between us." We pulled up anchor, piloted **Ariadne** out through the harbor entrance, and raised full sails, feeling the thrill of wind and boat fashioning a song of harmony. The sun shone on the ocean surface, the glittering rays seeming to leap from the water. We were running downwind; my belly was quiescent. Jackson and I sat in the cockpit, each of us on one side of the tiller. The steady winds kept the sails full, and we were content to sail smoothly in no particular direction, not trimming the sails to get the last half-knot of speed, just enjoying a leisurely drift to where the winds would take us. I could almost believe we were going to keep going, and then I thought, "Why not?"

"Jackson let's just keep going. We're stocked, the boat is ready. We have no possessions, nothing on land. Let's just you and I keep the sails full and follow the winds. Nothing is holding us in San Diego." I pointed to the compass, "Look, we're headed SSW, just where we've been dreaming of going. We can make a stop in Mexico somewhere before we head west and top off our food, water, and fuel." My voice fell to a pleading whisper, "Let's just do it now, right now. There's nothing, absolutely nothing, holding us here."

We couldn't jump. I could blame Jackson, as he laid out his excuses more clearly: he still had unemployment benefits coming; the boat wasn't quite ready; he was unsure about leaving his mother; and what if and what if? Who can say? I made noises of resignation, half-hearted arguments, sending accusatory looks that said, "Well, I tried, but you couldn't do it." Over the years, I have idly speculated about what would have happened if he had said, "Yes, let's do it," and we'd headed the bowsprit, like an arrow, south then west. Perhaps we could have set ourselves loose from our safe harbor. Today, this idle conjecture is best left in the ashes of the past to blow away into eternity.

Prolonged and painful conversations ensued. We both agreed that our relationship was troubled, and thus far, we hadn't been able to find our way out of our stuckness. Confounding that acknowledgment was the agreement that we did still love each other in some way. But I knew that I couldn't bear a future of looking into his eyes, day after day, and seeing the love and dreaming that had been the foundation of our relationship, that had sustained us unerringly toward our future, fade into a colorless, lifeless shadow of what could have been. I admitted to Jackson that I didn't see our dream of sailing away into a new and different life coming to fruition. "I still dream of the freedom we've imagined awaits us in the South Pacific, and" I added, "I think it could happen with Vicente. You remember he hinted he wants to return there and stay." This admission cut deep into Jackson's heart and psyche. I think it was those words that severed the cords on the curtain that had been hanging over us. It dropped precipitously, ending all hope. Break-ups are seldom easy or pretty, but we did our best not to hurt each other with accusations and recriminations. Inexorably, like so many who reach the end of a dream they can't fulfill, our dream died and took a little of our soul with it.

Once in a lifetime stars align, bodies align, psyches align, and an inexplicable fusion bursts forth from the cosmos. It is not an exaggeration to describe the relationship between Jackson and me as born from that kind of fusion. My love for him was the most potent love I had ever felt with a man. Our dreams, our politics, our laughter together, our love of nature and adventure, our fear for our country's future, our extrovert/introvert personalities perfectly aligned, and our bodies and sexuality fused, created a harmony not of this world. It was with Jackson that I was open and free to explore my sexuality and his. There had been no limit to what we had shaped, demanded, and given to each other. The special beauty was that our bodies knew, and our minds followed with no hesitation, and we brought forth from the depths of the other, the limitless. We often would remind each other, "You are the best lover I've ever had."

I still marvel at this powerful enchantment between us. Jackson was the ship where the sails of my soul had unfurled and been filled by the winds of affection that had carried me onward into the unknown waters of the felt, yet unnamed, tantric *Shakti Energy*. I am in gratitudinal awe and appreciation of Jackson and how much he enriched my life and Ron's and Pam's. To this day, he has never missed a graduation or wedding of these two young children who he took under his wing and nurtured and loved. (Just three years ago, in July 2017, Jackson and I danced together at Pam's wedding to her second husband, Joe. As we whirled around the floor, we laughingly remembered the nights of dancing together at **The Sandpiper**. We reminisced fondly about our years together and congratulated each other on the unique path we had each traveled since our separation some forty years past.)

THE DREAM FADES

If all this is true, why did I leave? The why will reveal itself over time, but finally, the *Restlessness* was pulling me inescapably into the unknown. As much as I was connected to and loved Jackson, I couldn't find the depths I longed to touch in both him and me. The voice in my dream of falling was speaking to me: *I've seldom found anyone willing to get into this journey and go all the way.* It was an inner voice, to be sure, but the words succinctly describe why I left Jackson for the promise of Vicente, who seemed willing to go all the way with me into the South Pacific dream of freedom, and willing to go deep into our psyches. I would have found it unfathomable if someone had told me it would be some thirty-plus years before I would find someone willing to truly, deeply, fully, go all the way with me into the not-yet-revealed place of manifesting *Shiva* and *Shakti* together into oneness. But, back then, all I could fathom was that I had to risk everything for an elusive promise.

Jackson decided to go north to Bellingham to be with his mom, reconnect with old friends, and perhaps search for new love and traveling partner. I wrote Vicente that I was available. Once he'd arrived in San Diego, we outlined a road trip all the way south to Argentina, where we intended to buy a boat and trace **Vikingo's** path through the Panama Canal. After that transit, rather than head north to San Diego, as Vicente and Emilio had done, Vicente and I would head west to the South Pacific.

In my psyche, the Pacific Islands held the promise of freedom in a land of blue water and white sands, of an idealized culture where our life would be limited only by our imagination. In my phantasmagorical world, I kept alive the dream of Ron and Pam joining me at some point, when I would fly them to Tahiti or the Marquesas. I wrote them often and apprised them of my plans and dreams. As the reader has no doubt surmised, my touch with reality was, at the most, tenuous.

I had one more detail to attend to before heading south. I had an IUD at the time and was bleeding clots during my period that was coming every other week. I considered getting back on birth control pills but had severe doubts about finding birth control pills in Mexico and other far-flung places, and I sure as hell didn't want to risk a pregnancy. It was abundantly clear that I had to seek another birth control method. I decided on a tubal ligation with an overnight stay in the hospital - a relatively straightforward procedure. I had no income and hadn't yet reached a settlement with Jackson about my monetary and physical contribution to **Ariadne,** so I made an appointment at a women's clinic for low-income women to consult about getting a tubal ligation, i.e., butterfly surgery.

The clinic assigned me to a resident surgeon, a young man very sure of himself and even a little intimidating. After he performed the pelvic exam, I sat up on the examining table, and he sat on his little mobile stool. There, seated in that classic configuration, a travesty occurred. He presented to me the possibility of removing my uterus as an alternative to tubal ligation. His argument went something like this, "Unlike the tubal ligation, they'll be no scars as the surgery will be vaginal, you'll have only an extra night's stay in the hospital that social services will cover, you'll have no future risk of uterine cancer, and no more periods." It all sounded so reasonable, and I admit that the last one was very appealing when I considered travel with Vicente to the south and across the sea. In the case of Dr. Someone, whose name I don't remember, I have concluded that he wanted to practice removing a uterus vaginally. Whatever his motive for doing this unnecessary and invasive surgery, when the tubal ligation was the better choice, it was a mockery of the feminine, and I entered into the conspiracy.

The profound question is, why did I go ahead? The masculine logic that had often served me well won the day. What I was unable to consider at that moment was that I was losing an essential female organ - the very womb that had carried my children, that had nourished them for nine months, that was an integral part of my female center. This unfortunate decision bears witness to the fragmented state I was in without being aware of the fragmentation. I was very far away from my feminine center.

When, years later, awareness of what I had done to my female body began to dawn, I blamed the doctor. It would take years of learning and growing before I took responsibility for the life-changing decision to remove my uterus. It doesn't excuse the doctor! But ultimately, the decision was mine. Female friends had sounded the alarm about what I was about to do, but my male logic would not be swayed. Sadly, as my future therapist observed, I would herald the transition from Jackson to Vicente by cutting out a part of myself. I waited to do the surgery until Vicente arrived to join me on **Ariadne.** I wasn't surprised that he was supportive of my decision. He accompanied me by taxi to the hospital and stayed the afternoon.

Going into surgery for the first time in my life was a powerful moment in which I felt the closeness of death. As I lay on the gurney, where we'd paused just outside the operating room, I looked up at the ceiling at the round overhead lights and thought, "This may be the last thing I see in my life." I sent all the love in my being to Ron and Pam. A nurse came and pushed the gurney into the operating room, and magically, after counting backward from ten as the anesthesiologist instructed, I awoke in the recovery room a little groggy. It was surreal to awaken from oblivion. I experienced a poignantly beautiful state as Ron's and Pam's faces filled my inner vision. In the morning, Vicente came to visit, and the day after that, we took a taxi to **Ariadne** with a strict admonishment that I must remain still. Vicente took care of me and our mundane life as we awaited my recovery and our subsequent departure.

As planned, Jackson arrived a couple of days before Vicente and I were due to leave. Though scars of the previous months still showed, the open wounds between Jackson and I had lessened. Jackson borrowed our friend's truck and drove us to the bus station. When we hugged goodbye, a part of me wanted to hold onto him forever, and salty tears fell as I tore myself away and turned toward the bus that would take Vicente and me south, nearly 6,000 miles, to springtime in Argentina.

11

1975-1979

Vicente

My Mettle Is Tested – Adventures on the High Seas

Vicente and I dismounted from the bus at the border, hefted our backpacks, made sure our money was well tucked away in the hidden pockets I'd sewn into the waistbands of our pants, and walked through the border crossing. Amid the cacophony of sights and sounds that greeted us, I reached for Vicente's hand, seeking a small measure of reassurance. He held tight as we threaded our way through the foot traffic on the narrow sidewalk. At the first curb, we were inundated by cries and motions of, "Taxi, taxi, best price, best price, come, come." The verbal flood quickly became hands tugging at our shirtsleeves, thin dark faces urging us to choose that driver over the others. Their pressing closeness felt threatening, and I clung tighter to Vicente's hand, afraid of losing him in the crush. "*Detengase! Detengase!*" he yelled at them as he vigorously almost violently brushed the fingers grasping our sleeves. Their eyebrows shot up at the fluent Spanish flung at them from this tall, hazel-eyed, light-skinned, bearded man. I recognized in the torrent of words his favorite swearing, "*Vete! Vete! hijos de puta.*" I was relieved when either the cursing or the violence his demeanor suggested sent them scurrying away, turning their attention to other prospective fares.

We boarded a bus in Tijuana for the long haul south. Arriving

VICENTE

in Mexico City tired from the bus's bouncing and heat, we treated ourselves to a somewhat upscale hotel and went out into the streets. We immediately satisfied our thirst with fresh-squeezed orange juice from a street vendor. We downed our drinks, savoring the cool sweetness as the liquid slid down our throats. It didn't take long for our bodies to reject what we'd consumed, and we spent the next few days in our hotel room, paths colliding as, fevered, we staggered from the bed to the toilet, vomiting and shitting out everything and then some.

From this ignominious beginning, an abiding simplicity defined the next weeks of making our way through Central and South America. Spending days in markets buying colorful woven clothes for each other, bouncing along in buses teeming with humans and animals, riding on more comfortable trains when we could, making love in hotel rooms. With each passing day, I left a little of the complexity and stress of "the transition" in the countryside through which we traveled. Fragmented parts of myself began a fragile coalescence.

Exotic places like Machu Picchu and Lake Titicaca echoed back to me from childhood geography books, now tangible and real. Riding that echo was the joy I felt in traveling with the man I loved. The perennial wanderer in me, hidden away for over a decade, thrilled as we journeyed from Panama to Quito, Ecuador, onto Cuzco, Peru, and into the mountains to Machu Picchu, where I basked in the remnants of a powerful spirituality. We returned to Cuzco and boarded the train. My excitement grew as the train raced across the altiplano into Bolivia and then crossed the border into Argentina.

A month and a half after leaving San Diego, we arrived in Mendoza, Argentina, Vicente's birthplace. I felt like the luckiest woman alive to be with Vicente on this grand adventure that would ultimately carry us to freedom in the South Pacific Islands. I could never have imagined the seismic jolt that awaited me in Mendoza, a jolt as powerful as the one in San Diego when the **Vikingo** had arrived.

In Mendoza, we stayed at Vicente's family home with his father, Dr. Rodrigo Sanz, a well-regarded surgeon in the area. The other household member was Lucia, their long-serving maid, cook, and household manager, who, more than once, would be my salvation in an untenable purgatory. The house stood on a quiet residential street cooled by surrounding shade trees. It was elegant yet modest in size. As we passed through the front door, Vicente opened a door on the left that led to the garage. We entered and he proudly pulled back the cover of his motorcycle. "I'm going to have a mechanic come over and get it running. It's what we'll use for transportation while we're here." I paused and lied when I said, "Cool." I had never liked motorcycles since the day I'd been riding behind Papa on a dirt road, my arms tight around his waist and he'd had to "lay it down."

Turning right, we entered the main living area, a large open room with an archway separating the living and dining areas. Dominating the dining room was a carved wooden table where each day Lucia would serve us, and Emilio Senior, the afternoon meal. I followed Vicente up the stairs to complete the tour. Three bedrooms and a bath curved off a large hallway. We dropped our bags in Vicente's old bedroom, in which we would sleep for the next month.

We entered into a social whirl of Vicente's friends and ex-lovers. It was a social milieu of seething waters, and like a babe thrown into the sea to either sink or swim, I was thrown into *l'intelligentsia de gauche*. When Vicente and friends would gather at someone's home or a café after a movie, the discussions ranged far and wide over politics, philosophy, books, world events, and there was much conjecture about the future of Argentina. I watched the admiration Vicente commanded wherever we went. I felt proud to be at the side of this returning hero admired for his daring and risk-taking. There was a story of money smuggling for leftist guerrillas which I never confirmed as myth or fact, and of course, his and Emilio's grand adventure sailing to America. I knew that daring in myself, and in that stratosphere of daring, Vicente's and my spirits met.

My pride of being at his side quickly devolved into invisibility as my very elemental grasp of Spanish left me out of conversations. If I asked Vicente to translate, he brushed me aside, whispering, "I'm not going to interrupt the flow of conversation." Once, when he suggested I meditate on the ceiling's cracks if I couldn't follow the flow, I opened my mouth to protest, but only the whimper of a wounded animal faintly cried out.

Those weeks in Mendoza, I was shrinking and sinking fast as night-after-night my loneliness intensified. One evening, just before 11:00, Vicente's distant relative picked us up and took us to his home for a formal dinner with him and his wife. She sat regally at the head of the table with a tinkling bell she would ring to call the maids with starched white aprons to serve us. In my nervousness, I accidentally broke an expensive wine glass that night. Vicente was ashamed, and though I apologized, I secretly didn't give a shit and was even a little pleased with myself. (In the future, as a trained psychotherapist, I would learn the psychological term for my behavior, passive aggressive.)

Abusive interactions between Vicente and me were subtle, yet constant. Though it was hard to see the parallel with my mother's story because the abuse was never physical, many were the moments when his harsh, derisive words cut me to the core. He criticized how I dressed, how I ate, how I carried myself, that I wasn't learning Spanish fast enough. He'd belittle me in front of others, as though he was ashamed of me, and yet he insisted I accompany him to evening socials. I meekly obeyed. His disdainful words took their toll, and already fragile, I began to doubt everything. I felt so alone, and our bizarre interactions crawled into my psyche like spiders and snakes that I couldn't brush away. One afternoon, when I couldn't bear the rage and hurt another moment, I went to Lucia, who felt like my only ally in Vicente's city. She had quietly observed the goings-on, as she had no doubt done all the years of living in her little room off the kitchen. She would cluck her disapproval at Vicente when he'd go off on his motorcycle to visit Elena, his ex-girlfriend, or to other private encounters.

This day she helped me figure out the bus schedule to a large central park. Stepping off the bus at the park entrance felt like a significant accomplishment, and I lightly chided myself for not taking the initiative earlier. The park was ablaze with summer flowers planted around the base of sinuous trees and along the dark gravel paths, edging bright patches of green lawn that defied the laws of luminosity. Scattered about were wooden benches inviting strollers into shade or sunlight. I wandered the whole of the park, looking for just the right place. Sensing "my spot," I sank onto a bench where sunlight and shadow cavorted across the landscape. I watched jealously as couples with arms entwined strolled by, kids played on the playground, and I thought achingly of Ron and Pam and wondered what the hell I was doing sitting there alone, on a bench, in a park in Mendoza, Argentina.

The park worked its magic and calmed the raging turmoil inside. I began to consider my options. I couldn't remember ever feeling so coldly excluded from a partner's life, and I couldn't comprehend how I had gotten to where I was. A plan percolated as the afternoon sun warmed me. I would get a taxi to the house right then, pack and disappear. Alternatively, I'd get through the night, and the next time Vicente left the house, I'd go. I could get a bus or train to Buenos Aires and somehow get the money to fly home. Who would send me the money? I had some money but needed a few hundred dollars more. But wait, I could take all of "our" money. Fuck Vicente: he owed it to me for the pain and suffering he was causing me. Instantly I hated the victim's voice I heard in my head as I pointlessly descended into the sad pathos of one spurned, full of hate and revenge.

Worst of all, I had allowed the fabric of my self-regard to be torn to ragged tatters. Vicente was like a mythical figure to me with his beautiful, svelte body, his storied childhood of privilege, his sophistication, his high intellect, his sureness of himself that allowed no doubt...and in the end, I couldn't leave. I couldn't leave the promise of his light shining on me and lifting me to the higher spheres where I imagined he lived. Compounding my reflections, and painting my thoughts with hope, was the promise of freedom in the beautiful islands of the South Pacific. And bottom line, I was hopelessly in love with him. I woodenly left the park and boarded the bus back to the house.

We had one more big blowout on an evening when I didn't want to go to another self-destructive social with him. Our yelling echoed throughout the house, and Lucia came to the bottom of the stairs and yelled up, "*Que pasa?*"

"*Está bien,*" Vicente assured her. He turned his attention back to me, insisting it was only my fear holding me back. I let him shame me into going. Like a good *Stepford Wife*, I obediently changed my clothes and followed him outside where the motorcycle awaited us. I climbed on behind him. Holding him tight around the waist as he skillfully wove through traffic, I once more considered leaving. In the end, I was unable to make the decision. I understood my mother just a little bit more.

A subtle balance kept me from sinking entirely into my self-pity and despair. I am an adventurer in my very soul, and what an adventure I was on with Vicente. While in Mendoza, we took unforgettable trips into the Andes Mountains to hike and camp and hunt guanaco. Those mountains of stone, so unlike the green Cascades of my youth, unexpectedly attracted me with their stark beauty of color and shape. I can close my eyes today and feel and sense the stone beneath me where, one day, I lay on my back on a rocky outcrop and watched the massive condors flying so close I could almost touch them. As I gazed at these majestic birds, tracing circles higher and higher on unseen drafts of wind, I flew upward with them and restored balance in my soul.

One trip, as we hiked with full backpacks into the mountains to hunt guanacos, we came to a humble gaucho farm that Vicente had visited often over the years. The señora and her daughter welcomed him, and in turn, they welcomed me and invited us into a nearby hovel. Inside, the rough cement floors were swept clean, and a few wooden chairs were arranged around an open hearth where a small pot hung suspended over the fire pit. The señora was a tiny woman, her weather-beaten face mirrored in the patched dress and apron she wore. She invited us to sit, blew on the coals in the fire pit, and added just one stick to the fire to heat water for maté. I'd never drunk maté before, nor did I know what it was, but I was about to experience it in its purest cultural form.

The señora spoke very little as she set a small gourd on the hearth and poured hot water over maté leaves she'd placed inside. She added a metal straw and brought the gourd first to me as the new guest, indicating I should suck on the *bombilla*, the metal straw. The utter simplicity of her gestures, the quiet in the room touched a place of gentleness in me as I slowly sipped the maté while she stood beside me. When I heard slurping sounds telling me the gourd was empty, I handed it back to her. She once again poured hot water over the leaves and handed it to Vicente. With her guests served, she refreshed the leaves, poured hot water over them, and passed the gourd to her daughter. And then, this nearly mythical being added hot water one more time, squatted by the hearth, and drank, gazing into the tiny flame. That hour, there in that humble home, did much to erase the pain of Mendoza.

And then there was the affluent gaucho family I would meet. One afternoon, as Vicente and I hiked down the mountain, our backpacks full of the butchered guanaco Vicente had shot, I heard bells and spurs jangling. Like a scene from a western movie, two men, fully decked out in their gaucho regalia, astride snorting horses, appeared atop a hill just in front of us. Seeing us, they leaped off their horses, and huge grins broke out as they embraced Vicente. I stared disbelieving at their colorful woven serapes, ponchos, neck scarves, blankets, and knives in their silver belts and hats. Were they for real? Oh, the backslapping, racing words, pure joy that swept me into another time and showed me another face of Vicente. Vicente introduced us, they mounted their horses, each reaching down an arm to hoist one of us astride, and we galloped down the hill to the family compound. Three generations of this gaucho family enthusiastically embraced Vicente. A barbeque pit built of stone awaited the fresh meat we carried. That night, we ate and drank and watched in delight as the family's young adults put on a show with improvised stage and curtains and costumes. How they'd known we were coming I couldn't guess, but what a fiesta we had! It seems impossible today that these gauchos, these friends of Vicente, existed. They had nothing to do with *l'intelligentsia de gauche*, and I was astonished at how Vicente was as comfortable with them as with his Mendoza circle. This man was unknown to me in so many ways, and yet, I must have intuited that the journey of discovering facets of him and myself, was well worth the despair that threatened to sink me.

Back in Mendoza, the floundering ship of our relationship was thrown a lifeline when Vicente announced, "We're going to Maipú for a couple of weeks before we go to Buenos Aires." He explained that Maipú was where his family had a summer home from the days when they had owned *fincas* (vineyards) there.

We climbed onto the motorcycle one more time and flew into the countryside to the village of Maipú in the northwestern part of the province. The house was cool in the summer heat, the yard full of flowers and trees. We ate fresh peaches from a tree he'd helped his mother plant when he was a young teenager. We sat in the shaded patio and read, and I wrote in my diary of happiness and love, burying away the hell I'd experienced while we were in Mendoza. We walked to the local empanada maker where we ate the hot treats direct from the outdoor oven, and to the little grocery store where we bought farm-fresh tomatoes and cucumbers, cuts of locally butchered beef. We cooked simple meals, drank the local wine, made love.

Vicente was different away from the city and his friends. In the bucolic countryside, my wounds began to heal. He seemed to discard his meanness like an old threadbare suit. He was kinder, calmer, and I re-discovered the man I'd fallen in love with back in San Diego. I felt hopeful and excited once again about the future we were planning together.

Returning to Mendoza from our two-week hiatus, we bought a little car and headed to Buenos Aires to an apartment that a friend of Dr. Sanz rented to us cheaply. What a thrill for me to live in this storied city on the Rio de la Plata. It didn't take us long to find our boat. Its owner had run the boat aground and just managed to get back to the boatyard and have it pulled from the water as it was sinking. Freaked out, the owner had abandoned the little ship at *Club Nautico,* where he was a member, and where we found the boat. It didn't take long to negotiate a price in American dollars, and this little ship was ours. We would change her name from **Raider** to **Le Petit Prince** after the character in the eponymously named book by Antoine de Saint-Exupery.

Reposed there in her cradle, the hull cracked from running aground, paint peeling and wood rotting, the graceful lines of this beautiful double-ender held us in thrall. It was a perfect little 31′ 10″ sloop. We propped a ladder against the hull and climbed aboard. Proud owners, we sat together in the cockpit, grinning from ear to ear. My eyes traveled along the deck to the tip of the bowsprit and back along the decks to where we sat. We leaned across the cockpit and fed our exhilaration into a long, sustained kiss. When we descended through the hatch, the interior held no surprises. It had the basic layout of small ocean-going sailboats: a tiny galley to the right, an even smaller head (toilet) area to the left, the chart table centered off the mast, and the bunks on either side. I crawled along one bunk to peer into the fo'c'sle where sails were stored and beyond that to the chain locker where the anchor chain was piled. I couldn't wait to start work on her!

Early mornings we'd drive out of town to the yacht club, where we worked long hours on the boat. At the end of each day, we'd joyfully evaluate the work and determine tomorrow's jobs. I can almost convince myself that my fear-fueled submissiveness had faded into the background. But then I remember Mateo. Mateo was Elena's brother and an old and very close friend of Vicente's from their Mendoza days. Mateo lived in Buenos Aires with his partner Luis, a young man full of laughter and wonder. The four of us often spent evenings together, either for dinner at our apartment or eating out and a movie. It's when I remember conversations with Mateo that I glimpse that all was not well. More than once, Mateo soothed my jangled spirit when he'd confirm that yes, he loved Vicente, but that Vicente could be *un pendejo arrogante* with his dissing, degrading, and criticizing of me that he would couch in the name of truth, of helping me see myself more clearly, of improving me. Mateo would take my wounds and wrap them in the healing balm of friendship and laughter, and I would remember my dream of the South Pacific no matter how elusive it seemed at times. With the stubbornness in me that has been both enemy and friend, I determined to hang on. Even from today's vantage point, I can't honestly say if my stubbornness was friend or foe during that year.

I often wrote to Ron and Pam, and once we set sail, I'd let them know our next expected landfall so they could write me c/o General Delivery. When we'd arrive to a town or city, I'd rush to the post office as soon as we had cleared customs. The kids wrote from time to time. I always wished for more letters but was content to know that their teen lives with Don were going well. Sometimes I'd send gifts from the local artisans, llama wool sweaters from Peru, ponchos from Argentina, and colorful batik shirts from Rio.

I stayed in touch with my mother as well, and she kept me current on family news. The time lag between an event and when I learned of it lent an illusory quality to the news.

> Journal entry March 25, 1976, Buenos Aires:
>
> *A letter arrived from mom today, "Your dear Grandma Trotto died February 25." In the letter, mom spoke of, ". . .her dear face, her gentle ways, her memory lingering on. . ." What a surreal way to hear of my grandmother's death that had happened a month ago, thousands of miles ago.*

Images and memories of Grandma surfaced throughout the next few days. And though she was still more alive to me than dead, tears would fall at those images, evoking a fond smile of remembrance and appreciation, and yes, love for my Grandma Trotto.

There would be another family death that year, sad beyond belief. Once again, I learned through a letter from my mother, this time informing me that Cameron, my little nephew of only 18 months, had drowned. I was heartbroken for my sister Gayle, unable to imagine the devastating loss of her child. How does a mother go on, I wondered? To lose a child has always been unimaginable to me.

What was perhaps even more inconceivable the day the letter arrived was Vicente's reaction to my tears when I told him the news. He asked, coldly, almost cruelly, "Why are you crying? Did you know your nephew? Was he so special? After all, it wasn't as though a brilliant child like an Einstein had died." I had no way to reply to him, as for the umpteenth time, I wondered who in the hell this man was? I left the apartment and wandered to a city park. Sitting alone on a bench, I privately grieved for little Cameron, my sister, Gayle, and her husband, Keith, and wrote them a letter.

Vicente's reaction revealed a part of him I was slowly coming to terms with - how his reason dominated his feelings. Sitting in the park that day, in shock at Vicente's response to the news of Cameron's death, I wondered how this beautiful man had turned into a tyrant that I both loved and hated. Some moments, I wasn't sure which was more potent, the loving or the hating. Undoubtedly, the love and the mysterious unfolding of *Shakti* was what carried me through the worst of times.

In 1976, Buenos Aires seethed with violence. In March, the Argentinian military staged a coup d'état that overthrew President Isabel Peron, Juan Peron's widow. She was placed under house arrest as a military junta seized power. In the days that followed, union leaders and other dissidents were disappeared, soldiers stood with guns at the ready, and armored tanks lined the streets. Fear gripped the city. Walking on the streets where soldiers guarded against the violence they had themselves created, residents kept their eyes glued to the ground. I was no exception. One day walking home with a bag full of groceries for dinner with Mateo and Luis, reviewing my list, I forgot where I was and looked up right into the eyes of a soldier patrolling at the corner. In the millimeter of a second, before I cast my eyes downward, I looked into the grim stare of that young soldier and knew he could squeeze the trigger of his gun in a nanosecond. My heart beat wildly as I tried to maintain my walking pace and not run. I dared not look back, just stared at my feet that at last reached the apartment door. I exhaled slowly as I turned the key, entered, locked the door behind me, and collapsed onto a chair in the kitchen.

Sometime in the next month, inside of that apartment, I staged my own coup d'état. One morning, Vicente announced that Elena, his ex-girlfriend, was coming to Buenos Aires and would stay with us. I pointed out to him that the small apartment could barely accommodate us. "Why can't she stay with her brother, Mateo? And where will she sleep?" I demanded to know.

Predictably, he exploded, "Stop being so negative; we'll work it out." And predictably, his explosion shut me up. It wasn't that I didn't like Elena, and under other circumstances, we could easily have been friends, but Vicente was an abyss between us.

On the first night of her stay, we cobbled together a bed on the living room floor with cushions and blankets from our bed. The apartment was sparsely furnished, as Victor, the owner, was wheelchair-bound and used it only occasionally when he came to the capitol from Mendoza. It was hard to keep the apartment warm with the one space heater we had. Each night, Vicente and I brought the heater into our room, and on the first night Elena was there, we did the same, assuming enough heat would filter out to where she slept on the living room floor. In the morning, she admitted she'd been cold, and had slept wearing two layers of clothes, with her coat as an additional blanket. "Well, then you move into the bed with us," Vicente announced, adding that it made no sense for her to be cold at night and unable to sleep. That fact I did not argue with, but with the rest, I had plenty of arguments.

When we finished breakfast, I made my decision. I gathered up the blankets from where Elena had slept, marched into the bedroom, and made up the bed. I placed our three pillows across the head of the bed: Vicente's, mine in the middle, and Elena's beside mine. I was fluffing the pillows, smoothing the bedspread when Vicente came into the room. He looked at the pillows. "Who are you to decide how we are going to sleep?" he demanded.

And though his voice had that edge of violence that usually made me back down, I turned from the bed to stare at him where he stood like a rock in the doorway. I grabbed the brass bedstead, drawing strength from the cold iron, and glared back at him. Without a trace of doubt, wanting to eat him alive, I spoke through gritted teeth, slowly enunciating each word. "We are not going to sleep with you between Elena and me, nor you next to only Elena. I will be in the middle." He stood looking at me for a moment wanting to challenge me. I didn't waver. With a huff, he turned and walked out of the bedroom. The muscles in my jaw relaxed. I turned back to the bed with a triumphant smile and smoothed out the last wrinkles. The three of us slept together for three nights until Elena returned to Mendoza. I didn't sleep much those nights, and I couldn't wait to drop her off at the bus station and send her home.

In the last months in Buenos Aires, driven by the state of the country and my visa that was due to expire, we worked feverishly to get the boat ready. We dared not take chances with my being in the country illegally. I was scared, and so was Vicente despite his innate bravado. Two days before my visa was due to expire, we launched the boat, did a little shakedown sail on the Rio de Plata, and returned to the *Club Nautico* in the late afternoon. Those last two days thrummed with fevered activity as we stocked up on food and water and made last-minute adjustments. In the early morning, on the day my visa expired, we set sail down the Rio de La Plata after going through customs. With sighs of relief, we set a course southeast, then north to Uruguay's southern coast. It would be an overnight trip, and we would use the auxiliary motor and the sails to navigate the 180 miles or so to Montevideo, Uruguay.

In the rush to leave the country, there had been no time to wrap up our life in Argentina, so once we'd gone through customs in Montevideo, secured the boat in a slip in the harbor, and established a relationship with the port authorities, Vicente returned to Argentina.

We needed to sell the car, clean the apartment, and Vicente had business with his father to attend to in Mendoza. Though I was nervous being there by myself, I was glad to be out of Argentina, and the port personnel were friendly and helpful.

As the days rolled by, the tension in my body disappeared, and I felt a smile on my face. I set up a routine of walking to the morning market in the city proper, visiting some landmark or other tourist spot, some days sitting in a park, and preparing **Le Petit Prince** for the voyage to Rio de Janeiro. I felt safe in the harbor with the locked gate, and in the quiet of the evenings, as **Le Petit Prince** rocked gently against the boat's fenders, my thoughts inevitably turned to Vicente. I missed him and worried about him as I recalled the dull faces of the Argentinean military posted along streets and buildings, the tanks in front of the *Casa Rosada* the presidential palace, as well as the heavy military presence that lined the main boulevards. And I had no doubt he would be spending time with Elena in Mendoza and probably nights.

Three weeks, and an aching three days later, I heard his voice calling, "Diane, Diane. Come unlock the gate." Relieved, angry, happy to see him, I threw myself into his arms as soon as he came through the gate. He hugged me back, kissing me with the passion of absence. He put his arm around my waist as we walked to **Le Petit Prince**. I asked no questions.

Within a week of Vicente's return, we completed the last details on **Le Petit Prince** and left Montevideo for the almost 1,200 nautical miles to Rio de Janeiro. On this trip, with no anti-seasickness medication, I learned of my seasickness pattern. We were instantly running close to the wind with the boat heeled over. The winds stayed steady, and my seasickness stayed steady as well. For three days, I vomited, my stomach was quiescent for a while, I'd eat broth and crackers, and then vomit again. I was miserable. Unlike aboard **Ariadne**, I had nothing for the seasickness, and I worried about my future boat life. It turns out, to my unbounded relief, I was only seasick the first three days out. In the future, occasionally, with favoring winds when we set sail, I didn't even suffer the indignity of those three days!

In Rio de Janeiro, **Le Petit Prince** anchored in the protected harbor, without the stresses of sailing, soldiers with guns, or ex-lovers, we re-discovered the power of our physical loving. I opened to his touch that stroked away my fears, and I recaptured my capacity for passionate merging.

"Big feelings," he'd say. "Big feelings are what matter to me, not little feelings." I remember sometimes making love, I'd open my eyes, searching to meet his, but in a strange surreal way, what I saw and felt was Vicente observing himself as he orgasmed. I reflected later that perhaps he was witnessing "Big Feelings" and wondered if there was room for another. In conversations, he touted "Big Feelings" as if the concept was an undeniable truth. As elusive and ill-defined as this mantra was, I chose to view it as profound and did my best to comprehend his view. Yet, in quiet moments, his grand pronouncement about "Big Feelings" left me uneasy about the way it seemed to belittle the day-to-day feelings and experiences we shared.

Our weeks in Rio were right out of a tourist brochure. The tram up Sugarloaf Mountain, beaches teeming with beautiful people, walking the multihued city streets, and of course, *Carnaval do Rio*. What wasn't in any tourist brochure was the prosperous city center's terrible shadow, the *favelas*. Looking out across the high rises of Rio to the surrounding hills where the *favelas* crept and cramped their way up the hillsides broke my heart. Boxes of whatever material the people could find stacked on top of each other like a child's structure of blocks that threatened to topple from a mere breath. Most of the *favelas* were without electricity or running water. Yet, despite these deficiencies, all year long, men, women, and children sewed and saved for the days of *Carnaval do Rio* where dance, song, poverty, wealth, beauty, hope, plus copious amounts of *cachaça,* all swirled together in a mélange that expressed the city of Rio de Janeiro as nothing else.

Despite my conflicted feelings about the city's devastating inequities, the vitality and excitement of Carnival thundered into my cells, and my body shivered in the cacophony of sounds, colors, and movement. The dancers' beautiful dark skin accented by costumes of every imaginable hue and the decorated floats were beyond my wildest imagination. The dancers and musicians held my attention and heart, and when I chanced to look into their faces, through the deep lines of poverty, I saw the tracings of pride and fulfillment in their art, in the companionship of their friends and neighbors, and in the phantasmagorical costumes they'd designed and sewn, and now wore with pride. The assault on my senses of the music and dance was captivating; everything in movement, bodies, feathers, floats, even the streets, and I welcomed this unknown, extravagant expression of tantric *Shakti Energy* into my very core.

Fabled Adventures on the High Seas

Leaving Rio de Janeiro, just the two of us wrapped in the cocoon of **Le Petit Prince**, marked for me the real beginning of our adventures on the high seas. Unless one has spent time on the open ocean, away from the demands of land life, it's impossible to imagine the timeless, peripatetic life of offshore sailing. When I'd left the USA, I hadn't considered how long I'd be gone. I just had the vague idea of a year during which Vicente and I would go to Buenos Aires, buy and prepare a boat, and set sail for the South Sea Islands. Though my ideas were vague, I assumed I'd fly to see Ron and Pam along the way or fly them out to be with me. In my wildest imagination, I could never have guessed at the events that would turn the estimated one year into three.

Mine and Vicente's three-year saga on the high seas could be a book in itself. "What to include?" I ask myself. The answer comes back clear - the manifestation and maturing of tantric *Shakti Energy* must again direct this choice - engagement of the senses that ocean sailing demands, the passion of my love for Vicente, dancing and music from Rio to Trinidad, and the voluptuous abandon promised by the South Pacific.

When we set sail from Rio, I re-discovered true companionship with Vicente. The simplicity of our life, the absence of others, the power of nature that both caressed and buffeted us all conspired to bring out the best in us as lovers and partners. With just the two of us wholly dependent on each other for survival and well-being, it was as if a sea-fairy had waved her seaweed scepter and dissolved Vicente's penchant to be abusive and put me down. She touched me as well to remind me of my competency and power. Over the years, though I cannot pretend to know all there is of Vicente, I know he had a need to be in control of himself and his environment. I have often mused that perhaps my emergent tantric nature, anathema to his high intellectualism, pushed an unconscious need to crush and demean me, this unruly creature he was living with.

That said, in this sea-going iteration of Vicente and Diane, we lived in the wonder of the sea and ports of call. Salvador da Bahia, Brazil, is the apogee of all our ports of call. I found it to be a place of natural cheerfulness. It was there I learned the countless words and gestures to express the feeling, "All is well." While in Bahia, we painted on the stern of our dinghy the expression, *Tudo Bem,* "Everything is well and good." Simple things like traveling on a bus became a "magical mystery tour." A passenger would tap out a rhythm on the seat where he sat, another would begin to flick a matchbook, another snap his fingers, others use their voices, and soon smiles and swaying swooped all of us up into pure, simple joy.

One night, as we floated at anchor up a small river, a soft baritone voice drifting across the water awakened me. I slipped out of bed and silently peered out the hatch. In the mist, I saw the outline of an older man in his small fishing dinghy, singing to the night. His voice resonated with mystery and communion with the river, the moon, the fish, his boat, his very soul. It was a singular moment of grace that the river and its people bestowed.

In Bahia, Vicente and I walked the city streets and ate *abará,* deep-fried bean fritters, or the delectable sweet *beiju,* a tapioca-based crepe that we bought from the large, animated women sitting at their stalls. We sat on the steps of a church, caught up in the life energy of the people of that city. Never before or since, when I have sat on a street corner in cities of the world, have I felt such well-being. It's hard to convey the feeling when one's heart is deeply touched and opened to a peoples' spirit, but in Bahia, I felt a spiritual aliveness because of the deep resonance I had with the people and culture.

We would spend five months in Salvador da Bahia. Over and over, we were blessed by the generosity of the Bahians. I remember with gratitude the tiny boatyard outside of the city where the owner gave us a section of a tree trunk for a new bowsprit, as ours had cracked. Over our protests, workers helped us shape the wood into a bowsprit on which Vicente carved curving vines and hanging grapes. With the boatyard owner and workers, we shared barbeques, music, and laughter. We met their families, who generously invited us into their homes. The town, the river tributaries, the islets all formed the beautiful topography of Salvador da Bahia. Ultimately though, the true essence of that magical city was the men and women that defined its flavor and generous spirit.

No matter the idyllic nature of a person or place, there is always the shadow: in this case, it was the ugly picture of power. While we were in Bahia, a US Navy aircraft carrier, accompanied by a flotilla of submarines and other military ships, arrived with much fanfare. We joined the Bahians to tour the aircraft carrier. Climbing the ladder to reach the deck, though I didn't want to be, I was duly impressed by the sheer size and power of that ship and the steely-eyed pilots with whom we spoke. As though to balance the mighty military, I was delighted when a young navigation officer was equally impressed that we navigated the open seas with only a sextant. When we left him, we'd arranged to take him and two of his navy friends for a day-long charter to one of the nearby islets.

The next day, we rowed to the dock to pick them up, expecting excited, happy faces and were surprised at the long sad faces that met us. It seems that one of them had had his watch stolen by a street urchin. Not realizing what this would mean, he yelled at the kid. Before he had even a moment to give chase, a shot rang out, and the urchin dropped dead just a few yards away from where Brett stood. In horror, he realized what had happened. A local policeman, concerned about the young American sailor being robbed, had simply shot and killed the boy. The authorities had little use for the young homeless kids that survived on the streets. What I remember most from that day was the young man's lament as he sat alone on the deck, "Dead for just a watch. Killed for just a watch." It was incomprehensible to him, and he was inconsolable, though perhaps the most healing thing he could have done that day was to listen to the quiet of the wind in the sails, the bow cutting through the water, and the calls of sea birds.

A month after our 6-month visas expired, we reluctantly departed for French Guiana. Raphael and Coraline, sailing friends from Marseille, France we had met and hung out with in Rio, had told us of the availability of stainless-steel cable in Kourou, French Guiana, left over from the construction of Guiana Space Center. Stainless cable was just what we needed to do repairs on our fraying galvanized cable.

From port to port, the pattern of my body's response to the seas' motion held fast. However, despite nausea and vomiting, I had to be functional, and with my macho stubbornness, I did what was needed on deck, though doing anything below wasn't possible. Miraculously, my body would adapt after the requisite three days, and no matter how high or rough the seas, my stomach was calm below decks, above decks, or hanging on the bowsprit gathering in a sail. For that, Vicente and I were both grateful.

We often set the self-steering, and days would pass uneventfully, trimming sails, taking sun sights throughout the day, gazing at the stars from empty horizon to empty horizon, and then becoming alert as we neared our next port of call. In the long days at sea, I had time and space to read books I'd put on a list to "read someday when my life was less demanding!" Vicente and I delved into endless vistas of knowledge as we read C. G. Jung, Krishnamurti, Alan Watts, and others. Our shared interest in Eastern spirituality lent itself to endless conversations. I found it thrilling beyond words to sit together in the cockpit and bounce ideas and questions off each other.

Sailing on rolling seas, I would often wedge myself between the bowsprit stays, and holding onto the bowsprit overhead, my feet would dip in and out of the ocean as a pod of dolphins played and gyrated where the boat's bow broke the water's surface. I watched in fascination as they darted right in front of the boat and dove away so close to where I clung to the bowsprit that I could look into their eyes and project my astonished delight onto them.

As if to balance this tranquility, there were the storms whose predictable pattern we came to know intimately. Sailing under sunny skies with steady winds blowing, we'd spot thin wispy, seemingly innocuous, grayish clouds floating across the sky - the harbinger of a storm, and we'd prepare ourselves and **Le Petit Prince** for what we knew was coming.

On the long trip from Salvador da Bahia to French Guiana, I watched one afternoon as those wispy forms scurried across the sky, turning to dark menacing clouds. We quickly reefed the mainsail and shortened a stays'l (staysail - foremost sails that fly from a cable at the bow and/or from a cable at the end of the bowsprit). The winds began to howl, and white caps rose higher. In this storm, we were *running downwind*.

Sailing through storms is a complex and ever-changing situation that I can't even begin to describe in detail. However, to help orient the reader, I note the following: *Running close to the wind* - the boat is around 45^0 off the direct line of the wind, the sails are pulled in tight, and the boat is heeled over with the scuppers sometimes underwater. *Reaching* – the wind direction is over the boat's side, slightly aft, my favorite and most relaxed sailing conditions. R*unning downwind* – the winds are directly behind the boat. I always found this the most challenging, as I'll explain.

Sitting at the tiller, I was bound in a terrifying fantasy that I'd get us sideways to the swell, and the wave would flip us over into the depths. Strangely, that same terror awakened my senses to an exquisite acuity.

I sat in the cockpit, white knuckles on the tiller, watching aft as 20-foot waves built and rushed at us. Crazily, amidst this deep tension, I shivered with a strange ebullient triumph each time a wave lifted **Le Petit Prince** to the horizon and, as the wave crested, flung her down into the trough where she disappeared into its open maw, only to be caught up and lifted again.

Each time my watch was over, I fell, exhausted into a bunk. Inevitably, after a restless catnap, I'd pop my head out of the hatch, look up into the sky, and ask, "Still blowing? Is it over yet?" Vicente would do the same after his break because even if there was a strange thrill at the power of nature, we both felt how vulnerable we were to nature's capriciousness. After this storm, as with so many others, we were dog-tired and grateful when we could once again take a sun sight, set the self-steering, and sail peacefully across the ocean.

We sailed into Kourou, dropped anchor, and went ashore. Talking with the locals, it soon became evident that our hunt for Kourou's stainless steel treasures was a bust. After just a couple of days, we raised anchor and sailed south to Cayenne, the largest town and French Guiana's capital, where we planned to meet up with Raphael and Coraline. This harbor would turn out to be the weirdest port of call in all our sailing days.

When we arrived in Cayenne, though Raphael and Coraline would soon leave to return to France, they introduced us to a circle of French physicians and nurses who worked as paid volunteers at a local clinic. Vicente spoke French, so communication was easy for him. With my two years of college French and these new friends' college English, my communication with them was manageable.

If Kourou was a monetary bust, Cayenne would prove to be a godsend for our coffers. Vicente was the first to get a job, one few people would have dared to undertake, but he was excited. A French mining company found him to be the perfect candidate to go into the jungle, armed with a Geiger counter, to search for uranium and other metals or elements. Four or five *Boni* would guide him. We learned from the locals that the *Boni* were descendants of escaped slaves who had disappeared into the tropical forest beyond their white owners' reach and created vibrant communities. The *Boni* guides knew this habitat intimately, and Vicente had a passing familiarity and love of the jungle from his days hunting in the Paraguayan jungle. The match was a good one, and the work paid exceptionally well.

"Are you sure about this?" I asked him, knowing he would be deep in the tropical forest and utterly dependent on the *Boni* for everything from food to getting back home. He reassured me he was excited and confident of what lay ahead. The day he was to leave, I rowed him to shore and walked with him to his departure point. I was nervous, Vicente enthusiastic.

I don't remember how I found my job. Ultimately, Cayenne was a small community, so connections happened through word of mouth. I went to work for Sahlman Sea Foods, an American shrimp company. Six days a week, for three months, I entered its doors where I worked in the tiny, cluttered office. The Cayenne operation was run by a rough-cut American who was married to a Surinamese woman. He ran the company with an iron hand. At the shrimp company, I would meet Ted, an owner of shrimp boats based in Tampa, Florida, who would have an unexpected impact on Vicente's and my future. I'm not sure our acquaintance was serendipitous, but it sure seemed so at the time.

Anchored in the tiny harbor, along with **Le Petit Prince,** was a boat from Hungary: a husband and wife and their young child barely a year old. I marveled that they were from a landlocked country and dared to be sailing the seas with such a young one. Vicente and I had them over to dinner one night, and we became passing friends. With Vicente gone, I was glad to have another boat in the harbor.

Each morning, I rowed the dinghy to the end of the long L-shaped dock, locked it up, then traipsed the long swaying dock to the land where I would board a bus to work. Some evenings I would meet up with friends from the clinic for a movie or dinner. I felt safe being out after dark in the town.

One night after a movie with friends, I arrived late to the dinghy and rowed out to **Le Petit Prince**, happy to be home. I jumped into the cockpit and pulled out my key to unlock the hatch. A frisson of fear shot through me when I saw the broken lock hanging lopsided. I waited and listened. I heard no sounds. Hesitantly, standing to one side and keeping my head away from the opening, I pushed back the hatch. I paused, still no sounds; I sensed no movement and dared to pull open the small hatch doors and descend below. As I shone my flashlight ahead of me, I panicked. Someone had ransacked our home: mattresses were torn off the bunks, papers and books strewn everywhere, the galley cupboards emptied, and dishes and pans scattered on the floor. Even the head was in shambles. Terrified, I staggered back up the two stairs into the cockpit and banged the hatch shut. Looking across the small harbor, I was grateful to see the lights still on in the Hungarian boat. I called across to them, "Miklos, are you up?" His face appeared in the hatch. "Someone broke in and tore the boat apart. I'm scared. Did you hear anything?"

"I'll be right over." He jumped in their dinghy and rowed hastily to where I stood on the aft deck. His presence reassured me. He followed me down below, and I stared disbelieving at this assault on our sanctuary. As Miklos and I surveyed the damage, my eyes fell on the "ransom" note. I read it out loud to Miklos. The spelling was terrible, the writing a scrawl, but the message was clear. The thieves had our passports, and if I wanted them back, I was to meet them under the bridge over the river in two days at 2:00 am with $3,000 in cash.

Miklos stayed and talked with me for a while, and we agreed I needed to go to the police in the morning. He offered to let me sleep on their boat that night, but I assured him I was okay, and if anything happened, I'd blow a whistle. I followed him up the stairs and watched as he rowed back to his boat, my bravado fading as my adrenaline receded. Going below, fighting the edge of helplessness against this unseen threat, I soothed myself momentarily by restoring order to our floating home. Even though I was emotionally drained, sleep evaded me. Through that long night, I tried to dissolve my fear of these strangers who had invaded not only our home but the very core of my being, but I could not easily erase my feelings of vulnerability.

The next morning, I went to the police and handed them the note. The officers gathered around a man who looked like the chief and excitedly talked among themselves in French Guianese Creole. When the consultation concluded, the chief stared long and hard at me as if taking the measure of who I was. He then asked if I would be the bait and meet up with the perpetrators so they could catch them. He assured me the cops would be hidden close by, and no harm would come to me.

I must not have been in my right mind because I agreed and set up the 2:00 am appointment. I didn't go to work but instead went to the hospital cafeteria to meet up with friends and ask for their advice. They were unanimous, "Don't do it!" We debated and came to an agreement – I would go but take one of the handguns we had aboard for self-defense. I had only shot my little .22 revolver once when Vicente had taken me to practice one day in Mendoza. What my friends were proposing was beyond frightening; however, the next day, on the appointed day of the rendezvous, I went to the police to let them know I would be taking a gun. In truth, I was hoping they would nix the idea.

When I walked through the door of the police station, the three officers lounging around the office clamored around me, "Why weren't you there? We waited for you. Why didn't you let us know you weren't going to show up? We were out there waiting for you and them!"

"But it's tonight," I stammered. "The note said two days."

"Yes, right, so, 2:00 am this morning was the second day!"

Ah-hh, I put it all together. They were right. I was apologetic as I explained my confusion. Secretly, it felt like divine intervention. It had been a horrible idea from the start. I informed them that as far as I was concerned, the case was closed, that I had no interest in doing anything further, and that I'd start the process of replacing our passports with their police report.

I had ridden out storms at sea that made my heart palpitate, but this threat from humans was much more disturbing. I kept the small .22 beside my bed, loaded with the safety on, and prayed I wouldn't have to use it. I wondered if I could. I imagined I would just close my eyes and pull the trigger. The Hungarians anchored close by brought some measure of reassurance as I anxiously awaited Vicente.

What a relief when Vicente returned from the jungle a week later, and I told him my tale. While the initial break-in was upsetting to him, he was livid with the cops. "Thank god you didn't go to the bridge that night! What a crazy idea. I would never trust the police. I can't believe they even proposed that to you." I nodded my affirmation. We raved in outrage until, having exhausted the subject of cops'n'robbers, we dared crow about the fact that they hadn't found our money, nor the two handguns that we'd hidden in a compartment of the chart table that we had carefully constructed before leaving Buenos Aires. I asked Vicente if he needed to return for the next foray into the jungle. "You know we need the money, and it pays well, so I think I should go back. It's not exactly a picnic for me, you know."

"Hum-mm. Well then, don't go back. What's it like anyway?"

"Well, we tramp through the thick forest all day, I follow the *Boni* as they cut a path with machetes, and I sweep the ground with the Geiger counter. Just before dusk, the *Boni* find a place to spend the night, we put up hammocks, and then they go out and shoot whatever small game they find - a monkey, birds, ground animals, or whatever and then they throw it into a pot and boil the hell out of it, and that's what we eat. It's rather tasteless but filling after a day tromping through thick jungle. Then we get into our hammocks and close up the mosquito netting though even then, some little things get through. In the morning, we eat the soup again, pack up, and hike on to somewhere." He paused, "But you know, despite all that, I like being out in the jungle, especially at night listening to the jungle sounds. I think I should go back for at least one more excursion. You'll be okay. Right?"

"Well, okay. It's been a couple of weeks, so I don't think the men will come back. Who knows, maybe they saw the cops staked out that night." Being together, tucked into the floating home we both loved and in which we had invested our heart and soul, everything seemed possible. Vicente left a few days later. With the infinite capacity we humans have to forget, I settled once again into secretarial life and quiet nights aboard **Le Petit Prince** until his return a couple of weeks later. Turns out he would make one more trip, and I would continue to work to fill our empty coffers.

When we quit our jobs, we were still woefully short of the funds we'd need for our indefinite future – day-to-day living, bringing Ron and Pam to visit somewhere, re-outfitting the boat for the long sail across the Pacific, and a nest egg for emergencies. We never landed on an exact figure - neither of us functioned that way - just figured we needed some few thousand dollars. Serendipitously, the solution materialized one evening at dinner with Ted, the shrimp boat owner, and his wife. Did we ask? Did he suggest? Who remembers? By dessert, the four of us had sealed a deal that would enable Vicente and me to make some serious money. We would wend our way to Tampa, Florida, and meet up with Ted at the start of shrimping season. Leaving **Le Petit Prince** docked (it would turn out to be in St. Petersburg, Florida), we would go out on one, just one, month-long trip on one of his shrimp boats to learn the ropes. Then he would assign us a boat – Vicente as captain, me first mate, and he'd help us find an experienced second mate, this being the essential crew of a shrimp boat. The promise of big bucks, which we needed for our trip across the Pacific to the South Sea Islands, forbade any doubts. We were ignorant; Ted was not. It was an insane and flawed proposal from every perspective.

Re-outfitting **Le Petit Prince** and stocking up on food, we left the harbor of Cayenne. We headed east to the open ocean, where a safe distance out from shore, we would turn north northwest to Trinidad & Tobago, giving a wide berth to where the Amazon River, carrying logs and trees emptied into the Atlantic. These years later, I don't remember the actual time between the various jumps from anchorage-to-anchorage, port-to-port. Sometimes the passages were days, sometimes a week or two. But each time, once my belly settled, a timelessness born of the sea and skies carried me across an unseen threshold into *Shakti Energy*. The sensuousness borne of the southern hemisphere's warmth sent our clothes into storage, and we sailed naked day and night. With the sea our home, with only the two of us and **Le Petit Prince** meeting the ocean's gifts and challenges, we found a oneness in which we acted in concert with the sea's moods. On days of steady winds, as the self-steering kept us on course, already naked, we'd clear away dishes, lower a wing of the table and slip into one of the narrow bunks. Our gorgeously tanned bodies, muscular and soft at the same time, mirrored the other. His tongue gently circled my breasts and nibbled at my hard, salty nipples. He licked my belly and sucked my clitoris to erection. I took his salty cock into my mouth, and as he grew hard, my hunger for our joining in this ocean of the senses demanded he enter me. I shouted my pleasure into the wind and waves as they joined with my orgasm to carry me into *Shakti* bliss.

In the infinite ocean, I was sure nothing could ever impinge on my happiness. At night, sitting in the cockpit bathed in the horizon-to-horizon canopy of stars, as **Le Petit Prince** cut through the ocean, with not even the whisper of another human voice, I began to know silence. These ecstatic moments alone and making love with Vicente whetted my appetite for the freedom I was sure awaited us in the South Pacific.

We arrived as planned in Trinidad to partake of another Carnival that would bear only a slight resemblance to *Carnaval do Rio*. There were the costumes and floats, to be sure, but more modest and fresher. I didn't feel the taint of the moneyed white elite of Rio and the international tourists. But what set the Trinidadian Carnival above all others for me, was the incomparable steel pan drum bands in groups from 20 to 100-strong. Those drummers created the unique experience of Carnival in Trinidad.

Before the sun had crested the horizon in the early morning hours, Vicente and I rowed ashore to find the energetic center where the Carnival parade would begin. The mass began to move even before dawn, and Vicente and I joined the Trinidadians to dance in the streets as dawn broke. There is no way to describe the magic of that sunrise except to say that I lost awareness of my body as I gyrated, bumped hips, and flung my head back in untamed ecstasy to the other-worldly music of the steel drums. What joy to feel *Shakti* energy moving through me, erasing all separation from Vicente, from the dancers and drummers, and the very drums themselves. That frenetic transcendent energy grabbed all people and things and the street itself in its net of delight. For three days, tantric *Shakti* reigned supreme in the unfettered music, whirling, spinning bodies, the unrivaled visual feast, and the happiness permeating the very air we breathed.

When the music and dancing stopped, the island would not release us, so we let the days roll by as we walked, listened to the locals' stories, and shared in their pride of country. We listened to drum practices that drifted from a neighborhood or stared transfixed at a workman sitting outside his home while he pounded and tested the surface of the cut-down oil drum, listening for the range, from deep bass to tenor, he was seeking. On this land, with the people, all our senses were assailed and demanded we open to them, to which I said YES. Aboard **Le Petit Prince**, feeling our very pores opened by the island and their people, we leisurely found the expression of *Shakti Energy* in our lovemaking. I could almost taste the Vastness. I reached for it and felt the promise. I felt satiated by this total immersion of all my senses in life itself. Those days were some of the most sensual and carefree of all the years Vicente and I were together. Nothing in us, or the environment, marred the totality of sensual intoxication. And then it was time to trim our sails and set our course north.

I have a worn and frayed cotton placemat in my keepsakes, a simple tourist article that we bought somewhere in the Caribbean. Written in bold letters in the northeast corner is its title, THE WEST INDIES. It's a pseudo map with Florida in the northwest corner and Trinidad & Tobago in the southeast. The landmasses are in greens and yellows, edged in sea blue. Prominent is a dotted red line that Vicente painted, tracing our trajectory as we sailed through the Caribbean

Islands and the Bahamas. The thin red line brushes the landmasses where we dropped anchor or docked in a local harbor. I smile as my fingers trace the red line that translates into the places and the transits in between, from Trinidad & Tobago, Grenada, St. Lucia, Dominica, Guadeloupe, Antigua, St. Kitts, and then a long leg to St. Thomas of the US Virgin Islands where we prepared for the jump to the Turk Caicos, and then into the Bahamas. Today, the people and places blur into a collage of green mountains, blue seas, and the dark, handsome faces of the island residents, of local gastrointestinal pleasures, and the occasional not so pleasurable tastes, appreciated anyway.

Somewhere along the red line, my finger pauses as I remember a terrible sea of red we sailed through where a colossal whale was in the throes of dying. Nervousness and sadness vied for our attention as the leviathan body roiled around us. Gratefully, that wouldn't be our only whale experience in the islands.

We paused in the Turk Caicos islands to restock and then trimmed the sails for the Bahamas. Our charts of the island archipelago, though recently printed, were woefully ancient. The ocean bottom hadn't been surveyed for a very long time, and the reefs had grown and expanded over the years. To add to the challenges of sailing those islands, cays, and islets were the strong currents. It was late afternoon, and we were pressing forward to reach an anchorage when that sound every sailor dreads - the scrunching and scraping of boat keel running aground - pierced our concentration. We quickly killed the motor as the boat came to a complete stop perched atop a bed of coral. **Le Petit Prince** hung perilously on the shelf. Crouched in the cockpit like stalking cats, we waited. At last, feeling her settle into a rhythm like a rocking chair, we sprang into action. With the dark of night imminent, we decided to stay right where we were and dropped an anchor, grateful for calm seas and minimal tide changes. There was nothing to do but go below, have a bite to eat, and be rocked to sleep.

We awoke with the sun and, climbing into the cockpit to survey our world, what a sight and sound met our eyes. Humpback whales were blowing and breaching all around us. Feeling a creature that huge so close to our matchstick boat made my heart flutter momentarily from fear. But surrounded by the reproductive display of these magnificent creatures of the deep, my whole body was soon aflutter with the euphoria of this natural wonder. I was breathless watching these mammoth 40-50-foot beings fling themselves into the air and then flop back into the water with a thunderous splash. We wanted to relax and enjoy this ocean theater but, there was the predicament of being stranded on a reef surrounded by whales! From the boat deck, surveying our surroundings, we noted that deep in the ocean's clear blue, the reefs readily revealed themselves. We turned our attention to the task at hand.

Winching in the anchor, unlike when **Ariadne** had run aground on hard granite rock, we were able to ease the boat off the crumbling reef. With contact between the propeller and the water, Vicente took a station on the point of the bowsprit, holding fast to the stay where usually a sail would fly. I took the tiller and the engine throttle. Slowly ever so slowly, I put the engine in gear, the prop turned, and **Le Petit Prince** eased forward. Vicente called back to me, "left, right, ahead, left, left more, slower. . ." and I guided the tiller. It was nerve-racking for both of us: Vicente gazing at what I couldn't see and gauging the depth, and I moved the tiller where he couldn't touch, working together as one. Under our shared guidance, **Le Petit Prince** moved out of the reef to deeper waters, where we carefully steered clear of the whale playground.

It wasn't long before we reached the previous day's intended destination and dropped anchor in the cove of an uninhabited cay. We spent days snorkeling, spearfishing for lobster or fish, reading, rolling in soft sand, reveling in this life we had chosen. We pulled up anchor and found another uninhabited isle and anchored offshore where we once again swam and spearfished for meals that we barbequed over an open fire on the beach. We walked on hillsides of green and mentally prepared ourselves for Florida and whatever it held. We passed two months in these isles and cays and finally turned the bow of **Le Petit Prince** northwest to the USA.

We sailed into the Florida Keys where, after passing customs, we spent a few last days sightseeing and relaxing. With reluctance, we finally sailed **Le Petit Prince** out of the harbor and turned north for the comparatively short sail to Tampa Bay, then docked **Le Petit Prince** in St. Petersburg, Florida, where I called Ron and Pam. Shivers of nearness raced across the phone line, and when I heard their voices, I was so overcome I could barely speak. I have no memory of the words or how long we talked, but I have never forgotten the feelings that nearly laid me low that day: hope, joy, regret, and impatience to reunite with them. I ended with the news, "Vicente and I are going out shrimping to earn some money, and as soon as we're back, I'll call you. We'll see each other soon! I love you both so much."

"We love you," they yelled into the phone receiver they each held to their ear.

As we sailed from the Bahamas to Florida, Vicente and I talked about how to best navigate the immigration system to allow him to earn money in the US. Being in a committed relationship made the choice easy. We would get married. Thus, with very little ado, within days of our arrival in Tampa, we applied for a marriage license, and for the second time (first time with Don in Coeur d'Alene, Idaho), I stood before a justice of the peace and said, "I do." Vicente and I went out to dinner to celebrate our new status as husband and wife. Though our marriage was grounded in love, it was also a marriage of convenience, as right after the marriage, Vicente began the green card process. I happily took Vicente's last name, Sanz, not wanting to bear Don's last name. (One day, I would discard all the men's names that I'd attached to Diane.)

Ted directed us to where his shrimp boats were in dry dock for maintenance. We went to work right away, scrapping, painting, and doing other odd jobs from dawn till dusk. In the rough world of the shrimping community, Vicente and I were outsiders and unwelcome ones at that. Worse of all, we were the "ugly Americans" of the shrimping culture, and unfortunately, we failed to notice the dissonance, focused as we were on the grand plan we had formed with

Ted. At the last minute, the captain of our shrimp boat, an older seasoned shrimper we'd met and liked and who had agreed to take us on and teach us the ropes, had to cancel when his wife became gravely ill. Because boats were already departing for the month-long trip into the Gulf, and captains' availability was almost non-existent, Ted hired Horace just two days before the departure date.

We met him aboard the shrimp boat where we were already installed. Horace was a big man, towering well over six feet, his bulk more muscle than fat. I guessed him to be in his early 40s. His neatly cut hair reaching just below his ears, and his baby-soft features, made him an almost handsome man and belied his heavy presence. As we extended our hands in greeting, he grasped each one angrily. He was unhappy about something! He brought Bobby, recently out of jail, having served a two-year term for assault, onboard as his first mate. We departed for what I have come to call "The month from hell."

Once at sea, when it was way too late, Bobby quickly apprised us of our situation. Typically, a captain chooses his crew, but in this case, as a condition of captaining the boat, Ted required Horace to take Vicente and me as 2nd mate(s). "Well," Bobby drawled, "Horace has a girlfriend his wife doesn't know about, and he always takes her as his crew. He's furious that he has to take you two instead of her, besides the fact that you two know almost nothing. And there's the added insult that he has to teach you how to captain a shrimp boat! I mean, you get it, no?" Oh, how we wished we'd known this before leaving port. Very likely, we would have made a different decision!

"I don't know how you're going to handle it," Bobby continued, "I guess just try to do what he asks. I'll help you however I can." He was true to his word, and I was grateful for Bobby's wisdom and occasional intervention with Horace. Yet always, for his survival, Bobby was on Horace's side in the mini-war that raged aboard that boat.

Vicente and I were woefully and dangerously ignorant about the rules of shrimp boat fishing in the Gulf. First and foremost, the captain is the absolute master of the ship. Horace, our captain, began a reign of terror. He was a violent man in the best of circumstances, and the current situation increased his violence to where he could barely contain it, and then not always. For thirty days, Horace would heap every kind of indignity on Vicente and me that he could get away with, even physical violence. I was terrified of him, and I was stupid as well because I'd cop an attitude that would infuriate him, and he'd take it out on Vicente. Vicente, in turn, begged me to stop pushing Horace.

Horace himself finally put the brakes on my not well-hidden anger and disdain for him. He and I were standing in the galley. He was screaming at me about spots left on the silverware (he was obsessive about cleanliness and germs). Idiotically, I pointed out the spots were simply water spots. With one hand, he grabbed the book I was carrying and hurled it across the galley and raised the other in a tightly clenched fist aiming for my face. I remember thinking, "This is going to hurt." Blessedly, a force held him back, and he dropped his arm. It was as if the tension in his arm landed on his tongue, and the worst imaginable vitriol flew from his mouth, nearly knocking me over. I wisely bowed my head and shut my mouth until he dismissed me with an angry wave of his hand.

One afternoon when he was threatening Vicente with violence and had a knife in his hand, I knew I had to let go of my arrogance, my insistence on being right, my hatred of him as a man that had total control of our life, right down to petty details like only allowing Vicente and I plain oatmeal for breakfast after the night's fishing, in contrast to the sausage, eggs, toast, and coffee Horace and Bobby were enjoying in the wheelhouse. Our very lives depended on me getting control of my own violence and anger. I began to learn about exercising control over myself rather than unconsciously trying to control everything around me to feel safe. It was a paradoxical challenge, and Horace was my teacher.

For me, Horace's violence toward us was a simple mirror of the violence of shrimp fishing. I remember my shock the first night when we hauled up the nets that had been trawling the ocean floor. As the full net swung over the boat's deck, the neck of the net opened, and sea life poured like a thunderous rain squall onto the deck. I stared in awe at the wiggling pile, alive and quivering, and wondered how we'd save all that life. It turned out we wouldn't.

Horace handed each of us a low stool and bucket, and Bobby showed us how to cull the few shrimps from the writhing sea life. As we sat there plucking the shrimp, a death pall settled over the pile as the "by-life" died off. We had small wooden scrappers with which we would push this "by-life" out through the scuppers. By the time we had finally worked our way through the pile, the mass was inert. Everything was dead. Night after night, this slaughter continued, and we were only one boat of hundreds. For thirty days, Vicente and I helped each other survive what we had so unwittingly chosen. I kept track of the days in my journal, and he would ask me, "How many days left?" Some days when I would tell him, he'd reply, "That's what you said yesterday." No, I'd assure him it's one day less. When we could find moments alone in the bunkroom, we'd surreptitiously touch and hug and know the unique closeness that strife and danger can bring.

Thirty days after leaving Tampa Bay, after chasing shrimp the whole way to Louisiana, we entered a cannery port. Workers unloaded the shrimp, and we waited for Horace to come with our pay. Ah-h, another lesson learned in how the industry worked. The boat owner paid the captain, and then the captain paid his crew. There was nothing written, only wage guidelines that captains generally followed. I don't remember the percentages usually given the second mate, but I do remember that what Horace paid us fell woefully short. He came aboard the shrimp boat where we were still staying, handed Vicente an envelope, turned on his heel, and hurried up the dock. We went into the bunkroom, and I stared as Vicente counted out $300. Stunned, we went to Ted and begged him to do something, but he pointed out it was the captain's prerogative, and his hands were tied.

We had been on a fool's errand. We tucked our tails between our legs and drove with Ted back to St. Petersburg, where **Le Petit Prince,** like the old and dear friend she was, welcomed us aboard and held us close in the wood and brass of her body. For the next few days, we simply basked in the solace she gave us and wondered idly about what to do next as we didn't have money to go much further.

Having lunch with Ted one afternoon, he said that he and his wife were driving to Galveston, Texas, where they had a home. He suggested we sail there, and he'd do his best to help us get work in the boatyards. (I'm guessing he felt at least partially responsible for the unrealistic promise he had made to Vicente and me in French Guiana.) Wanting to keep our dream alive, giving new meaning to the old saying, "clutching at straws," we made quick preparations and set sail for Galveston. I consoled myself with the thought that at least we were still heading west. And now, at last, guessing we'd settle in for a while in Galveston, my plans to see Ron and Pam took center stage. I was determined that no matter what our financial situation, I would be on a bus north as soon as I could.

A faint blush colored the sky as we approached Galveston Harbor. Then, like a star-filled sky, thousands of individual lights began to appear. We lowered the sails and kicked the diesel engine into service to navigate the miles-long channel to the port. I stood on the bowsprit, holding on to the jib stay. *"Red Right Returning"* I reminded myself as my eyes strained to pick out the channel guides from the thousands of other lights of the city and harbor and yell to Vicente at the tiller, "a little starboard, a little port."

As soon as we'd secured **Le Petit Prince** to a berth, I filled my pockets with quarters and searched out the nearest payphone. Unlike the call from Florida, this time, my plans were definite. Ron happened to pick up the phone and to hear his voice and share the news that I'd be seeing them soon, overwhelmed us both. I listened to the muffled tears on his end and did my best to keep my tears from bursting into uncontrolled weeping. Pam wrested the phone from Ron, and they passed the phone back and forth as we began to dream of our reunion.

A week or so after settling into a more permanent berth in the Galveston Bay harbor, Vicente and I bought a little Volkswagen station wagon, and he drove me to the Greyhound bus station. I boarded a bus for the nearly three-day trip to Seattle and then on to Bellingham.

When I arrived in Seattle, my dear friend Barb from college picked me up at the bus station. I settled in with her and called Don's number the following day. When Don heard my voice, he called Ron. "Hello, mom," Ron spoke with restraint, and I could hear in his voice that his dad was close by. I adopted the same mood, which seemed to alleviate his hesitation and no doubt his fear of disappointing one or both of his parents, both of whom he loved dearly. I sensed a change in his voice, and when it came, our hearts, closed by the years of absence, cracked open, and he laid out plans. "I'll call you back as soon as I've talked to dad and checked my work schedule. Pam will probably be able to go to Bellingham to Gramma's house tomorrow. Do you think Gramma Davis will be able to pick her up?"

"Yes, yes, of course," I replied. "I'll head up to Bellingham tonight, and we'll meet her bus. Have her call me at Barb's with her arrival time." I hung up the phone and sat transfixed, not breathing, holding onto Ron's voice. The promise of seeing and touching them, oh so close, was almost unbearable. When I let my tears fall, breath came, and I dared allow unimaginable happiness to seep into me.

When the bus pulled into the Bellingham depot late in the afternoon, my eyes were glued as the bus door swung open, waiting, waiting for the first sight of her. What a shock when a beautiful 14-year-old teenager, not a pre-teen sprite, stepped down the two stairs and searched and found my eyes locked on her. We laughed, we cried, hugged, and marveled at each other. There were no words from either of us in those first moments, our tears saying it all. "Let's go have lunch," my mom interjected. She drove us to her favorite "all you can eat" restaurant, and there, over lunch, Pam and I, mother and daughter, our words questioning and probing, hesitant smiles dancing back and forth, bodies leaning in and pulling back, our matching dark brown eyes leaping across space and time, we reunited. Ron drove up the next day. And though we suffered the same stumbles and hesitations as Pam and I had, our initial conversation and his maturity beyond his sixteen years allowed us to leap over the chasm of separation quickly.

Despite the awkward and even shy moments, innate trust and love soon won out, and we were, in those blessed times, simply mother and children adoring each other, laughing together, telling stories of our lives. What delight to get to know these two beings that had grown and blossomed while I was away. A slight shadow, an ache in my heart, of guilt and regret for the years I'd missed, flitted around the edges of my joy. It would be decades before I would find peace with the separation I had engineered.

I would stay in the northwest for about a month and a half, spending almost every weekend with Ron and Pam. I was in no hurry to cut short this reunion with my children. Knowledge of my alternate life with Vicente, far away in Texas, dimmed in the penumbra of my mind.

I had also called Jackson from Galveston, and he had come north from his home in California. What a reunion he and the kids and I had! We took a weekend trip by ferry, then boarded a small fishing boat that took us to the island where Tortuga, one of our deckhands on the Neah Bay to San Francisco sail, was homesteading. Another great reunion. Whenever Ron and Pam came to Bellingham to visit me, Jackson would join us, and we'd grab a meal together. Out of time and place, this slice of life carried us back to the years of being a family aboard **Ariadne** sailing the Pacific Northwest waters. Jackson's teasing and stories riffed between us. Though our family had broken apart, Ron and Pam's love for Jackson was vibrantly alive, and, as they told me later, they were at a loss as to why I was with Vicente instead of Jackson. I knew why, but adult complexity is often opaque to the simple logic of one's children.

Jackson and I hung out together whenever we could. When he'd come to pick me up, my mother looked askance but was always polite and didn't ask questions. I didn't try to explain the inexplicable. Jackson and I visited old haunts and old friends and once again joined our bodies in lovemaking, usually at his mom's place when she was at work. Open relationships were not in hers or my mother's lexicon, and neither would have approved of Jackson and I sleeping together. Fortunately, I had matured over the years and saw no reason to throw my relationships in my mother's face as I might have done when I was younger.

The ancient magic captured Jackson and me; our passion had faded but little. And oh how we laughed together. God, it felt good when I was in Jackson's arms; Vicente ceased to exist. Jackson and I added an exclamation point to our reunion when, as in days of yore, I lied to mom, telling her I was staying with a friend. Instead, Jackson and I stayed two nights aboard our friend's converted tugboat that was berthed across from where **Ariadne** had been docked. When Jackson and I sauntered down the dock, as we had hundreds of times before in a forgotten past, we shared a flood of memories.

Aboard the tugboat secured in its berth, Jackson and I were in timelessness, and we re-discovered – well, almost – the old magic and orgasmic ecstasy. As before, my body willingly rose to his caresses, his wide full lips finding mine as we hungrily sought each other's center, and savored orgasms shot through with joy and laughter. I marveled to be once again opening my legs and heart to him as he slowly, or sometimes explosively, entered me. I reveled in the quiet aftermath, lying together and listening to music. Sometimes, gifts of intimate simplicity find us, and though they may not withstand the ravages of day-to-day reality, they enrich us, and so those nights with Jackson did for me. Ah-h yes, the idea of being back in a relationship with him drifted alluringly through my mind. However, I knew better, and like an impatient parent, truth intervened and shattered my childish fantasy.

One afternoon, when Jackson and I were having a beer and a Reuben sandwich at Cap Hansen's Tavern, one of our old haunts, Jackson presented a risky plan. I had no way to reach Vicente, so I made a unilateral decision and said, "Yes." When I returned to Galveston, just as I'd hoped, Vicente was all in with the plan that would, at last, pull together the nest egg we needed to sail west into the land of our dreams.

This time, when I said goodbye to Ron and Pam, unlike our parting those years ago in San Diego, I had a plan and a timeline. I couldn't apprise them of my forthcoming nefarious activity, but I could promise them that I would be back in the United States in a few months. Knowing this eased the pain of parting.

About two weeks after I arrived back in Galveston, Jackson and his partner, Charlotte, came to stay with us for a few days. Aboard **Le Petit Prince**, with Vicente and I sitting across from Jackson and Charlotte, I was taken back to that first time Vicente and Emilio had sat across the table from Jackson and me. Extraordinary, I thought, how things change and yet remain the same. There was a level of comfort and appreciation for all we had been through together, which was the foundation of "The Plan." It was simple on paper.

At that time, *Panama Red* was one of the primo marijuana strains, and we were about to be part of the supply chain. Vicente and I would sail south to Panama to a small island off the coast where Jackson had contacts. We would send a letter to Jackson giving our departure date with the trip's projected duration from the western Panamanian Port of Balboa. **Le Petit Prince** would sail to this designated island off Panama's west coast and load the boat with *Panama Red*. In a set window of time, the pick-up boat, Jackson and Charlotte aboard **Ariadne**, would meet us in an anchorage at Santa Catalina Island, located off the coast of Long Beach, California. We'd unload the haul onto **Ariadne,** and Vicente and I would quietly sail back into Mexico to prepare **Le Petit Prince** to enter the USA through customs in San Diego. Jackson would front the money, arrange for selling the marijuana, and we'd split everything 50/50. If all went well, we would see each other at Santa Catalina Island.

It is essential to remind the reader that law enforcement's attitude and our "hippie" cultural attitude toward marijuana were lax in those years. Smoking marijuana was a fact of life and almost a non-issue, though that would begin to change with Reagan's "War on Drugs." Vicente and I carefully weighed the odds of getting caught, what possible prison time we might face, and the financial gains proposed.

Though a risky way to get the funds together for our dreamscape of the South Pacific Islands, we didn't calculate the risk as being too high, so we were all in! And thus, the grandest of adventures began.

In Galveston, we outfitted **Le Petit Prince** for the trip south through the Gulf, then through the Panama Canal, and the long sail north. Ah-h, but before we arrived in Panama, there was the trip south from Galveston. The beauty of long-distance sailing is that you can't know for sure what Mother Nature will throw at you. Through all the glorious and challenging years of sailing, both on **Ariadne** and **Le Petit Prince,** there were only two times I felt death dancing oh so close around me. The first encounter happened on the trip south to Panama.

The trip from Galveston to Panama was a taxing 20-day voyage. Strong following winds and big waves continually washed over the decks. We kept the hatch closed, and portholes bolted down tight, but there was no way in an old boat to completely stop the seawater from dripping a little here, a little here, slithering through a porthole that leaked. One of us might be transiting into the cockpit just as a fierce wave crashed overboard. Whoosh, a deluge of water would enter below. At some point, we stopped thinking in terms of getting dry after a watch and falling into a bunk with damp sheets was immaterial because your clothes were equally wet. Though the winds blew steady, their force demanded there always be someone at the tiller watching the compass and holding the ship on course. It was a miserable trip. Every piece of clothing, towels, bedding, even dishes was drenched. With just the two of us, sleep time was sacrosanct unless there was an emergency that would require all hands on deck.

One evening as I sat at the tiller, dusk shading the skies gray, I watched as heavy thunderclouds began to gather ominously overhead. Vicente was down below sleeping. The rain started to fall, big drops challenging the ocean's surface, making splashes as if for one moment they be mightier than the sea.

I heard the thunder before I saw the first flash. Like I had done as a child, to calculate how far away the storm was, I waited for the next flash and began counting seconds before the thunder rumbled across the sky. There weren't many seconds, and very quickly, my counting was to 0. The continuous booming roar shook the boat; the vibration in my ears split my head as the lightning flashed overhead. And then, as I peered through the sheets of rain, I beheld lightning hitting the ocean, sending up little flares on contact. How many feet away was it? 10, 20, 30, 100? I couldn't calculate through the roiling and pelting rain, but there was no doubt that the lightning bolts were exploding close to the boat. With whispered dread, childhood stories surfaced that lightning is drawn to the highest point in its vicinity. Our mast was unquestionably the highest point. How could the next lightning bolt possibly miss us? Or what if it ran across the water to the boat? I knew water was an electrical conduit, especially saltwater. I was frightened from my head to the tips of my toes. The refrain, "I don't want to die alone," kept repeating in my brain. I desperately wanted to awaken Vicente. I vacillated. "Wake him up?"

Another voice spoke, "No, he'll think you're stupid."

"But...." the other voice said, "I want him here beside me if anything happens, I don't want to die alone."

"And what will he do?" the voice chided me. "Don't be ridiculous."

"But maybe he's better on deck rather than down below if lightning does strike and the boat catches fire."

"You're just making excuses," the macho voice rejoined.

I wasn't a believer in prayer, having thrown that out with my church membership long ago. But I think there's an urge in most of us when we feel our life is on the line, to turn to something ungraspable as the last hope. I talked to the weather gods and goddesses, telling them I felt death close by and I didn't want to die. The tightness in my chest swelled as I held my breath like a free diver plunging into the ocean depths, my lungs bursting until my body demanded breath. In the sensory overload of the storm, I don't know if we sailed out from under the cloud, or it sailed away overhead, but the thunder and lightning calmed, and my high tension unwound bit by bit. The bullet-size raindrops dwindled to gentle drops, and gratitude to the spirits of wind and wave, and **Le Petit Prince**, trickled from my every pore. Each time we passed through challenges, my affection and delight in her strengthened. I would often talk to her, pat her, thank her. She was a living spirit, and I could feel my spirit conjoined to hers.

It took us a week in Panama to dry out the boat, wash saltwater from all our clothes, and spread them on the deck to dry in the sun. Before signing up for our passage through the canal, we sailed for the San Blas Islands, where we lingered for two weeks snorkeling and spearfishing in pristine blue waters, barbequing our catch, stretching out and making love on the white sands of isolated islets.

On the islands where the indigenous Guna people lived, we walked along narrow dusty paths. The children laughed and danced around us, and the women invited us into their huts to show us the beautiful molas they'd made that formed the bodice of their dresses. We giggled with them when they held a dress up to me, as most of them were quite a bit smaller than me. Chatting with many of the women in Spanish, we bought unique and gorgeous molas, some already part of a dress. What impressed me most about the Gunas was that though the simple wooden pole huts were densely clustered along dusty walking pathways, an air of tranquility permeated the villages. I remember thinking that their communities defied the common western perception of the dilatory effects of overcrowding! Leaving that storied archipelago of islands that had been like a celebration before Lent, we sailed back to Panama.

Back in the anchorage, we signed up for our transit through the canal, and while we waited, I got out my hand-crank vintage Singer sewing machine and went to work sewing sail bags. I made a total of nine in anticipation of filling them with *Panama Red*.

Boats like ours pass through the locks behind a ship whose length allows a smaller boat to share the space. Our excitement was high when the port authorities notified us that our turn had come. The ship we would accompany through the locks turned out to be the ***Jeanne d'Arc***, a French naval training ship traveling to the South Pacific. Ahh, I thought, soon we'll be sailing in that direction. I took it as an auspicious sign that we would set out for the South Pacific once we had completed our escapade.

That remarkable passage through the engineering marvel of the Panama Canal is anchored fast in my memory. We were required to hire two more line handlers. We found two young women who, like many others, hung out in Panama specifically to help with a transit through the seaway. Also aboard was the required pilot who, for the 40 miles from entering to exiting the locks, would be the captain. How small we were perched 100 feet below the walls of our water passageway. At the pilot's signal, workers way above us on the channel walls tossed four "monkey fists" with messenger lines to the port and starboard sides where the four of us awaited, nervous and ready to capture them when they hit the deck. All four "monkey fists" landed within easy reach, and each of us grabbed ours and tied it off to a cleat. As the sluices closed, water poured into the lock. The boat rose, and the experienced workers on either side of the canal gathered in the lines, keeping them taut to avoid **Le Petit Prince** drifting to starboard or port and crashing against the iron walls. The exact process was repeating aboard the ***Jeanne d'Arc***. French sailors, arrayed along the training ship's stern, cheered as the two ships ascended together.

The process would be repeated through two more locks until we had risen 85 feet above sea level to Gatun Lake, the artificial lake over which we would transit the 21 miles across the Isthmus of Panama. As the workers quickly gathered in the lines and turned us loose, we waved goodbye with hollered thanks and smoothly entered Lake Gatun to meet our appointment with the locks on the west side of the canal.

It was a beautiful day, and our pilot generously allowed us to sail so long as we could maintain our speed at six knots. Though we had guaranteed to the port authorities that we carried enough fuel to make the transit, Vicente and I weren't 100% sure that was true. The pilot allowing us to sail removed the specter of being stranded on the lake with neither wind nor engine power. The ***Jeanne d'Arc*** quickly distanced herself as her big engines kicked in. The sailors amassed on the stern waved and whistled as they left us behind. A couple even tossed their hats overboard. Watching three women working aboard a sailing vessel in bathing suits had undoubtedly broken the monotony of their long voyage from France to Tahiti and the Marquesas. Our journey ahead would be long, but seldom would monotony settle in.

Because the **Jeanne d'Arc** had already gone through the locks on the Pacific side, we were scheduled to go through the western locks with another ship. We arrived right on time and slipped in behind the big cargo ship for the downward journey. This time water rushed out of the series of locks, and the rope handlers reeled out their coiled lines as the water dropped through first one chamber, across the small Miraflores Lake, then down through the two chambers of the Miraflores Locks. We sailed into the Port of Balboa, paid our two women crewmembers, left them and our pilot on the docks, and anchored out in the harbor where we spent two nights. Refueled, restocked with water and food, we mailed the letter off to Jackson and prepared ourselves as well as we could for the deep-water adventure that lay ahead.

Timing our departure from the western harbor of the canal so that we would be leaving the island designate with our cargo as evening fell, we pulled up anchor and motored out to raise the sails and catch the winds. The small island appeared on the near horizon, and we sailed into a tiny, protected anchorage with a barely visible dock. We tied up and waited. Three men appeared, and we made our rendezvous with the Panamanian growers. We gave them gifts Jackson had sent, inspected the crop as we all worked feverishly to fill the sail bags and load them onto **Le Petit Prince,** counted the money into their hands, and as evening fell, we sailed out of the little cove.

Those miles sailing away from the island were tense aboard **Le Petit Prince**. We scanned the horizon, searching for ship lights that might be Federales. As the night wore on, neither of us could sleep, so we talked of our dream, and we reiterated the story we would tell if we were caught so as not to implicate Jackson. With each nautical mile, we dared our little grins to broaden. Concerned only with putting distance between the law and us, we pushed **Le Petit Prince** with full sails and trailing winds into the midnight hour. I mused to myself how altogether incomprehensibly insane it was that we weren't watching out for sea-going pirates, that we were the pirates. That was a little mind-boggling even for my adventurous spirit! By morning we felt we'd put a reasonable distance between ourselves and Panama, so we pulled out the sextant, took a sighting, set our course, and trimmed our sails. We settled into what would be 55 days at sea with **Le Petit Prince's** fo'c'sle filled to the limit with *Panama Red*, the gold standard, along with *Acapulco Gold*, of the weed of the 70s. We felt that the most dangerous part of the journey was over.

12
1979

Emancipation of the Dreamer from the Dream

As **Le Petit Prince** wended her way north northwest, I read and journaled, recorded dreams, cooked and sewed, and took my watches at the helm. My favorite times were sitting in the cockpit, warmed by the sun, embroidering flowers and curls on shirts I'd sewn for Ron and Pam. On the back of each shirt, I'd stitched a *mola* that I had acquired from the Guna Indian women during the days sailing the San Blas Islands. I couldn't wait to hand the shirts to them.

Our south to north transit from Panama to San Diego, California, with the winds steady out of the northwest, meant we would have to run close to the wind most of the trip. There are choices in how to sail up the coast of Central America: 1. A boat can hug the shore and sail into the harbors and anchorages that line the coast. 2. A boat can do short tacks (trajectories) back and forth, a little west-northwest, then come about and run east-southeast, repeat, and repeat endlessly. 3. Or one can make long extended tacks before coming about and tacking back. We chose the third option. On the first tack, sailing north-northwest, always close to the wind, we sailed within 600 miles of Hawaii. At this almost arbitrary point, we came about and tacked east-southeast toward the western coast of Central America. We would make one more long tack, north-northwest, then finally we would turn the bow east-southeast and sail into a small anchorage on the coast of Mexico.

Running close to the wind, our bodies adjusted over the days to the boat being heeled over, the leeward scuppers of the boat deck skimming near the water's surface. The winds held steady, so for days on end, with only minor adjustments, we left the steering to the self-steering mechanism we had built. These were long leisurely days and nights sitting in the cockpit or sometimes on deck soaking up the sun by day and at night gazing meditatively at the horizon where stars disappeared into the sea. We had long conversations about Jung, our nighttime dreams, and planned for our trip west, where we'd go first, how long we'd stay. Once a week, we'd rub dry shampoo into our hair and then shower with a gallon of water each. Vicente would pour just enough water over me to wet my skin, scrub me all over with soap, and then he'd slowly pour the remainder of the gallon, first over my head, and then let it trickle over the rest of my tanned body. In turn, I would serve him. These weekly showers were the perfect foreplay to our lovemaking as **Le Petit Prince** sailed us surely and safely toward home and financial promise.

I was a good sailor, and we trusted each other explicitly no matter the conditions. We took sun sightings to determine our position a couple of times a day. I always felt such satisfaction when peering through the sextant, I'd moved the arm of the sextant to bring the sun's image down to the horizon and say, "Now." In that instant, Vicente would press the button on the chronometer. Sometimes our roles were reversed, but either way, after the sighting, we'd go down below, read the sextant, make calculations with the aid of the Celestial Almanac tables and plot our position on the chart. Outside was the broad expanse of blue from horizon to horizon. On the chart, that broad expanse of blue was translated to latitude, longitude, degrees. A tiny dot that we marked on the chart each day denoted **Le Petit Prince** on the endless ocean of blue.

Onboard our 31' 10" home, we seldom thought of our boat's size until we sailed across shipping lanes. Massive ships that would grow from a tiny dot on the horizon to leviathan monsters dwarfed our tiny ship. At night, sailing in the shipping lanes, all our senses were on high alert, and when we'd see a ship's lights in the distance, we'd watch their course and adjust our trajectory accordingly. If one of those ships happened to run us over, those aboard would feel only a slight bump as though we were driftwood.

On this sojourn, in the daytime brilliance of sun and sea, muted nighttime light of stars and sea, the sound of **Le Petit Prince** moving through the water, Vicente and I lived in a beautiful bubble of deep relating. Thoughts of our cargo hardly entered our awareness. Not once during the whole journey did we feel the urge to open a sail bag, pull out a bud, and roll a joint. I was high on life.

Yet, disturbingly, my dreams sometimes told a different story than "a beautiful bubble of deep relating." The earliest of the dreams came in the summer of 1977. In the dream, I'm trying to scramble aboard **Le Petit Prince** from the ocean, and though I call out to him, Vicente won't help me. I see sharks, and I am panicked. I know I'm going to die and cry out for Vicente to help me, but he ignores me.

The second dream came a year and a half later and left little room in its meaning.

Dream - Winter 1979 – Sailing to San Diego from Panama
I am swimming in a swimming pool, seem to be the only one in the pool, then swim over to the side and am relaxing in the water at the side of the pool. Suddenly I feel someone above me poolside pushing my head down, holding me underwater. I am fighting like crazy to surface; my breath is running out. Finally, with a surge of strength, I get the hands off me, or maybe I duck out from under them and sputtering, I break the water surface. As I'm gasping, wiping the water from my face, I look up just in time to see Vicente's back as he hurries out of the room. I realize it was him trying to drown me.

Yet, until the final sail into a tiny bay in Mexico, I refused to give up the South Pacific dream of sailing to a paradisiacal world with Vicente. I refused to believe my dreams' seriousness and insisted on telling my unconscious that all would be different once we had money. "And besides," I'd argue with myself, "I've found the man that dares to be a partner in this dream and adventure. No one else has dared follow through. We're in tune with each other right now, so enough already!"

As we approached the landmass of Mexico, forces began to exert pressure on our apparent tranquility. Like locusts appearing on the horizon, warships surrounded us, battleships, cruisers, carriers. Planes buzzed overhead; loud booms erupted. And though rationally we knew it had nothing to do with us and our cargo – I mean, it wouldn't take an entire navy to arrest one little sailboat - it was nerve-wracking to sail through the panoply of ships. With binoculars, we made out that some ships were flying American flags, some Mexican flags, and we surmised we were in the middle of joint military maneuvers. From all directions, thunderous shots rang out, and the rumblings of the enormous engines reverberated through the water. We held **Le Petit Prince** steady as we sailed through and beyond the theater of war games. As outside events are often mirrored by internal events in powerful synchronicities, following our exit from this pseudo war, Vicente dropped a bomb that detonated in my psyche.

Sitting in the cockpit, **Le Petit Prince,** on course for the little bay we would enter to disguise her, Vicente cleared his throat. "I don't want to go to the South Pacific."

"What?" I demanded shrilly. My eyes searched his for clarity, "What are you saying?"

"Well, I've been thinking about my future over the past days as we're getting close to the end of the trip, and I realize I'm ready to do something different. There's a writing project I've been pondering, and I want to put my attention and time there. You know, I've been travelling for years now, it's time to stop moving . . ." He halted mid-sentence. I waited. He offered no further words.

"But what about our dream to sail to the South Pacific TOGETHER? We'll finally have the money. This voyage west is what we've talked and dreamed about these years since we left San Diego."

"That was then; this is now. I want to use the money to go to the mountains somewhere and have time for my writing project." His tone admitted of no argument.

"What about us?" I weakly questioned. I wanted to say more, but something stopped me, perhaps the memory of the dream of Vicente drowning me. And yet, like a drowning person, I clung to a wispy straw of hope that we could stay together, and in some phantasmagorical edifice I'd build, I wouldn't feel drowned by him. I made one last effort, "Are you sure?"

"Yes, I'm absolutely sure. You know I've made two long-distance sailing voyages, and I'm through with the sea. At least as far as I can imagine my life in the future." I couldn't argue with his observation and could even understand it a bit.

No sleep came that night to calm my torturous thoughts, the substance of which the reader can easily surmise. Through that night of tossing with the boat's motion, grateful for my watch sitting under the stars, I contemplated my future. By morning I had decided what my path would be.

We sat in the cockpit finishing our morning coffee like hundreds of other mornings aboard **Le Petit Prince**. "As you can imagine, I didn't sleep much last night after your pronouncement. I don't want to keep **Le Petit Prince** and try to get to the South Pacific alone. And as I must accept it's not my destiny to see that promised land, I've decided to go to France. Once we're back in the USA, since neither of us wants to sail, let's sell the boat, and as soon as accounts vis-à-vis our share of the marijuana sales and the boat sale are settled, I'll be moving to France." I paused, and as he said nothing, I continued, "For reasons very different from the call of the South Pacific, Paris too has called to me." I waited; Vicente gave no response. It was then that the driving force behind my decision surged forth, "In truth, I want to go there and be alone, so alone, I weep and wail. All my life, I have been with a man, going from one relationship to another, starting with my father, Don, RT, Jackson, you. I want to be alone, alone, alone." The rising vehemence of these last words left no question about my decision. My *Intent* was strong as I took responsibility for the decision my dreams demanded. I was chagrined, yet also grateful that Vicente had taken the initiative to usher in our new directions. The hoped-for money, originally intended to fund our trip to the South Pacific, would now instead serve our separation.

I spent hours as we sailed the last leg of our voyage, sitting in the cockpit or on deck, staring at the horizon, and contemplating the words that had burst from me, "I want to be so alone I weep and wail." The words were perhaps overly dramatic, but I came to realize they were the words of that child of long ago, who sat alone in the Sun Room, and made the decision not to need anybody and had uttered the promise to herself.

I will not be touched ever by the need to be seen and loved.
I am an island, and no one can ever cross the ocean around me and touch me.

Though it wasn't clear at the time, I came to recognize the dramatic words as a cry for space to build the foundations of self-love, to open my heart, and to rebuild my ego. I welcomed the challenge to test and tear out the roots of my decision.

Two days later, we entered the isolated little bay in Mexico we had chosen on the chart. We dropped anchor, relieved to see we were the sole occupants. We were right on target with our timeline and set to work to transform **Le Petit Prince**. With scrub brushes, we cleaned off the barnacles and algae that had accumulated on the waterline and keel during the trip that would be a signal we'd been at sea for a long time. We freshened up the decks and painted the yellow hull white with brown trim. Unscrewing the **Le Petit Prince** nameplate from the stern, we replaced it with an already prepared plaque with numbers that were part of the American boat registration system. And finally, we took down our Argentinean flag and hung an American flag.

Along with the race to leave the Panamanian island of marijuana growers, our next maneuver was the second riskiest part of the trip.

EMANCIPATION OF THE DREAMER FROM THE DREAM

With this subterfuge of transforming our boat, we intended to create a picture, an impression. We hoped that as we sailed into American waters through the night, and as dawn broke, we would be viewed as just one more pleasure boat out for a day's cruise. Timing was everything as we left the bay in the darkness and set sail for Santa Catalina Island, one of the Channel Islands south-southwest of Long Beach, California. It would take many hours of sailing, and we hoped the winds held steady, though we had some fuel for motoring if that became necessary for our rendezvous with **Ariadne**.

As we were counting down the hours till we reached the islands, a violent storm arose. It would be the worst storm of our three years of sailing. We had no choice but to turn **Le Petit Prince** out toward the open seas. We decided to "heave-to," meaning we set the jib in tight, reefed the mainsail way down, firmly tied the tiller, and battened down the hatches. We went below and waited. The boat creaked and groaned and strained, monster waves crashed across her decks, water dripped through unseen cracks. Sitting on a bunk, I could see the mast moving where it passed through the deck into the keel. I talked to **Le Petit Prince**, thanked her for our voyage, and asked her to carry us through this one last storm. Vicente and I talked of what we should do if serious trouble arose like a broken mast, broken steering, or the boat taking on water, and we had to start setting off flares, our only mayday option. We reluctantly agreed that we'd throw the bags over with weights, though it wasn't a solution we relished, nor were we sure we could do it in these storm conditions. It was with disbelief I contemplated this last hurrah to raise money, sinking to the bottom of the ocean.

I thought of storms as generally a 3-day affair, and I didn't see how we'd get through that scenario. Never before had we been forced to wait out a storm, hunkered down below. Completely battening down the hatches with no one in the cockpit was new territory. Feeling every creak and groan, listening to the angry winds tearing at our little boat, both of us tuned into our small ship as never before. Minutes were hours were minutes as my ears strained to hear even the tiniest of unfamiliar sounds that would herald disaster. Occasionally, one of us would hold tight to the railings along the bulkhead as the boat's motion threatened to throw us down and retrieve crackers and chocolate from our dwindled food resources. My ears strained to detect any shift. About 20 hours into the storm, I thought I sensed something. "Is it lessening?" I asked Vicente.

"Yes, I think so, I think so. The boat seems to be creaking and groaning less."

"Dare we hope?" I asked into the void. And if in response, I heard the winds yield ever so slightly, heard less water sloshing over the decks, felt the boat's pitching soften. We were on deck as soon as we dared, raised the stays'l to half-mast, and turned the bow east toward Santa Catalina Island. Prayer or no prayer, I thanked the powers that be, and most especially, I thanked our little ship. It was early evening when we sailed into the designated island bay and dropped anchor. We quickly noted that **Ariadne** wasn't in the harbor. Guessing she wouldn't be arriving that night, we made a simple dinner and succumbed to the sleep of babes.

In the morning, I popped my head out of the hatch to the soft sun of dawn and gazed around at the green and blue palette of island, sea, and sky. Too impatient to cook, we quickly made coffee and ate a cold granola breakfast. Grabbing snacks and water, we launched our dinghy, rowed to shore, and chained *Tudo Bem* to a cleat on the little dock. From the shore, we hiked to a high spot facing east and settled in to scan the arriving boats. It was just after noon when through binoculars, I saw the familiar outline of **Ariadne**. Vicente and I yelled, pointed, and hugged as if a liberating army had sailed into view. We hurried downhill and rowed like crazy to **Le Petit Prince**. A couple of hours later, **Ariadne** sailed into the anchorage. I jumped up and down and waved like a crazy woman. The tears coursing down my cheeks were warm salty beads of joy that I licked and savored. Ever since we had passed through the war games, changed our boat's identity, and sailed through this final storm, the frayed edges of my nerves were about to explode. Sweet relief flooded my contracted soul.

Jackson expertly sailed close, dropped his anchor, and drifted back until **Ariadne** was alongside **Le Petit Prince**. Then, like other boaters, many there to party and play, we threw out the bumpers and lashed the boats together. Jackson and Charlotte came aboard, and the four of us shared dinner and a bottle of champagne they'd brought. We regaled each other with sailing tales and toasted our venture, our boats, each other, and of course, the cargo **Le Petit Prince** carried. Then, laughing at the irony, we went forward, pulled out a couple of buds, rolled a joint, and tasted and tested our *Panama Red*!

When the night grew late, and one by one, boat lights were extinguished, and the outlines softened in the darkness, barefooted and wordless, we transferred the sail bags to **Ariadne**. In the morning, Vicente and I stood on the deck of **Le Petit Prince** and waved goodbye to Jackson and Charlotte as they carried our valuable cargo the last leg of its long sea journey, safely into a Long Beach marina. Once **Ariadne** was well on her way, Vicente and I pulled up anchor and headed south back to Mexico.

We entered the same isolated bay where we had transformed our boat and spent a few days reversing what we'd done just days before. We repainted the boat the original colors of yellow with green trim, screwed to the stern our beautifully carved wooden name plaque, **Le Petit Prince**. On the backstay, we re-hoisted our tattered Argentinean blue and white flag, along with the required courtesy flag of the country of entry, the stars and stripes. Leaving the little bay's tranquility, we embarked on the final sail aboard **Le Petit Prince**. For the last time, we pulled up anchor, determined our compass heading, trimmed the sails, and sailed forth. That last leg of our years-long journey was an achingly sad and poignant time. Filled with nostalgia for the ineffable adventures we'd shared over the previous few years, I did my best to let go as each nautical mile brought us closer to San Diego.

We sailed into San Diego Harbor, where we had each arrived so many years ago, Vicente from the south and me from the north. I opened to the welcoming arms of this old friend. We tied up to the customs dock, and Vicente, as the captain, sought out the customs officials. By the time they arrived, my mood was light and welcoming, and they were equally cordial: unsuspecting and conversational. Our papers were in order; they neither saw nor smelled any red flags. While they reviewed our documents and passports, they told us how impressed they were that just the two of us had made that long voyage. They stamped our passports, and when they'd disembarked, one of the agents turned and smiled at me, "Welcome home."

We motored away from the customs dock, entered the San Diego Bay anchorage, and dropped anchor where the saga of Vicente and Diane had begun. Everything else would be anti-climactic. We hugged, smiled, made love, and headed to the Red Robin for hamburgers and *pina colados*, where years before Jackson and I, and Emilio and Vicente, had sat and talked and laughed, eaten hamburgers, and Vicente had made a toast to *pina colados*.

In our last two months together, with no relationship stresses, no coup d'états, no storms demanding minute-by-minute attention, no boat maintenance, no illegal cargo, no financial concerns, our time together bordered on a celebration of a relationship survived and even well-lived. We'd occasionally make love, more like old friends than lovers. Though unspoken, there was a tacit agreement that our job now was simply to wrap things up as impeccably as we could. In the future, we would have one last encounter that would be less amiable, but thankfully, that future was unknown.

Vicente and I bought a bright blue Ford station wagon a few days after arriving in San Diego anchorage. As soon as **Le Petit Prince** was secured and we'd found someone to keep an eye on her, we drove north to Bellingham, landing at my mom and Bill's. Driving through the gate, seeing their cozy home and well-kept gardens surrounded by a sweeping lawn, intricate and complex emotions swallowed me momentarily. I was the eternal prodigal daughter arriving on my mother's doorstep returning from that first adventure in the summer of '61. I was returning now in 1979 with a new husband from whom I'd soon be splitting. And in a weird way, I was just stopping by.

Mom came out on the porch to greet us. Though it had only

been six months since I'd seen her, it felt like years, as so much had changed in my life. Our hugs were long and hard. I introduced her to Vicente, my husband, and she gravely shook his hand. "I'm glad to meet you. Are you hungry? Do you want coffee?" We went inside, and I introduced Vicente and Bill. (The truth is that while I was glad Mom had Bill's companionship and support, he always remained a background figure for me as I didn't much like him.)

"Coffee would be great, mom. Good to be home. I'll put our things in the bedroom. By the way, Ron and Pam are driving up tomorrow. I guess they can sleep on the couch or in your trailer, right?"

"Yes, of course. It'll be great to see them. How long will they stay?"

"A few days, I hope. It depends on Ron's work schedule. Vicente and I will probably be here for a couple of weeks. Hope that's okay." Not giving her time to respond, I continued, "I want to show him the northwest, and the kids know Vicente, so it'll be fun to be together with them."

"Oh, how do they know him?" she asked."

"Well, it's a long story. I'll tell you over lunch, okay."

"Sure, that's fine."

At Mom's, I witnessed another iteration of Vicente that blew me away. He was curious about Marian! The two of them would often sit together, and he'd question her about her life and listen attentively to every word, and she positively glowed from the attention. In one of life's ironies, Marian turned out to like Vicente more than she'd ever liked Jackson.

Vicente and I wiled away the days and weeks in the northwest, sightseeing in the San Juan Islands aboard ferries and driving on land from Vancouver, Canada, to Seattle, Washington. Whenever they were available, Ron and Pam joined us. At last, the eagerly-awaited call came from Jackson - the sale of most of the marijuana was complete. Hallelujah! We retraced our steps south to reconnoiter with him and Charlotte in northern California. Spending a couple of days with them, we celebrated success and parsed out the money. From there, our coffers at long last full, we drove to San Diego. The only remaining task was a car for Vicente, and when we'd completed that, it was time for me to go.

On my last night aboard **Le Petit Prince,** Vicente made dinner, and we shared a bottle of wine. Sitting across from him, I could only conjure beautiful memories. We folded out the single bunk into the double bed we'd shared in so many countries and across the many moods of the sea. As we undressed and slipped into bed, I could almost believe we had a future together. Making love that night, though one might think it was poignant and heartful, truth is I was lost in thoughts of what could have been, intersecting with what was to come.

In the morning, we motored to a dock and tied up in a guest slot. Vicente helped me carry my possessions off **Le Petit Prince**. When I collected the last box and turned to climb the stairs out the hatch, my legs refused to move. I leaned against the chart table and bowed my head as the tears flowed. I was glad Vicente was outside, and I was alone to feel the depths of my sadness. "It's over," I whispered to myself and willed my feet to take the few steps to the stairs and climb out the hatch closing the book on my sea-faring life. I loaded the last box into the Ford and turned to Vicente to say goodbye. I rested in his arms one last time: our kiss goodbye was more mellow than passionate. Nevertheless, my heart was in my throat as I drove away from our little ship, my eyes glued to the rearview mirror as **Le Petit Prince** receded. I would miss her gentle embrace and sure-heartedness in the face of all the ocean had thrown at us and the loss of a magnificent dream aboard her.

Leaving San Diego, where Jackson's and my dream had died, and Vicente's and mine had begun and died, brought the close of an era. Vicente would be my last relationship where I would succumb to a man's power because I had been unable to recognize, to remember, the powerful *Shakti* energy in me and had relinquished that power to another. It took me a long time to fathom the abusive nature of Vicente's and my relationship. I was so enamored of his power and confidence that sometimes I was amazed that he had chosen me. It would be even more years before I could relate this sentiment to that of the young girl, who, though her father abused her, was proud that he had chosen her.

And finally, I can sum up why I chose to be with Vicente in one word: *Intent*. He embodied masculine *Intent*. Though I felt hurt by the shape of his *Intent*, there was no denying his wielding of its power. That day I'd sat with him in the cockpit of **Le Petit Prince** and laid out my future in France, I graduated into a conscious embodiment of feminine *Intent*. I didn't necessarily gauge it at the time or consciously define what it meant, but looking back, all the pieces fit into my *Intent* toward wholeness and the full expression of *Shakti Energy* moving inside me. This was the journey I was on, and the brightness of my future buoyed my spirit.

13

Summer 1979

End of an Era

The sea had taught me how to meet fear. I had learned that fear didn't exist in the midst of challenging, even dangerous situations. My fear only flourished in idle imagining. Thus reassured, in 1979, I would launch into the loneliest and yet richest time I could imagine. I would feel psychologically unbalanced at times - be afraid I was losing my mind. Still, I would find the strength to fight my way through, in part because of the trial by fire of that year in Argentina with Vicente and the incomparable voyages aboard **Le Petit Prince**.

I arrived back in the northwest a few days after leaving San Diego. To account for the money I now had, I simply informed everyone I had sold my share of **Le Petit Prince** to Vicente. (It would be many long years before I dared acknowledge where the money had actually come from.) With part of the largesse, I bought five acres of land in Alger, Washington. With the remainder of the funds, I would support my inner and outer explorations for several years.

Not far from the property I bought, my brother Don and his wife Penny, who were living in Washington DC, where Penny, a lieutenant in the navy, was stationed, had seven acres. They had cleared a large site and installed an extended single-wide trailer. The clearing was surrounded by towering Douglas firs, with a stream running through the land whose faint sounds drifted up to where I was ensconced. Though it was primitive, I was grateful for the roof over my head, the stream from which I would haul pristine water, and the nurturing ambiance of the forest.

Serendipitously, I discovered an intensive summer course in French

END OF AN ERA

through Western Washington University, where I had earned my BA a lifetime ago. Laurent and Anne, two young women from France, taught the class by speaking only French with us for three hours each day. Perfect! I would reconnect with both of them when I went to live in the south of France. Meantime, once again, into my lap, spirit delivered what I needed.

Though reluctant, their dad allowed Ron and Pam to drive up and spend weekends with me. From the mundane, taking them shopping for school clothes, to the exotic, taking them to my French class's end-of-semester party where we danced and sang together, I felt like the luckiest woman alive. I listened eagerly to details of school, and they questioned me of my sailing adventures. When I would recount a tale, I'd ask them how that was for them. They would reassure me that they wanted to hear everything. They agreed they were doing great living with their dad, though they would hint from time to time that sometimes Carol was difficult. If I questioned them further, they simply shrugged and said it was okay, and I didn't press them. (I would only learn of how challenging it had been when, as Carol was dying from throat cancer in 2004, she apologized for how mean and parsimonious she had been with them, especially Pam. It was a powerful healing time for the three of them, and though I had stayed out of the kids' relationship with Don and Carol, I was touched and grateful for this gesture Carol had made at the end of her life.) We visited old sailing friends from our days of living aboard **Ariadne** when Ron and Pam were kids, and I smiled proudly when our friends exclaimed over the delightful, mature teenagers Ron and Pam had become. Most important of all, we lovingly re-tied the severed strands of our family of three.

I was unformed in many ways, still looking for my grounding, so I honestly admit that at this point, seeing that they were doing great with Don, I didn't consider staying in Bellingham or Seattle. The three of us talked about it, and both kids were accepting of my journey and reiterated that they were comfortably settled into being typical teenagers in the middle-class life of their dad and stepmom. The unvarnished truth is that in these years, being a mother was the background to being a seeker of knowledge, not only of new countries and places but also into the most hidden corners of my psyche: a calling that had an imperious quality I could not ignore.

While in the northwest, I had an intention born of my fatigue living in a man's world. I determined to "be with a woman." To this end, one weekend, I went to a coastal town on the northeastern end of the Olympic peninsula. Several friends from my Washington sailing days had boats docked there and lived in that little community by the sea. Two of the women had a successful boat business, and I drove to see them as soon as the ferry landed. One of them, Zoe, was the darling of everyone who knew her. She would laughingly say she'd had sex with most of the women and men in the northwest sailing community of which Jackson and I were charter members. The weekend was a reunion of old friends, sharing stories and futures, and as I flirted unashamedly with Zoe, I was holding my breath. Would she consent to initiate me into sex between women? When the social evening ended, and she invited me to spend the night with her, I was atremble with excitement and curiosity. I was already turned on when we doused the lights and snuggled into her futon on the floor. It wasn't the ultimate sexual experience for either of us. She apologized for not being more available to me. I simply thanked her for her willingness to invite me to her bed. So, if not with blazing colors and seeing stars, nevertheless, the initiation happened, and it intimated and opened my body and mind to another *Shakti* energetic possibility.

Before I left for France, I would have one more night with a woman, a friend of my brother, David. He and I were hanging out at the local gay/lesbian/straight bar playing pool, drinking beers, when across the pool table, a look passed between Lorraine and me, and just like that, we went home to her house. Unbeknownst to me, she had no experience with women. There was a comical aspect to our having sex, me after one experience being the experienced one! Unlike with my earlier friend, there was a flame we fed. Together, touching and laughing, we gave a joyful definition to the expression, "a roll in the hay." Her breasts were so large that I wasn't sure how to suck them, how much I could take into my mouth. In the end, our clitorises were both hard and extended, so we mutually masturbated each other to satisfaction and fell asleep tucked together. In the morning, she was shy, almost embarrassed she had had sex with a woman. I was content and cheerful.

Being in the embrace of a woman after the Vicente years was freeing. Vicente's sense of male entitlement was so deeply ingrained in his very cells that it admitted no argument, and I could seldom fight against this sense of himself. The passionate, feminine power inside of me, though she had found expression in lovemaking, was adrift in other aspects of Vicente's and my relationship, so she retreated to a corner of my being to fight another day. As the dream from our sailing days had shown, Vicente hadn't quite drowned me, and the first step I took in that fight was to seek a connection with women! I smile at the memory of Lorraine's big breasts. Perhaps that is what inflamed me that night across the pool table.

At the end of the summer of 1979, I gave the blue Ford to my brother, David, to use until I returned. We drove to Seattle and stayed the weekend with Barb, whose home had become my second home. On Sunday, my last day in the northwest, David, the kids' favorite uncle, and I drove to Fall City and picked up Ron and Pam. The mood was celebratory as the four of us went to a nearby mall, had dinner, and went to a movie. When I dropped Ron and Pam off at their home in Fall City, I gave each one an envelope with $1,000 inside. (The kids told me later that Don was unhappy with what I'd done – that he resented me waltzing into their lives and giving them gifts and playing while he was doing the day-to-day work of raising two teenagers. I understood his position but didn't play into his umbrage, filled as I was with the happiness of the days Ron and Pam and I had together.)

Monday morning, I boarded the train, my favorite mode of travel, for New York City. For several days, in my sleeper compartment and often socializing in the dining car, I eagerly traveled across the USA from west to east for the second time. I spent a day and night in New York City, then boarded the Russian ocean liner, **MS Mikhail Lermontov**, for the 8-day voyage across the Atlantic to Le Havre, France.

14

1979-1980

France

The Chrysalis

Cocooning in the South of France

Outside the train station, I waved down a taxi and proudly gave my destination in French. *"A la guerre."* The driver looked at me puzzled, repeating my phrase with an insolence I would often encounter as I spoke in my fledgling French with a strong American accent. I frowned, and he repeated my phrase, his frown competing with mine. Then I heard what I had asked of him, "To the war." This time, to my *"A la gare,"* I added, *"A la gare por Paris."*

"Ah-h, d'accord." With an exasperated sigh, he added, *"a la gare."*

My original phrase, *"A la guerre,"* turned out to be prophetic. In the coming war whose outlines I had intuited when I'd petitioned the infinite for the experience of ". . . being so alone I weep and wail," I would struggle to integrate my childhood dramas, insecurities, and parental craziness. In this years-long descent into the unknown, dreams would be a guiding light, and before I left for France, the unconscious sent me a dream that succinctly described the yet-to-be-defined process of opening my heart to myself and the world.

FRANCE

Dream Aug. 9, 1979, Bellingham
Together with my family in a car. I see an evil man with a knife. He gets in the car with us, a scuffle, and I somehow get his knife and am now driving. We arrive to a magical place. I run inside and find a friend dressed like an Arabian genie. His servant comes, and they both take their "wizard shields" and get ready to fight the evil man. "There he is," I shout. "he has the knife." And then I open the door. The evil man jumps inside and grabs me and stabs me with his knife on my back opposite my heart. I awaken and can feel the spot where he has stabbed me. There is no pain; rather, it is like something powerful has touched me on that spot.

In my family context, the evil man with a knife is the stilted and damaged ego of my childhood. I'm the actor who gets the knife away and drives (taking this exploration into my own hands). I arrive in a magical place of transformation, with the masculine in the service of this transformation. In this gossamer intertwining of seeming evil and magic, the dream says that it is time to destroy the old to make space for a new heart-centered ego structure. It showed me that from seeming evil and violence, the heart will open. The dream gave me hope.

This dream into the shadow world of my psyche was just one of a plethora of prescient dreams and experiences that would remind me of the vastness I could access to guide me. In the year and a half, I lived in France, like a dust mote captured inside a cocoon, I would reflect and do my best to incorporate the dream messages into my life. And one timeless day, a transformation would split open the cocoon.

After just a day in Paris, leaving its luscious bountiful table for another day, I headed south to the *gentilesse* of the French countryside. Arriving in Aix-en-Provence, with my nascent French, I found a room to rent, enrolled at *l' Université de Aix-en-Provence* to audit classes, and bought a used bicycle. I settled into student life with other international students, determined to avoid speaking English in order to advance my French language skills. This international circle of friends was perfect, as French was our common language.

In Aix-en-Provence, I was determined to pursue my childhood ambition to be a serious writer. I labored to give birth to 6 or 7 short stories and submitted them to various magazines. I received brief refusal letters. I guessed I hadn't yet found my voice. In abandoning my ambitions to write, my aloneness gained a new level of desolation.

> Journal entry Nov. 2, 1979
>
> *There is a strange floating feeling that envelopes me, isolates me - a little physical, a little mental, without reason, without time, a little scary. Hours later, I still feel the feeling and realize I'm missing touch - perhaps to ground me? Like a reluctant sleuth, I'm uncovering the aloneness I'm seeking.*

The panacea for my aborted writing attempts was the clarion call of adventure. On an early spring day, I outfitted my bicycle with saddlebags, a handlebar box, added a small backpack on my shoulders, and rode out - destination Nice, France. Ten halcyon days passed as I pedaled miles and miles along the southern coast of France, feeling the hard breath of wind as I flew down a hill after an arduous climb, arriving in an unknown town or village, finding a small hotel, enjoying wine and dinner and resting for the next day's ride. The silence I experienced reminded me of sailing on **Le Petit Prince** or **Ariadne,** except that I was alone with no trace of loneliness.

In one of the small, elegant hotels, I was surprised to find a hot tub. As soon as I'd had dinner, I headed to the Jacuzzi to relax my road-weary muscles. I joined a family of three already soaking, chatted with them briefly, then closed my eyes and settled back. I noted the family's conversation indicating that the parents were going to their room, and the twenty-something son was staying. I learned his name was Gabriel. . .and here we leave the story of Gabriel to be told later.

Soon after my return from my road trip, I knew I was through in Aix-en-Provence. I had initiated my life in France in the languor of the south, but I was intoxicated with the thought of Paris. An ostensible reason for choosing France was my attraction to the existentialists. I was reading Sartre, Kafka, and Simone de Beauvoir in English. I was hopelessly enamored with everything about Simone de Beauvoir: her writings, her lifestyle, her philosophy, and her feminism. I determined to go to Paris and read her definitive work, *Le Deuxième Sexe,* in French. I wanted to live in her city, talk in cafes, and take lovers. (I arrived in France in love with the existentialists and in particular, Beauvoir, thinking I was one of them. The irony is that in surrendering to my existential despair, I would discover that in my core, I wasn't an existentialist at all.)

Before I left the south of France, I had a remarkable dream with elements of lucid dreaming that was a disquieting picture of my fragile psychological state. In the dream of Nov. 1979, I am hiding behind a couch at my mother's house when a knock comes at the door. She throws a blanket over me as dangerous men enter. Someone rips the blanket away. I am afraid and want to awaken but decide to stay in the dream and discover what is scaring me. I wrote about the dream's ending, "I feel their faces leering above me, moving around like snake heads. I peer intently and finally make out the grotesque faces of four children with their faces painted white with mime paint. I awaken, groaning."

At the time, I was avidly reading C. G. Jung's writings, and when I came across the following passage, I thought, "Oh my god, so this is what's happening. This is why I'm in France." Jung writes:

> *If, in a dream, numerous homunculi, dwarfs, boys, etc., appear, having no individual characteristics at all, then there is the probability of a dissociation.* He continues, *On the other hand, if the plurality occurs in normal people, then it is the representation of an as yet incomplete synthesis of personality. In this case it appears that the self is still in the process of development.*

By dissociation, Jung means the splitting of the self into its component parts or complexes. These "children" in my dream all have mime paint with no individual characteristics. As Jung indicates, my psyche was either splitting apart, disintegrating, or I was "normal" and simply in the process of moving toward a synthesis of personality. In the future, this differentiation would seem moot! Paris would be a powerful geographic center for the movement toward what Jung describes as "... a complete synthesis of personality." (Eight years later in another dream, these same leering figures will reappear, transformed.)

From the intellectual existential despair and, yes, depression that drew me ultimately to Paris, I would one day leave France with new hope and excitement.

Exploding Out of the Chrysalis

In Paris, over and over, I rushed to answer ads, *'a louer'* (to rent) in papers, notice boards, and brochures. The competition for studio apartments was fierce. I was grateful to at last rent *une chambre de bonne* (a room for domestics) in the 10th arrondissement on the Rue Lafayette. The small room on the 5th floor of an apartment building, originally designed as a maid's room, fit my psyche's needs like a glove.

Across from the entrance, a dormer window overlooked Paris's rooftops. My eyes shifted inside the room. Clustered in that tiny space was a double bed, wardrobe, a hobbit-like kitchen table and two chairs, a cramped corner shower stall. Beside the shower was a sink where I'd wash dishes and brush my teeth, with a mini-refrigerator underneath. Adjacent, a one-burner stove sat atop a small cabinet. Tucked under the cabinet was a shelf with a few dishes, one pot, and a frying pan. Two empty shelves beside the cabinet completed the tableau.

In the remaining empty corner, I would construct a little shelf for the objects I always carried with me that made any space "home," and under the dormer window, I would build a shelf for my books. Outside my room, just kitty-corner from my door, was the shared W.C., an old-fashioned squat stall. Two other hall doors opened onto two more *chambers de bonne,* each occupied, as was mine, by a woman. Unquestionably, I need expansiveness outdoors whether it's the sea or open spaces to walk. However, I've always preferred small living spaces.

I enthusiastically settled into the rhythm of a *Parisienne.* After breakfast, I'd take the elevator down, greet the concierge who always seemed to be looking out her window, pass through the building's entryway, and cross the street to the neighborhood vendors. At each shop, a simple stall that opened to the street with an iron grate door lowered when the grocers weren't there, I'd browse and chat as I bought the day's groceries. Most enchanting of all was *le fromagerie*, the unending variety of cheeses I'd never even guessed existed. I would sample them all, my favorite being the mold-encrusted goat's cheeses. With my cloth bags, I'd move onto *le épicerie verte, la boulangerie, le magasin de vin*. Returning home, I would take the elevator to the 4th floor where it stopped, slide open the iron gate, and climb the stairs to the 5th floor. When I unlocked the door, groceries in hand, the room welcomed me. It was both my refuge and my pressure cooker. *La vie Parisienne* agreed with me, and I dreamed of living permanently in Paris.

Mid-morning, shopping done, baguette and cheese in my backpack, I'd board the metro to a destination I'd chosen to sharpen my sensual acuity, and bring light into my "dark night of the soul." The museums were a feast for my eyes and soul. At the Centre Pompidou, I was thrilled to discover a Salvador Dali exhibition. I gazed at the enormous canvasses I'd only seen in art books, entranced by the brush strokes and textures and the sheer audacity of his work. I repeatedly returned to the Impressionist paintings - their brilliant colors, soft lines of light and shadow that urged the viewer to enter the moment – reflecting my ambitions to live in the moment, not in the past or future. I often spent the afternoon at the Musée Rodin, where the sculptures and gardens conspired to illuminate the sublime. The sprawling parks, some sculpted and some seeming almost wild satisfied my need for nature. At sidewalk cafés, I'd sit engrossed in the movie-like scene of Paris streets.

My rambling would often take me to the magnificent Notre Dame. I'd first climb the stairs to the balconies and look out over the rooftops of Paris, and then, like a long-anticipated dessert after a lavish meal, I'd enter the nave and find a seat in the back. The cathedral's interior, where streaming light illuminated the glory and brilliance of the stained glass in every corner, I would peer intently and let the luminosity draw me into a deep and desolate meditative space. Yes, in all its splendid diversity, Paris provided succor to my seclusion that, though wished-for, nevertheless left me melancholic.

In this enticing exotic city, filled with unknown dangers and promise, I was the 18-year-old in San Francisco, in an unfamiliar environment where I was seeking something I couldn't put into words. This time though, I didn't have Peggy at my side. When she and I had gone to San Francisco, the term "freedom" was the operative word embodied by our shared ambition, "Be a perennial wanderer." Here in Paris, freedom was still the operative word, though it was couched in the idea of loneliness. There would be moments of depressed, suicidal ideation as I struggled in solitude to hold onto my sanity. As the months wore on, the purpose I'd set for myself, "...to be so alone I weep and wail," entered an even more stark chapter.

Tucked away in my nest on the fifth floor, a tale I'd kept hidden from myself pricked my conscious awareness; I was drinking like Dayton. At lunch and dinner, *comme une vrai Parisienne*, I always accompanied the meal with wine. I would tip the bottle and pour the liquid into one of the two wine glasses I had bought until I was, well, yes, mildly to majorly intoxicated. I used alcohol to obliterate my primary identity and shift into an altered state. In my alcoholic haze, I was often maudlin, and I'd experience loneliness in every corner of my being. I felt it in body sensations, saw visions of it in my dreams, smelled it even. There were two parts of me: one on the edge of wanting to end the pain and desperation, and another that knew I was right where I needed to be. I couldn't guess how the scales would tip.

While external activities enriched my conscious mind, one could even say kept it occupied, the unconscious had free rein, and ran like a wild horse on a rangeland of mystery. My dream life accelerated with dreams of violence, killing, dying, sexual encounters, and orgies. As I would write them down, I would feel shame and embarrassment at the scenes my unconscious was throwing up. I tried to reassure myself that this was simply the unconscious getting my attention: that I was metaphorically dying and also alive with sexuality, intuiting what I would come to know as sensual *Shakti Energy* - the vehicle for my awakening.

By late spring, several incidents pushed my loneliness to almost unbearable, mind-numbing dimensions. A man, a government bureaucrat whom I'd met in the park and often walked and talked with, turned on me when I refused his advances. He insisted I was a stupid manly American woman, lacking a French women's femininity, and understood nothing. That I didn't belong in Paris, and why didn't I go home to America? With his words burning in my brain, I saw myself a failure as a wannabe woman in France emulating Simone de Beauvoir.

And there was the night I waited in a cavernous nightclub for a friend who had invited me to meet up with him and a couple of friends. I found a seat, grateful to be ignored by the young women sitting around me in the arrangement of chairs and couches I'd chosen. For two hours, I ordered drinks and waited, my eyes glued to the door. When it was almost midnight, I knew they weren't coming. I picked up my purse and jacket and skulked across the floor to the door, sure everyone was thinking, "Look at that 35-year-old woman slinking to the door. How pathetic." Outside, feeling vulnerable and lost, unable to face navigating the underground, I spent precious money on a taxi.

And lastly had been a letter from my sister, Laura, when she innocently shared a little news of Ron and Pam of which I was unaware. Along with my daily drinking, these incidents coalesced to set off a pivotal event a couple of weeks later.

Sitting in my room one evening, I viscerally experienced evil presences lurking in the dark corners of my room and knew I'd reached the breaking point. Somehow, only the goddess knows how, I summoned a tendril of sanity, and decided to go to a movie. I resolved that if I didn't meet someone or a shape-shifting event didn't occur, I would consider giving up and going home. Perhaps it was time to retreat.

I debated between a French or an American film and decided I didn't have the mental bandwidth to listen closely to French, so I chose, *The Rose*. The theater wasn't too full, and before the lights lowered, I quickly surveyed the moviegoers, wondering, who or what might be the person or event? Watching the movie in the anonymous darkness of the theater, carried into my psyche and that of Janis Joplin, I couldn't stop the tears when Bette Midler sang *The Rose*, feeling the words as an expression of the pathos of my life. Watching the disintegration of Bette Midler's character was like seeing a version of myself.

Wiping my nose and drying my eyes as the lights came on, I arose and exited the theater into a warm spring Paris night. Wending my way through the ubiquitous evening strollers, I descended to the metro. When the train arrived, I chose a random car, stepped inside, and paused to survey the passengers. And like a long-awaited epiphany, there he sat. My eyes took in his tousled light brown hair (I would learn it was a perm), pale blue eyes set in an adorable youthful face. But what ambushed my attention was the softness emanating from his very being. I had never been attracted to this quality in a man.

From those long months of despair, I emerged boldly from the chrysalis of aloneness at this moment somewhere in the Paris underground. With seductive intention, as I would over and over when the right man appeared to join in my tantric unfolding, I walked down the aisle, nodded, and took the seat across from him. *"Bonsoir,"* I greeted him. He returned the greeting, and I jumped into the opening and inquired in my best French, "Weren't you at the movie, *The Rose*?" He looked a little startled and replied yes. I carried on in French, "What did you think?"

"You're American, aren't you?" I replied in the affirmative. In English, his proficiency about equal to my French, he said he had been to America the summer before. He loved America. And thus, our conversation launched, I felt his keen enthusiasm equal to mine.

As the train approached my stop, I stood up, and with little to lose, I spoke. "This is my stop. Would you like to come have a drink at my place so we can keep talking?"

"Mais, oui," he replied, and his beguiling smile shot an arrow straight into my heart. That chance meeting, or perhaps not chance meeting, opened the doorway into Paris and friends. That night reaffirmed for me the power of *intention* that had come at my breaking point. The war, *la guerre*, was far from being over, but I had forced a retreat.

A Love Affair

His name was Jacques Denis. The three significant men in my life up to that point, even including Lyle, fit the moniker "macho men." I would often find myself overtly or covertly in opposition to their machismo. In the incubator of Paris, the hints that I didn't need a man to compete with, to be male-identified with, whispered. Jacques Denis was the herald of this shift.

I had been living in a self-imposed tundra of winter ice, cutting holes through the crust, dropping a line into the dark ocean of unconsciousness, fishing for what I could, pulling the catch up into consciousness, and facing my demons of the deep. Now it was time for the warm caresses of springtime, the hot sun of summer. The blossoming love between Jacques Denis and me melted that tundra of ice as we would move and dance our lives together night and day.

We made love that first night, and he stayed the night. We were both delighted and even a little surprised to awaken together. We talked intimately as we lay in the freshness of the morning. Most remarkable of all was when he spoke of several operations he had suffered through as a very young child and that his mother had left amid the operations. I wondered about the trauma for him, but it was clear that he had come to accept this traumatic history. There was no apology in his voice, no remorse for what the medical profession had imposed on him. I was so turned on by his honesty and tenderness, his lack of machismo, and my hand followed my heart's desire as it slid from his testicles to his penis that was already hard. Our lovemaking was sweet and gentle, just like him. Even my orgasm, which oftentimes was intense and raucous, was quieter, my groans softened to tender grateful moans of pleasure.

Jacques Denis introduced me to his closest friends, and they instantly included me, so un-French in some ways. I learned that they were all teachers in the public school system, a couple of them, including Jacques Denis, in schools with a high Arab population, politically far left, and committed social activists, joining protests in the streets. Wow, this was a dream, connecting with this part of the Paris scene.

The sexual orientation among his friends was diverse, and I saw such ease among them: a straight couple, Marie and Javier; a gay couple, Arnaud and Guy; a single lesbian, Nicole; and a single straight woman, Colette. In early August, Marie and Javier, Nicole, Colette plus Jacques Denis, and I traveled to the countryside to a big farmhouse they had rented for two weeks. Like all *Parisiennes* that could, they left Paris during August.

When we drove up the hill to our retreat, a few remaining wildflowers lined the road. It wasn't far to the farmhouse. I remember the façade of white and gray limestone bricks covered with ivy. As we entered, the walls, floors, high ceilings were solid, as if they had stood for hundreds of years sheltering humans and animals. I was awed by the rustic kitchen, the chipped and worn tile floors, the old wooden family-size kitchen table with chairs of different styles and shapes that dominated the room, and the copper pots suspended on iron hooks from the kitchen walls. I had entered another century into a perfect womb of familial comfort. There were three bedrooms on the second floor, one on the first. Jacques Denis and I took a 2nd-floor bedroom. The atmosphere of that house permeated our bodies and the space around us and transported us to a more gentile time where there were no stresses, no cities, and no job demands.

Once unpacked, we shut the door, and smiling from ear to ear, we enticingly whispered to each other as we undressed and fell onto the quilt-covered bed. I opened to Jacques Denis's softness, and our shared joy subsumed us as our tongues and fingers traced the contours of our bodies. When he plunged inside of me, my body rose to meet his, and I melted into pre-orgasm. We rolled over, and I sat on him to take him deeper inside of me. His body moved in response to my thrusts, and my orgasm sang with hallelujahs of awe and gratitude.

The first morning at the farmhouse, like each following morning, we woke to the smell of coffee and warm fresh breakfast pastries. Jacques Denis and I joined the others around the big wooden table. As we all savored coffee and munched the fresh-baked pastries, someone inevitably asked, "Who dreamed what?" An animated discussion, with mind-blowing psychological adroitness, would carry us well into the morning. I was happy in this communal haven where intellectual curiosity, augmented by mindfulness of the sensuality of food, the aesthetics of how it was served, not-to-mention the variety of dinner drinks, opened my senses to novel delights of taste, vison, and language. This perfect tantrika education stretched my tantric soul into new shapes and expressions.

And then, a proposal from Jacques Denis sent me leaping into the skies like those whales I'd witnessed in the Bahamian reefs. The serendipitous opportunity of his proposal was beyond space and time. Couched in my plans for France, I'd held the prospect of going to India. Reading Alan Watts, C. G. Jung, Suzuki Roshi's **Zen Mind Beginners Mind,** and others had piqued my curiosity about this culture so different from the West, and I felt something awaited me there. And miracle of miracles Jacques Denis had a ticket to go to India for a month and, he asked, why didn't I go with him! And thus, his solo journey became ours together. I mean, how does that happen? Even today, I marvel that after the months of feeling so lost and alone, suddenly, a threshold had appeared, and I had stepped over into a bountiful world of connection.

When we got back to Paris from the countryside, I immediately bought my ticket to India. I would arrive a day after Jacques Denis and stay a month after he left, wanting more time to explore that exotic land. Curiously, before I left Paris for India, I would pay my rent three months in advance. Was I already guessing something?

In that spring and summer in Paris, I surrendered to this new man in my life, to a new way of being in a relationship. With Jacques Denis, I began to see the edge of competitiveness that had informed my other relationships. Instead, words like pliancy, affectionate acquiescence, and delight described how we were with each other as we moved about in his city. The stereotypical man woman tensions I knew so well were, for those few months, non-existent.

When Jacques Denis and I traveled in India and Nepal, the east would demand further surrender.

15
1980

India and Nepal
My Heart, My Body, My Soul Succumbs

With Jacques Denis

Surrender. To India. The plane door opened, and as I exited, I halted momentarily, unmoored by the blast of hot New Delhi air, the neon lights that glittered and danced beyond the airport building – the garish brightness and heat converging powerfully in my brain and body.

When I passed through customs and out the airport doors, the clamoring racket of sights, sounds, and strange aromas assaulted my senses. This country, in which I had just arrived, would whirl me away to an unexpected flight beyond the familiar, and I knew at that moment, I would find what I'd come for.

I was awed, excited, and nervous, wondering how I'd ever find Jacques Denis in the packed mass of people. Ah-hh, relief when Jacques Denis's form and his welcoming smile emerged from the crush of humanity. When I saw him in his white Indian dhoti and a gorgeous red and orange silk scarf twining around his neck, my heart swelled, and I held him tight, planting kisses on his neck and face. He laughed in delight and led me to a waiting bicycle rickshaw. We ducked our heads as we climbed in and sat on the tattered Naugahyde-covered seat. Jacques Denis held my backpack on his lap as the driver peddled us into the stream of cars, rickshaws, motor rickshaws, trucks, pedestrians, and cows. Eyes agog, mouth agape, I surrendered to the wisdom of the captain of our tiny rickshaw ship as he wove his way amongst various modes of conveyance and seething humanity. He would spot an opening, hidden to my eyes, and skillfully dart in and out, then peddle slowly, scanning for the next opening. I marveled at the seamless weave and dance of the streets and sidewalks that seemed to merge into one. There were no defining lanes or directions, yet somehow, with a visceral intelligence among people and machines, the traffic flowed. Yes, it really did flow! With my amped-up curiosity, I determined to touch this essential flow of chaos. Though I didn't have the words at the time, now I can say that if San Francisco felt like a city of modern tantric *Shakti* energy, this city exuded the quintessential flow of ancient tantric *Shakti* energy!

We arrived at our hotel, Jacques Denis paid the driver, and I followed him to our room, which would be one of many. The hotels we stayed in were non-descript – rooms clean, thin washed sheets, saggy mattresses, and scarred walls, the whitewash worn away. At night, lying in bed, I would listen to insects scurrying about, but in the main, our rooms felt like safe havens to spend a night or two.

Our metaphorical honeymoon was in full bloom. I was content with Jacques Denis's agenda; it was, after all, his trip; he had been planning it for months, and I hadn't taken time to study or think about where I wanted to go. From Delhi, we traveled to Agra and sought the Taj Mahal, doubtless the most enduring symbol of lost love. We bought marble inlaid pendants from family industries dating back centuries. We traveled to Varanasi, and one morning I slipped out of bed early, left Jacques Denis a note, and stepping outside, boarded a rickshaw to one of the Ghats (broad steps to the river) of the Ganges. Arriving at the river as dawn curved into day, I felt for the first time the India I longed for. Fascinated, I watched the Indians and their river: ordinary men and women, deformed beggars, wealthy men who would drop a few coins into the hands of the beggars when they emerged from the Ganges. All had come to bathe and worship, and in the flow of that sacred river, all were equal. The Ganges favored and cleansed each one as he or she needed. It was a muddy river, polluted with debris and occasionally a body. Morning peeing and defecation accompanied the morning wash and ablution.

Hindus' relationship with this river defies comprehension to the Western mind. Still, it was palpable that morning, and I let the otherworldliness of the connection between the people and their river include me for just a moment. At the bottom of the Ghat, I stepped in, bringing all the consciousness I could muster to the feel of water washing over my feet, my calves, and then lapping above my knees. I breathed in the smells that, strangely, weren't offensive to my refined western olfactory sense. Carried by the scene into the river of connection, my monkey mind halted its endless chatter. And then, as fleetingly as the hush of connection had penetrated my mind, so my thoughts severed the link. I lost my footing, stumbled, fell into the river, and onto the shore of physical reality.

Wading ashore, I climbed the Ghat and chose a place not far from one of the burning pyres to dry out and witness the cremations. I watched as male relatives carried the body of a deceased family member, wrapped in fine cloth, to the pile of wood. They laid the body on the funeral pyre, spread flowers across the shroud, and then someone lighted the fire. I didn't understand the ceremony's details, but I was startled to realize the cremation had an almost festive air along with the mourning and tears, and I saw this complex mood in virtually all the services.

I tore myself away from this essence of Indian life and took a rickshaw back to the hotel. Jacques Denis had left me a note, and I found him at breakfast reading an English novel. Still spellbound by the Ganges and its people, I barely sat down before words gushed out as I excitedly shared my experiences. When I paused long enough to notice the effect of my unstoppable torrent on Jacques Denis, I saw his eyes downcast, his shoulders slumped, his fingers playing idly with his teacup. I stopped instantly. "Oh, Jacques Denis, I'm sorry. I've barely said good-morning or acknowledged you. I was so caught up in my story!" I stood, and from behind, wrapped my arms around him where he sat. I bent and kissed the curls I adored and then leaned in and kissed his lips and whispered, "You're the best. I missed you."

He laughed lightly, "Yeah, I missed you too. I was surprised when I found your note, though it's true I wouldn't really have enjoyed what you describe. Let's have breakfast, and then I want to take one of the boats along the river. The guidebooks say that they will stop and take us to little shops. I especially want to buy silk, and we can have vests or shirts made cheap."

"Perfect. That'll be great. Silk is my favorite, and I'm excited we can get it here for so little." With that, we turned attention to the menu to order breakfast. I wished we'd been able to share the experience at the Ganges, but I was glad we'd quickly aligned our moods and repaired this hairline fracture in our honeymoon edifice.

For the last week and a half of our month-long trip, we flew to Nepal. In 1980, Nepal was still relatively untouched by the gross commercialism that would bury authentic Nepal. Arriving in Kathmandu, I felt I had discovered Nirvana. Gone was the cacophony of Varanasi or New Delhi. In central Kathmandu, the street sounds - vendors, music, pedestrian voices - seemed muted. We found a local hotel and, taking our first walk around the city, we saw, rising amid the shops and hotels and restaurants, the Kathesimbu stupa (a stupa is a sacred Buddhist dome-shaped structure). Straightaway, I entered the stream of Nepalese that were clockwise circumambulating the prayer wheels at the stupa's base. I brushed my fingers, turning the prayer wheels, and chanting the mantra I'd learned, *OM Mani Padme Hum*.

The unfolding of events in Kathmandu seemed pre-ordained, and it all began, quite innocuously, at the Swayhuanath temple and stupa, one of the most sacred stupas for both Buddhists and Hindus. As I climbed the 365 stairs to the stupa grounds, the raucous chatter of the howler monkeys chattering in the trees and leaping on the handrails, their audacity at grabbing at food, whether in your hand or your bag, dominated my attention. Nearing the top of the stairway, I was stunned by the stillness that descended like a silky cloud around me. The magnificent stupa filled every corner of my vision as we stepped onto the grounds of the temple complex. I felt Jacques Denis beside me, and our hands joined as we absorbed the wonder of the shape and color before us. I stood in the same silence I had experienced in the middle of endless oceans, when a starry sky kissed the dark expanse and water and stars met on the horizon. I didn't yet have the words "inner silence," but that didn't preclude me from having the experience.

In Kathmandu, Jacques Denis and my different traveling styles began to abrade ever so slightly, and a contrasting emotion rattled my psyche, discontent. My discontent was about me, not him; he was happy sitting in a café with his English to French dictionary, reading and enhancing his intellect, going shopping, content to leave me to go exploring. I had a more difficult time allowing him his preferences. Our schedule saved me from an indulgent dissatisfaction – it was time to go to fabled Pokhara, a place no western hippie seeker could miss.

The 7-hour bus ride equaled any roller coaster ride I'd ever taken. The towering green and white mountains surrounding our vehicle, the road climbing and descending, careening through blind curves - the ride was as terrifying as it was beautiful. No one who has taken that ride ever forgets it! I had taken bus rides in the mountains of South and Central America, would take a modern coach in the cold winter in Switzerland, where we were the last vehicle through before the pass was closed due to a storm, but nothing compared with that wild ride in 1980 from Kathmandu to Pokhara. I stared down cliffs hundreds of feet high as we bounced in and out of deep potholes, and I was thrown from side to side, bracing against the pitch that threatened to dump me into the aisle. When we began the last descent into the valley where the mystic town of Pokhara nestled, I bowed my head and said a prayer of thanks to the mountain spirits.

Pokhara enraptured me: the gravel streets that would get muddy in the rain, the buildings strewn haphazardly along the roads, their walls built of soft red bricks often crumbling around the edges, side by side with concrete structures. And the prolific signs in Nepalese, some with English translations, painted on buildings or on a wavering board daring the winds to carry it away.

Exiting our hotel the first morning, young kids selling "magic mushrooms" met us outside our door. That first day we smiled at the treasure in their outstretched hands and said no. At breakfast, we learned that the local kids would go out in the morning to the pastures, gather the mushrooms, and sell them to westerners, who would then take them to a particular café where cooks would make a "magic mushroom" omelet. The next morning when the young kids held out grimy hands with fresh mushrooms, Jacques Denis said no – drugs hadn't been part of his cultural milieu. But for me, coming from America, this was familiar territory. I said yes and carried my handful of freshly plucked mushrooms, still with the residue of cow dung clinging to the roots, to the restaurant, and handed them off to the cook.

When the mushrooms came on, I couldn't sit in the café, so bidding Jacques Denis goodbye, as he sat happily with his coffee and book, I walked into the dreamscape of Pokhara, the world bright with possibilities. That first morning of the mushroom omelet, I rented a rowboat at one of a cluster of lakes in Pokhara and paddled along the water's edge. Seeing a trail, I headed to the shoreline, jumped out, pulled the small craft from the water, secured it, and set off. Climbing on an indistinct trail, I spotted a clearing, and off to the side, hidden by a few small trees and bushes, I spied a waterfall falling noisily into a pond. Ah-hh, magic mushrooms indeed! Shoes off, I risked taking off my blouse and waded in. The mushrooms enlivened my senses, and when I lowered myself into the cold mountain water, it transported me out of time into bliss. When goosebumps reminded me I had a body, I crawled like a human amphibian to the pool's side and slithered out to sit and let nature transform me. My eyes took in the visual beauty of mountains, water, green, blue, white, and my body imbibed the vibration of that beauty as well. I spent a couple of hours in and out of that magic pool. Rowing back to town, I found Jacques Denis at the café. He was reading his novel in English, as determined to improve his English as I was to improve my French. I understand that drive. And especially for him in Nepal, where the locals' second language was English.

Nevertheless, there was a verbal disconnect between us as we attempted to include the other in the day's doings. Judiciously, we left words aside, touched into our hearts, and attuned to each other. I sat across the table from him, and we smiled and chatted. Exiting the café, we walked with arms around the other: life was good, and that night, our lovemaking was sweet and passionate as we gave ourselves over to the magic of human love.

The following day, I enthusiastically searched out the kids, consumed my mushroom omelet with its earthy taste, wondering idly if the cooks had washed off the cow dung. Minutes after the last bite, I strode once again to the lake, rented a rowboat, and paddled to the same sacred spot where I bathed and played. When the journey's peak had worn off, I found my shoes and sat down to put them on. What a shock when I stared at my feet and was creeped out to see white wiggling things attached to my ankles and feet. Yikes, ugh-hh, what were they? They hadn't been there yesterday. I tried to flick them off with a snap of my fingers, no luck. I pulled at them, and fortunately, they had not yet burrowed too deep, so most came off. I gingerly put my shoes on and descended to the waiting craft. At the rental place, I asked the attendant about the creatures on my ankles, "Leeches," he smiled knowingly. I'd never seen or heard of a leech.

When I found Jacques Denis, I was brimming with news and excitement of the day's escapade; the leeches, the beauty that made it worthwhile, the calmness of the lake, the pool. "Hey," and using my most enticing voice, I asked, "why don't we both go out tomorrow? Maybe you can try some mushrooms. What do you say?" I was bubbling, and the pot boiled over. He stared at me, eyes blazing soft and icy, and closed his book as he uttered the words, "*Tu pèses sur moi.*" (You weigh me down.) My mouth fell open in shock. I was a weight on him? It is one of those scenes that hangs out in my brain like an old, faded photograph. I see Jacques Denis sitting at the table, so darling in his white hjoti, the red and orange silk scarf around his neck, his knees crossed, the empty coffee cup on the table between us. He looks steadily at me, unmoving, not granting a breath of redemption,

"Tu pèses sur moi." His repetition of that distressing phrase sent my monkey mind spiraling. My inner critic attacked me for encumbering anybody. I was deeply offended he had labeled me as such. I had always tried not to be a burden to anybody. Hadn't I always taken care of myself? Not asking for help from anyone? (Obviously, these observations had no truth to them. I had been helped all my life, but I had difficulty acknowledging others' help at that time in my life.)

"I'm sorry, I really am. I didn't mean to weigh you down, to be a burden." We stared, stunned and wordless. Gratefully, one of us dared break the impasse. He apologized for his words, and I apologized for trying to make him do things my way. I breathed with relief as our honeymoon enchantment won out, and the sun shone again.

We left Pokhara a couple of days later and once again endured the infamous bus ride. Our spirits were not so light, and the tossing around seemed less humorous. The next morning, we headed again to the Swayambhunath Stupa to meet Jacques Denis's friends traveling in Nepal. When we crested the top of the stairs, the stunning visual feast captured me anew. The two of us walked and talked, held hands, and were at ease. Jacques Denis went to a café to await the friends from his hometown, and I continued exploring.

I heard voices chanting and followed the sound to a small temple opened on one side, allowing locals and tourists to observe the monks. They sat in a semi-circle, some with texts in front of them, chants floating back and forth, their voices accompanied by the music of conch shells. The youngest monks, perhaps 6-7 years old, sometimes followed the elders but just as often smiled shyly out at the spectators. I heard a young Nepalese man explaining in halting English to a blond, blue-eyed man about the ceremony. I politely invited myself into the conversation and was instantly included by both of them. The young Nepalese man stood between the two of us talking animatedly, and my eyes sought out what he was describing with occasional peeks at the other whose own glances met mine. The young Nepalese paused in his elucidation and introduced himself, "Hello, I'm Krishna." I remarked on the powerful musical sound of his name. "Yes," he said, grinning, "I'm named after Lord Krishna. I'm the eldest son, and that is my place in the family." He added proudly, "My parents see big things for me, and I won't disappoint them." Turning to the blond stranger standing beside him, he added, "This is Sven. He's from Denmark."

"Hi, I'm Diane. I'm from the United States. That's interesting what you were saying about the chanting." (It seemed as good an entrée as any.) The three of us talked a few minutes more, then Krishna departed for the family-owned café in the stupa complex where he worked. He urged me to stop by. Sven and I began to walk and talk and smiled a lot at each other. He had a distinctive way of peering at me sideways. I wasn't sure if it was shyly or slyly. As we meandered, engrossed in conversation, we came unexpectedly upon Jacques Denis and his friends. It was awkward. I introduced Sven. Jacques Denis looked askance at him. I knew he was justifiably unhappy I'd disappeared for so long while he and his friends waited and had been forced to go looking for me. Proprietarily, Jacques Denis took my arm and, turning to his friends, he introduced us and added, "Let's go have lunch."

I turned to Sven, "Nice to have met you. Please thank your friend for the tour."

We spent the day with the friends, eating and sightseeing. The next evening, I took the taxi with Jacques Denis to the airport. We hugged each other and disappeared together into a long kiss goodbye. I whispered, "I'll miss you. We'll see each other in Paris. I'll call you when I'm back. Okay?"

"Yes, yes. Call me. I'll see you in Paris in a month. Travel safe." He flashed his most endearing smile as he turned to climb the stairs. At the aircraft doors, he waved. I smiled and threw him a kiss as he disappeared through the passageway. All passengers aboard, the doors closed, the engines revved, and the plane taxied down the runway and disappeared into the clouds.

INDIA AND NEPAL

Sven

Outside the airport at Katmandu, I motioned for a taxi, took a few moments to haggle till we reached an agreement on the fare, and climbed in for the half-hour ride back to the city. I changed rooms to a less expensive room with a smaller bed as I was now no longer sharing travel costs. I spent the afternoon listless and alone, missing Jacques Denis like crazy, vacillating between possible dreams for us. My romantic, picture-perfect vision was that he and I would set up house together in Paris, and yet, if I was brutally honest with myself, our travels together had forced us to thresholds we hadn't quite been able to cross. His words swirled in my brain, "*Tu pèses sur moi.*" And, though loath to admit it, the words were a little bit true for me, about him.

The next day, a new day, I considered the coming month and where I would go and contemplated the tantalizing possibility, called Sven. I remembered he'd said his birthday was the next day, though how that came up in our brief conversation is a mystery. "Well, why not?" I proposed to myself. For a third time, I climbed the 365 steps up to the Swayambhunath Temple and Stupa, and this time I was more intent on finding the café of Krishna's family than taking in the holiness of the scene. I found the café and asked the young boy tending the restaurant if Krishna was around. "I go get him. You want coffee, tea?"

"Tea would be wonderful." He busied himself behind a bamboo curtain and emerged with a steaming cup of tea.

"I go now, get Krishna," and he was gone out the door.

Retrieving my journal and pen from my small backpack, I tore out a blank page and wrote, "Hello Sven, Happy Birthday. I'm here at the temple for the afternoon, maybe we could meet here at the café, say at 2:00, and I'll buy you a birthday lunch, or perhaps we'll see each other where the monks are chanting or somewhere around. *Namaste*, Diane." Krishna arrived. I gave him the note for Sven, murmuring, "*Namaste*," as I bowed and thanked him, launching my *Intent* into the winds of adventure, my heart trusting we'd find each other if it were meant to be.

We found each other where the monks chanted. I learned that he was staying with Krishna's family, who lived in one of the apartments surrounding the temple. I invited him for a birthday dinner in the town center. We descended the steps together and stayed in lockstep for the next two months.

Our first night together, we jammed into the single bed in my room, making love almost hesitantly. Lying beside him, I felt his quiet sensitivity and softness, not unlike Jacques Denis, but different in that I sensed a man with a ruggedness born of his Danish heritage. Alive with sexuality, I gazed at his tangled blond hair, my body longing to kiss his tantalizing lips, yet content for the moment to simply gaze and soak him in and wait for his sleepy eyes to open. He must have sensed me staring as suddenly his eyes fluttered open. I smiled as I bent and kissed him. The languid sensuality of the morning transformed in an instant: our bodies were pressing hard, kisses demanding, our fingers probing and pressing. I rolled on top of him and brought his penis to stimulate my clitoris and then into my waiting vagina. Sitting atop him with my head thrown back, leaning forward over him, we moved together to orgasm. Lying together post-orgasm, I felt I had found in Sven the perfect balance between sensitive and macho and that intangible frontier into pure ecstatic oneness I'd broached before, felt possible, and enticed my seeking soul.

Over breakfast, Sven invited me to stay with him at Krishna's family's home at the Swayambhunath Stupa. "Are you sure it's okay?" I couldn't imagine the family would welcome a stranger.

"I'm sure it's okay. My friend Jens and I were both staying there. We were going trekking together, but he ended up going back to Denmark. He couldn't handle India." Then as if he'd pulled the thought out of thin air, he asked, "Hey, why don't we go trekking together?" His question blew my mind. We'd known each other less than 24 hours, and two weeks trekking together? It reminded me of another adventurer whose male friends had failed him and who had turned to me to complete the dream. I happily entered Sven's vision

INDIA AND NEPAL

as I had entered Jackson's. Trusting what spirit had delivered, I decided to go trekking in the Himalayans with Sven.

I packed up my things after breakfast, and we climbed to the temple complex. The family, father, mother, three daughters, and Krishna lived in three rooms with a small cooking area. At night, the main living space transformed into a bedroom, and Sven had been sharing that space with Krishna. The parents insisted that we, a couple, have their bedroom's privacy, and they would share the girl's room. We protested vehemently, but in their reserved Nepalese manner, they unequivocally refused our entreaties. When we moved our backpacks into the parents' room, my embarrassment was excruciating, and I wanted to flee. Sven seemed at ease, so I took my cue from him, but my discomfort remained, and I determined we would leave as soon as we could organize our trek and relieve them of their self-effacing generosity.

As we settled in the first night, I whispered to Sven, "Where is the bathroom?" He matter-of-factly informed me that the green area in the back of the building was the toilet area. My eyes widened. I thought he was joking. How could it be that this family, the owners of the small restaurant where I'd penned my note to Sven, and the father employed as the electrician to the king, did not have indoor plumbing? My "ugly American" naïveté was in full view.

I wanted to insist Sven come with me down the dark stairs, around to the back of the building where I must search for a place to squat, but I clenched my lips to halt my demand. (Clearly, I was already intuiting a quality about this man that would often challenge me.) Gathering my courage, with my little travel flashlight in hand, I quietly tiptoed through the curtain that was the bedroom door, opened the door to the outside, and nervously crept down the stairs. Out back, the grasses and plants were calf-high, and the terrain sloped away. I couldn't tell how steep it was, so chose a spot not far from the building. I dug a shallow hole with my heel, doused the light, and squatted. It seemed forever before I relaxed enough to let go and pee and defecate. I used some leaves to wipe and hoped they weren't toxic.

Then like a cat, I scrabbled some dirt over my leavings, turned on the light, and quietly retraced my steps to the bedroom.

Over breakfast in the family-owned restaurant, Sven questioned me again, "Are you sure you want to go trekking with me?"

Barely waiting for the words to leave his mouth, I replied, "Yes, yes, that sounds wonderful. I've been considering how to spend my next month here in India and Nepal, and I'd read about trekking and was wondering how to manage it. I wasn't all that excited to go alone. Oh my god, I'd love to go with you into the mountains."

Then, in practical Sven fashion, he added, "I need to lay out the rules if we're going trekking together." The rules were that he would set the pace and itinerary, and if I couldn't keep up, he would leave me at the nearest village. Hum-m, I was a little surprised and yet appreciated how he laid it all out so succinctly. The Danish cultural more of equality between the sexes carried a hidden implication of each person taking care of herself or himself and I would occasionally find it challenging. It lent a particular color tone to our interactions, and sometimes I'd have to reassure myself that his seeming indifference to my wellbeing had nothing to do with whether he cared for me or not . . though I would learn that shades of his personality were also part of the dynamic.

The month was October, and the monsoons had passed. The forecast for that time of year where we would be hiking promised to be sunny and warm though not hot. Within a couple of days, we boarded the bus for Pokhara, the main departure point for trekkers. On our expedition, I would be caressed by nature's majesty and fall in love in extraordinary circumstances. Being with Sven in the Himalayan mountains cut to the core of my psyche and hooked a hidden web of tantric *Shakti Energy* whose meaning, and bonds would take me years to unravel. Lastly, I would stumble into Tibetan Buddhism. (Looking back from today's perspective, it is the tantric practices of Tibetan Buddhism (*Vajrayāna Buddhism*) that had intuitively impressed me with the desire to go to India and Nepal. One day I would recognize this tradition as a description of my true self.)

With Sven, whose spirit of adventure matched mine, I had the traveling partner I craved. Our first morning in Pokhara, we brought our freshly purchased mushrooms to the restaurant, ate the earthy omelet, and headed to the lake. Sven rowed us across the placid waters and at my "spot," we pulled the boat ashore, climbed the short path, and emerged at the little waterfall. I had loved being there alone, but now sitting with Sven, being at the pool by myself, paled in comparison. Stripping down naked, daring to go into the water despite the leeches, laughingly splashing and entwining our bodies and pulling the leeches off as soon as they attached, I gazed at the vibrancy of nature through the emerald-clear glasses of the mushrooms and lost myself in the grandeur of our natural castle on the hillside. I couldn't wait to be in his arms making love.

Late afternoon, we returned to our rustic hotel room, and as the lights flickered in and out, we cheerfully lit candles, smoked a joint, and greedily succumbed to our lust and love. We savored that magnetic pull, and the urge to tear each other's clothes off, held in check by the marijuana, lent an exquisite edge as fingers and lips brushed delicately until our passion mounted and swept away the languor. With my breasts hard and nipples erect, my clitoris vibrating against his cock, he seemed to shyly await my invitation. My eyes said, "YES," and as he entered me, his groan of satisfaction echoed my own. Feeling him move inside of me, his pushing demands driving deeper and deeper, I cried out his name as my orgasm exploded. In this breathless moment, surrounded by those indescribable mountains, feeling the sacredness of the valley, the demands of sensual transcendent *Shakti Energy* nailed me willingly to the cross of our loving. By day our eyes feasted on the snow-covered Himalayas. By night our fingers feasted on the outlines of each other's body. This binding of *Shakti* magic, cast in the fires of our bodies, and the commanding nature of those mountains, would not be easily unbound.

Sven had researched and planned the trekking expedition with Jens, and I was thrilled to step into the opening Jens had left. Sven assured me our tennis shoes would suffice for the trek into the mountains as neither of us had hiking boots. We packed only the essentials: a first aid kit, water bottles, a sweater, one change of clothes, a couple of changes of socks, two sheets I'd sewn together to make a sleeping pallet liner, a light sleeping bag we could unzip for a cover, and finally some gorp we had made. Sven even had a little flask of whiskey, and we had some opium that the locals recommended for diarrhea if we should be so afflicted. Most importantly, we had the all-important map to guide us.

Our destination was a Tibetan monastery in the mountains. There was to be a gathering of monks and a festival in one of the high-altitude refugee villages where the sacredness was as viscous as the air was thin. Sven had calculated it would take us 5-6 days to make the trek. "Enchanting," I said to him. So we began a peregrination of grace in the breath-taking Himalaya Mountains.

A noisy, smokey bus took us from Pokhara to the foothills, where we disembarked to rough gravelly ground and were quickly onto the mountain path. We walked and sometimes paused to let the mountains work on us, to close our eyes and feel the nameless power wrapping itself around us. Each day, as evening approached, we would enter one of the Tibetan refugee camps that had, by the 1980s, become villages. In each village, Tibetan prayer flags bobbed and swayed in the wind as if trying to break free of their moorings. The narrow dirt streets were lined by houses of mud and wood that felt as though they simply rose from the earth itself. On inquiring, a resident might direct us to a kind of hostel, but more often than not, we were pointed to a particular home where, for a few rupees, the woman of the house would give us a bowl of rice and dal, and a place to spread our sleeping bag. Sometimes there was a Sherpa or two sharing the meal and floor with us. Mornings, we ate a rice breakfast, and found the tiny store, ubiquitous in the villages, to purchase food for the day. As we hiked, we learned to ignore the leeches insidiously hidden under our socks and shoes, especially mine. What a welcome relief when early in our trek, at a hostel, a young Tibetan saw the leeches and showed us how to use a bic lighter to burn them off. Was that a gift! Sven smoked, so bic lighters we had aplenty.

We watched and learned from the Sherpas. They carried heavy loads, supported by a band around their foreheads and a strap around the waist, and moved with a graceful, steady pace. There was no rushing to get somewhere other than where they were—quiet teachers reflecting the quiet that imbued their lives. We hiked accordingly, no rush, no time pressure.

We crossed rivers, sometimes scarily finding ourselves waist-deep with the water pulling at our backpacks, fighting against the voracious appetite of the river to pull us down. We held tight to each other against the river's raging flow, and I felt that nothing could conquer us, nothing could challenge us beyond our ability to respond and extract ourselves. There were the suspension bridges with missing boards, frayed ropes over deep gorges. Crossing over, I only dared a glance downward. If I stared too long, I grew dizzy and frozen. As I neared the other side of these bridges, all I could think was, "Oh shit, we will have to cross back over that bridge…..if it's still here." Those crossings weren't for the faint-hearted!

At one point, the trail opened to a vista that made me feel I could reach out and touch a snow-covered mountain whose peak disappeared into the clouds and carried me upward to the heavens. I halted, and for an instant, became something other than myself. Sharing this experience with Sven, feeling that he felt this grace as did I, was a moment as sublime as the ecstasy of our orgasmic lovemaking. It never lasted long; it was like a glance allowed to a stranger in a room of hidden mirrors.

Sven had excellently researched his, now our, trekking to coincide with the *Mani Rimdu* festival, the most important festival for the mountain Sherpas. We walked into our village destination through snow patches that never melted. The sun, piercing the thin air at the high elevation, around 12,600 feet (3800 meters), bounced brilliantly from the snow. Houses of mud bricks were clustered around the temple and scattered up the hillside. As always, in the villages on the trekking path, there was someone who spoke English, and he directed us to a house where we rented a room.

Each day we would go to the monastery and vicariously experience the almost continual ceremonies. The monks blew on the dungchen, the long trumpets that they would rest on the floor or a wall outside, and the higher notes from the conch shell players merged with the low sounds of the dungchen as if rising from the very ground itself. Through my feet, my body vibrated from the extravagant melody of sounds echoing around the room or into the valley. I was ecstatic.

Today I reflect on a favorite sutra from the **Vijnanahairava** that gives words to the experience I couldn't describe to myself back in 1980.

Sutra #52 - *Focus on the universal fire, fierier and fierier that raises from your feet and burns away all impurities. When there is nothing left but ashes blown by the wind, know the peace and joy of infinite space that is the Self.*

In those mountains with Sven, I tasted what I would come to call the transcendent *Shakti*.

The last morning, as we were out walking, some women motioned for us to follow them. We accompanied them out of the village and up a hillside above the monastery to a cave we had to bend at the waist to enter. Inside the cave, keeping us behind them, with hands clasped in prayer, they bowed toward the stone, and we did the same. The women indicated some flat rocks, where we should sit, and then they moved aside and pointed. A flame danced on the surface of a thin stream of water trickling from the cave wall; fire and water joined in synchronous motion. I stared in wonder and released my thoughts into the chants of the women and the visual delicacy of the dance - present to the mystery without trying to explain it scientifically or theoretically, watching the elements in harmony in space itself.

When the *Mani Rimdu* festival ended, we retraced our steps: re-crossing the swinging footbridges that were still there, re-crossing rivers, trekking up mountains, sleeping in huts with villagers, until we arrived back in Pokhara. Reprising the bone-jostling bus ride, we returned to Katmandu and traveled to India by train.

Hand-in-hand with the glory of India was the dark shadow that slammed me full-on when we emerged from the train station in Mumbai. For several blocks, beggars' eyes and hands reached for us, hovels of cardboard, tin, pieces of wood lined the streets, and as I peered into the lean-tos, I saw women cooking on tiny stoves, some over fire pits in the cramped space, children lying on rags. I have seen poverty in many cities, but in Mumbai, I witnessed abject poverty beyond my ability to comprehend. I was ashamed I had ever considered myself to have lived in poverty. I wanted to escape this shadow world and was relieved when we boarded a rickshaw that carried us away from the impoverished humanity struggling to survive on those streets. After just two days in Mumbai, feeling overwhelmed, we dared buy train tickets without assigned seats. We couldn't find a seat in the scramble to board, so like other travelers without seats, we found a spot on the floor.

As night fell, bodies began to stretch out, and I lay with most of my body across my backpack, as did Sven, my hand touching him. Soon bodies were lying across my legs, and every way I shifted, I compacted tighter with anonymous bodies. I didn't think I'd slept, and yet in one moment, I awoke, and Sven wasn't there. I trembled in terror and despair and didn't dare move. I waited, and I waited, my despair reaching panic, and I couldn't stop the tears of aloneness, abandonment, anger, and, most of all, fear. What if something nefarious had happened to Sven? When the dawn's light fell over the sea of bodies, Sven appeared. I was more angry than relieved, a wild banshee wanting to wail and claw at him. "Where were you?" I demanded through clenched teeth.

"I went to find somewhere with a little more space."

"But you just left me. Why didn't you take me with you?"

"You were sleeping, and I knew you'd be fine." There was that incredible Danish quality that I both loved and hated. Words died, and I just held onto him as the train chugged into the station, and the writhing mass, of which we were part, rose and slithered as a twisted snake, crowding at the door until it opened and disgorged us.

In our travels, we went as far south as Goa, where in early mornings, we bought fresh fish from fishermen just pulling their boats onto the sand. We spent days lounging on the beach, swimming, cooking, eating with even more gusto, and thrilling to each other's body beyond cares and limits. I wanted to stay forever, side-by-side with Sven, on the seashore in a little hut, lost in timeless sensual ecstasy. But time does intrude, and we left Goa to begin our journeys home – me to Paris, Sven to Denmark.

Before I drift away from India, the image of the Taj Mahal appears. Revisiting that monument to love during a full harvest moon with Sven, sitting side by side at the reflecting pool, made me want to weep in ecstatic bliss. We watched the moon appear on the horizon and climb slowly over the heart-stopping purity of the white dome: moon and building reflected in the quiet pool, a fabric of shimmering gold, fire, and water. Our two months together had been a seamless movement from one peak experience to another, even with the challenges. Our last experience before leaving India and Nepal, the full moon at the Taj Mahal, closed this chapter in a grand heart-stopping gesture.

At the airport in New Delhi, we said our goodbyes as we turned to an indefinite future. Aboard the aircraft flying home to Paris, as I drifted through memories of Sven and me, finding hardly a tear of discontent in the fabric of our relationship, I refused even the suggestion that it was over.

16
End of 1980

Paris to Denmark
Shakti - Open Heart and Sexuality

Three months away. It was good to be home: to take the elevator, climb the stairs, unlock the door, and cross the threshold into my womb room. I dropped my backpack and stretched out luxuriously on my bed, and basked in the joy and receptivity that India, Nepal, and the Himalayan mountains had wrought in my body and psyche. Those months in the East had heightened my appetite for sensuality in all its forms, for love, for firsthand experiences beyond my imagination. The freedom to eschew all limits that Peggy and I had sought in San Francisco and never quite found, I now found in Paris. I was the resurrected 18-year-old of San Francisco, open now to imbibe all the enticements of Paris. In the months to come, *Shakti* sexual love energy would flow from me out to the world. My inner critic would try to devalue and judge what I was feeling, but a resilient, determined, and loving part of me celebrated the experiences and emotions to come.

I'd let Ron and Pam know I was going to India and Nepal and had sent them postcards, but there had been no way they could contact me. As soon as I was back in Paris, I called them, we caught up on our lives, and I promised we'd see each other soon. I listened carefully when they assured me they were doing great, scanning for any signs of unhappiness, but Ron and Pam both sounded congruently content. They did add that they couldn't wait to see me. (In one of my journal entries, I lamented that Ron and Pam wouldn't be coming to France to visit as I had hoped.)

In June 1980, around the time I met Jacques Denis, Ron had graduated from high school, where he had been a star athlete in the pole vault, high jump, as well as wrestling and senior class president. Pam, who would be entering her junior year, was proud to be on the varsity volleyball and baseball teams and was exploring that exalted state of "first love." Through the stresses and strains of my psychic growth, my children were the unshakeable monolith that gave value to everything I was undertaking. However, on re-entering Paris from the East, pulsating sexual *Shakti* energy filled my heart and overlaid the heart space that held my children. Soon though, the heart circle of Ron and Pam would explode open and descend on me with affectionate fury . . .but not quite yet.

Awakening my first morning in Paris, Jacques Denis's face swam into my vision. I sank into memories of us in my room, in my bed. When we'd parted in Nepal, he'd reminded me of his 6-month sabbatical and that I should track him down through friends. Of his friends, I was closest to Nicole, so I called her that morning and asked her over for dinner. She happily accepted my invitation.

In my fantasies of dinner together, there was the tantalizing thought of sleeping with her. It may seem a curious thing. After all, I'd left Sven just three days before full of love and affection for him. I'd left Jacques Denis in Kathmandu a couple of months earlier with our love connection strained but felt. And now I wanted to touch and be touched by Nicole. I was a vessel that had been cracked open, filled with wonder and curiosity and impatient for endless loving and laughter and sharing.

Even today, I can't explain how I knew Nicole was attracted to me. She'd always been very discreet - I was Jacques Denis's girlfriend, and she was his close friend. She knew from the farmhouse that he and I were totally into each other, but a connection had somehow insinuated itself into Nicole's and my psyches.

Nicole arrived with dessert and flowers in hand. I laughed at the surprise on her face when she looked around the tiny room I called home. "*Oui, c'est petite,*" I acknowledged, "*mais, toutefois, c'est confortable.*" (Yes, it's small, but comfortable nevertheless.) "She is as angelic-looking as I remember," I thought to myself. I smiled back at her shy smile, gazed into her pale blue eyes behind round glasses, and noted her gorgeous shape, the ever so slight roundness of her hips, and her boyishly short hair.

Nervously, she pulled one of the two chairs from the table and sat down. I handed her a glass of white wine and shifted attention to the simple, elegant dinner for two I was preparing: fish and rice with a salad to follow. We sipped red wine with the cheese plate and topped off the meal with the chocolate tarts she'd brought. Like old friends, our conversation flowed easily. When we'd cleaned the last chocolate crumbs from our plates, I picked up the dishes from the table, turned around, and set them in the sink. Turning back to gaze at Nicole, I saw my smile reflected in hers. I took her hand and pulled her up from the table. "*D'accord?*" (Okay?) I questioned. (We spoke French together.)

"*Mais oui, bien sur*" (But yes, for sure). The words were barely out of her mouth when mine was on hers. We wasted little time getting our clothes off and falling onto the bed. I confessed to her I hadn't much experience making love with a woman. She laughed and led me into our lovemaking. What I remember most is that we made love all night long. I loved her beautiful, firm breasts. What a joy to suck on her nipples, to hold her breast in my hand and bring as much as I could into my mouth. When my hand slid down to her wet vagina, it took my breath away to feel that warm wetness, to push my fingers up inside of her, and finally to slide down her body, kissing licking until my lips found her clitoris, and my tongue played and coaxed it erect like the little penis it was. She reached down to my wet vagina, found my clitoris, and I brought my hand to hers. In mutual masturbation, I orgasmed into the long-awaited enchantment and thrill of making love with a woman – one I cared for, who loved me, one with whom I could be fully passionate. Whatever my fantasies had been about being with a woman, making love with Nicole fulfilled those fantasies. Drifting into sleep, my body entwined in Nicole's, the flow of *Shakti* energy that saturated my being was like being held in the arms of mother earth herself. When I awoke and felt Nicole's naked body warming mine and saw our bodies bathed in the morning light, my hands reached out, and my eyes followed the curves of our bodies that rose to the touch of our hands. Our lovemaking matched the sun's ardor as it announced the new day.

I would learn much about Nicole throughout those last months in Paris because, as with Jacques Denis, we were together from that first night. As a teacher, the school year dictated her work schedule, so in the morning, I would sleepily say, *"Bonjour mon ami,"* and wish her a good day. Though not grand, her studio with the tiny kitchen attached was larger than my room, so we spent most of our time at her place. I resumed my outings to museums, where I gorged myself on the beauty humans wrought on canvas, clay, and bronze. I sat and walked in the parks, from the formal Jardin du Luxembourg to my favorite green area of the city, Parc des Buttes-Chaumont. Like exposed nerves, all my senses were tickled to their euphoric limits, and I acquiesced to their madness.

Returning to Nicole's neighborhood, I'd buy groceries for our evening meal, over which we shared intimate conversations. I learned that Nicole's mother had committed suicide when she was 12, and I glimpsed the lingering pain in her eyes as she spoke. Her father had never remarried and had raised Nicole and her younger sister alone after their mother's death, and Nicole remained very close to him. She told of having a few sexual experiences with boys in high school that had left her cold and that in college, a woman had taken her home from a party, and they had sex. "Being sexual with a woman for the first time, I thought, oh this is how it's supposed to be; this is what the pleasure of sex is all about. I was so happy." She smiled, "And I've never been interested in sex with men since!" She then confessed that when we were all at the farmhouse, and she and I had gone bike riding, and she'd taken a nasty spill, when I'd helped her to her feet, put my arm around her, walked her back to the farmhouse, and led her to her bed and ordered her, "Sit down," cleaned and bandaged her wounds, she'd fallen in love with me.

For my part, I confessed that I had sought a relationship with a woman to balance having struggled in a man's world to find my feminine center, and that our relationship was everything I'd hoped it could be. I laughed, "I so adore your beautiful body and spirit." I talked of Ron and Pam, how I had left them, my guilt feelings, and how I missed them more and more each day. I didn't hide my time with Sven, though I didn't give details either. I said I thought mine and Jacques Denis's relationship was over, though I still loved him as a friend.

Each night when we made love, I wanted to bring her to orgasm. She wasn't overly orgasmic, and I was sure, if I patiently loved her, touched her, sucked, pinched, rubbed, pushed as deeply into her as I could with my fingers, she would come and know rapture. When I acknowledged that my fixation on orgasm was about me and not her, I harmonized with Nicole into pre-orgasmic timelessness – this was the sensual gift she gave me. When the longing for orgasm would seize me, I'd lie on my back, every part of me open. Her fingers would push inside of me, her lips suck my clitoris until the orgasmic impulse blasted away all separateness, and I heard the whisper of ecstatic oneness that orgasm brought.

On the other hand, what Nicole loved most was our kissing. Our lips buzzed and burned as we nearly swallowed each other's tongue and nibbled at the other's lips. Our kissing would often render us breathless, and when her mouth would slide to my breasts, I would lightly orgasm. I couldn't get enough of physical loving with this woman.

Nicole and I intimately shared *la vie quotidienne* (day-to-day life) – walks in the neighborhood, movies, and meeting up with friends. The openness and tenderness I experienced with Nicole, this amazing young woman, was a new and fabled land, and I reveled in the discovery of two female bodies together; of the intimate psychic connection of two women; of a resonance that echoed from one to the other. This energetic flow between two women was the nectar that my soul hungered for to heal the past.

When Jacques Denis arrived back in Paris, I asked Nicole to let me tell him about us, and she was relieved. I was enraptured with Nicole, and though I was excited to see Jacques Denis, I also felt a guilt-fueled dread. I knew, unequivocally, that we would not be in a couple relationship, but even if not in love, I loved him and regretted the hurt I was to cause that afternoon.

As we exchanged kisses and hugs, my heart fluttered, the memory of "us" whispered afresh in my body. We ordered lunch as our conversation meandered along mundane lanes of re-acquaintance. Then he took the gamble, "You know Diane, for me, our relationship wasn't over when we parted at the airport at Kathmandu. Yes, the last couple of days we were together, things had been a little strained, but I figured once we were both back in Paris, we'd work it out: that the strain had mostly to do with our ways of traveling. When you sent a letter saying you were extending another month in India and Nepal, I remembered the guy you'd introduced me to at the temple complex, and I guessed you were with him. I was so hurt at the thought of the two of you together."

It was my turn. "Yes, you guessed right. I did stay and travel with him for two months. We'll talk about it, but first, there's something more important I need to tell you." I sensed his body stiffening as I paused to gather my courage. Doing my best not to be apologetic, I hemmed and hawed, then, as I've always done when words refuse to form, I counted, one, two, three. "Umm, well, Jacques Denis, since I've been back, umm, well Nicole and I have been together, I mean together in every way. I'm pretty much staying at her place."

I waited, my eyes fixed on his, determined to be honest and speak candidly as he'd always done with me. His eyes grew moist. I could barely stand the emotions swirling like a snake around us, and I could do nothing to change my betrayal. As I had been unable to explain to my mother and friends why I was leaving Don, so I couldn't explain how I could love each of the three of them, him, Nicole, and Sven, at the same time. "Jacques Denis, talk to me, please. I'm so sorry. I'm just so sorry how this is working out. I care about you, and that must sound like a bunch of shit, but I do. I would be devastated if you were out of my life."

When at last he spoke, he didn't hold back or pretend he was brave and tough. No, the very thing I loved about him shone through. With disbelief at what I'd just confessed, his voice accusatory, the words came. "How could you do that? I mean, we were good together until the end. I feel so betrayed, so angry at you. When we said goodbye in Nepal and our long kiss, I guessed all was well. How could you just jump into bed with him and then Nicole? I want to jump up and leave right now."

"Please don't leave. I mean, I understand if you need to, but if you could just hang in with me. I doubt there's anything I can say that will ease the pain."

"You're right. There's nothing you can say. I'm just trying to take it in. I'd thought when we met today, we'd be talking of a possible future together. I mean, what you've done is incomprehensible to me. I mean, I figured we'd get over whatever you did with the guy in India, but I never imagined you'd be with Nicole. Not in a million years." As we sat there in the café, at an impasse, our gaze turned to the street. We watched the passers-by, the fashions, and the traffic. It was a way through the morass of anger, hurt, pain, and guilt. Emotions hovered between us, suspended and waiting.

We wouldn't sort it out that day, but finally, when I reached a hand across the table, he didn't pull back, and I felt hopeful that our friendship was intact. And so it was. We would be in each other's lives for the next few years, circling in the same group of friends whenever I was in Paris. Though there was hurt, there was relief as well. His words, *"Tu pèses sur moi,"* still rang true to some degree, as the weight he'd felt was our different energies colliding. Our energies weren't a match - where my energy felt kinetic to him, his energy felt to me like *existential ennui*.

I hadn't realized how the unresolved relationship with Jacques Denis had lodged between Nicole and me. Once I'd cleared the fog with him, Nicole and I were freer than ever to love. Her exciting return from school each day, sharing wine and good food, and the evening lovemaking wove a web of delight that turned me into a giddy schoolgirl.

Meanwhile, an invisible hand was pulling me back to the USA. There was no precipitating event or thought process - just a knowing that it was time to reconnect with Ron and Pam and even my mom and brothers. I knew that I couldn't leave Europe without seeing Sven. We'd had a couple of brief calls that included suggestions of future possibilities. With my return to the USA imminent, I called him with more than an innuendo, "I'm going back to the USA, and I'd like to come to see you first."

Without hesitation, he urged, "Yes, yes, come anytime for as long as you want." It was decision time. Was I coming back to Paris? Were Nicole and I a possibility? Would Sven and I find love in Denmark as we had in India and Nepal? Should I ship things back to the USA or keep things in Paris - each choice pregnant with implications. Nothing seemed obvious. One afternoon, as I sat with a coffee watching the streets of Paris, the message shot across my awareness. "Send everything home." That was the signal for which I'd been waiting. Finally, I had something definite in my indefinite future!

When I told Nicole I'd be leaving to go back to the USA and my kids, her disappointment was acute. When she learned I would return home via Denmark, she risked asking, "Why?" I offered lame excuses, and we chose to avoid further discussion, choosing instead to be more intensely together in every precious moment.

I spent a few days packing up my room, sending boxes home, and taking last walks around Paris. The last evening with Nicole before my departure, our lovemaking was steeped in the poignancy that partings bring. Our kisses carried an eroticism of joy and sweet sorrow, and after making love, we slept, as we always had, with her curled in my arms. On our last morning, I arose when she did, and we had breakfast together. Even the croissants and coffee were steeped in the tender and poignant. I kissed her goodbye and assured her I'd be writing when I was back in the USA. Unbearable melancholy hung heavy between us as she opened the door to go. We kissed goodbye, and then I had to shut the door to cut off the unanswerable questions in Nicole's eyes.

Sven met me at the train station at Aalborg, Denmark. I descended, saw him, and ran into his arms. He pulled away slightly to introduce me to a woman at his side. I frowned for a moment until he explained that the woman, Erica, was his best friend's girlfriend and had driven him to meet me as he didn't own a car.

Sven lived in a two-story house with his friend Jens with whom he'd gone to India. As with most homes in Denmark, when we opened the door and stepped into the big family kitchen, a welcoming blast of warm air hit me. Sven led me into a large room, and my eyes went immediately to the long wooden table around which sat a group of several guys and two women. Beer bottles, full ashtrays, a bowl of marijuana, and plates with cold cuts, eggs, and I wasn't sure what else covered the tabletop. Voices rang out shouting welcomes, their effusive and genuine warmth echoing the blast of heat from the kitchen. Someone pulled out a chair, someone else handed me a beer, followed quickly by a heaping plate of food. Another person passed the condiments. I felt like royalty as I gorged on the abundance and joined the merriment. I have entered people's homes in many lands, strangers, friends, yet no welcome holds a candle to how Sven's friends received me that evening. Sitting around that solid dark wood table smoothed by generations of hands, listening to Danish and just as often English, the unrestrained jollity, I was happy. Living in Paris, I'd felt like I had come "home," but being with these Danes implied a whole new definition of "home."

When I felt myself slipping into a dreamy state drifting from the conversation, and the group showed no signs of flagging, I whispered to Sven that I was a little tired. Instantly he was ready to join me in bed, and we went upstairs to his room. When we collapsed onto his single bed, my body memory came alive. A sweet brief joining, and I fell asleep in his arms. The world, my life, felt complete; there was nothing to add and nothing to take away.

Being with Sven in Denmark, the fairy tale world of Hans Christian Andersen, the Danish author who, among other tales penned, *The Ugly Duckling,* subsumed me. On Christmas Eve, we went to an uncle's home where his mother's family had gathered for a Christmas repast of roast pig, potatoes, and the favored boiled cabbage. Pumpkin or apple pie was supplanted by the traditional *ris a l'amande,* a cold rice pudding with whipped cream and homemade hot cherry sauce. My palate vibrated with the cold of the pudding cut with the heat of the cherry sauce, and I was in one of Andersen's fairy tales.

On the day after Christmas, Sven and I bussed to central Alborg, where Malthe, Sven's two-year-old son, lived with his mom. We brought him to Sven's for a few days. Malthe would chatter away, an alphabet salad of words and sounds, and I would chatter back. We would laugh and play nonsensical games where language didn't matter. One morning, though it was winter cold, we dressed in heavy coats, boots, gloves and went to the ocean. As we stood at the gently sloping beach throwing rocks, noses running, lips numb, I learned to my astonishment that the highest point in Denmark was about 561 feet – minuscule for a girl raised in the northwest mountains! "Wow, wait till you see the northwest," I impetuously exclaimed to Sven, having no doubt it was in our future.

Two days later, we dropped Malthe off at his mom's and boarded a train for Copenhagen to spend four days exploring that gorgeous city. In every square, there was a Christmas tree, each one brilliantly lit. Deep in this winter wonderland of Hans Christen Andersen, I could imagine that *Little Match Girl* huddled alone and cold, selling her matches in front of the quaint shops. And then the brilliant flash as the box of matches flared, and her grandmother appeared and carried her to be with God.

Sven and I celebrated New Year's Eve and the start of the new year in an upscale restaurant where the proverbial Christmas tree sparkled with lights and tinsel. The glow from the roaring fire in the stone fireplace reflected modestly in our eyes. We toasted the coming year, and I imagined, like that brilliant flash of fire that heralded ascent to heaven for the little match girl, that our toasts, raised against the burning fire, heralded a divine future with Sven.

In contrast to the glitter of a traditional Christmas and New Year's Eve, we spent our last day at Christiania, the internationally known commune, occupying an abandoned military area. Christiania was the high point for Sven, as he is communal in his very bones. Walking into Freetown Christiania, we wandered the streets, admired the unique and sometimes haphazard structures, bought and smoked marijuana, sat in cafés, talked and read about this storied and successful commune. Both faces of Copenhagen inspired me, yet perhaps most telling, is that today, some 40 years later, the day in Christiania colors my memories most vividly.

Back in Aalborg, cozied in at Sven's, he and I began to talk of a future. Several things were on the table, but first and foremost was the idea he would move to the United States with me. There was the question of Malthe, but we agreed he would come to visit, and who knows, we thought, maybe he could live a year or so with us. Sven loved the idea of living in America. I felt that with him at my side, I could confront all the things I hated about my country: the income inequality, the environmental destruction, a government becoming more and more reactionary and violent – the very conditions that had pushed Jackson and me to dream of sailing away to a new life nearly a decade ago.

Uninvited and unwelcome, in the middle of the visions of our glorious future together, a land mine exploded. Sven received a job offer for a position he had applied for in Kristiansand, Norway. It was a dream job for him at an avant-garde clinic for short-term mental patients. He would be the social worker who would help residents prepare to move back into society and rejoin their families. He made no effort to hide or contain his enthusiasm. Jens was there when Sven opened the letter and read it aloud in Norwegian. Sven relayed the message in English, and then he and Jens switched into Danish, and

ON BE(COME)ING A WOMAN OF WISDOM

I knew the animated discussion was about the clinic, the job, and moving to Norway. I disappeared inside myself. It wasn't that Sven intended to ignore me or leave me out, but this unexpected event overtook him and gathered him up in her arms like a welcome lover.

It was no surprise that the itch to go home, lurking just under my skin since I'd left Paris, burst forth and erupted a couple of nights later. Sven's friends were gathered around the big wooden table just as they had been the evening I arrived – an impromptu party to celebrate Sven's new job. Plates of cold cuts, the infinite supply of beer and marijuana, and the full ashtrays again cluttered the tabletop. I did my best to engage in the gaiety of the evening, but my fake smiles and laughter nearly choked me. I turned to Sven, "I'm going for a walk. I need some air."

"Sure, okay, you want me to go with you?"

"No, no, I need to be alone."

"Okay," he replied affably.

I donned warm clothes, boots and mittens, a scarf, and a hat against the night's cold that mirrored the coldness in my heart. I walked and walked over flat farmland, flat yards with houses barely breaking the flatness; even the sky felt flat and oppressive. I began to talk out loud to myself, and as the houses grew sparse, my voice rose with the emptiness. "I hate this flatness. I hate it. I'm sick of all of it. I want to go home. I just want to go home. I want to see Ron and Pam and speak English with English-speaking people." My litany went on and on, and as I walked, I welcomed heavy tears. I remembered the deep ontological sadness that had swallowed me in Paris but whose symmetry had been broken by Jacques Denis. But this time, even the warm edge of love and companionship in the house I'd just left couldn't arrest my soul's ache.

Perhaps intentionally, I lost track of what corners I had turned, what lone homes I had passed. Wandering in the flat spaciousness ironically soothed the ache, and as I shifted from inside to the outside world, the cold began to seep into my bones, and I grew a little nervous. In the darkness, I tried to gauge the most probable route back. Turning 360°, I decided to retrace my steps to the corner in the distance and then decide whether to turn right, left, or go straight. I don't remember what I chose or how long I wandered, but something in me intuited the "way home." Out of the darkness, I heard him calling, "Diane, Diane." I paused to listen to where his voice came from and walked towards it. The flashlight broke the darkness, and then his figure emerged. I went to him, threw my arms around his neck, pressed hard against him. His willing arms encircled me. "I was worried about you. You were gone for a long time."

"I, I got lost, I'm lost, I want to go home, home to Bellingham, to my kids. I've been away too long." I was nearly floating out of my body and was grateful when he put his arm around my waist, and I glided beside him back to the house. Outside the door, I paused, "Wait just a minute, I need to make myself more presentable. I just want to go home." The words came out again of their own volition. And though I was babbling nonsensically, I couldn't stop. "I want to go home. I want to be with Ron and Pam. I want to go home. Please, I want to go home." One part of me was chastising myself for the drama. Another part was fighting down the hysteria rising in my throat at the thought of entering back into that warm house where Sven's friends were celebrating the gut-wrenching event that had torn my dreams asunder. The faint image of reuniting with Ron and Pam saved me further embarrassment at this display of self-pity in front of Sven. I was learning that because I had so little compassion for myself, buried as it was by the unsympathetic parental triad lodged in my psyche, I would inevitably go to a place of self-pity to find a small measure of compassion.

Sven held me like a baby, his voice cooing as if to a young child. "It's okay, it's okay. We'll get your ticket tomorrow. You can be on your way home as soon as you want. Come on, let's go inside. We don't have to say anything. No one will think anything." He gave a little laugh, "They're so drunk and stoned they probably think you left just a few minutes ago." It made me smile in the dark. I kissed him.

"Thank you. I'm sorry to cause you to worry. I didn't know how much I was missing home."

17

1981

Full Circle

Ricocheting across the Globe

Northwest Washington, USA: Nourishing Our Cores

On the train rides to London, the flight out of Heathrow, flying the Great Polar Route, seeing the familiar pattern of Seattle lights, I had time to restore a measure of emotional balance. Retrieving my backpack from the arrivals carousel, impatient to clear customs, and finally emerging through the swinging one-way doors, I spotted my two beautiful children, waving and smiling to welcome me home. I paused for a moment to take them in. Ron stood over 6', Pam 5'8", the same height as me. Though unmistakably brother and sister, they were differentiating from the near-twinness of their childhood. Ron's demeanor was slightly more serious than I remembered. His dark brown eyes that had become deep-set like his dad's sparkled with curiosity. He stood tall and thin, his shoulders straight, and I noted he still took the lead with his sister. Pam's face was rounder and fuller, her lips smiling and eyes laughing though I saw a determination in them. She had filled out and carried herself as a proud young woman. I noted that her vitiligo (a condition where patches of skin lose pigment), a disorder she shared with her dad, was more apparent on her face and arms. She'd once said to me in her early teens when we were talking about this disorder, "Mom, when I start to feel bad about my vitiligo, I just think of kids that don't have arms and legs to get vitiligo on, and I'm grateful." Hugging them through tears and laughter of pure unadulterated joy, I never wanted to let go.

Out of the corner of my eye, I recognized their close friends, James and Junior Anderson, standing nearby. I turned and greeted them with light hugs. Ron took my backpack, and I was home at last. Resourceful beings that they are, Ron and Pam had arranged for me to spend the night with the Andersons in Fall City, as clearly, I couldn't stay at Don and Carol's house. In the morning, the three of us, in Ron's truck, headed to Bellingham for the weekend.

My mom, in her inimitable quiet way, had organized a welcome home lunch. Her house was small, so we couldn't gather around a table. Instead, we filled our plates with the pot roast and veggies she'd prepared and decamped to the living room, eating off of TV trays. The number of family members gathered that day was relatively small as only David and Don, out of seven siblings, now lived in Bellingham. However, they were both married, and David had two stepchildren, and Don and his wife had two young ones. With Ron, Pam and me, Mom and her husband, Bill, and my nieces and nephews full of energy and laughter, we filled the house with a heartwarming racket. After eating, some of us gathered at the table to play hearts, a family favorite, and others went outside to entertain the kids. I felt like a pilgrim returning from an aimless sojourn into a land of milk and honey. I basked in the love and wellbeing these moments brought me. None of this detracts from the closeness with friends in Paris and Aalborg, but I cannot pretend that at that moment, there wasn't an extra measure of comfort with the familiar people and places that were the ground of my being.

During the weekend at mom's, with Ron as the architect, the infrastructure that would support my time in the northwest was conceived, fleshed out, and initiated. Ron worked at the local supermarket in Carnation, Washington, a little town about five miles from Fall City, where he and Pam lived with Don and Carol. He had befriended Ned, a grizzled 70-year-old bachelor who still lived in the house where he'd grown up. His property was about two blocks from the rural town center where Ron worked. Ned's house sat on an acre of land,

and Ron had the vision of parking my brother, Don's, 17' camping trailer on said pastureland. He called Ned from Bellingham that very day. "Sure, sure," Ned agreed, no doubt intrigued at this novel idea.

Saturday evening, after dinner and games, Ron huddled with my brothers, and they organized the whole shebang, even down to the cesspool. On Sunday afternoon, Ron and Pam headed back to Fall City, and I remained at Moms. She and I spent the next day and a half talking non-stop, signaling a growing closeness between the two of us. Perhaps because of the years away, my reuniting with my children, or simply my maturing, I became curious about her for the first time in my life. I didn't ask intimate questions, that would come later, but sensing my interest and curiosity, she became more animated and even dared ask me about Paris and India, which was new for her. I happily shared innocuous stories seeing no need to create unnecessary walls that might have sprung up if she learned of my tantric nature.

On Tuesday morning, we borrowed Bill's truck, and with my brothers, hitched up Don's trailer, threw into the truck bed some sewer pipes, and a 50-gallon oil barrel in which they had drilled holes. The three of us, me in the blue Ford station wagon that David had handed back to me, and David and Don in the truck, hauled the whole collection to Carnation. Before they left to return to Bellingham, David and Don helped me set up my hobbit house. The next afternoon, Pam and I dug a trench for pipe and a hole for the 50-gallon oil barrel that would be my septic tank. I draped the trailer's tiny interior with silk cloth from India to hide the plastic and added the objects I always traveled with to make a room or apartment, or trailer in this case, into a cozy home. It would prove to be one of the more eccentric living situations of my life! Ned, my landlord, appreciated as one of the town's characters, drove an old red Ford truck, in the bed of which was a 5' sculpted outhouse he'd built. Each year, his proudest moment was when he joined the tractors, motorcycles, simple floats, local marching bands, and show horses to drive his battered truck in the local 4th of July parade, grinning from ear-to-ear as he waved to the crowds lining the streets.

Ned would often lean across the pasture fence and call out that he had something to show me. I'd dutifully follow him into his house, where in the dining room and living room, there was a narrow path through stacks of papers and magazines. He'd show me some artifact that had belonged to "mama" then sit down at his old, out-of-tune piano and play an old folk song and sing. His singing done, I'd find a reason to go back to my trailer and wave goodbye as I pulled the old, rusted screen door shut behind me. We were an odd pair, to say the least – Ned living in the past and me constantly pushing into the future.

Carnation would be a feast of familial love. Ron and Pam popped in often to talk, and on sunny days we'd spread blankets outside the trailer to relax in the sun's warmth, talk, and sometimes smoke a joint together. Evenings, I might cook for us, or we'd go out to eat, and they sometimes stayed the night, the table and banquettes making into a bed for Ron and the couch making into a double bed for Pam and me. The kids were the much-needed antidote to the loneliness I had welcomed when I'd left Vicente a seeming lifetime ago. Between the three of us, love blossomed exponentially into unfettered joy as if to make up for the missed years.

In the future, we would need to process the hurt and pain that came from my sending Ron and Pam to live with Don. But for now, during this time in Carnation, we lived the closing chapter of their childhood, immersed in joy and companionship as we discovered who each of us had become since that day I had put them on a plane in San Diego some five years before. It was the first time I dared acknowledge the grief over how much I had missed of their lives and that those years were irretrievable. But they were blossoming, and the bedrock of our love and connection was firm and growing. Knowing that assuaged my grief and guilt.

Other little vignettes of daily life in Carnation flit around: Ron bringing a prom date by to introduce her and take pictures; the afternoon when Mom and Bill visited me, and we went together to Pam's baseball game. Wow was that a memorable outing! Mom, Bill, and I were sitting in the bleachers with our eyes glued to the action on the field. The batter connected with the ball and Pam threw off her catcher's mask for the play as a runner dashed for home base. The shortstop scooped up the ball and hurled it to Pam, who had planted herself between the third-base runner and home plate. I watched in slow motion as Pam turned for a glance at the runner just as the ball hit her face so hard it lifted her off her feet, and she fell to the ground unconscious. I ran onto the field, leaned in close, "Pam, Pam. . . " Her eyes fluttered open, blood was pouring out of her mouth, and she spit out a tooth that someone had the wherewithal to pick out of the dirt. The ambulance arrived in minutes, and holding her tooth in a little water cup, I rode with her to the emergency room. She was unbelievable, never shedding a tear, while I fought mine like crazy as the sirens echoed in my brain. The emergency room sent us straight away to the dentist, who reinserted the tooth and braced it in. (She has the tooth to this day!) We rushed back to the emergency room to have her lip stitched up. Mom and Bill had followed us through it all, so after the emergency room, we drove Pam to Don and Carol's. I hugged her as I reluctantly handed her off to them, and Mom and Bill drove me home. Ron stopped by the next day to say Pam was doing fine and that he'd bring her over that night.

My day-to-day life was almost orgasmic in its joyful simplicity and the psychic healing I awoke to each day. Unavoidably, in quiet moments, the background noise of Sven would surface. We'd made no promises when we parted. We'd acknowledged our love for each other and said we'd write. I'd wished him success in his new job and his move to Kristiansand, Norway. I wrote almost weekly. Once a week, refusing to let myself go more often, I walked the two blocks to the post office. Approaching the counter, I would request my mail via General Delivery. With bated breath, I'd quickly go through the two or three envelopes. There was often a letter from Nicole, occasionally a letter from Jacques Denis, but the name I scanned for never appeared. Weeks went by until unable to bear his silence any longer, I wrote a letter demanding he write me and let me know how he was and send me an address other than c/o the clinic as I hated writing him there. I was like a tragic romantic heroine of the 19th century pining for a romantic love lost in the nether world of time and distance.

The long-awaited letter from Sven arrived. He sounded happy and excited about his job, liked living in Norway, had found a Danish community, and was busy. He avowed his love and added that he missed me. Reading and re-reading his letter, I was perplexed about where we stood and could find no clarity sitting there in the trailer, so I took long walks along the nearby Tolt River and trails through the forest adjoining Ned's property. Feeling the wordless wisdom of trees, the rushing river tumbling towards the ocean, sitting quietly on a rock, nature pulled tendrils of confusion from my brain.

Nature's power to bring clarity to my questioning was amplified when I joined Ron and his friend, Dan, on a hike up Mt. Si, a nearby mountain just over 4,000' high. We followed a steep trail up through an old-growth forest with a 100 foot-plus scramble to the top. I managed this daunting ascent up the steep rock promontory on all fours. I joined Ron and Dan at the peak where they sat with legs swinging over the abyss. Sitting beside Ron on that narrow ledge, I dared to glance at the view across the small town of North Bend, with rivers snaking across the valley and Seattle beyond. Mt. Rainier rising to her full majesty beyond the farmlands took my breath away, and I wanted to stay just to contemplate my favorite mountain in the northwest. But perched atop that rock, 4000' high, the empty space above the land pulled at my belly, and my pulse raced as my acrophobia wrapped itself around my chest. My voice shaking, I managed a half-smile, "I'm going back down. I'll wait for you below the rocks. It just makes me too nervous, and I don't want to spoil your good time." As I crab-crawled backward away from the edge, I could hardly bear to leave Ron so cheerfully chatting with Dan, my fear wanting to pull him away from his perch so far above the valley.

Whew, my body relaxed as I entered the forest shade and sat

beside the path. Was it the forest stillness, my heart palpitations, or awareness of death that finally made me face the churning undercurrents that surfaced each night? My dream life had been shouting at me, the images seeming to intensify every night.

Most startling of all was a grotesque dream in early spring where I was fishing at Birch Bay, a playground of my youth, and pulled up a fish called Gangrene Fish. Some men observing, to whom my eyes pleaded for help, said to me, "You must kill it yourself." I know the truth of what they say, but as I'm flaying it, the fish turns into a man with the likeness of Jesus. I struggle mightily, painfully, and at last, with blood flowing copiously, I am able to slit the throat of the fish turned Jesus. I awaken crying and yelling.

As I reviewed the dream, my association with Birch Bay was that it was where I had first experienced the *frisson* of *Shakti Energy* when, at twelve years of age, I'd sat on a sandy beach with my first boyfriend, Bob, and our kisses had taken my breath away. I had longed for more – to not only kiss but to touch our private parts. We had been too shy. And now, in the psychic setting of Birch Bay, I am fishing into the unconscious. What I pull up from the sea is a rotting entity that I must kill in order to realize my tantric nature that had sprung up so unexpectedly on the beach at Birch Bay. In the dream, this gangrenous fish turned Jesus, is the ultimate Christian religious authority of my childhood years. Though it was a struggle, in the dream, I found my intent and was able to destroy the rotting entity, the Father, Son, and Holy Ghost – masculine and religious authority in all its forms.

A second dream that came just a few days later pointed out a path. In the dream, I'd left my purse with Vicente and Jackson on a café windowsill, and as I walked across a bridge, a man with a military hat stole my purse. I started to chase him and then realized the purse had only my passport and about $50 so decided to pursue him no further and simply report the theft at the post office. Standing in line I encountered a cousin on my father's side. Turns out we both live in Paris, and she tells me to come to her house and says, "It's easy to find. It's right by where the Nietzsche Tours start."

FULL CIRCLE

In this dream, I rejected the identity tied up in my purse with passport and money that I had left with the two most powerful men in my life, and that was then stolen by a man. (Sven was the only man I was ever in relationship with that did military service.) I discover an unexpected guide at the post office, a woman in my father's lineage. We can view this psyche constellation, Papa, my psyche animus (unconscious masculine), and his niece, my psyche anima (unconscious feminine) living in the same house in Paris, my soul city, and that integrating the two in wholeness, is my "Nietzsche Tour."

During my years of travel, I carried Nietzsche's book, *Thus Spoke Zarathustra*, tucked away in my backpack. Though Nietzsche's ideology is vast and complex, I knew my dream drew on his challenges to traditional religion and morality and conventional social and political doctrines. Going on a "Nietzsche Tour" meant I had to go beyond cultural, family, and religious constraints in order to become whole. The dream insists I must give up my male-identified self and stop looking to men to give my life meaning, and instead manifest the tantric nature of *Shakti Energy* in this being named Diane.

Seated near the summit of Mount Si, I took courage to face my fear of rejection from Sven, my fear of taking a decision not based on following another's lead, my fear of being made a fool, of making a mistake, i.e., I took responsibility for what I wanted in my life, rather than stay frozen in old stories that had deeply structured how I lived. I noted in my journal on April 30, I *have finally decided and written to Sven saying I want to be with him here and now. I mailed the letter today*. As I reflect back, I note that in the dream I am at risk of losing my identity again to a man, to Sven, but as the dream shows, I let the identification with Sven go as well. That will be my challenge in this new relationship.

His return answer came within two weeks. "Yes, come." His agreement pulsed across earth and sky, and I began to plan my trip back to him. I talked with Ron and Pam about my decision, eliciting their thoughts. They were incredibly supportive, even happy for me, insisting, "Yes, go! We'll come visit. It'll be fun. We'll meet Sven and travel in Europe."

"Yes, yes, that'll be great. I can't wait. As soon as I'm settled, we'll start planning your visit." My mood was light and loving because I was light and loving, and affection flowed easily with my children who stood excitedly on the threshold of adulthood. When I left, since I saw Norway as my home in the foreseeable future, I signed over the blue Ford station wagon to Ron and gave Pam $500.

Spain and Paris: Closing Doors

I took a circuitous route to Norway, my new home, stopping first to visit Jackson in northern California. I also planned to visit Nicole in Paris and Vicente in Spain before boarding a train north to Kristiansand, Norway.

After an overnight trip from Seattle, I arrived in Yreka, California, to spend a week with Jackson and his girlfriend, Charlotte. Jackson picked me up at the bus station, and we drove through Ft. Jones, then up winding mountain roads to his extended acreage of redwood forest and streams. He and Charlotte lived in a small rustic cabin whose rusticity included hauling their drinking water from the sizeable stream flowing close by the cabin. (Eventually, when he married his long-term girlfriend, Barb, in 1992, he and Barb would build a beautiful log house.)

During the summer days, we hiked in the hills, chopped and stacked wood, and visited his super-cool neighbors. Jackson has a gift for folksy and funny storytelling, so evenings after dinner, seated by the fireplace, the three of us smoked marijuana and laughed uproariously at his stories. I entertained them with tales of my travels to exotic lands and love affairs. We were family in our closeness and camaraderie. When I told him I'd be seeing Vicente in Spain to settle finances from the sale of **Le Petit Prince** and the last of my marijuana share, which, as we'd agreed, Jackson had sent with Vicente, he wasn't optimistic of my success. "You know Vicente and I disagreed about the money from the marijuana caper, and we couldn't come to an agreement. Vicente was intractable around the money."

"In what way?" I questioned. "I mean, we all agreed on a 50-50 split. It doesn't seem too complicated."

He was circumspect and would only say, "You'll see." It sounded a little ominous, but I chose to ignore his words, sure it wouldn't be like that between Vicente and me. On departure day, Jackson drove me to the Greyhound bus station, and when we hugged, I felt him heart to heart as a friend who would always be in my life. A few days later, after a rather taxing cross-country bus trip (I swore it would be my last!), I happily boarded the plane for the cross-Atlantic trip to Paris.

I had strongly hinted in my letters to Nicole that I would be going to Norway to join Sven. As soon as we'd settled into her now-familiar studio apartment, I gently, if such an action is possible, fleshed out the obvious. The moment the words were out, we both went into denial. That first night together, passion and my fondness for her, her love for me, conspired to ensure we tore off our panties and shut out the future. Our hands found the sweet spots, and we brushed and squeezed and massaged away mental obstacles. We walked in the Bois de Vincennes just outside of Paris, visited our old café haunts where we sat street-side and watched *Parisiennes*. We were solicitous and caring with each other. I didn't feel unfaithful to Sven and wasn't surprised at that.

One weekend Nicole and I drove in her little Citroën to visit Jacques Denis, who was newly married and teaching in the suburbs. What a reunion we had! We went to the market to buy food, cooked together, played games, and drank wine and Pastis. When I bid Jacques Denis goodbye, I suspected our paths would not cross again, and so it was. I spent a last weekend with Nicole in Paris, a weekend whose echo would linger on, and then I boarded the train to Spain.

I was apprehensive and curious as I rode west to Vicente's new home in Capileira, a small village on the southern flank of the Sierra Nevada, an hour or so southeast of Granada. In July 1981, finding

Vicente in the hills somewhere above the town was like climbing a mountain with no signposts. In Capileira, I kept asking in formal Spanish, *"Lo conocéis Vicente Sanz?"* At the local bakery, the answer was finally, *"si, si, lo conozco."* (Yes, yes, I know him.) Eventually, with the miracle of sign language and goodwill, the baker directed me to a man with a car who filled the role of a taxi in the little town. As he drove, he explained that Vicente lived in an old, remodeled farmhouse nestled somewhere on a hillside. He pointed out that it was nearly impossible to drive up the hill we were climbing in the winter.

Arriving, I noted that Vicente's aesthetic sense showed even from the outside. Adjacent to the whitewashed adobe home was a swimming pool that undoubtedly met Vicente's need for water in those desolate landlocked mountains. He came out of the house, smiling happily to see me. I was hopeful as we hugged, and he led me inside. The interior was lovely - polished clay floor tiles in a soft rose, a big kitchen with rustic table and chairs, a modern propane stove, a narrow stairway up to a loft, and charming little circles and squares molded into the whitewashed adobe walls where tiny figures nestled. Opposite the kitchen area was the original fireplace, albeit restored to be more heat-producing. Faith, his partner from California, came forward to greet me, arms out, with a big hug and kisses - one American to another. When she hugged me hard to her soft, round body, I intuited her happiness at being in the company of another American woman and her loneliness as well. (Vicente had often proclaimed how he loved Reuben's women: soft and feminine and round. In Faith, he had his Rubenesque muse.) Tucked away in the mountains of Spain, Vicente had begun his writing project. I later learned from Jackson that Vicente had fulfilled his ambition, publishing several texts on spirituality.

The afternoon of the second day, Vicente and I sat companionably at the pool's edge after a refreshing swim, and I broached the subject of money. "Vicente, I went over the accounts with Jackson vis-à-vis the marijuana, and he said you still had the last of my share. The other thing is my share of the sale of **Le Petit Prince**. Remember when we parted, you didn't want to sell right then, so I agreed you would pay me half when you sold it. You wrote that you had sold it, and I can use that money now as I'll be living in Norway and not working."

His body had gone rigid, and at that moment, a creeping suspicion crystallized. He had never intended to give me my half of the sale of our sailboat. With a stony glare, he sniffed as he often did as a prelude to speaking. His riposte insinuated that I had insulted him. His words came like poisoned darts straight to my belly. It's impossible today to describe the invective that came at me. Nearly spitting, he hurled these last words, "You're just a bitter old gypsy wanderer who wants my money. You won't get it because it's not for you to decide what I owe you or not. I decide, and I can tell you, I don't owe you a penny, not a fucking penny." In one motion, he bolted up from the side of the pool and strode to the house. The hills echoed back my stunned, paralyzed silence. The power of his conviction once again left no room for discussion. His vitriolic rage landed on me with an ear-splitting crack, and I knew I had to get off the mountain fast. I headed to my room, packed, and asked Vicente to drive me to Capileira. Faith begged me to stay another day; I politely declined, stared at Vicente, and challenged him to deny me a ride out of this mountain hell.

"Okay, if that's what you want. Look, there aren't many busses in and out of Capileira, so why don't I drive you to Granada."

"Yes, why don't you," I replied, my voice dripping with derision and scorn. I figured this was not a time to cause myself additional pain and hassles by being stubborn, insisting that Capileira would be fine, thank you.

We didn't speak for miles as I stared out the window seeing nothing of the passing lands. His voice felt distant when he spoke, "Diane, look, I'm sorry, but I just don't feel I owe you anything." I had no answer, no argument left in me, but there was a grit inside me - the vow that never again would a man render me powerless. I understood that the best I could do right then was to admit to the financial loss. As we drove, he tried to make conversation. I refused his entreaties about how Ron and Pam were doing or how Jackson was. I was a silent, angry witch cursing him. How grateful I was to see the outer limits of Granada. At the train station, I insisted, "You don't need to get out of the car. I'll get my backpack." As I slammed the door, I managed an ill-felt, "Thank you for the ride." I watched as his car merged into traffic, whispering into the air, "Goodbye, Vicente, my one-time lover, boyfriend, and partner in crime." My nostalgic thoughts could not dispel the potent taste of bitterness his words had left.

Blessedly, over the following days in Madrid, I began to let go of the bitterness, knowing it was hurting me, not him. From my clean humble hotel on one of the side streets in the town center, I ventured out to the museums and the lively streets. Evenings, I'd taste the nightlife of Madrid, drinking sangria, eating paella, and turning away flirtatious men. The evenings out, the quiet breakfasts before a day museum hopping, helped dispel the toxicity that clung to my skin. It wasn't just the money that had been part of my financial plan for the months ahead. I was equally upset about the powerlessness I had felt when I tried to wrest from him what was rightfully mine. Before heading north, I stopped in Gaudi's Barcelona, where the sheer audacity of Gaudi's colors and forms relieved my rancor. When I stood at the highest point in the Sagrada Familia, Gaudi's other-worldly cathedral, I flew into the clouds and chose to leave my bitterness in the sacred power of the cathedral.

Norway: Throwing Open the Most Treasured Door of All

The trip from Barcelona to Kristiansand was like a fever dream. The clickity-clack of train wheels seized my brain, turning it to mush until the moment when the ferry docked in Kristiansand, and I saw Sven waiting on the pier. I was exhausted from the transition from Washington to Norway that had begun a very long time ago, but the sight of him standing there in his familiar blue parka with the rabbit fur-lined hood chased away any vestige of fatigue. When he smiled, lifted me off the ground and swung me around, I felt like a transitory bird that had come home from the journey south to incubate and birth new life. Sven put me down, picked up my backpack, and hailed a taxi outside the terminal.

His, now our, home was a one-bedroom apartment just a couple minutes' walk from the clinic where he worked. Closing the door to the outside world and entering our bedroom, we fell together onto his mattress and made love. I sighed contentedly as our passion quietly joined us, body and soul. I was home. I fell sound asleep, ebullient in the promise of the home we'd make together. He kissed me in the morning, said there was food in the refrigerator, and he'd see me in the evening after work.

I found a card table in a closet and set it up in a corner of the bedroom that looked out over a garden. I unpacked my little portable typewriter and set it on the table. I imagined sitting and writing while Sven was at work and welcoming him home in the evening when we would sit down together to dinner and talk and then make love every night. It seems a little silly now, childish even, but I had not a sliver of doubt that this relationship, created in a sacred space beyond our western world, must, at its core, be the most magnificent and sustainable love story ever!

The apartment was a well-designed space with cozy living room and adjacent dining room with sliding glass doors onto a patio that gave onto a small grassy backyard edged by woods. On the second day, while Sven was at work, I headed out to a path I had spotted at the edge of the yard that disappeared into the woods. As I meandered over sloping hills and through deep trees, I suddenly emerged onto a small lake - well, I guess I would more accurately describe it as a pond. White water lilies covered the surface, their green leaves brilliant and shining in the sun. The water was clear, and the proverbial frogs sat on the lily leaves, croaking their approval of the blessed day. I sat down and listened and gazed at this seeming secret that was just mine. I would wade into the pond, cool and refreshing in the summer heat, and stretch out luxuriously on my back, and close my eyes in contentment. (This little pond would record the seasons of nature and my mind. The lily flowers would fade, the leaves would turn gold and yellow, floating down to the pond leaving the trees barren. In winter, a thin layer of ice would drape the pond in silence.)

Sven was happy! He loved his job, and each evening he would come home and excitedly relate his day, his interactions, his patients, the successes he was having helping people reintegrate back into their pre-clinic life. I shared in his excitement and told him of my day learning the bus system, enrolling in a Norwegian for Foreigners class. I would tell of my delight in Kristiansand. It was a lovely city, pedestrian streets dominating the waterfront of the fjord lined with fishing boats where I'd buy cod or mackerel directly from the fishermen.

Sven had planned a two-week trekking trip into the mountains terminating at a cabin belonging to one of his bosses who had given him the key. I was amazed that he had only been at the clinic for six or seven months and was already able to take two weeks off. Not the American way!

Anja, a Danish friend, drove us to the trailhead. As we unloaded our gear, she saw I didn't have a sleeping mat and offered hers. "Oh no, I don't need it. I sleep great on hard ground."

"Are you sure?"

"Oh yes, yes," my ignorant macho self declared, unaware of what it was like to sleep on the cold ground. I would lament that decision on many a freezing night!

The mountains of Norway swept us into nature's wonderland. We hiked each day, and when we were hungry, we'd select a place to stop for lunch, usually beside a stream to cook, eat, refill canteens, and wash dishes. One day we stopped by a small lake where Sven hauled out his fishing pole and caught some trout for lunch. We joked about the urban hunter returning home with the day's sustenance.

Hiking cabins were available along our route, but we generally chose to pitch our tent in a sheltered spot for the night. But a rocky overhang couldn't keep out the ground's chill. I had a down sleeping bag; Sven had a better one. He had a sleeping mat; I didn't have a sleeping mat. And there was the rub. The cold from the ground seeped through the tent floor, my sleeping bag, and whatever clothes I was wearing right into my bones. Damn, those nights were bitter cold!

On those chilly mornings, I woke up grumpy, masking my anger with Sven, who I thought was being selfish in not trying to find a way to share his nighttime snuggly bag and mat. I hinted to him a couple of times, but it didn't register, and regrettably, my macho self couldn't ask directly, informed no doubt by Sven's attitude that at times looked like indifference. I chose to give him the benefit of the doubt that it was just how Danes were, i.e., that he wasn't indifferent to my well-being, he just assumed I'd tell him directly if I needed anything. And honestly, I wasn't sure which was more correct. The anger aimed toward him was, in part, diverting my anger at myself for refusing Anja's mat. We occasionally paid for sleeping bunks at the self-service and no-service huts that were part of the hiking and cross-country skiing system in Norway. Snuggled in the warmth of the huts, I slept deeply, and the small travails were forgotten.

Toward the end of our trek we reached a long-awaited destination - glaciers. I had never hiked on glaciers! As we walked, we carefully tested each place we stepped with our hiking sticks, ever vigilant for any crevasse lightly covered with snow. On top of the glacier, snowfields reflected the sun, while the blue ice seemed to absorb the light that danced like snow fairies under the glassy surface. We walked in quiet wonder inside of glacier caves, eerie ice blue and white. The sound of a glacier's unseen movements was like being in a tunnel of breaking ice and rushing water. Occasionally, the ice emitted eerie moans. Traversing those vast expanses of ice, simultaneously transparent and solid, sounds seemingly held in a hidden warren of ice and space, my thoughts were muted into stillness.

Hiking, fishing, cooking, looking out on ice-blue glaciers, meadow flowers, the trekking huts, snowfields, green meadows, tall forests – I experienced the Norway of my fantasies. My paternal grandfather was Norwegian and only a second-generation American. As we hiked, I could imagine that this was the world of my ancestors.

Just as our maps indicated, like the atoll that appeared on a blue ocean so many years ago, so the cabin Sven's boss had loaned him appeared one late afternoon. It was one of several cabins built throughout the area on the edge of a small village. Sven unlocked the door onto a perfect Nordic hideaway. Before food or even lovemaking, we shed our wet clothes and climbed into the steaming hot tub.

For days we basked in this warm and cozy resting place. Cocooned inside the cabin one day, we swallowed the little paper squares of LSD I'd brought with me from the USA. We stayed within ourselves for the first two or three hours. Then we flowed outward toward each other with talk, laughter, shared hallucinations, and at the end of the day, joined our heightened awareness into hours of lovemaking, dozing, and wonderment. I was loath to leave that idyllic setting where nature, my innate sensuality, and our love had conspired to rouse the *Shakti* to the brief bliss of oneness.

I was coming to understand that in the blissful heights of sex, through my unbounded pleasure and craving to reach the sublime, I brought an intoxicating quality of present-ness to lovemaking. I felt and saw how men especially responded to me. I found a potent aphrodisiac in knowing I could take men to those heights, that I could leave them at a loss for words. What they didn't realize was that I hungered so for the state of transcendence through sex that I gave everything to whomever I was with and took back in equal measure. The music of this symphony didn't always carry over into day-to-day life. Nevertheless, in those moments of bodies touching, hands and mouths exploring that forced my back to arch in invitation and receive a lover's penis deep inside my physical being, transcendence was promised - especially with partners I loved with all my being. And so I was with Sven in the cold reaches of Scandinavia.

Back in Kristiansand, like a vaporous phantom, mundane life imperceptibly began to erode the unfathomable magic on which we had built our relationship. I'd sit down at my table each day to write, but no matter how I started on each story, it was dead within a few paragraphs. I would rip the paper out of the typewriter and crumple it into the wastebasket. It seemed I had the perfect situation, and the prospect of failure weighed heavily on me, not unlike how I had weighed on Jacques Denis. I fought the inevitable depression as my colorless writing days were like gray-out compared to Sven's palette of color at the clinic.

I doggedly found ways to keep my gathering angst at bay.

How delighted I was one day hiking along the familiar trail to the pond when I spotted the toadstool with its brilliant red cap covered with tiny white dots and its lacy skirt just under the cap: yes, the fabled Amanita Muscaria mushroom. I kept the mushrooms secret and would take a bite of them from time to time. Those forbidden mushrooms helped my mood.

Sven had bought a little boat and motor he kept in a nearby lake. On weekends we would pack a lunch and set off with his fishing pole in hand to one of the many small islets dotting the lake. I was content to sit back and enjoy the sun and nature around us while he fished. A couple of times, I took the boat out myself. That relieved my angst.

I took hot baths every afternoon, remembering that this had been part of Vincent Van Gogh's treatment when he had been in a clinic in Saint Remy. Those baths helped quash the scream I'd seen so perfectly depicted in the eponymous Munch painting.

Day after day, I tried to write. The contrived and convoluted sentences increased my anguish until I felt the only way forward was to quit. I was intrigued and hopeful when Sven set up hypnotherapy sessions for both of us with the clinic's psychologist. I met with him several times after the hypnotherapy session, and he lent helpful interpretations to my dreams. At one session, I confessed my discouragement with my writing, saying I was ready to give up. He insisted that I must keep writing, saying, "Your dreams show a very imaginative and creative part of you. Don't give up. You'll find your way." That gave me hope and kept the scream at bay.

When Sven arrived home each day, I happily shared his enthusiasm about his work, but more and more, his work became the sole focus of our evenings. Our time didn't feel about us. Some nights he went to bed early so he could get up early, and we didn't find time for the physical intimacy I desired. Nearly every day, I hiked to the pond to find the solace it gave me. The lilies had given way to a carpet of autumn leaves. It was getting colder.

An entry in my journal highlights Sven's angst - I wasn't the only one in a painful puzzling state. What was becoming abundantly clear was that the utter delight and connection we had found in each other, in the magical kingdoms of Nepal, India, Denmark, and the mountains of Norway, were failing to carry over into our day-to-day life in Kristiansand. I saw and perhaps admitted to the writing on the wall before Sven could.

> Journal entry September 23, 1981
> ....*then I am afraid in the dream, and I awaken when I yell, "help."*
>
> *Strange thing – I yelled, awoke, and was kind of panting from the fear. I wished Sven would put his arms around me and hold me as Jackson and Vicente used to do. I thought that he must just be sleeping sound. Then suddenly he got up from the bed and went to the kitchen. Since I was awake too, I got up and went out to the kitchen and got a glass of water. He was drinking milk. As I went back to bed, I said, "I had a strange dream." No response.*
>
> *When he came to bed, I asked, "Have you slept yet?"*
> *"No, not really."*
> *"So, you heard me when I yelled in my dream?"*
> *"It wasn't really a yell. I thought you were dreaming of making love."*
> *"No, I was afraid in my dream."*
> *"Oh, I didn't know," he said.*
> *"Too much going around in your brain?" I asked*

"Yeah, I guess so."
"Are you thinking of work tomorrow?"
'No."
And so it ended. Earlier in the evening, he'd told me how he had felt himself getting angry three times that day – once with his chief and twice with patients. He was surprised, he said, because ". . .it's not my usual self." I suspected his anger was related to "us," though I couldn't guess at the specifics and conjectured he hadn't made that same connection.

Despite the unconscious processes in both of us, we nevertheless had amazing and loving times together until the writing on the walls, now with red markers, was scribbled everywhere. One morning in early November, I took a thermos of hot chocolate, stopped at a bakery, loaded up on pastries, and headed to the lake where Sven kept the little boat and motor. I shoved the boat into the lake, jumped in, pushed out from the shore with an oar, started the small outboard, and headed for an island beach. Once there, seated on a log on a crisp cool fall day, I reviewed everything of Sven's and my relationship, from our meeting at the Swayambhunath Stupa to our current life in Kristiansand. I was terribly unhappy and couldn't see a future for us in the day-to-day we shared. If I imagined my days and years without Sven, I felt even more lost, rudderless even.

I'd had a letter from Pam telling me how much she missed me, and what a hard time she was having at home with Carol, her stepmother. Sitting on that beach, looking out over the blue lake, welcoming the cold nippy air, relieving it with sips of hot chocolate, my path became clear. It was time to go home for good. I outlined plans and a schedule for myself, how I would tell Sven. A dark cloud lifted; hope took hold as I pushed the boat back into the water and turned the bow toward Kristiansand.

After dinner, I opened the conversation, "Sven, I need to talk to you. You know I haven't been able to feel at home here; we've talked about it. I loved your life and friends in Aalborg, but it's not the same here in Kristiansand. People in Norway are different from the Danes. The mood is different, and unlike Denmark, it's a conservative and insular culture. Today I took the boat out and sitting on an island shore, I made the painful decision to go back home to America. Pam needs me, and I am content that I am going back to be with her, but I'm broken-hearted to leave you because I love you beyond words. And I get that Norway is your home now, but I am not at home here."

Stunned, he stammered, "You can't just decide that by yourself. We have to talk about it. You can't just announce that. I didn't know you were that unhappy. Why haven't you talked to me about it?"

With an icy coldness that I needed to fortify my intent and give me courage, I replied - and oh how I remember the words, the tone of my voice, where we were sitting on the couch turned toward each other - "Well, I didn't want it to be true, and we can talk about it, but I've made up my mind." Wow. I was Vicente sitting there with my words admitting of no argument. And yes, we did talk because the coldness wasn't in my heart. I acknowledged my love for him but insisted that life in Kristiansand, Norway was untenable for me. "More importantly," I added, "my daughter needs me."

In the last few weeks with Sven, just as had happened with Vicente when we'd decided to separate, the mood lightened, and each evening I happily prepared dinner for us and welcomed him home with love and attentiveness as he recounted his day. We began to make tentative plans when we would see each other again in the USA. We made love in the night, each evening carrying the message, ". . . maybe this is the last time." Each day I found time for the half-mile hike to the pond. The last time I was there, the water was icy cold. I could see the ice crystals that had formed at the edges. Winter had come.

As I prepared for my return voyage, my interest in Jiddu Krishnamurti's teachings, which I'd read over the years, burst to the forefront, and I determined to stop off at Brockwood Park Krishnamurti Educational Center in England outside of Winchester. I wrote to the school, and they gave me dates to visit, and around that, I planned my return.

At the pier, Sven and I said to each other like a wedding vow, "I love you." Standing on the deck waving goodbye, as the ferry slowly maneuvered away from the dock, an inexplicable phenomenon broke over me - copious tears fell unabated. Aboard the ferry and on the train to Aalborg, where I stayed with Sven's friends overnight, tears continually spilled from my eyes. I couldn't understand it, couldn't explain why I couldn't stop crying. I was glad to be secluded on the train to Berlin in an overnight berth because more than two days after leaving Sven waving goodbye at the dock, I still cried uncontrollably. What was this thing that pulled at the foundations of my being, that pushed tears spilling onto the book I was trying to read? I kept reminding myself that I was the one that had made this decision, but it didn't matter – I still cried and began to imagine I was going insane. On the plane from Berlin to London, the fount of tears at last dried, a much-needed respite from the craziness of this nearly deranged emotional part of me over which I'd had no control. (Clarity about this ending would finally come some 25 years later when I reconnected with Sven by phone in the midst of a systematic review and letting go of relationships in my life.)

A week at Brockwood Park Krishnamurti Educational Center blew me away. I stayed in a student room in the Cloisters, with a bed, desk, built-in drawers, and closet. Sweeping lawns sloped into farmlands. Above, sat the beautiful original estate home, gleaming white, majestic, speaking of another age, now transformed into a residential school of international students. I learned that all the staff, from gardener to Dorothy Simmons, one of the founders and school principal, earned the same small stipend. Room and board were free, and students and staff alike shared in the daily chores of gardening, cleaning the grounds, and washing dishes.

Though I'm embarrassed to admit it, in that short week, I found Samuel – the perfect antidote to my despair at having left Sven. We were both guests, so we naturally tuned into each other as we sat in the large common room on couches and chairs arranged around a mansion-sized fireplace. A wood fire warmed us and put fire in our eyes. With little on our schedules, Samuel and I walked together in the afternoons and talked together in the evenings. And then, I don't rightly remember if it was on the third or fourth day, as we roamed the fields that edged the magnificently manicured lawns of Brockwood Park, he spread his coat on the ground. Our simple kisses soon aroused us both, and there in the grass of a sunny winter's day, we had sex, simple, uncomplicated sex between friends who felt an attraction to each other. I was impressed with his penis size, not so big that when he plunged deep into me, it hurt, but a perfect fit, and I was surprised when I orgasmed. I hadn't expected that. We managed one more outing into the grasslands before my week was up. Samuel and I promised to stay in touch. There is nothing like a brief passion for burying the sadness of lost love.

The day before I left Brockwood Park, I had a brief interview with Dorothy, the principal, and expressed my desire to one day be part of the staff even though currently I was headed back to Washington state to make a home for my teenage daughter. Dorothy invited me to come back the following September to help prepare for the yearly gathering under the big tent when Krishnamurti arrived to give talks. Flying from Heathrow to Seattle-Tacoma Airport, closing the door on Europe, I re-entered the open door of America. It was a benchmark moment, marking where I had been and my passage into an unknown future. I had no plans beyond arriving at the airport in Seattle and making a home for Pam.

Jackson and me aboard *Ariadne* 1973

Ron, Pam, me in cockpit of *Ariadne* the day they left for Don's

Me at the tiller of *Le Petit Prince* sailing in the Pacific

My mom, Marian, with her grandkids, Ron 15 and Pam 13

Pam and me with Ron and Debbie at their wedding 1983

Dayton and Marlene 1973

Me in front of my tipi in northwest Washington

18

1981-1982

Hiatus

Ordinary Life Enriched by the Unpredictable

It seemed that Pam, albeit unconsciously, was just waiting for my arrival stateside. I had arrived at my friend Barb's in Seattle intending to bus up to Bellingham for Thanksgiving when Pam called in tears. "I got in a fight with Carol. She slapped me across the face, and I slapped her back. It was just one too many times. The bitch kicked me out of the house, and I'm at my friend Tess's. What am I going to do?" By now, the tears had changed to anger. "I'm glad to be out of that house and away from her. I'm going tomorrow to get my things."

And thus, in the panorama of my life, the path appeared. "Okay, look, it's Thanksgiving weekend. I'll call David and see if he can come get us. What's Tess's number? I'll call you right back." I called my brother David in Bellingham, and he promised to pick us up the next day. Crazily, by the time David and I got to Fall City from Seattle, where he'd picked me up, Pam, a life architect like her brother, had a plan! Janet, Tess's mom, had agreed to rent the upstairs apartment to Pam and me. When we picked up Pam, I met Janet. We talked, liked each other, and settled on the rent and a move-in date after Thanksgiving weekend. I had just enough money with me to give her the first month's rent. I shouldn't have been that broke, but because of Vicente's having cheated me of many thousands of dollars, I was now living on the financial edge.

At the end of the Thanksgiving weekend of eating and talking with family, I felt grounded and ready for a life in Fall City with Pam. I borrowed a couple of thousand dollars from mom to see us through the next month or two. We would need to be frugal, and my calculations depended on me getting a job right away, but I wanted to borrow the minimum from my mom. David generously agreed to drive Pam and me back to Fall City. The first stop was at Don and Carol's, where Pam dashed in and collected the boxes in which she'd hastily crammed her things, then we drove the mile or two to Janet's place. I had only my backpack (the rest of my things were coming by ship from Norway), so with just our personal belongings, settling into our new home was a breeze.

Janet's newly built home was situated on a hill with a long, almost pretentious, driveway. Located about a half-mile out of Fall City proper, it aspired to an incongruent *gentilesse* in that little rural town. I was grateful for this quiet landing place for Pam and me. The furnished upstairs apartment was fresh, shiny, and invitingly cozy. We settled delightedly into the space that boasted novel designs like heated hardwood floors, vacuum cleaner hoses attached directly into the walls, and more simple accommodations like a small kitchen with stovetop burners and a table and chairs for four. The bedroom was Pam's, figuring she needed more privacy than I did, and I set up my "bedroom" in an alcove off the living room. Janet owned a new and used furniture store and kept the inventory in her basement, so over the next few days, she helped us choose what we needed to finish furnishing the space.

In an instant, I went from being a lover-oriented, somewhat narcissistic traveler to a mother-of-a-teenager, homemaker-oriented life. I welcomed and embraced the change. For the next two years, tender necessity was the guiding principle. It would re-awaken the *Shakti energy* embodied in motherhood - secondary in my natal birth imprint, but still strong. I was once again a single mom with a child to support and nurture.

Within a week, I'd found a job with Borg-Warner Leasing as an accountant clerk. We were an office staff of four: the boss, Malcolm; the collections person, Lucy, 2nd in command; and Susan, the contracts clerk, hired about the same time as I was. Those first weeks, the grit of my grandmother took over. There was no room for self-pity or lamenting what I had chosen or what had chosen me. That grit, that determination against all odds to unflinchingly meet what life puts on your plate was Grandma Trotto all the way. So, with alternate *Shakti* energy, one colored by duty, love, and grit, I plunged into the alien corporate culture of my job.

The Borg-Warner office was in South Center, a vast shopping mall and office complex, south of Seattle, just a mile from Sea-Tac airport. Without a car, my most immediate challenge was the 30 miles to work. Fall City was rural, and busses ran through the tiny city center from other small city centers. With a quick review of bus schedules and routes, I established my transportation routine. Mornings, I would walk the half-mile to Fall City proper, board a bus to Issaquah, and with a good connection, arrive at South Center from where I'd walk the quarter-mile to work. Links for the reverse trip were less favorable. Fortunately, there was a local café in the small town of Issaquah where I spent an hour reading and drinking tea as I waited each evening for the connecting bus to Fall City.

When Pam and I moved in, fortuitously, Ron and his friend Dan were looking for a place to live. In conversation with Janet one evening when Ron was visiting, she suggested that the two boys could stay in her basement, where there was a full bathroom, in exchange for refinishing furniture destined for her store in Bellevue. Ron happily accepted, and the next day he and Dan carved out a living/sleeping space among the furniture and moved in. I was grateful for her generosity in sharing her abundant space with the four of us.

Quotidian hardships were erased by the evenings' pleasure when Ron and Dan would join Pam and me upstairs for dinner and the weekends of being with both the kids. We flourished as we cooked, conversed, worked, laughed, and supported each other in nesting domesticity. We would have a short 3-month residency before a collision of world views would jolt our cozy heaven.

Janet and I and the girls would often hang out together. She was unhappy in a relationship; it seems there were issues around her boyfriend's wanting to be sexual. During one intimate conversation among the four of us, Tess, Pam, and I were all on the side of, "Just go for it. What's the problem?" Janet demurred, intimating that I was "loose" in my attitudes around sex, and the girls were young. Low-key irritations began springing up from Janet, all directed at Ron and Dan, the men in the household. The crash was inevitable.

I arrived home from work one evening, and as I reached my hand to turn the doorknob, the door was yanked open, and a blast of icy cold wind nearly knocked me off my feet. "I want you out of the house now. Leave tomorrow! And your son needs to be out tonight." Janet's screaming diatribe pierced the air sending me into shocked bewilderment.

When she stopped for breath, I slipped in my question. "What's happening? What is going on? Why do you want to kick us all out? Please don't go there," I implored her. I couldn't help but remind her that we had paid rent until the end of the month.

My interruption seemed to sober her momentarily, "Well, well, okay, you and Pam can stay till the end of the month, but" her voice rose, nearing hysteria once again, "I want the boys out now!"

"Well," I responded reasonably, "they can't leave right now. I'll talk to them, and we'll work something out in the next day or so."

She mumbled and grumbled, finally stepped aside to let me enter the hallway, and as I climbed the stairs, hurled after me, "They need to be gone by the weekend."

"Okay, the weekend then." Shit! I wondered to myself what the fuck had happened. What had they done? Ruined furniture? Gotten drunk? I couldn't even guess what had set her off. I opened the door at the top of the stairs, where the three of them, Pam, Ron, and Dan, sat glumly at the table. I smelled dinner cooking. That was a good sign. Obviously, they had heard the screaming. I looked at them, puzzled, "My god, what went down?"

Words tumbled out from all of them. It seems that the four teenagers, Ron, Dan, Pam, and Tess, had all been outside on a blanket enjoying an unexpectedly warm afternoon. Ron and Dan each had a beer; okay, they were technically underage, but they hadn't been restricted from drinking beer at the house. Apparently, Tess was lying face down on the blanket, and Ron was massaging her shoulders, neck and I don't know, maybe just at the moment, Janet appeared he was touching her butt. For Janet, the scene stank of sexuality, and she was infuriated that Ron was molesting her daughter. Screaming at them, she'd broken up the gathering of these vibrant young sexual beings, sent Tess to her room under protest, and ordered Ron and Dan to get their things together and leave. It seems that Pam had smoothed the situation a bit, and the three of them had fled upstairs to wait for me to come home.

Though at the time, I was indignant, today, I am more charitable toward Janet. Raised in the south, still holding to certain conservative southern ideals, there was a mighty culture clash that Janet couldn't tolerate. She was terrified of raw sexual energy, of touching and turning on. For Ron and Pam, sexuality was appreciated, and having smoked marijuana with Jackson and me, they were, in their way, grandchildren of the '60s. It was too much for Janet.

Ron was devastated as most of Janet's ire had fallen on him. He couldn't bear the thought of having caused hurt and was miserable that he had upset Janet, who had been so generous to him and Dan. As the five of us sat over dinner, camaraderie, and even a little quiet giggling, plus the simple joy of having a parent who understood and didn't condemn, smoothed over the remorse and anger.

Serendipitously, Ron and Dan had just found jobs at a roofing company, and on the weekend, we all four went on a rental search. The boys found a little house in North Bend, and by the end of the month, Pam and I had moved into the recreation room in the basement of another of her high school friends, Becky. Once again, I met the mother, Lorna. We liked each other, agreed on the rental amount and move-in date at the end of the month. It was a bit primitive: a pool table filled the "living room," there was a defunct dishwasher that would serve as the cupboard for dishes, a two-burner propane stove sufficed to meet our cooking needs, and in the adjoining laundry room was a deep sink. A large sliding glass door provided us with a separate entrance, so our space was private. Unlike at Janet's, Pam and I would each have our own bedroom, separated by a large bathroom. That was a plus. In the "dining space," a huge picture window gave out over a small valley, and in the early mornings, as I prepared for work, I would sit at the table with my coffee and breakfast staring out over the valley. A pair of robins had built a nest in the bigleaf maple at the edge of the lawn where the valley sloped away, and each morning I gave witness as the female built the nest and settled in for the two-week brooding period. After the hatching, I watched, fascinated as the parents brought food, the chicks' short, featherless necks and heads showing just above the edge of the nest as the parents' beaks disappeared into theirs. This robin family felt like a reflection of my family life in Fall City, where I happily nurtured my two near-adult children. Smiling with the resonance, I would leave that tender scene and walk, the now shorter distance, to the bus and work.

I can't pretend work was a joy; it was a job, and I gave my best. I found it mildly interesting from time to time, but what kept me there was supporting a home for Pam and me as she finished out her senior year at Mt. Si High School. She had a steady boyfriend by now, enjoying the first forays into sexual intimacy. Her dad helped her buy a car, and that improved our errand running! I felt the bountiful nature of family when my brother offered me an old Nash Rambler he had, and I jumped at the gift. The last year that Ramblers were produced was 1969; it was now 1982, so I cannot even guess at the age of that faded turquoise blue specimen.

Today, Ron and I still double over laughing when we remember the car's maiden drive from Bellingham to Fall City. Those old Ramblers had a vacuum system to operate the windshield wipers that, in this car, were pretty much defunct. When a torrential northwest downpour pelted us, the wipers didn't have a prayer to meet the onslaught of the raindrops on the windshield, so we pulled over to the side of the road to wait out the deluge. As we surveyed the dark skies, it was soon apparent that the relentless rain was not about to abate. Ron's solution was to take his shoelaces out of his shoes, open the door and lean into the sleet while he tied a shoelace to each windshield wiper. As I drove, our arms out the windows, we manually pulled the wipers back and forth across the windshield. We kept our eyes glued to the road, squinting between smeared raindrops. Yes, one could lament that it was dangerous, but poverty dictates creative solutions!

John – Lover and Friend

In the spring of 1982, John Lopez came into my life. We were both oddballs tucked away in Fall City. In the hidden web of connections we all move through, I met John through a friend of a friend, who, on discovering where I lived, exclaimed that he had a friend living in Fall City in a tipi. I went with him one afternoon to meet his friend who would soon become my lover and dear friend until his untimely death in 1989.

My friend invited John to join us for lunch. I found John fascinating, mysterious even. He had a reticent manner as if he had a secret that he might let you in on. His mouth and his eyes sparkling like stars conspired to create the intimation. He was tall, over six feet, slightly round and soft, with a laugh that would suddenly break out from his smile. His dark hair fell around his beatific face. In a seeming incongruity with the gentleness that emanated from him, he was a construction worker.

A week or so after our first meeting, I walked the mile to the field where his tipi perched in a pasture. Thrilled to find each other in this rural enclave of cows and farmland, it didn't take us long to fall into bed together. Hidden away in his tipi on the weekends, we joyfully rollicked and played together. At a future point, I would note to him that he was always a little drunk or a lot drunk when we had sex. He didn't argue the point. He identified himself as a conscious alcoholic, and I agreed with him in some strange, inexplicable way. Undoubtedly, that is what drew him to Chogyam Trungpa Rinpoche's Buddhist teachings, who was himself an alcoholic.

I wasn't interested in becoming a practicing Buddhist, and unlike John, I couldn't find my way into taking on Trungpa as a guru of "crazy wisdom." However, I gratefully accepted John's invitations to meditation practices at the Shambala Center in Seattle. Shambala training billed as a secular arm of Trungpa's Tibetan Buddhist tradition, fit my inclinations, and I began meditating in earnest. I joined in weekend-long meditation marathons during which my knees painfully protested, and my unstoppable monkey mind ran amuck. I think the best part of the meditation weekends was Sunday night when John and I and others would seek out the nearest bar. I might have given up meditating except for John's commitment that encouraged my own. Though the meditation modalities I would practice in the ensuing years would take many forms, John laid out the original intent for me. A quarter of a century later, I would come back to Tibetan Buddhism with a fresh view.

A deep affection grew between John and me. At times I was convinced we were in love, and in our way, perhaps we were. At one point, when he was moving to a large 3-bedroom house with a roommate, I strongly hinted, well not hinted, I outright suggested we consider living together. Hindsight would prove the wisdom of his "No, I don't think it would work out." I would come to see that his heart belonged to Cynthia, his first and only wife, also a practicing Buddhist. A couple of years earlier, she had divorced John and moved to Colorado to be near Trungpa's spiritual center.

In the seven years we were in each other's lives, I traveled often, and over time and distance, loving letters flowed between us. Knowing he was in Seattle added a comforting dimension to my life, and I loved our easy companionship of lovemaking, meditating, and socializing whenever I returned. When John passed away, among his things, I found a little silk-covered book of Shakespeare's love sonnets I'd bought at Stratford-on-Avon and sent to him in 1984. On the inside cover, I had written, *Far apart in time and space, close together in our hearts. Love, Diane.*

In the late summer of '82, with Pam and I living in Lorna's basement, and John living in his tipi, two visitors arrived from overseas at nearly the same time. I talked with John about their coming and that I wouldn't be able to see him much. He said he'd miss me. I assured him as soon as the visits were over, I'd be back with him and would come over between the visits. As though to cement our commitment to the future, he fixed us a drink, and as soon as we'd downed our whiskies, we madly tore off our clothes and literally fell over each other into bed. Our lovemaking had a violent edge to it that afternoon as though we wanted to imprint on the other the memory of our passion. Swallowed into the incomprehensible mystery, I would once again, with these two visitors and John, be lovingly engaged with three beings at once. But before that, an experience in late spring hit me with much more force. I witnessed how *Shakti Energy* and *Shiva Energy*, the great feminine and powerful masculine universal energies, were manifesting in my children, now two young adults.

On the always welcome weekend away from Borg-Warner, I was unwinding in the morning sun out on the patio, coffee cup on the table beside me, a book in my lap, when Ron came around the corner of the house, "Hi Mom." I noticed an uncanny glow around him that seemed to have little to do with the sunlight.

"Ah-h Ron," I got up, delighted to see him, gave a big hug, and invited him, "Sit down, do you want coffee or anything?"

"No, no thanks. Actually, I've quit drinking coffee. I've come to share important news with you. I just came from church, and I've made the decision to answer the call of Jesus. I'm going to be baptized into the Seventh-day Adventist church. It'll be in a couple of weeks, and I want you to come."

If I hadn't already been sitting, I would have disappeared into the ground as if a ton of bricks had fallen on me. "What? Really? Tell me. . . ," was about all I could muster from my stunned silence. Over the months, we'd often had spirited discussions, even sometimes finding common ground between Christianity and my brand of spirituality that was a mixture of Krishnamurti and the sorcery tradition postulated by Carlos Castaneda. Ron was familiar with Castaneda, having read a couple of his books, and I was familiar with Christianity as presented by the Adventists.

"I've been studying the Bible and going to church with Dan, and as you know, our boss at Anderson's Roofing is Adventist. It's the right path for me. The Christian teachings quiet the unease in me and lighten my depression. You know how I fight that, and I feel blessed to be turning my life over to Christ. Will you come to my baptism?"

I wish I could have responded differently, enthusiastically right in the moment, but I couldn't, and we always did our best to be honest with each other. "Um-mmm, well, let me think about it. You know how I feel about the Adventist church. My own experience wasn't loving or good or even very spiritual in the end."

"Yeah, I know," he said lightly, seemingly unaffected by my reticence. "I know you'll come, really, but anyway, let me know. I love you. Gotta go, there's a church potluck at the Pastors."

We stood up, hugged each other close, "Love you too."

I watched him walk to his car and collapsed into my lawn chair, my gloom a sharp contrast to his glow. My inner dialogue roiled thunderously in my brain. All awareness of the beautiful summer day disappeared into my uncontrolled monkey mind. "If only," I kept telling myself, "if only I hadn't sent them to live with Don, I could have steered his spiritual yearnings in another way. He could have found the solace for his spirit in Krishnamurti or the ancient sorcery tradition. If only, if only . . ." Then I began to attack myself with a vengeance – the psyche disturbance of that inflection point in my life when Ron and Pam went to live with Don was a long way from being resolved. "I can't believe he's choosing the Adventist Church." I continued muttering to myself. "I hate that church, the arrogant and demeaning attitude the congregation had to Grandma and us kids. It's such repression of vital energy." Every bad memory of my years being a Seventh-day Adventist found a voice. The more I let my mind wander through the past-perceived ills toward me from THAT church, the more upset I became. "Jesus," I swore to myself, "enough already. Go take a walk, meditate, do something!" Digging deep, mining a tidbit of buried goodwill toward myself, I came back to the little valley below where tall yellow grasses poked above their bed of green. I refilled my coffee cup, and with a sigh, picked up my book. When it didn't hold my attention, I went inside and spent the afternoon cleaning.

In the evening, when Pam returned home from her day floating down the Snoqualmie River with her friends, she barely had time to hang up her suit and towel before I started in. "Ron is going to be baptized into the Seventh-day Adventist church. I can't believe it. I just can't believe it. Of all things, that church, and he wants me there to witness his baptism?" my voice was incredulous.

Pam just stared at me, "Mom sit down." I sat at the table like a guilty child. Something in me knew I was off base. "This is an important moment in Ron's life," Pam said firmly. "It's his chosen spiritual path. And you of all people, who talk so much of finding the right path?!" She was way more incredulous than I had been. "Of course he wants you, his mother, there to witness this commitment he's making. Of course, you're going; we're going." Her demeanor, her voice left no room for argument. I was chagrinned at my narcissistic response to Ron and grateful for Pam's wisdom.

Two weeks later, the three of us sat together in a pew in the Spring Glen Seventh-day Adventist church outside of Fall City. As the church service drew to a close, the Pastor announced that a baptism would follow. Ron quietly slipped out of the pew as a church Elder invited us, the congregation, to retrieve a church hymnal from the little racks tacked to the pew in front of us and open the page to a given number. We sang together in joyous hallelujahs for this baptism we were about to witness. The curtain of the baptismal font opened. Framed in the window, I saw the Pastor standing in his black robe. The water reflected on the font's back wall, and as Ron descended the short staircase into the font and entered the water, the reflection danced and swirled around the two of them.

Just as the Pastor was about to say a prayer and immerse Ron, a gentleman in the congregation stood up. (I was to learn he was the prime mover and shaker in the area's Adventist community.) We all listened as he declared, "Pastor, I want everyone to know the mettle of this fine young man. Our church is blessed to have him among us." As he sat down, the quiet tears, already wetting my cheeks and Pam's, shifted to a flood of pride and happiness that the community saw and felt Ron's divine spirit. The Pastor spoke a few words about Ron and how he had come to God, and he praised the glory of God. I could see Ron's eyes close as the Pastor placed the white cloth over Ron's nose and mouth, intoning, "I now baptize you in the name of the Father, the Son, and the Holy Ghost. Amen." He dipped Ron into the waters of transformation, and as he raised Ron up, water dripping from his hair into his eyes, I felt the spirit moving. I was so proud and touched by this gentle being that I was blessed to bring into the world and who had now chosen his own path to spirit. Ron turned, and his eyes sought mine. Our tears melded together in understanding. It was, and still is, one of the high spiritual moments of my life and one of the most excellent teachings of love through my two children: Pam's loving wisdom when mine failed me, and Ron's loving commitment to a life of spirit in his way, not mine.

After the service, we joined most of the church at Ron and Dan's house for a potluck. I was impressed by how these two young men had pulled together this celebration of abundance and good cheer, and I was proud when people shook my hand and congratulated me on the fine young man I had raised.

Pam's response to Ron's baptism, her mothering, protecting spirit is who she is at her core. Even in grade school, she had been a fierce mother bear of critters and distressed humans. She is an ardent conduit of *Shakti Energy* - voluptuous spiritual earth energy. Ron, a tender conduit of heaven's spiritual energy, is the ultimate manifestation of *Shiva Energy*. They would both have to fight hard to manifest their true selves in our material world, as any of us must if we dare to take up the mantle of awareness.

Old Loves Reemerge

As the reader may have guessed, Sven and Nicole both crossed the sea to America that summer. Sven came first for a month in late June, and Nicole would come for three weeks, a week after Sven left. In America, unlike Norway, because I had only been at my job a little over six months, no vacation time was forthcoming.

Pam and her boyfriend graciously took on hosting duties showing Sven around the area, taking him inner tubing on the Snoqualmie River, hiking up Mt. Si, where a lifetime ago, I'd decided to write to Sven about going to live with him in Norway. After work, I pushed the ole Nash Rambler home to have every minute with him I could squeeze out of a day. One weekend we headed up to Bellingham to visit family. A memory bursts forth of an afternoon looking through stacks of picture albums my mom had. We came across a picture of me taken the summer before I'd left for France. I am sitting on a blanket on a summer day playing with a young niece and nephew. The photo captured Sven's attention, and staring at it, he murmured with a kind of breathlessness, "You are so beautiful." That was only the second time in my life a man had said those words to me. This time I could hear them, and my heart burst.

It seems there are always "flies in paradise." The two times I took Sven to parties, he wasn't shy about flirting. When I questioned him, he replied he wanted to experience everything about America, including other American women. Consequently, one night he went on a movie date with a woman from a party. I think that's when I began to realize that America was the true lure of his trip, not just me. I was hurt and saddened because each morning during his visit, I stayed in our bed to the last second, jumped up, dressed, and drove to work, sometimes carrying his smell inside of me from our early morning loving. Throughout the day, my reveries of "us" made it hard to concentrate on the mundanity of accounting. But as the days wore on, though it was subtle, I felt his enthusiasm for "us" waning. The subtlety of the shift – a slight inattention when we'd talk, sensing him drifting away when we'd make love - didn't allow an opening to consider what was going on, so we drifted in the half-light of a dying love.

In the last week of his visit, the impossible-to-speak-about, deep connection between us frayed – not a big break, just a wearing away. Blessedly, this dashing of my dreams on the hard rocks of reality freed me a little, and I began to untie the *Shakti* energy I'd woven into my story with him. I wasn't sad to drop him off at the international terminal at Sea-Tac, and we knew this time, our goodbyes were final.

I prepared Ron and Pam for Nicole's visit. I hadn't talked much of her previously. I let Pam know that Nicole and I would be sharing the bed, that, in fact, we were lovers. Though she was surprised, as I'd never talked of my attraction to women, she took it in stride. With Ron, the discussion was more delicate. He was more innocent than his sister around sexuality - was a little shy about it. Another element was his total commitment to the Seventh-day Adventist church's precepts, whose views defined homosexuality as a sin, but then again, so was pre-marital sex. But, as always, being the loving, accepting person he is, with a slight frown, he nodded his head yes that he understood, and he was okay with her coming and looked forward to meeting her.

Nicole intended all along to make this trip about seeing America from east to west, tying it up with a bow on the west coast with me. She'd landed in New York and spent almost two weeks traveling across America by bus and train. I loved her spirit of independence and adventure. I arranged for her to spend four days on the ocean with Jackson as he moved a boat he had bought from one port to another. When she and I spent a weekend at my mom's house, I didn't push the envelope by making love, though we did sleep together: innocently as far as my mother was concerned as there was just one guest bedroom. Our lovemaking, more sweetly nostalgic than wildly passionate, we saved for my bedroom at home in Fall City.

Saying goodbye at the international terminal at Sea-Tac, Nicole and I knew a phase of our relationship was over. We held a deep affection for each other and sensed we would see each other again as friends.

Like a fairy creature gathering gauzy wisps of possibilities, I gathered up these tendrils of another time, tied them together, and released them to the wind. John was waiting.

19
1982-1983

Love Stories
The Innocent and the Vulgar

By August 1982, Ron had traveled south to northern California to work and learn at a natural healing center, and Pam had graduated from high school. I'm not sure how Pam determined it was time to move on, but by mid-July, like an insect waving its antenna to explore and test its environment, she was once again scouting for a new home. During the two-plus years we shared our lives between 1981-83, I would follow her to four different living situations. This time, leaving our basement abode at Lorna's, we landed in Redondo Beach, Washington, less than a block from the ocean, where a couple of restaurants, a general store, and a bait and tackle shop fronted the waterfront dock. Our new domicile was a big old four-bedroom house with a generous kitchen and living room and an inviting front porch surrounded by a stretch of green grass. Pam and her friend Cristina had found it, and along with Karen, a friend of Cristina's, the four of us moved in. The house location was perfect - close to my work, to Pam's community college, and Cristina's work, and with the fresh breeze and smell of the ocean wafting in through the open door.

The old Nash Rambler was limping along, but I was afraid it would stop running and leave me stranded on some highway or country road. With trepidation, I entered the world of credit buying and purchased a little red Datsun – critical for my freeway commute. When I'd been married to Don, buying on credit had seemed a no-brainer for him and had led us into the morass of "payments due and overdue," and I was left to deal with the ubiquitous calls of creditors. My complaints to him had fallen on deaf ears. When we'd divorced, I had promised myself to never be in that situation again, so I calculated my finances carefully and decided I could just make payments on a car.

About the time we left Fall City, John left as well, moving into Seattle proper. We'd meet up after evening meditations at the Shambala Center and go out with our close friend, Chuck (a Catholic priest who had left the priesthood and was now in the meditation circle of Trungpa's secular form of Buddhism, Shambala) for beers and snacks. John was thrilled to be working for NOAA on one of their research vessels, so he was often out to sea. Whenever he was home, we found every moment we could to be together. Between his travel and my work, there never seemed enough daytime hours to be together to eat, play, and meditate. The nighttime hours of lovemaking felt even more precious. I loved waking up in his bed, my eyes drinking in his gentle countenance with his dark hair spread on the pillow. I'd marvel at the contrast of his peaceful sleep and our feverish, usually alcohol-fueled lovemaking of the night. In those early days of our relationship, I was committed to my life with Pam, and neither of us had a desire to commit to each other - we were at ease together as close friends, confidants, and ardent lovers.

Three memory imprints, mostly about love, ripple across time from Redondo Beach. A most sublime memory is of Ron's arrival from the natural healing center with a darling young woman named Debbie. They had come to ask their parents' permission to marry. They relayed to us a sweet and trusting story. Ron had been praying for a young woman to come into his life, a woman he could love and that loved him.

Meanwhile, in Eatonville, Washington, Debbie's parents had encouraged her to answer a missionary call from their friend running a natural healing center in California. Debbie was seriously dating an older man that the parents adored, and they saw a bright future for their daughter with him. However, they were always ready to answer a missionary call that came their way, whether for themselves or their daughter, so they sent Debbie south.

Debbie arrived at the center, and for Ron, it was love at first sight. Soon Debbie was falling in love with him and wrote to her parents about this nice young man working and studying there. Though there was no outright declaration of love, the parents smelled it. They grabbed Andy, the prospective bridegroom, jumped in the car, and sped south to California. Her parents had Andy primed to pop the question. Alas, it was too late. Awkward words and actions cut the visit short.

Ron and Debbie had known each other for only a few months when Ron asked her to marry him and join him in a life of service. Debbie said yes. Now they had come back to the northwest to get their parents' permission, and their first stop was with me. I loved Debbie from the first moment we met. Cut from the same mold as Ron, she was a sweet, gentle soul that flawlessly mirrored his.

Over time, they have become nearly indistinguishable from each other, so close do their spirits resonate. At first, Pam felt a little jealous that the older brother she adored had placed his affections on someone else. It wasn't long before she proclaimed to all of us one night at dinner, "I thought I was losing a brother, but I see that I'm gaining a sister." Pam and I gave permission with a big resounding YES and YES. The meetings with Debbie's parents, Kathy and Henry, and Don and Carol didn't go quite so smoothly. Before Ron and Deb returned to California, Henry and Kathy had secured their promise to "wait a little bit." It was late October 1982 - they would be married on March 20, 1983.

At Redondo Beach, Pam met Travis, who, with two friends, had docked their fishing boat at the harbor pier. As the weather turned cold, they became regulars at the house, grateful for the warmth and comfort their craft did not provide. The three young women of the house and the three young boatmen fell into an easy camaraderie. Most every night, we were seven for dinner, and after eating, I would retire to my room, and the young adults would enjoy evenings of laughter and stories as they passed a joint and quenched their thirst with cheap beers.

Within a few weeks, Pam and Travis fell in love and declared themselves a couple. Travis was a quiet, sensitive young man who seemed to have his head in the clouds. As the relationship grew, I judged that Pam had to mother him, and I wasn't happy with the dynamic. However, as it became clear they were committed to each other, I made a conscious decision to learn to love Travis, as he was the partner my daughter had chosen. I reasoned that if I loved her, I could love him. "And" I wisely reminded myself, "she needed to grow and love in her way." (Decades after breaking up, Pam and Travis would re-connect as friends. Travis told Pam that she had saved his life, and he was grateful for her love. And as the karmic circle spins, Travis, in his turn, would help Tanner and Isaiah, Pam's sons, when they were going through a rough patch in their early 20's.)

The last event from that time that left perhaps the most profound imprint was Papa and Marlene's unexpected arrival. I'd barely arrived home from work one Friday afternoon when an RV pulled up and parked in front of our house. When the driver's door opened and Papa climbed out, I stared out the window dumbstruck. He was like a nearly forgotten stranger from long ago that had wandered back into my life. I stood transfixed until they knocked and called my name. When I opened the door, Papa grabbed me, hugging me close. "Diane, honey, I'm so glad to see you." He held my arms as he stepped back, "You look great." He smiled disarmingly, and I noted he'd gained a little weight but seemed relaxed and happy.

"Oh, thanks." I slipped from his hold and turned to Marlene and hugged her lightly. She hadn't changed, still soft and round, her smile often breaking into laughter, her round blue eyes taking in the world with the curiosity of a child. I liked her. She was easy to be with. And I was fascinated with the adoration that lighted up her face when she looked at Dayton. Certainly, I'd never seen my mother, Marian, look at him that way.

I stepped back, "Come on in. Can I get you something to drink? Water, beer?"

"Beer sounds good. We've just driven from seeing Uncle Les at UW Hospital in Seattle." Uncle Les was Papa's younger brother, and they were very close. "You know he had a heart attack and was legally dead for four minutes. It's a miracle really. He's still in the hospital, but they expect he'll have a full recovery. His heart attack is what precipitated our trip north. We've been staying with Grandpa Johnson and visiting my other siblings." He paused for a moment, "Grandpa had David and Don and their families over one day for lunch, and Don gave me your address."

"Oh, okay. Well, that's amazing about Uncle Les. Your family must have strong hearts. I remember Grandpa Johnson's massive heart attack and his full recovery." With that, I handed them each a beer. Thanking me, they pulled out chairs and sat down at the kitchen table. I slipped into a chair across from them.

"Yes, right. That was something, wasn't it, how Pop bounced back from his heart attack? I think you're right that our family has strong hearts, though I hadn't thought of it much. Pop said you come to visit him whenever you're in Bellingham. I'm glad you stay in touch with him."

Staring at my beer bottle, I halfheartedly pulled at the wet edges of the bottle's label. "Yes, well, I love going out to see him. I remember one time I arrived, and he was out on the barn roof replacing some shingles. He's amazing." Conversation halted. Uncomfortable, I picked up my thread, "Hey, did you read that long letter Arly sent out for Grandpa a couple of years ago? He wrote he was almost 84, still collected the wood for their 'earth stove,' had a large garden, and did all their yard work. And I think after his heart attack, in the late '60s, he became a vegetarian. Right?"

Relieved to have a question to fill time and space, Dayton confirmed my question and then relayed other family news and stories. Hearing footsteps on the porch, three pairs of eyes darted to the door as Pam, just returning from her college classes, pushed it open. She paused at the door taking in the scene, then greeted her Grandpa Johnson and Marlene with surprise, "Wow, what are you two doing here? I'm guessing that's your RV, right?"

"Yup, that's ours," Papa responded. "We drove it up from California, mostly to see my brother, Les, who had a heart attack. You remember him, right?"

"Yes, of course, in fact, when my dad worked on Bainbridge Island where Les and Kay live, he'd go visit them at his lunchtime. You remember my dad, right?"

"Sure, I remember Don. Small world, huh? How are you?"

"Great, mostly just going to school studying Recreational Leadership." With that, she turned to the refrigerator, got herself a beer, and joined us at the table.

Over beers, we all loosened up a bit and were soon reminiscing about the time Jackson, the kids, and I had sailed into Goleta, California, and spent time with Papa and Marlene. Papa especially was nostalgic. "Sure was great sailing with you guys to San Diego from Goleta. You know Marlene and I are talking of building a boat." I didn't pick up this thread, mostly because I wasn't interested. Papa, perhaps sensing my indifference, changed gears, "Hey, you guys hungry? I'm thinking we could order fish'n'chips from the restaurant we saw on the waterfront or maybe go there to eat?"

"Well, I'd vote to stay here and order out. We haven't eaten there, but it's probably good; after all, it's a seafood restaurant on the water." I turned toward Pam, "What's your preference? If we go there, no more beer," I laughed lightly.

"Right, so yeah, I'm good with eating here."

Papa stood up, leaned over Marlene, his hands on her shoulders, and kissed the top of her head. "Hon let's go get some food. Okay?"

I stared as they shared an endearing smile only meant for the other. "Yeah. Sounds great." Marlene turned to Pam and me, "Anything else you want? Maybe more beer?"

Pam jumped in. "Make sure you get lots of tartar sauce, and yeah, maybe more beer."

With that, Papa and Marlene left. Pam and I changed into comfortable clothes and set the table. As the four of us ate together in the Redondo Beach kitchen, with the alcohol flowing freely, the mood shifted. By the time we had licked the last grease from our fingers, Papa was smashed. The violent drunk was gone, replaced by a pathetic slobbering drunk. It was an improvement - my body wasn't stiffened in fear of being punched or slapped or having to fend off his sexual innuendos.

Emboldened by the alcohol, like a predator lying in wait, I jumped. "Papa, do you remember that time a long time ago when you came to Grandma's house on a Sabbath afternoon drunk and demanded David come live with you?"

"Humm, not really. That must have been a long time ago." He took a swig from his beer. "Why bring that up now?"

"Seeing you so drunk brings it all back, though at least you're not violent and threatening Pam or me. I haven't forgotten how you threatened me that day, and Don faced you down. Nor have I forgotten the nights of being afraid when you came home in a drunken rage. I hate seeing you so drunk!" And then, just as I had done on that Sabbath afternoon some twenty years ago, I laid out the evidence of how he had been a terrible father. With additional information I'd garnered over the years from mom and my sisters, I brought new ammunition in the case against him . . .and yet I held back the most salient part - the afternoon he'd sexually abused me. At one point, as our voices and my anger escalated, Marlene turned to Pam, "Let's go for a walk and leave these two to work this out. I have a flashlight; we can go check out the waterfront." I saw how relieved Pam was to leave, and I was grateful for Marlene's wisdom.

And so we were left to fight it out. With Pam gone, I attacked mercilessly, and Papa shrunk back from my rancorous rampage. He seemed about to speak, and I stopped him by now yelling across the table. "You abandoned your sons. The beatings and threats to mom I witnessed as a child are still vivid. And you've never taken responsibility for your violence!" His usual bravado faltered for a moment, he cast his eyes down, and then, to my shock, he raised his glazed eyes to mine and insisted he had never hit mom, saying I should ask her, and he hadn't really abandoned his sons, he just wasn't welcome at the house. His dishonest audacious responses added fuel to my fire and yet. . .and yet I was unable to go to the depth of my rage and hate, and I left him wiggle room. He tried to divert by talking about how much he loved me. That's when the red rage blasted from my being. I yanked the beer bottles off the table, "This conversation is over!" I spit out at him.

"Wait, wait," he begged me. "Okay, okay, maybe some of what you say is true, I don't really remember." I turned violently away from him and stormed upstairs. Later, I heard murmuring voices when Pam and Marlene returned. Eventually, I heard the front door close and guessed Papa and Marlene had gone out to the RV, and I drifted into a troubled sleep. When we arose in the morning, we had all slept off the alcohol residue, and I managed a measured civility. Papa and Marlene left after breakfast; I brushed aside Papa's hug as I wished them well in their life together.

A couple of days later, I wrote to Papa and laid out in detail all I had tried to convey verbally. I wanted him to have the words in front of him, not to be able to argue with me. I gave no return address and let him know contact between us was over. Inexplicably, or perhaps not, while I could attack him for his abuse of Mama and his physical violence toward us kids and hint at inappropriate behavior with his daughters, I couldn't quite confront Papa with the details of his sexual abuse to my person. Shame is a potent inhibitor of truth.

We'd been at Redondo Beach just a little over six months when Karen announced she was moving to Seattle to be close to her new job in Edmonds, north of Seattle. Cristina too wanted to move north to be closer to her new boyfriend. Pam and I needed to stay in south Seattle, close to her school and my job. On a Saturday morning, when I came downstairs, Pam had made us breakfast, something she only did occasionally. We sat down at the table, and she served us coffee and French toast with fresh strawberries. I laughed lightly, "What a treat. Thank you, hon. Is this a special occasion?"

She took a breath, smiled, and bursting with enthusiasm, rushed to answer me, "Well, yes, it is a sort of special occasion – at least for me," she added impishly. "Since we're going to be moving, Travis and I want to move in together. " She then outlined, as she had so often in the past, a living situation for her and me, with the addition of Travis. She acknowledged she still needed my financial support and suggested that the three of us move into a two-bedroom apartment. Travis would pay a third of the rent and groceries. When I questioned how he would contribute as he didn't have a job, undeterred, she informed me that he did have some income from selling marijuana and that they had talked it over, and he was already looking for a job. Her trusting carefree mood was contagious.

"Well, I'm happy to continue supporting you, and I'm fine with the three of us living together. If you feel confident Travis can pay his third, then let's do it!"

"Thanks, Mom. I think it'll work our great." With that, Pam set out on a mission to find us a place to live. It didn't take her long to find a two-bedroom apartment located just north of Redondo Beach. The complex was brand new and was offering a 6-month introductory deal. Pam excitedly described a habitat utterly opposite to the Redondo Beach house - in place of drafty walls and creaky floors, everything was fresh and tight, wall-to-wall carpeting covered floors instead of linoleum, and replacing the wood stove we chopped wood for to keep it burning on cold winter days, we only had to flip a switch for heat or air-conditioning in the summer. The sprawling complex offered a gated entry, and most exciting of all, the resident facilities included a swimming pool, Jacuzzi, and tennis courts. "I love it, and I think you'll love it too," she gave a little laugh, "well, I hope you will."

"Okay, let's go look at it, and I'm willing to sign a 6-month lease at their introductory offer."

The three of us moved in at the end of the month. I must say it was good to be out of the drafty old house and into a place where one only had to turn up the thermostat to be warm. Travis was only too happy to move off the even colder and cramped boat he'd been sharing with the brothers. We all quickly availed ourselves of the facilities, including John. Though he poo-poohed the modern, rather yuppie apartment complex just a little, he loved coming down on weekends to sit with me in the hot tub, hang out in the pool and then make our way across the grounds to the apartment. We'd sometimes join Pam and Travis for dinner, then bid them good-night, close my bedroom door, and thrill to each other's body as we made love and quietly orgasmed.

Not long after we moved in, preparations went into high gear for Ron and Debbie's wedding in Eatonville, Washington. As I hadn't had much contact with my sisters, Rochelle and Gayle, over the last few years, I was surprised to learn that they and their families were coming for the wedding. But then again, Ron was the first nibling of his generation to be married, and they were thrilled he was marrying an Adventist girl and couldn't wait to meet her.

As our home was less than an hour from Eatonville, Pam and I welcomed both families into our home and turned our living room into a dormitory. Fortunately, the room was large as there was the sticky oddity that Travis and Pam's bedroom had to stay locked as Travis was growing psychedelic mushrooms in their closet! Nevertheless, in shared conviviality, everyone found a place to throw a sleeping bag or bedding on a couch or the floor of the main room. Daytime, all the bedding and sleeping bags were gathered up and dumped in a corner, and mealtimes, we sat on the couches balancing plates on knees.

We caravanned to the Seventh-day Adventist church in Eatonville and met up with my brothers and their families, Mom and Bill, and Jackson with his mother, who had all driven from Bellingham for the day. In the church, decorated with living rhododendrons that Debbie would eventually plant in a future home, I was content sitting with so much of my family to witness the marriage of Ron and Debbie.

During the ritual, faces glowed and tears flowed. At the end of the ceremony, when Ron and Debbie each took a lighted candle and together lit a single candle then blew out their individual candles, Pam and I squeezed our joined hands and eyes to hold back our emotions that threatened to become extravagantly obvious. Over time, Ron and Debbie, two people united as one in their love of each other and resting on the foundation of their Adventist faith, was who they would become.

Don Carlson's mother, Doris, had flown up from California and had come from Fall City with Don and Carol. They'd also driven Edna, Carol's mother. There was a priceless moment during the picture taking when someone near me remarked, "Why are there so many grandmothers." Lined up with Ron and Debbie, glowing and smiling, were six grandmothers – Doris, Ron's paternal grandmother, Marian, Ron's maternal grandmother, Dorothy, Ron's adopted grandmother through Jackson, Edna, Ron's adopted grandmother through Carol, Tilly, Debbie's maternal grandmother, and Julia, Debbie's paternal grandmother. I turned to the woman with an enigmatic smile and replied, "There's been lots of loving realignments in Ron's family."

One nearly overwhelming detail of this most joyous of events was when I received the wedding invitation. I delightedly opened the embossed envelope and was reading aloud when the words, *Ronald Lee Carlson, son of Don and Carol Carlson*, slipped out before I even realized what I'd said. I was stricken when I didn't see my name as one of the parents, and my heart missed some beats. With my head, I understood Ron's longing to fit into the idea of a Christian nuclear family and his church community. Still, in my heart, the omission hurt and was exacerbated when I wasn't invited to be part of the receiving line at the wedding. I had some hard moments in the space between the ceremony and the reception when I went outside to brush away tears of sadness. Gratefully, I encountered Ron's closest friend, James, designated the official photographer, and he needed help getting people together for photos. I was happy to volunteer because most powerfully in my heart was to love and support Ron on this most memorable day of his life, and that easily erased my private hurt.

Back then, I knew Ron couldn't accept being in conflict with his dad. Conversely, I took comfort in the knowledge that Ron and I were able to talk openly together, to find common ground in our very different spiritual paths, and he knew we could always work things out honestly and non-confrontationally, no matter how sticky the problem. The wedding slight paled beside the true depth of our bond.

A month before the 6-month introductory offer on the apartment was due to end, and the rent to increase exponentially, circumstances in mine and Pam's life aligned. She and Travis wanted to set up a home together, I was ready to quit Borg-Warner, Brockwood Park in September was on the horizon, and I anticipated spending the summer months living on my land in John's tipi as he saw no further use for it in his future.

Meantime, just before we broke up our household, I determined to go to Ojai, California, for the series of Krishnamurti talks. I hadn't gone to Brockwood Park in England the previous September as I'd initially arranged with Dorothy Simmons, the principal. I had happily chosen to stay in the northwest, being a mother and friend to Ron and Pam. In May of 1983, using my hard-earned vacation, I headed for the Krishnamurti talks in Ojai. I was aware that Dorothy would be there for the talks and intended to approach her about my coming to Brockwood Park in the near future.

Old Pain – New Promise

I also intended to track down my father who was living near Ojai in Oxnard, California, and was building a sailboat at a boat storage facility nearby. A few weeks before, I'd visited Grandpa Johnson on his farm in Ferndale, Washington, where he lived with his second wife, Inez. He and Inez had met at a social for widowed men and women and fallen in love and had been hesitant to marry too soon after Grandma Johnson's death. His daughter, my aunt Arly, insisted that they were hardly young and why stand on ceremony and delay their marriage, so they were married in 1975, just six months after Grandma Johnson had passed away from cancer.

At this visit, in May 1983, he was 86 years old and still sharp as a tack. I knocked on the door of the double-wide trailer where he and Inez now lived. Several years ago, they had bought the manufactured home and parked it on an open field on the farm close to the old farmhouse where his youngest son, divorced and unemployed, now lived. Grandpa and Inez welcomed me, and when I bent down to hug them as though they were young children, I remembered as a child being curious that Grandpa was shorter than Grandma Johnson. And now he actually towered above Inez! We sat together in the living room, and Inez brought us glasses of orange juice and cozied up with Grandpa on the couch. I smiled at the two of them sitting together like teenagers. Grandpa, still inquisitive, wanted to know everything of my life, and then, as though waiting for an opening, he told me how devastated Papa had been with the letter I'd written. He added, "Dayton hopes that someday he'll be able to talk to you. I know Dayton loves you and wants to be in touch with you. You know, he and Marlene are building a sailboat and want to sail. Your sailing experience has inspired him, and strangely they want to sail away just like you did."

"Yeah, he mentioned that when they visited last year, but you know Grandpa, I don't like that he's doing what I did, so I didn't ask about it. In truth, I'm uncomfortable with the idea we have the same dreams and his dreaming my dream feels like it sullies my life, illogical as that may sound. I'm just angry at him for how he was as a father and husband. It was pretty bad."

Grandpa stared intently at me as though urging me to listen closely. "Yes, I understand. You know, when he was a child, our life was a hardscrabble one. He was born in a hut I'd thrown up with a dirt floor in the middle of winter in Montana on some abandoned land. Times were hard, so neither Dayton nor the next two or three kids had much attention from Madge or me. We were just struggling to survive and keep clothes on their backs and enough food on the table. It got better when I got the job at the cement plant, but by then, more young ones needed our attention, so Dayton, Les, Judy, and even Bert (the four oldest Johnson siblings) had to pretty much take care of themselves."

He paused, "I know when Dayton was married to Marian, he didn't always behave well, but he's changed and wants to make amends. I think it's a testament to how much he admires you. You know, you and Dayton are a lot alike, and I don't think that's a bad thing." Listening to Grandpa Johnson talk lovingly of his son, my father, touched me, and I began to consider making peace with Papa. I couldn't have known it at the time, but today I am eternally grateful for that decision.

The last time I visited Grandpa Johnson in spring 1988, he and Inez were living in a retirement center. He was 91 years old, and though he was in a wheelchair, his mind was as alert as ever. Even today, I vividly picture this last time I saw him. I was in Bellingham, visiting from Seattle, and had joined him and Inez for lunch in the facility's, almost elegant, dining room where the sun streamed in through large picture windows. Each table for six was covered with white tablecloths and napkins, with a small bouquet in the center. Inez didn't say much, just leaned in close to Grandpa over the arm of the wheelchair. Seeing them entwined together like animated dolls, I marveled again at how tiny they were. I moved my chair near Grandpa and held his hand as we talked over coffee. At one point, he looked intently into my eyes, "You know Diane, I'm over 91 years old, and I'm getting tired. I don't understand why anyone would want to live to be 100. (A goal his family talked about.) We sat together in silence, my heart bursting with affection for him.

I squeezed his hand, "Grandpa, I think I understand, but I know I'm happy you're still around, and I'm sitting here with you." He smiled at my words. In November of that year, I would return to Bellingham for Grandpa's funeral.

Letters had passed sporadically between Samuel and me, and when I'd written I was coming to the talks in Ojai, he invited me to stay with him, and I accepted with curiosity. I remembered his shy little-boy countenance, the blue eyes, thoughtful way of speaking, and his seeming awe about our lovemaking when we'd both been passing through Brockwood Park in December nearly two years ago. When he met me at the station in Ojai, I smiled as I stepped off the bus and embraced him warmly, planting a big kiss on his lips. He hesitated, then pulled me tightly to him and kissed me back fervently. When we pulled apart, he dropped his eyes, picked up my backpack, and hailed a taxi. We soon arrived at his one-bedroom apartment. "What a nice apartment," I complimented him. "Where shall I put my stuff?"

His reply caught me off guard. "Well, hmm, well, it's not going to work for you to stay here, okay? And when you kissed me, it really affirmed my decision. Truth is, I can't tolerate us being so connected during the talks."

"Wait, wait," I stopped any further words from him. "I mean, what the hell?" I stared at him feeling we were in parallel universes. "Why didn't you write me? I mean, we'd agreed we'd be together. I was looking forward to getting to know you, and there's the issue that I've made no arrangements for housing. What's going on? Why am I now ejected from your place? This isn't making any sense." I paused my diatribe.

He replied calmly, "Well, I've decided to be celibate, especially during the talks, and we'd acknowledged we'd sleep together, and I knew we'd be sexual, so it won't work to have you here. I'm sorry, but that's where I'm at. You know, going to the talks during the day and then having sex at night, well, I mean you have to admit that having sex doesn't seem all that spiritual from what K says."

We argued hotly and loudly, but I got it that he wasn't going to budge. I sighed angrily to myself at his conversion to celibacy. "Look Samuel, maybe I could stay and sleep on your couch. We don't have to sleep together... There is no need for us to be sexual, really."

"Look, I'm sorry. It won't work. Us being together would be a distraction from the talks. There's a campground nearby, and you can borrow my camping gear, and . . . blah blah blah." I didn't hear him any further as the wheels in my brain turned, trying to deal with this new wrinkle in my expectations. I wondered how he intended me to travel from this campground to town for the talks since he didn't have a car to drive me.

That night, I lay on his couch fuming, furious that he hadn't let me know earlier and barely grateful he'd allowed me to stay this night. In my mutterings, I admitted to myself that I didn't really care about being sexual with him - though I was irritated with the sanctimonious attitude he'd laid on me. As I struggled to sleep, I heard Grandma Trotto's voice in my head talking about men's uselessness, how one just had to take care of things herself. By morning I had a vision of what to do.

Sitting in the kitchen nook, as if I was a military officer and he a foot soldier, I ordered him, "Okay, Samuel, since I can't stay here, you're going with me to walk the waterfront and find my dad, and hopefully, he'll have a car I can borrow. I see no other options at this point. I certainly can't afford to rent a car for ten days." With a mixture of relief and consternation, he agreed.

We took a bus to Oxnard and began walking the ocean shoreline, looking for something that fit the description my grandfather had given me. The morning sky was blue, the sound of the ocean surf calming, and the sun warm but not hot. I took off my shoes and shuffled through the sand, sometimes walking where it was wet and cool, then wandering to the warm, dry, gritty powder. Nature, as always, brought some balance, and I felt compassion toward Samuel. I admitted to myself that though we were the same chronological age, he was like a lost boy who had been happy to moor himself to me when we'd found each other during the Brockwood Park visit. I could see that the thought of us living together in his home for close to two weeks was too much for him to contemplate. Looking back, I can only marvel at how Samuel's decision was a gift to me in the way it led me to Papa.

After about an hour's walk, I spotted a catamaran obviously under construction in a small boatyard and angled toward it. I squinted against the sun at a figure that emerged on the boat's deck and descended a ladder to the ground. I recognized my father and called to him by his name, "Dayton, hello."

Papa was shocked as if a ghost had emerged from the ocean's edge. He came toward me hesitantly as though waiting for a signal that I was real. I crossed the last few steps through the sand, and holding him at a distance, I lightly hugged him. (Later, over dinner, he admitted that after my letter, he thought we'd never see each other again and that he'd been heartbroken.)

I introduced Samuel and explained why I was in southern California. Once he got over his shock, Papa proudly showed me their 40' catamaran. Samuel, unsure what to do, followed me when I climbed the ladder with Papa and went down below into the cabin. I noted to Papa how different it was from a single hull design. I admired his carvings along the bulkhead, the beautifully finished table and settees, and the varnished kitchen nook. The three of us walked along the deck; the boat felt solid and well-built. We joined Marlene on the ground where she was painting the hull a soft yellow and inspected the mast that was laying alongside the boat on large sawhorses with the rigging already attached, just waiting to be stepped. And wonder of wonders, as we talked, I realized the boat launch was scheduled for the very day I was to fly out of Ventura. At that point, I asked Papa about borrowing a vehicle. He instantly offered to loan me their truck, for which I thanked him profusely. We agreed that on launch day, I would come to the boatyard to attend the big event, and then they would take me to the airport. My reunion with Papa was a blessed one.

He and I dropped Samuel off at the bus station and went back to the boat to lock up tools and equipment and pick up Marlene. The three of us piled into the truck cab and headed for dinner at a nearby seafood restaurant. The waitress led us to a booth. I sat opposite Papa and Marlene, looking at Papa with doubting eyes and listening to every nuance in his voice. I was keenly aware of interactions between the two of them, and as we ate, my distrust gave way to hope.

What made the meeting unique and heart-opening was that Papa and Marlene were reading about Dianetics and, as a result, were doing a cleansing fast that meant no alcohol for two weeks. I delighted in this sober version of Dayton. Our afternoon and evening together remain to this day one of the fondest memories I have of Papa. And while it didn't balance the karmic scales, I was grateful for those few hours. Though I still couldn't get the words out that were so personal about me, Papa and I talked honestly. Reluctant and ashamed, he took responsibility for his past behavior as an alcoholic, abusive, and irresponsible father. He even thanked me for my letter. I felt his apology came from his heart, and I let it into mine. It was all I'd ever wanted.

Throughout the evening, watching Papa and Marlene smiling at each other, Papa listening intently when she spoke, and feeling he had pulled back his sexual energy from me, I was happy for them. I am eternally grateful for that glimpse of who Papa could have been, of who he was for some brief moments. I felt accepting, even a little proud, of being his favorite daughter. This acceptance would sadly be erased the next and last time I saw him alive.

Ironically, I was grateful for Samuel's decision to kick me out of his place. His reticence to be close with me during the talks was the right call. I just hadn't known it! Ah-hh the machinations of spirit when my eyes are averted by drama. I spent a second night at Samuel's, and an early morning phone call affirmed a camping site was available at Wheel Gorge campground. The place was gorgeous, quiet save for the soft rustlings of small animals, birds warbling, and the drifting voices of other campers. I pitched Samuel's tent on a slight rise that overlooked a green valley. A stream flowed close by. I was content.

As they had been in the past and would be in the future, the talks that year were held in The Grove, an area Krishnamurti called "A sacred place," and which he insisted must be treated as such – it wasn't a place for picnics and parties. When I arrived at The Grove, a few people that would quickly grow to hundreds were seated on the ground in front of a low platform covered with woven wool rugs and set between large oak trees. I found a spot on the grassy area, sat down, and let the whispers of the beautiful oaks descend.

Sitting there in the grass, surrounded, and shaded by the magnificent oak trees, I was breathless when Krishnamurti entered the grove, stepped onto the platform, and sat in a simple wooden chair that rested atop the rugs. It felt surreal to be seated on the ground in front of Krishnamurti in the flesh. I was mesmerized by his voice as he carried us through seemingly random paths and byways - ". . .truth is a pathless land" - and led us back to his central theme of the day. When he concluded what he called "our conversation," we all sat quietly until he'd left the grove. Only then did the crowd stir. With the others, I stood up, and Samuel and I found each other. After each gathering, we'd have lunch together at his place or in a nearby restaurant to debate and do our best to understand what we had heard that day. Each time I happily bid him goodbye as I headed for my camping site in Wheel Gorge.

On the last day, I had a meeting with Dorothy. She was gracious as always and hugged me. I told her how my daughter was now a young adult, I would be quitting my job soon, and I asked her about my coming in September for Krishnamurti's talks at Brockwood Park, England. She invited me to write and request to be a volunteer before and during the talks. I was ecstatic and assured her I'd be there.

The next day I packed up the tent, camp stove, sleeping bag, and mat that Samuel had loaned me, said a thankful goodbye to the park that had nurtured me, and delivered the camping equipment back to Samuel with profuse thanks. Our farewell was final - there would be no reason to stay in touch.

I drove from Ojai down the hills to Oxnard and found the marina where Papa and Marlene would be launching their boat. I was running late and hoped I hadn't missed the moment when the little ship slid into the water and Marlene broke the traditional bottle of champagne over the bow and christened her **So What**. In explaining the name, Papa had said there had been many naysayers about their plans and dreams to take early retirement and move onto the **So What** and sail away, and to all objections, he would proudly proclaim, "So what." I liked that. I sped down the mountain to celebrate their new beginning with them before I flew north.

As I climbed out of the truck and looked around, a puzzling sight met my eyes. There was no boat floating beside the dock. I looked around and saw the *So What* pulled off to the side resting in the transport cradle. A group of men sat around in lawn chairs, a collapsible card table in the center covered with beer and whiskey bottles, glasses, and a plastic dish with burns on the side overflowing with cigarette butts. I spotted Papa among the men and hurried over. "What's happening? Why isn't the *So What* floating in the water by now?"

From his chair, his blurry red eyes looked up at me, "Oh Diane," his slurred words told me all I needed to know. I stared, my eyes instantly glittering with irritation as countless voices, clamoring, slurring, told the tale. It seems that when the canvas cradle lowered the vessel gently into its ocean bath, and Marlene broke the champagne bottle and christened it *So What*, and even as heartfelt cheers burst forth from the friends there to celebrate, *So What*'s waterline was fast disappearing below the sea's surface. The men guffawed, took swigs from their bottles, and continued the story. Dayton had climbed aboard, saw where water was pouring in through a poorly caulked toilet fitting and yelled, "We need to haul it out." The boatyard personnel had sprung into action, raised the launch cradle, and transferred the *So What* into the transport cradle that had brought it to the launch site. The celebratory drinking of this premonitory event had turned into a macabre wake. That's when I arrived. It soon became clear Papa was in no condition to drive me to the airport.

"Where's Marlene?" I asked. Papa indicated their RV that they'd brought to the boatyard to provide a facility for the party. I hurried inside and found Marlene and her sister, themselves pretty drunk. "Papa said you'd take me to the airport," I blurted out. I was already calculating whether I had enough money to pay for a taxi. Marlene wasn't drunk enough to hide her sadness and worry about what had just happened. As could be expected, my request for her to drive me to the airport added to her unhappiness. She also knew Papa was in no condition to drive and intimated that she and her sister had come inside to get away from the men. I mentioned the time restraints I was under. Marlene understood and pushed herself up from the settee with an audible sigh. I regretted the added strain of my request and tried to compensate, "Thanks Marlene for doing this. I'm really sorry it got pushed onto you. I'm happy to drive."

"It's okay." She smiled faintly, "You driving will give me a chance to sober up. Let's go." The three of us quickly headed to the truck.

Papa and his drunken friends were between the truck and me. It seems they had decided to decamp to a bar and had called a taxi to get them there. Papa saw me and grabbed me as I tried to slip past him. He pulled me to him. The smell of booze and cigarettes nauseated me, triggering the bile of Dayton memories. Putting his face to my ear, he whispered, "I have always loved your mother, but she just grew too old for me." With those words, he clamped his mouth on mine, and before I had time to react, he thrust his tongue into my mouth. Horrified, vomit in my throat, I shoved him away. His friends caught him as he staggered back, and holding his collapsed form, they poured him into the back seat of the waiting taxi. Did his eyes look pleadingly at me to forgive, to understand, to conspire with him? A drunken unknowingness, a shared secret?

That last scene, his drunken smile, and glazed eyes as he fell into the taxi, was frozen in my enraged soul until the day, in November, when my brother called to tell me that Papa and Marlene had drowned.

20

Summer 1983

Tipi Living

Healing Alone In Nature

When I'd asked John about buying his tipi, he'd loved the idea of passing it on to me and offered to help me set it up on the five acres of pristine forest I had bought with the marijuana bounty. A half-hour drive south of Bellingham, the land was located well off the highway and a couple of miles from the village of Alger, an old logging camp which boasted a bar, gas station/store, and a few houses. It felt like the perfect place to spend the summer before I left for England.

On a Saturday in late May, after I'd given my two-weeks-notice at Borg-Warner, John loaded his tipi - now my tipi - onto the top of his car, and we drove north from Seattle to where David and Don and a few friends joined us at the property where I would stake my claim. Earlier that month, my brothers and I had cleared a large circle and smoothed the ground for the tipi raising.

Dressed in shorts and shirt on this warm pre-summer day, John directed the project; 25' lodge poles were joined together, and near the top, he bound the small ends with leather. We raised the bundle of poles upright and holding them straight, spread them evenly apart at the base. We wrapped the canvas skin around the poles and wove the sides together with lacing sticks, beginning just below the smoke flaps. One of the guys drove stakes into the ground to anchor the tipi, and another dug a gutter around them. We installed John's oil barrel stove and stovepipe in a fire pit of rocks in the center of the interior, and by the end of the day, there stood my new home. The lodge poles reaching to the sky, the smooth sticks joining the two sides together, and the gleaming, glorious white shape pointing upwards as the afternoon sun shone its blessing wove together a promise. As dusk descended, John and I laughingly closed up the tipi and made love in that circle of harmony. I felt blessed by this elegant shelter that had been John's in Fall City and would now be mine. In the morning, I fixed us breakfast and cleaned up. We paused once more to make love, then headed south to our mundane, seldom-magical lives.

I returned to the tipi a week later to take up occupancy for the intervening three months before I left for Brockwood Park in England. It would turn out that the summer of 1983 was one of the wettest summers in the northwest, and at times it sorely tested my patience. However, my stubbornness and the majestic forest saved me. Each morning, I would build a fire with dry twigs and keep it going throughout the day with wood I collected from downed trees on the property. The glowing stove created a cozy warmth despite the rain drumming on the tipi.

This time alone in the tipi contrasted sharply with my days alone in Paris. Someone had left me a half case of beer from the tipi-raising, but I hadn't the slightest interest in drinking. Ease and wellbeing supplanted the desperation of Paris. The beautiful art and grand architecture that had relieved the tedium of being alone in Paris was replaced with the humble tipi structure and the unparalleled magnificence of nature. When I could, I was outside clearing trees with my brother's little chain saw, hiking and exploring my five acres, and drifting into neighboring five-acre lots. I fell in love with one huge maple tree tucked away toward the back of the property. I would hike to the tree, talk to it, sit with my back resting against the trunk, and meditate or masturbate, orgasming into oneness with that tree and the forest around me. Evenings, the fire cast dancing shadows on the tipi walls, smoke drifted lazily from the stovepipe, and my two kerosene lanterns set on the table by an open book glowed softly. I affirmed that for me, a round structure, primitive in its accommodations, was total perfection. The poles leading upwards carried the mind and spirit through the opening at the top, and my soul was fed, at once on fire and space, in that cone of silence.

My brothers, David and Don, visited occasionally, and I was surprised one day when my mom and Bill, out for an afternoon drive in Skagit Valley, stopped by. They admired the tipi from outside, my mom murmuring tepid approval, "It's nice." Once inside, they hesitantly lowered themselves onto the low futons, seeing no doubt the difficulty in getting up. I proudly showed them the details of my unique living space: the poles leading the eye up, the cozy stove with a warm fire in the center of the circle, the low table I'd made for futon level eating and working. I even showed off the various cloths and rugs I'd used to cover the dirt floor. Though Bill was non-committal, Mom expressed appreciation of these details. After I'd made us sandwiches for lunch, when the time came for them to leave, I was happy to give mom a hand, and Bill managed to scramble up on his own.

Travis, Pam's boyfriend, had given me a mescaline capsule. One morning, waiting to be sure of a sunny day, I headed out to the nearby stream to sit and meditate and travel to where the mescaline would take me. As the capsule dissolved in my stomach, the medicine flowed into my bloodstream, carried right to my core, expanding my perception out into nature's sounds and movements. Suddenly, with my senses amplified, I felt exposed and unprotected. I knew the setting wasn't right, so I hurried down the little hillside to my tipi. Once inside, I laced the opening shut, laid down on the futon, and closed my eyes. With no warning, I realized I was out of my body. I hovered overhead, marveled at my prone body so still below me. My "eyes" drifted along a silver cord from my out-of-body awareness to my physical body. Idle speculation accompanied this alien separation. I wondered with curiosity, absolutely no alarm, what would happen if I cut the cord. Would I experience ego death or actual physical death? I considered for an infinite, timeless moment if I should test it out. I contemplated how wonderful it would be to have an ego death. The prospect was glorious, and yet, I wasn't ready to leave the earth plane if to cut the connection would mean a severing of my non-physical self from my physical self. I decided not to risk it, and slowly, as the mescaline dissipated from my body and mind, I experienced an incredible sense of wellbeing and curiosity.

John would later help me understand my experience. On his next visit, hanging out over morning coffee in the sacred belly of the tipi, I told him of the experience. "Oh wow," his eyes widened, "the silver cord is in lots of Eastern philosophy. It's what connects our astral body to the physical body. You should read up on it. I think when we leave the earth, that cord is stretched and stretched and then finally is severed, and we pass into death, though I'm not sure."

After my inconclusive research, I wasn't sure whether to be ecstatic about this experience or terrified. However, both then and now, I was thrilled at this glimpse into transcendence. That same longing for the transcendent has been the driver of my desire for the orgasmic state of oneness - A oneness that promises wonder and wellbeing in daily life. That afternoon, with the mescaline running through my body, as had happened with the LSD, I crossed the threshold into the transcendent.

Though desperately seeking, I hadn't yet discovered the transcendent apogee where spirit and sex would one day carry and sustain me. However, at this moment, the promise of Brockwood Park Krishnamurti Educational Center tasted sweet in my mouth, and I couldn't wait to absorb the divine guidance and joyful right living I was sure awaited me there. In my naivete, I imagined there was no shadow world in that spiritual utopia.

Epilogue
Winter 1983

Dayton's Death

When my father died, a blast of energy hurtled from him to me and severed something that had bound me to him. It was as if a door kept locked against hidden horrors had been sprung open to reveal, not a pig stye of filth, but the promise of a brighter day. It would turn out to be a benchmark moment in my tantric quest to express the power of *Shakti Energy*.

It has taken me decades to come to the place where I can tell this story of Papa, my father. I have hated him, rejected him, fought with him, used every tool available to me – psychology, forgiveness exercises, energetic maneuvers, medicine work - to reach the view of my father you will read in this Epilogue.

I know this story through the Coast Guard transcript of communications with Papa and Marlene via shortwave radio that the Coast Guard generously shared with our family. I know it through my years of sailing the oceans with a partner, of tossing and turning through fearful storms. I know it through visits when I witnessed the deep love between Dayton and Marlene. I know it through glimpses of depth in my father that we, his young children, seldom saw. And finally, I know it because I am, in part, my father's daughter.

So from me, Diane, his second daughter, here are the last events in Dayton Johnson's life, eldest and most favored son of Lester and Madge Johnson, as he passed to the other side.

The waves are crashing bigger and bigger; the storm is growing, he is working furiously to repair the tiller connection to the rudder while Marlene, his beloved, is below on the radio with the Coast Guard. They've been in contact almost five hours, she letting them know their position as far as they could determine it, the Coast Guard searching, trying to find them, but greatly hampered by the huge breaking swells and gusting winds.

Dayton looks up from deep in the trough of a wave to see the highest wave yet running toward them about to break over the deck. He estimates it must be 30 feet tall. Grabbing hold of one of the cleats close by, he bends his head into the wave as it crashes over him. At the last moment, his hand slips off the wet cleat, and he grabs for the railing cable as the water carries him along the deck. It cuts deep into his hand, and he can't hold on any longer. Amid-ship, the foaming water forces him onto his back as his lifeline tightens; a second of eternity passes as his lifeline twangs and stretches. It holds. He lets out his breath as the boat begins to lift up and up toward the horizon and as it surfs down the face of another wave. He scrambles on all fours to the stern, and his heart sinks when he sees that the monster wave completely tore away the steering mechanism he was cobbling together. As one pontoon of the catamaran lifts dangerously out of the water, he knows their boat, their dream, is lost. They'll have to abandon ship to save themselves. Dayton crawls to the hatch, opens it quickly, and, half sliding, half climbing, descends the ladder yanking the hatch closed, but not before the frothy crest of a wave swirls its way into the boat behind him like a sinister shadow. The water was already sloshing around in the bilge, and now it swirls around his ankles.

"Honey, the last wave took the steering, or what we had left of it that I'd managed to put together." He tried to keep the panic out of his voice. "Without any steering and the water sloshing around inside, the boat is threatening to go over."

Marlene looked up at him with those wide robin's egg blue eyes, so trusting, without even a shadow of a doubt that he'll get them

EPILOGUE

through this storm. She was huddled over the chart table, maintaining communication with the Coast Guard, shivering even with her float coat on. She not only loved him with every fiber of her being, but she was in awe of his wisdom, his intelligence, and his ability to protect her. For his part, he loved her enduring trust in him, her admiration for him, and how, with her 5'4" height, she fit so comfortably under his arm when they walked together. But now he was worried about that very quality. How would her strength hold through what they were about to do? It was going to be challenging, but he believed with all his heart that they were going to make it; that once the Coast Guard found them in the life raft, and they were aboard the ship, getting warm dry clothes and a cup of hot coffee, what a story they'd have to tell! But in the meantime . . .

His somber gaze roamed around the inside of the boat, noting each detail he'd worked on over the years: the beautifully varnished teak, the compact galley, the bench seats Marlene had upholstered in a soft yellow. His eyes watered as he gazed at the carvings around the bulkhead he'd done that depicted the special moments as they'd built the **So What**. He was heartbroken, knowing that their journey together was ebbing away into a broken dream, but reached down deep and pulled himself back. "Honey, we're going to have to abandon ship. I'm going to go up and launch the life raft. When it's ready, I'll pop my head down and let you know. Where are we with the Coast Guard?"

"They're over the last the position I gave them, and we're not there. The Coast Guard says they will keep searching in widening circles because we've clearly been blown and carried far off from our last position. They can't bring a helicopter yet to help in the search cause it's too windy and dangerous but are hopeful they'll be able to find us soon."

"Well, stay on with them until the last minute, let them know we're going to go into the life raft, okay?"

"Okay, honey, I love you," she yelled as another wave crashed over the boat.

He waited until he felt **So What** drop into a trough, and then as the boat lifted, he yanked open the hatch, climbed out, and quickly clipped the lifeline onto the rope around his waist. Holding onto whatever cleat, rigging, or structure that was within his reach, he made his way to the life raft. His fingers stiff with cold, he briefly tried to undo the rope tying the life raft to the deck. What was he thinking? It didn't matter anymore to try to untie water-soaked knots. He pulled out his buck knife and quickly cut the ropes. The life raft slid easily off its pad. With a perfectly executed bowline, he tied the raft to the boat's railing, and lowering his head against the crashing waves that like insatiable demons with cold watery claws tore at his clothes, threatening to tear them away, he waited for a propitious moment to fling the life raft overboard. With each wave, the boat shifted crazily in the wash, and he knew it was only a question of time before one of the waves would turn them broadside to the next breaking wave, and the boat would go over. He fought down panic and focused on the job at hand. He judged the moment and pulled the cord to inflate the life raft as he tossed it overboard. With relief, he saw the lifeboat land in the water, filling with air in seconds just as it was supposed to do. He checked the knot where it was tied to the railing and looked out at the life raft one last time before he went down to get Marlene. His glance, meant to be momentary before he crawled to the hatch, was arrested in utter horror. The life raft was swiftly taking on water. For a brief timeless second, he hoped waves were swamping it. Then he saw the water pouring in through a broken seam.

Frozen in disbelief, he bowed his head, not in prayer, atheist that he was, but in utter despair. He was swept off into an unconquerable sadness and helplessness as he faced having to go down below and tell Marlene, many years his junior. Marlene, who had followed him unhesitatingly into this dream, who had gotten her ham radio license, painted, run errands, and tended their home as he had built the boat, and whose belief in his protection was unshakeable. In truth, he had never doubted he could protect and care for her, for them. Slowly he crawled back to the hatch. This time he didn't bother timing the opening; water inside was becoming irrelevant. Nevertheless, out of

EPILOGUE

habit, when he climbed below, he pulled the hatch shut. When he sat down, and reached across the table for her hand, their feet were wet in sloshing water. She looked up, her eyes questioning, "Everything ready?" Her voice was almost cheerful. He loved that about her, her eternal optimism and bright smile.

He squeezed her hand, "Darling, the life raft is leaking. It has a hole in it. By now, our life raft is a bunch of wet rubber hanging from a rope tied to the boat."

Though he wanted to look away from her, he forced himself to hold his gaze steady on hers. "Oh," she frowned. "Oh no, no. It can't be. The guy assured us it was good, and we checked when he repacked it. That just can't be," she insisted, refusing to believe what he was telling her, though knowing he wouldn't be joking.

"It is true," he said simply. "It's true."

Here I, Dayton's daughter and scribe, take poetic license as I dream into these final moments.

He had to look away, momentarily, from the sadness and shock in her eyes. He squeezed her hand tighter, raised his eyes to hers, and leaned in closer, his face just inches from hers. "We're going to have to jump overboard wearing our life jackets. We'll wear both a life jacket and our float coats, take off our shoes and anything else that might weigh us down, and hold onto the life preserver we still have on board. That way, we'll be buoyant and be able to ride the waves. The swimming part doesn't matter; mainly, we'll just have to be ready to hold our breath when waves break over us, and I'll be holding you tight to me. I'm going to leave the hatch open so the waves will quickly swamp the boat, and the next big wave will flip it over. Okay. Got me?" She nodded; no words came. "We'll stay clear of the boat, then when it flips over, it'll float, and we'll hold onto the hull until the Coast Guard gets here. Okay?"

Marlene found her voice, and miracle of miracles, her eternal smile of optimism, faint though it was, lighted up her face. "Yes, okay, okay, I've got it. When we jump overboard, we'll hold tight to each other. We're going to be okay; we'll just hold tight. We will. Then when the boat flips over, we'll hold on to it till the Coast Guard comes." They clung to each other, whispered over and over their love and their gratefulness for each other and the years they had had together, echoed each other's thoughts that they wished there had been more time, and though it was only a faint hope, they hoped there would be more.

And now we return to what is known.

"Wait, one more thing before we go topside." She pressed the button to speak to the Coast Guard, and with strength and power in her voice, she spoke into the little microphone. On the other end, the Coast Guard captured this moment. "Hello, this is the **So What**. The boat is taking on water and is sinking. Our lifeboat leaked and sunk, so we are going overboard wearing our life vests and float coats. When the boat flips, we're going to hold onto it. I pray you find us soon. This is the **So What** signing off." She switched off the ham radio and followed Dayton out the hatch leaving it open for the relentless Pacific waves to swamp their boat. She was shocked at the force of the wind, closing her eyes against the spray flung onto the decks. Holding tight to Dayton's hand, his other hand holding onto the life preserver, they leaped overboard into the tumultuous waves.

As the cold fury of the Pacific Ocean closed over them, a mysterious vibrating tidal wave of energy throbbed out across the ocean, across the land to faraway England.

Three hours later, the Coast Guard helicopter, flown by dedicated pilots that had waited impatiently for the winds to subside enough to go searching, spotted the upside-down catamaran. Forty feet away, they found Dayton's body floating face down, man and ship peering endlessly into the dark depths of eternity. They took pictures that found

EPILOGUE

their way into the newspapers as they reported on the storm that had taken several lives. They never found Marlene's body and assumed sharks had found it first. The Coast Guard retrieved Dayton's body. Eventually, waves and wind carried the boat to the shoreline where the tail-end of the storm beat the **So What** unmercifully against the rocks until the carcass of their dreams sank to the bottom of the sea. The storm dissolved back into the formless obscurity from whence it had emerged, leaving flotsam and detritus scattered along the shore.

Days later, beach walkers would curiously examine strange shapes a sailor might have easily identified - the polished end of a tiller, tangled strands of rope knotted to a wooden peg, a round post splintered beyond recognition as the mast it had once been. The casual afternoon strollers, wondering at the detritus strewn on the shore, would finally recognize the shapes when they discovered a tattered life preserver bearing the faint words, **So What**. One in the group remarked that she had read in the paper about a boat sinking and the people on board lost at sea. And those beach walkers would pause a moment longer, think how sad it was, and then, glad to be alive, lift their faces to the sun, and spread their arms to feel the gentle breeze blowing onto the shore.

End Notes

The sutras from the Vijnanabhairava Tantra are compiled by the author from various texts which include:

1. Odier, D. (2005). *Yoga Spandakarika, The Sacred Texts of the Origins of Tantra.* (Rochester, Vermont: Inner Traditions).
2. Singh, J. (1981). *Vijnanabhairava or Divine Consciousness.* (Delhi, Varanasi, Patna: Motilal Banarsidass).
3. Saraswati, S. (2003). *Sri Vijñāna Bhairava Tantra: The Ascent.* (Munger, Bihar, India: Yoga Publications Trust).

Introduction: *Defining My Tantric Quest*

4. Jung, C.G. (1965). *Memories, Dreams, Reflections.* (United States of America: Vintage Books Edition by Random House).

Chapter 5 – Junior High: *Heaven And Hell Seamed Together*

1. Midler, Bette. "The Rose." *The Rose.* Paul A. Rothchild, 1979. CD of the movie soundtrack.

Chapter 6 – High School: *Intuiting Freedom* OR *It's All About Sex*

1. Midler, Bette. "The Rose." *The Rose.* Paul A. Rothchild, 1979. LP of the movie soundtrack.

Chapter 7 – San Francisco Dreaming

1. Schlachter, T. (2016, February 4). *In the USO's Early Years, Hostesses Provided a Wholesome Morale Boost.* Retrieved from uso.org

2. "When You Wish Upon A Star.

Chapter 8 – The Prodigal Daughter Returns: *Marriage-Children-Taking Responsibility*

1. Peggy Lee. "Is That All There Is." *Is That All There Is*. Phil Wright, Jerry Leiber, Mike Stoller, Dave Cavanaugh, 1969. LP.
2. Jung, C.G. (1960). *Synchronicity – An Acausal Connecting Principle*. (United States of America: Princeton University Press).

Chapter 14 – France: *The Chrysalis*

1. Jung, C.G. (1969). *The Archetypes and The Collective Unconscious. (Collected Works of C.G. Jung Vol. 9 Part 1)*. (United States of America: Princeton University Press). 165

Characters

Primary Characters

Immediate family
Anna - Grandma Trotto, Marian's mother, my maternal grandmother
Marian – my mother, Mama
Dayton - my father, Papa
Rochelle – my oldest sibling
Laura – third sibling, born after me
David - fourth sibling, oldest brother
Don – fifth sibling
Gayle – sixth sibling
Martin – seventh sibling, youngest brother
Baby boy Johnson – stillborn last child of Marian and Dayton

Ron – my son, Ronny
Pam – my daughter, Pammy

Debbie – Ron's wife

Immediate Family – secondary characters
Grandma Johnson - Dayton's mother, Madge
Grandpa Johnson - Dayton's father, Lester

Lara - Dayton's 2nd wife
Gladys - Dayton's 3rd wife
Marlene - Dayton's 4th wife

Grandpa Trotto - Marian's "father," Peter

CHARACTERS

FF - Marian's unknown birth father

My husband, Don's, family
Doris – Don's birth mother
Earl Carlson – Don's father
Ginny Carlson - Don's stepmom
Carol – Don's second wife

Relationships, lovers, sexual encounters in chronological order

Grade school thru San Francisco (1961)
Bob Helgoe – childhood sweetheart
Harry – camp meeting love
Willy – high school boyfriend
Nicky and Steve – first boys Peggy and I met in San Francisco
Lyle – lover in San Francisco and his sidekick Art
Tamara and two gangsters - #MeToo experience

Marriage thru Vicente (1979)
Don Carlson – boyfriend, husband
RT – affair at end of my marriage
Jackson – relationship after divorce
Grant – brief interlude during break-up with Jackson
Vicente – relationship after Jackson

Paris thru Brockwood Park and back to Paris (1985)
Zoe - first woman lover
Lorraine – second woman lover
Jacques Denis – relationship – 1st Paris sojourn
Nicole – relationship – 1st Paris sojourn
Sven – relationship in India, Denmark, and Norway
Samuel – Brockwood Park visit
John Lopez – lover and friend - Fall City and beyond

Friends
Peggy Linn - throughout
Theresa and Nicole – junior high & high school
Rebecca – Bellingham during marriage
Barb – friend from college to today
Chuck – John Lopez's and my close friend

Secondary Characters

<u>Chap 5</u>
Earl Linn – Peggy and Sherry's dad
Sherry – Peggy's sister, Rochelle's friend
Mr. B – Junior high orchestra teacher

<u>Chap. 6</u>
Tommy – Peggy's boyfriend, Willy's friend

<u>Chap 8</u>
Dr. Z – delivered both my mom's and my children
Rudy and Annie – Don's and my older friends

<u>Chap. 11</u>
Emilio – Vicente's childhood friend and sailing partner
Lucia – live-in maid with Vicente's family in Argentina
Elena – ex-girlfriend of Vicente
Mateo - Elena's brother, Vicente's friend,
Raphael and Coraline – sailing couple, became Vicente's and my good friends
Ted – shrimp boat owner Vicente and I worked for
Horace – captain of the shrimp boat Vicente and I worked on
Charlotte – one of Jackson's girlfriends

CHARACTERS

<u>Chap. 17</u>
Ned – grizzled landlord in Carnation, WA

<u>Chap. 18</u>
Tess and her mom, Janet - Pam's friend and her mom, owner of our 1st apt. in Fall City
Becky and her mom, Lorna – Pam's friend and her mom, owner of our 2nd apt. in Fall City
Travis – Pam's boyfriend in her 20s

Acknowledgements

Thank you to the generous friends and family who supported me, read, and gave me invaluable feedback - Don and Alene Johnson who began reading even before this current iteration of my memoir and were always gracious and helpful; Darien Donner, for our long conversations that encouraged me and showed me the value of this book for others striving to manifest *Shakti Energy*; Nisha Zenoff, who excitedly awaited each chapter and encouraged me with spot-on advice and deep compassion; Francoise Bourzat whose words, "I am LOVING the book as I am reading it!" spurred me on; Aharon Grossbard who insisted a good editor always makes a better book! I feel loved and supported by each of you in your brilliant genial ways.

Thank you to Dorothy Wall, my trusted editor, for invaluable knowledge and professional acumen that smoothed and polished the rough edges of my prose and helped me eliminate the unnecessary.

Grateful thanks to Anna Gatmon, who pushed me to take the first steps to write this iteration of my life story.

Heart-felt thanks to Joe Shahan, stellar graphic artist, kind soul and devoted son-in-law, who skillfully edited and organized the photos, created the beautiful cover, and rescued me from technical illiteracy.

To my daughter LaRae (aka Pam), and my son Ron, and his wife Debbie, who bring light into the world and to my soul - my heart bursts in love and appreciation of who you are. To my two grandsons, Tanner, and Isaiah Fleming, thank you for being compassionate stars of your generation. And finally, to my partner, William, the first reader of each word, who believed in the book from the beginning and lovingly insisted I dedicate every moment I could to writing. Thank you my beloved.

www.ingramcontent.com/pod-product-compliance
Lightning Source LLC
Chambersburg PA
CBHW071100230426
43666CB00009B/1769